FOSTERING SUCCESS OF ETHNIC AND RACIAL MINORITIES IN STEM

To maintain competitiveness in the global economy, United States policymakers and national leaders are increasing their attention to producing workers skilled in science, technology, engineering, and mathematics (STEM). Given the growing minority population in the country, it is critical that higher education policies, pedagogies, climates, and initiatives are effective in promoting racial and ethnic minority students' educational attainment in STEM. Minority Serving Institutions (MSIs) have shown efficacy in facilitating the success of racial and ethnic minority students in STEM and are collectively responsible for producing nearly one-third of the nation's minority STEM graduates.

In *Fostering Success of Ethnic and Racial Minorities in STEM*, well-known contributors share salient institutional characteristics, unique aspects of climate, pedagogy, and programmatic initiatives at MSIs that are instrumental in enhancing the success of racial and ethnic minority students in STEM education. This book provides recommendations on institutional practice, policy, and lessons that any institution can use on their campus to foster better retention and persistence among minority students. Higher Education leaders and administrators interested in encouraging achievement among racial and ethnic minority students in STEM education will find this book a welcome and timely addition to the discourse on promoting minority student success.

Robert T. Palmer is Assistant Professor of Student Affairs Administration at the State University of New York, Binghamton, USA.

Dina C. Maramba is Associate Professor of Student Affairs Administration at the State University of New York, Binghamton, USA.

Marybeth Gasman is Professor of Higher Education at the University of Pennsylvania, USA.

FOSTERING SUCCESS OF ETHNIC AND RACIAL MINORITIES IN STEM

The Role of Minority Serving Institutions

Edited by

Robert T. Palmer, Dina C. Maramba,
and Marybeth Gasman

Routledge
Taylor & Francis Group

NEW YORK AND LONDON

First published 2013
by Routledge
711 Third Avenue, New York, NY 10017

Simultaneously published in the UK
by Routledge
2 Park Square, Milton Park, Abingdon, Oxon OX14 4RN

Routledge is an imprint of the Taylor & Francis Group, an informa business

Library of Congress Cataloging in Publication Data
Fostering success of ethnic and racial minorities in STEM : the role of minority serving institutions / Edited by Robert T. Palmer, Dina C. Maramba, and Marybeth Gasman.
    pages cm
    Includes bibliographical references and index.
    1. Science—Study and teaching (Higher)—United States. 2. Engineering—Study and teaching (Higher)—United States. 3. Technology—Study and teaching (Higher)—United States. 4. Mathematics—Study and teaching (Higher)—United States. 5. Minority college students—Recruiting—United States. 6. Minorities—Education (Higher)—United States. I. Palmer, Robert T., editor of compilation. II. Maramba, Dina C., editor of compilation. III. Gasman, Marybeth., editor of compilation.
    Q183.3.A1F675 2013
    507.1'173—dc23
    2012012563

ISBN: 978-0-415-89946-8 (hbk)
ISBN: 978-0-415-89947-5 (pbk)
ISBN: 978-0-203-18103-4 (ebk)

Typeset in Bembo and Stone Sans
by EvS Communication Networx, Inc.

Printed and bound in the United States of America on sustainably sourced paper by IBT Global.

This book is dedicated to the scholars, practitioners, faculty, and educational policymakers who work tirelessly to advance the psycho development and academic success of underrepresented students in K-12 and higher education.

CONTENTS

Foreword   *xi*
   Freeman A. Hrabowski III
Preface   *xv*
Acknowledgments   *xxi*

1 Charting the Course: The Role of Minority Serving Institutions
   in Facilitating the Success of Underrepresented Racial Minority
   Students in STEM   1
   Robert T. Palmer, Dina C. Maramba, Marybeth Gasman, and
   Katherine D. J. Lloyd

2 Minority Serving Institutions and STEM: Charting the Landscape   16
   Frances K. Stage, Valerie C. Lundy-Wagner, and Ginelle John

3 Impact of Institutional Climates of MSIs and Their Ability to
   Foster Success for Racial and Ethnic Minority Students in STEM   33
   Terrell L. Strayhorn

4 Engineering the Academic Success of Racial and Ethnic Minority
   Students at Minority Serving Institutions via Student–Faculty
   Interactions and Mentoring   46
   Darnell Cole and Araceli Espinoza

5   Model Programs for STEM Student Success at Minority Serving
    Two-Year Colleges   59
    Soko S. Starobin, Dimitra Jackson, and Frankie Santos Laanan

6   Teaching to Teach: African American Faculty, HBCUs, and
    Critical Pedagogy   72
    Roland W. Mitchell, T. Elon Dancy II, Dana Hart, and Berlisha Morton

7   Supporting the Dream: The Role of Faculty Members at
    Historically Black Colleges and Universities in Promoting STEM
    PhD Education   86
    Shannon Gray

8   Community Building: Minority Serving Institutions and How
    They Influence Students Pursuing Undergraduate STEM Degrees   102
    Alonzo M. Flowers and Rosa M. Banda

9   Academic and Social Integration for Students of Color in STEM:
    Examining Differences between HBCUs and Non-HBCUs   116
    Idara Essien-Wood and J. Luke Wood

10 Broadening Participation in STEM: Policy Implications of a
    Diverse Higher Education System   130
    Lorelle L. Espinosa and Carlos Rodríguez

11 Action Research: An Essential Practice for 21st Century Assessment
    at HSIs   149
    *Alicia C. Dowd, Misty Sawatzky, Raquel M. Rall,
    and Estela Mara Bensimon*

12 Asian American and Native American Pacific Islander Serving
    Institutions (AANAPISIs): Mutable Sites for Science, Technology,
    Engineering, and Math (STEM) Degree Production   168
    Robert T. Teranishi, Dina C. Maramba, and Minh Hoa Ta

13 Collaborative Partnerships in Engineering between Historically
    Black Colleges and Universities and Predominantly White
    Institutions   181
    Christopher B. Newman and M. Bryant Jackson

14 Cultivating Engineering Student Success at an HBCU: An
    Empirical Study on Development   192
    Kenneth Taylor and Robert T. Palmer

15 Achieving Equity Within and Beyond STEM: Toward a New
     Generation of Scholarship in STEM Education   209
     Juan C. Garibay

Afterword   *221*
     Shaun R. Harper, Ph.D.
About the Editors   *224*
About the Contributors   *226*
Index   *233*

FOREWORD

Freeman A. Hrabowski, III

UNIVERSITY OF MARYLAND AT BALTIMORE COUNTY

Several years ago, I had the privilege of speaking at the commencement exercises of my alma mater, Hampton University. I found myself thinking about the lessons that university leaders from across the country can learn from historically Black colleges and universities (HBCUs) and other minority serving institutions (MSIs). While close to 90% of African American college and university students are enrolled at predominantly White institutions (PWIs), HBCUs account for almost a fifth of the nation's African American bachelor's degree recipients. Nearly a third of all Hispanic bachelor's degree recipients graduate from Hispanic serving institutions (HSIs). These institutions, along with the nation's Tribal colleges and universities (TCUs), have demonstrated long-term success in preparing many of the nation's minority leaders. This book allows those of us at PWIs to learn from them, especially regarding the social and academic needs of minority students. It also allows educators at MSIs to benefit from best practices used at other institutions

Many of the lessons I learned at Hampton shaped the philosophy of education underlying the Meyerhoff Scholars Program, founded at the University of Maryland, Baltimore County (UMBC), to recruit and educate African Americans in science and engineering. It was at Hampton that I learned the importance of putting students first, expecting the most of them, giving them the support that they need to succeed, and emphasizing leadership and service to others. Any institution that has been successful in educating minority and other students in science, technology, engineering, and mathematics (STEM) understands that these students grow when they are challenged intellectually and receive support, both academic and personal.

Fostering Success of Ethnic and Racial Minorities in STEM: The Role of Minority Serving Institutions focuses on the strategies and institutional characteristics of MSIs associated with minority academic performance in STEM areas. The initial chapter establishes the importance of this subject and explains why this enhanced performance is critical to the nation's competitiveness. Key lessons examined in the book include (a) an emphasis on various aspects of campus culture that can affect academic achievement, including, for example, peer culture and faculty–student interaction; (b) the importance of preparing faculty to teach students from a range of racial and ethnic backgrounds; (c) the critical role of minority-serving 2-year institutions and their relation to 4-year institutions in supporting the development of students in STEM areas; (d) the essential role of assessment in understanding the academic performance of these students, including retention and graduation in STEM areas.

These strategies can be effectively used to change the culture of an institution. In the 22 years since the Meyerhoff Scholars Program was founded, UMBC has been recognized for a variety of innovations related to student success in STEM areas, and the University is now the leader among PWIs in the number of African American bachelor's degree recipients who go on to earn PhDs in the natural sciences and engineering. No doubt the success of our campus led to my being invited to chair the National Academies committee that produced the recent report *Expanding Underrepresented Minority Participation: America's Science and Technology Talent at the Crossroads*.

The *Crossroads* report builds on the National Academies influential *Rising Above the Gathering Storm* report, which argued that the nation's continued global competitiveness in STEM will depend on the investments we make in research, innovation, and talent development. At the core of the STEM workforce challenge is the country's changing demographics. As a result of a congressional mandate, the National Academies created the Committee on Underrepresented Groups and the Expansion of the Science and Engineering Workforce Pipeline to explore the role and value of diversity in the American STEM workforce, and to identify best practices for broadening participation. Expanding participation is critical for several reasons. First, as more STEM graduate students who are not U.S. citizens return to their own countries, the future of the nation's talent pool becomes increasingly uncertain. Second, the groups that are most underrepresented in STEM are also the fastest growing in our population, particularly Hispanics. Third, increasing the participation of these groups will contribute substantially to the nation's future competitiveness.

However, the problem is daunting because while underrepresented minority groups make up almost 30% of the national population, they represent only 9% of college-educated Americans in STEM occupations. The underrepresentation is exacerbated by the progressive reduction in representation along the academic pipeline. In 2007, underrepresented minorities comprised almost 40% of K–12 public enrollment, a third of the college age population, 26.2% of undergraduate enrollment, 17.7% of STEM bachelor's degrees, and only 5% of STEM doctorates. Furthermore, the United States ranks 20th out of 24 countries in the percentage of 24-year-olds who earn a first degree in the natural sciences or engineering, with only 6% holding such a degree.

Even more troubling, fewer than 3% of underrepresented American 24-year-olds had earned a first degree in the natural sciences or engineering. The *Crossroads* report suggests that we need to quadruple or even quintuple these percentages to remain competitive. To fix the problem, we will need to focus on education from pre-K through high school, improving college awareness about STEM opportunities, providing more financial support to make higher education affordable, and focusing more attention on academic and social support. While the report looks at the roles of different types of institutions, it is very clear that a number of MSIs have been particularly successful in preparing minority students for graduate school in science and engineering. For example, the leading 10 baccalaureate institutions for African Americans who earn STEM PhDs are HBCUs. Similarly, the top two baccalaureate institutions for Hispanics who earn PhDs in these subjects are HSIs in Puerto Rico. Nevertheless, most Blacks and Hispanics who earn STEM PhDs completed their undergraduate degrees at one of America's PWIs (there are more than 3,000), often with, at best, a handful of other minority students completing STEM degrees. Using lessons learned from these successful MSIs can help both PWIs and other MSIs become more productive. This book takes the important step of documenting the strategies that have helped MSIs to be effective.

For many institutions of all types, increasing the number of minority students excelling in STEM fields will require transformation of the institution's culture. For my own campus, the process of culture change began with a variety of focus group discussions involving students, faculty, and staff concentrating on the underachievement issues of minority students. These conversations were very important because, although culture reflects subjective values, changing a culture requires rigorous analysis. It begins when an institution's faculty and staff look at themselves carefully to identify strengths and weaknesses, recognize challenges to be faced, and determine how to respond to those challenges in order to reach desired outcomes. Taking an inclusive approach involving faculty, staff, and students can help harness the creativity of those groups. Any institution that is successful in educating minority students in STEM will attribute that success to (a) the active involvement of faculty, (b) an emphasis on study groups and peer support, (c) an emphasis on hands-on research for students, (d) constant opportunities to reflect on the experiences of these students, and, most important, (e) regular assessment of these initiatives.

Finally, institutionalizing culture change will require campus support to be strong and broad so the change can be sustained beyond any one group of leaders. While it is certainly the case that PWIs can benefit from strategies used by MSIs, many of the lessons discussed here can assist both types of institutions in improving the performance of underrepresented groups. I would argue that all of us in higher education can do much more. This book provides strategies and pertinent advice that can be helpful to any university interested in enhancing the success and academic performance of students.

PREFACE

This book is the first of its kind to provide an in-depth examination of the role of minority serving institutions (MSIs) in the production of underrepresented racial minority (URM) students in science, technology, engineering, and mathematics (STEM). Indeed, while countless articles, reports, and policy briefs have noted the significant impact that MSIs have on the success of minority students in general and STEM specifically, this book discusses the ways in which MSIs are able to facilitate the achievement of URMs in STEM. Indeed, this book is essential for postsecondary institutions seeking to improve educational outcomes among URMs in STEM. In particular, faculty who work with students in URMs will find this book critical as they support student learning and success in the classroom. Similarly, student affairs practitioners, college administrators, and educational policymakers will find this book essential as they work with faculty in and out of the class to support student success in STEM.

This volume consists of 15 chapters. The first chapter, "Charting the Course: The Role of Minority Serving Institutions in Facilitating the Success of Underrepresented Racial and Ethnic Minority Students in STEM," by Robert T. Palmer, Dina C. Maramba, Marybeth Gasman, and Katherine D. J. Lloyd provide the foundation for this volume. Specifically, in this chapter, they discuss the significant impact that MSIs have on the success of URMs in STEM. Despite resource deficiencies, they note that MSIs have shown greater efficacy in facilitating access and success among minority students in general and those majoring in STEM specifically. In fact, they argue that these institutions disproportionately produce a large number of minority STEM graduates. They conclude by providing an historical overview of MSIs and discussing how *some* MSIs might provide exemplary models of learning for institutions interested in advancing the success of minority students in STEM (Clewell, de Cohen, & Tsui, 2010).

In chapter 2, "Minority Serving Institutions and STEM: Charting the Landscape," Frances Stage, Valerie Lundy-Wagner, and Ginelle John argue that although MSIs are successful at disproportionately producing a large number of URMs in STEM, there is a scarcity of research that disaggregates the contribution of each MSI designation. They suggest that disaggregating the contribution by MSI designation is important because research has firmly documented the roles that HBCUs and HSIs play in minority STEM production; however, they argue, less is known about the contributions of Tribal colleges and universities and Asian American and Native American Pacific Islander serving institutions. Using data from Integrated Postsecondary Educational Data Systems and the National Center for Educational Statistics, they found that while all MSIs played a significant role in URM STEM productions, there were differences by designation. Their chapter concludes with a discussion and conclusion about the findings of their study.

Terrell L. Strayhorn argue that campus climate plays a critical role in the success of STEM students at MSIs. In chapter 3, "Impact of Institutional Climates of MSIs and Their Ability to Foster Success for URM Students in STEM," he delineates the impact that supportive campus climates at HBCUs have on positive outcomes for URMs in STEM. Through qualitative and quantitative approaches, findings from his study extend the understanding that URMs in STEM who feel a sense of belonging on campus are more likely to succeed. This chapter concludes with important implications for practice and policy.

Darnell Cole and Araceli Espinoza authored the subsequent chapter, "Engineering the Academic Success of Racial Ethnic Minority Students at Minority Serving Institutions via Student–Faculty Interactions and Mentoring." In it, they examine the effect that structured mentoring programs, student–faculty interactions, and campus climate have on degree attainment for students in STEM at MSIs. To examine this issue, they used quantitative analysis and data from the Beginning Postsecondary Student Longitudinal Study with students who attended MSIs and majored in STEM. Their results have interesting implications for practical and future research considerations for colleges and universities.

In chapter 5, "Model Programs for STEM Student Success at Minority Serving Two Year Colleges," Soko Starobin, Dimitra Jackson, and Frankie Laanan discuss the critical role that minority serving 2-year institutions play in promoting access and success for women and URMs pursuing careers in STEM. Their chapter also presents a case study, which provides characteristics that help women and minorities navigate their STEM educational trajectory, and identify commonalities between two programs that assist women and URMs with success in STEM. Their chapter concludes with salient recommendations for practice, policy, and future research.

Roland Mitchell, T. Elon Dancy II, Dana Hart, and Berlisha Morton consider the role of HBCU faculty in using pedagogical practices that are cultural inclusive and validating in chapter 6, "Teaching to Teach: African American Faculty, HBCUs, and Critical Pedagogy." Indeed, they argue that teaching modalities of this nature have a significant influence on teaching subjects, such as STEM. In their discussion, they urge faculty at various institutional types to employ similar pedagogical strategies to enhance success of URMs in STEM.

Shannon Gray explores the role of supportive faculty and success in STEM for Black students at HBCUs in chapter 7, "Supporting the Dream: The Role of Faculty Members at Historically Black Colleges and Universities in Promoting STEM PhD Education." Specifically, drawing on the voices of four PhD students at the University of Pennsylvania who earned their baccalaureate degrees from HBCUs, participants reflected on the supportive role that HBCU faculty had on their success in STEM. He concludes with important recommendations for institutional officials and faculty, which can be used to help facilitate the success of URMs in STEM.

In chapter 8, "Academic and Social Integration for Students of Color in STEM: Examining Differences between HBCUs and non-HBCUs," Idara Essien-Wood and J. Luke Wood use data from the Beginning Postsecondary Student Longitudinal Study, to examine academic and social integration patterns between students at HBCUs and non-HBCUs. Their results reveal that STEM students at HBCUs were better academically integrated than their non–HBCU peers. Their chapter concludes with salient recommendations that non-HBCUs could use to increase success among URMs in STEM.

Alonzo Flowers and Rosa Banda add to the scholarly discourse on MSIs and STEM in chapter 9, "Community Building: Minority Serving Institutions and How They Influence Students Pursing Undergraduate STEM Degrees." In particular, they delineate eight characteristics that universities should incorporate into their programmatic STEM initiatives to help the success of URMs in STEM. They also focus on the importance of MSIs building communities that cultivate the talent of URMs in STEM. They suggest that these communities can serve as linchpins that can be used to create important relationships with stakeholders and help increase success among URMs in STEM disciplines. They conclude with recommendations for practical considerations.

Lorelle Espinosa and Carlos Rodriguez emphasize the critical role that postsecondary institutions play in diversifying the STEM workforce, in chapter 10, "Broadening Participation in STEM: Policy Implications of a Diverse Higher Education System." They describe their involvement with the Broadening Participation in STEM Project, which served as a research and policy effort to address increasing the participation of women and racial/minority groups. Through the use of trend analysis of MSIs and qualitative data from stakeholders, they described the process by which the project worked toward recommending potential practices for higher education institutions to increase the participation and success of URMs in STEM. They conclude with policy, research, and practical implications for institutions seeking to improve participation and success among URMs in STEM.

In chapter 11, "Action Research: An Essential Practice for 21st Century Assessment at HSIs," Alicia C. Dowd, Misty Swatszky, Raquel M. Rall, and Estela Mara Bensimon argue for using action research tools as important approaches for institutional assessment with regard to the Hispanic serving institution (HSI) context. More specifically, they advocate for the use of two self-assessment instruments (SAIs); the Institutional Agent Self-Assessment Inventory for Increasing Latina and Latino Participation in STEM Fields and the Center for Urban Education's Culturally Inclusive Policies and Practices Self-Assessment Inventory (CIPPs-SAI). Further emphasized is placed on how these instruments serve as pivotal approaches to assessing individual and collective practitioner efforts toward creating culturally inclusive practices in STEM. Their chapter concludes with suggestions for further professional accountability for HSIs.

In their chapter, "Asian American and Native American Pacific Islander Serving-Institutions (AANAPISIs): Mutable Sites for Science, Technology, Engineering, and Math (STEM) Degree Production," Robert Teranishi, Dina C. Maramba, and Minh Hoa Ta, advocate for the incorporation of the Asian Americans and Pacific Islander (AAPI) population in the STEM and MSI discourse. To set the context, a discussion on the background on AAPI students and STEM is presented along with a discussion on the ways in which AANAPISIs have responded to the unique challenges and needs of AAPIs. A case study of a current AANAPISI, City College of San Francisco, is presented, which adds breadth and depth to how a STEM program has supported Filipino American, Southeast Asian American, and Pacific Islander STEM students. Their chapter concludes with implications for research and practice as well lessons that can be learned from AANAPISIs with regard to advancing the success of AAPIs in STEM.

In chapter 13, "Collaborative Partnerships in Engineering between Historically Black Colleges and Universities (HBCUs) and Predominantly White Institutions (PWIs)," Christopher Newman and M. Bryant Jackson discuss HBCUs and PWIs that have maintained collaborative partnerships through dual degree programs in engineering. They also provide specific examples of dual degree programs between PWIs and HBCUs and highlight the premise of these partnerships. They conclude by discussing some of the potential advantages and disadvantages of these partnerships and provide consideration for future research on this topic. Given that a new report by Education Counsel and the American Association for the Advancement of Science have urged colleges to create partnerships with each other to increase the rate at which women and minorities participate in science (Basken, 2012), Newman and Jackson's chapter is indeed timely. Kenneth Taylor and Robert T. Palmer authored chapter 14, "Cultivating Engineering Student Success at Historically Black Colleges and Universities (HBCU): An Empirical Study on Development." This chapter provides empirical evidence regarding the need for institutions to consider noncognitive factors that influence persistence for students in STEM. This chapter is based on a larger quantitative study that examined the relationship between identity development of Black engineering students at an HBCU and persistence. The results of this study revealed that identity development is important to the success of Black engineering students. This chapter offers important considerations for HBCUs and possibly other institutions seeking to increase persistence among Black engineering majors.

In the final chapter, "Achieving Equity Within and Beyond STEM: Toward a New Generation of Scholarship in STEM Education." Juan C. Garibay proposes a new way of thinking about the importance of increasing the participation of URMs in STEM. In particular, he argues that researchers, faculty, administrators, and policymakers should shift the discourse from increasing access and success among URMs in STEM because it has implications for America's economic competitiveness to one focused on democratic ideologies. He posits that this is critical because the current discourse serves the corporate interest rather than the needs and interests of populations of color. He concludes by discussing how institutions, such as MSIs could make changes in their STEM curricula, the cultures of their academic departments, and pedagogical strategies in order to produce graduates whose interests are aligned with the promotion of social justice and social change.

References

Basken, P. (2012). Colleges are urged to cooperate to bring more women and minorities into science. *The Chronicle of Higher Education*. Retrieved from http://chronicle.com/article/Colleges-Are-Urged-to/130946/

Clewell, B., Cosentino de Cohen, C., & Tsui, L. (2010). *Capacity building to diversify STEM: Realizing Potential among HBCUs* (The Urban Institute Report [NSF]).Arlington, VA: National Science Foundation.

ACKNOWLEDGMENTS

Robert T. Palmer would like to thank the authors who have worked tirelessly to respond promptly to feedback and for sharing their work in this volume. He would also like to thank his collaborative peers—Dina C. Maramba and Marybeth Gasman, who made this experience enjoyable and memorable. Finally, he would like to thank his mentors and friends in the academy who have supported his personal and scholarly growth and development, particularly Marybeth Gasman, Terrell L. Strayhorn, James Earl Davis, Dina C. Maramba, J. Luke Wood, T. Elon Dancy II, Ryan J. Davis, Marylu McEwen, Melvin Terrell, Fred Bonner II, Shederick A. Mcclendon, Jameel Scott, Tiffany P. Fountaine, Brenda Davis, Adriel A. Hilton, Praria Stavis-Hicks, Cheryl Rollins, Shaun R. Harper, Howard L. Simmons, Maurice Taylor, Herbert Brisbon, Christopher Weaver, Torrance Brown, James Moore III, Stephen A. Austin, and Lemuel Watson.

Dina C. Maramba would like to thank her family and friends whose unconditional love and support keep her grounded and inspired. She would like to thank the contributors who made this edited book project a success. She gives special thanks to Robert T. Palmer and Marybeth Gasman for making this a fun and exciting collaboration. She also expresses gratitude to her mentors and brothers and sisters in academia whose camaraderie has kept her motivated and balanced personally and professionally. To each and every one of them, she gives her utmost appreciation.

Marybeth Gasman I am thankful to my coeditors Robert T. Palmer and Dina C. Maramba for their hard work and innovative ideas. And as always, I am grateful to my sweet daughter Chloe for her love and humor as well as my good friend Nelson Bowman for his constant support. Lastly, I am thankful to my research assistants for their hard work and dedication: Thai-Huy Nguyen, Felecia Commodore, Shana Yem, Stephen Garlington, Claire Fluker, and Nina Daoud.

1

CHARTING THE COURSE

The Role of Minority Serving Institutions in Facilitating the Success of Underrepresented Racial Minority Students in STEM

Robert T. Palmer, Dina C. Maramba, Marybeth Gasman, and Katherine D. J. Lloyd

Introduction

There has been much discussion in various media outlets and public forums about the critical need to increase academic preparedness among underrepresented racial minorities (URMs) in science, technology, engineering, and mathematics (STEM) (Gasman, 2010; Harmon, 2012; Harper & Newman, 2010; Palmer, Maramba, & Dancy, 2011; Perna et al., 2009). Indeed, given that the U.S. Census Bureau (2008) predicts that there is expected to be rapid growth in the number of URMs over the next few decades (e.g., Blacks, Latino/as, Asian Americans, and Native Americans), researchers, policymakers, and educators have emphasized the importance of growing and nurturing the academic talent and potential of this population so they can effectively engage STEM education (Cole & Espinoza, 2008; Harper & Newman, 2010; Palmer, Davis, & Thompson, 2010; Palmer, Maramba, & Holmes, 2011; Perna et al., 2009). In fact, scholars have consistently argued that if America fails to increase academic success among URMs in STEM there will be negative implications for the country's economic growth and competitiveness in the global arena (Perna et al., 2009). Specifically, Museus, Palmer, Davis, and Maramba (2011) indicated:

> Several high profile organizations have warned that the nation's standing in the global economy is declining and the preparation of graduates who can contribute to its scientific and technological capacity is critical to preventing further decline and maintaining the nation's competitiveness in the international marketplace.... Given ... that minorities will make up an increasingly larger proportion of the STEM talent pool, it is essential for educators to maximize the success of these individuals if they are

to use the entire talent pool of potential STEM college students, college graduates, and professionals who can help maintain America's edge in the global marketplace.

(pp. 4–5)

Research has shown that academic readiness due to factors such as inadequate school financing (Adelman, 2006; Oakes, 1990), lack of participation in advanced placement courses (Adelman, 2006; Fergus, 2009), unqualified teachers (Perna et al., 2009), low teacher expectations (Fergus, 2009), lack of role models/mentors (Grandy, 1988), Eurocentric curriculum (Ladson–Billings, 1995; Tate, 1995), and premature departure from secondary education (Fergus, 2009), are some of the factors that stymie success among URMs in STEM. However, research indicates that URMs are just as interested in STEM disciplines as their White counterparts (Adelman, 2006). Indeed, some K-12 systems have harnessed the interest and potential of URMs by engendering programmatic initiatives to increase their academic preparedness (Museus et al., 2011).

Similarly, some higher education institutions have placed an earnest emphasis on increasing academic preparedness and success among URMs in STEM. For example, the University of Maryland at Baltimore County (UMBC) has established the Meyerhoff Program, which has shown efficacy in facilitating the success of URMs in STEM. Meyerhoff was founded in 1988 to increase success among Black students in STEM (Maton & Hrabowski, 2004). Research has shown that Meyerhoff provides knowledge and skills development, student motivation and support, monitoring and advising, and academic and social involvement to selected participants. Participants also engage in summer bridge programs, study groups, summer research internships, and have access to administrative and faculty support, community and family involvement, and mentors (Maton & Hrabowski, 2004).

Research indicates that Meyerhoff participants have higher grade point averages (GPAs) than nonparticipants (Hrabowski & Maton, 1995; Maton, Hrabowski, & Schmitt, 2000). Specifically, in a quantitative study where Hrabowski and Maton (1995) compared three Meyerhoff cohorts with historical cohorts at UMBC (before the Meyerhoff Program), they found that Meyerhoff cohorts had higher GPAs in their freshmen year of college than their pre-Meyerhoff counterparts. Similarly Perna et al. (2009) noted that Meyerhoff participants have achieved higher GPAs and earned admission into graduate programs at higher rates than nonparticipants. While the intent of the program was originally focused on promoting success among Blacks in STEM education, Meyerhoff has evolved to serve other student populations (Maton, Hrabowski, & Özdemir, 2007). Nevertheless, research has shown that this program has helped UMBC become a national leader in increasing access and success among URM students in STEM (Maton et al., 2000).

Notwithstanding the success that UMBC has had with the Meyerhoff program in increasing the academic preparedness of URMs in STEM, many higher education institutions are grappling with ways to increase retention and persistence among URMs in STEM. As Stage, Lundy-Wagner, and John note in chapter 2 of this edited volume, while this is true of all institutional types, it bears particular relevance to predominantly White institutions (PWIs; Harper, 2009; Hurtado, Milem, Clayton-Pedersen, & Allen, 1999; Palmer, Maramba & Holmes, 2011). Indeed, research has consistently indicated that the institutional climates of PWIs serve as an impediment to the academic growth and social involvement of URMs in general and STEM in particular. In fact, this research has noted that many URMs characterize the campuses of PWIs as chilly, alienating, unsupportive, and perpetuators of racial microaggressions (Smith, Yosso, & Solórzano, 2007; Solórzano, Ceja, & Yosso, 2000; Solórzano & Yosso, 2002).

Not only do these factors influence how URMs experience the institutional climates of PWIs, they also affect how URMs experience the institutional cultures of these institutions. Specifically, Museus et al. (2011) indicated, "Both the climates and cultures of [PWIs] and departments pose several challenges for [URM] students, suggesting that many of the challenges encountered by minority students are deeply embedded in the fabric of college campuses and STEM fields" (p. 70).

Indeed, while research has shown that having supportive and engaged faculty is critical to the success of college students in general and STEM specifically (Cole & Espinoza, 2008; Essien & Wood, chapter 9 this volume; Fries-Britt, Burt, & Franklin 2012; Gray, chapter 7 this volume; Newman, 2011), Cabrera, Colbeck, and Terenzini (2001) explained that "a classroom climate permeated by prejudice and discrimination on the part of faculty and peers [at PWIs] has emerged as an explanatory factor accounting for differences in college adjustment, majoring in hard sciences, and persisting in college between White men, women, and minority students" (p. 334). Similarly, Seymour and Hewitt (1997) stated, on campuses where there are few URMs in STEM, minority students were more likely to question whether they belonged, wonder if their peers viewed them as competent, were less inclined to seek support, and were more likely to experience loneliness without a peer with whom to share their experiences.

Despite the challenges that some PWIs experience in facilitating the success of URMs in STEM, some minority serving institutions (MSIs) have shown efficacy in facilitating the success of URMs in STEM education (Harmon, 2012; National Academies, 2010). Specifically, many educational institutions that serve predominantly minority populations, such as historically Black colleges and universities (HBCUs); Hispanic serving institutions (HSIs); and Tribal colleges and universities (TCUs) are effective in facilitating the educational attainment of minority students in general (Contreras, Bensimon, & Malcom, 2008; Gasman, 2008; Harmon, 2012; Nelson Laird, Bridges, Morelon-Quainoo, Williams, & Holmes, 2007; Palmer & Gasman, 2008), specifically in STEM education (Contreras et al., 2008; Perna et al., 2009).

For example, although HBCUs comprise 3% of the nation's institutions of higher education (Palmer & Wood, 2012), they prepare most of the nation's Black leaders in critical areas, such as science, mathematics, and engineering. In fact, Perna et al. (2009) indicated that "in 2004, HBCUs were the source of 22% of all bachelor's degrees to Blacks but 30% of the bachelor's degrees to Blacks in STEM fields" (p. 5). Even more noteworthy is that HBCUs make up 17 of the top 20 leading producers of STEM baccalaureate degrees among Blacks. Moreover, while HSIs represent 4% of all postsecondary institutions, they enroll approximately 42% of all Latino students (Harmon, 2012), and award nearly 40% of all baccalaureate degrees to Latinos—20% of which are in STEM fields. According to Dowd, Malcom, and Bensimon (2009), given the large numbers of Latinos that HSIs serve, they are positioned to provide critical pathways to STEM fields for this population. In fact, Congress has recognized HSIs for the important roles they will play in increasing STEM access and success among Latino students (Dowd et al., 2009). Further, while there is not much empirical research on the role of TCUs (Gasman, 2008; Guillory & Ward, 2008), some research suggest that TCUs produce the largest pool of American Indians who eventually complete their PhDs in science and engineering (National Academies, 2010).

Collectively, MSIs are responsible for producing nearly one-third of the nation's minority STEM graduates (Institute for Higher Education Policy [IHEP], 2009). According to a report by the National Academies (2010), MSIs provide a sensitive climate that consists of peer support, mentoring, role modeling, cultural relevant curricula, and that places an earnest emphasis on teaching—all of which play a significant role in the educational outcomes among URMs in MSIs (Contreras et al., 2008; Palmer, 2010; Palmer, Davis, & Thompson, 2010; Palmer & Gasman, 2008), specifically in STEM (Contreras et al., 2008; Perna et al., 2009).

MSIs' success among URMs students in STEM is noteworthy, but consistent with their mission in providing access and success to higher education for URMs, especially those who are underrepresented, first-generation, and low-income (Gasman, 2008; Gasman, Lundy-Wagner, Ransom, & Bowman 2010; Harmon, 2012; Palmer, Davis, & Hilton, 2009; Palmer, Davis, & Thompson, 2010). A recent report from IHEP (Harmon, 2012) indicated that collectively MSIs enroll more than 2.3 million students or close to 14% of all students, which include Black, Native Americans, Latino, Asian American, and Pacifier Islander American students. While these accomplishments are noteworthy, equally impressive is that MSIs are able to achieve these outcomes while lacking resources comparable to those of their PWI counterparts (Gasman, 2008; Harmon, 2012; Kim & Conrad, 2006; Palmer, Davis, & Thompson, 2010; Palmer & Gasman, 2008; Palmer & Griffin, 2009). Indeed, given this chapter's focus on MSIs, the next section will a provide historical context on HBCUs,

HSIs, TCUs, and Asian American and Native American Pacific Islander serving institutions (AANAPISIs).

Historical Overview of HBCUs

Before the Civil War, most colleges and universities were slow to open their doors to Blacks, especially in the South (Roebuck & Murty, 1993). Some Black Southerners were able to pursue education in what were termed "clandestine schools," which provided an opportunity to read, recall, and recite biblical passages (Allen & Jewell, 2002). When the Civil War began, less than 5% of 4.5 million Blacks were literate (Brown, 1999). Furthermore, there were only a few colleges and universities that catered exclusively to Blacks. Cheyney State University of Pennsylvania, founded in 1837, was one of the first colleges created to serve the educational needs of Blacks. Other Black schools established before the Civil War were Lincoln University of Pennsylvania, Avery College, and Wilberforce University (Brown, 2001).

After the Civil War, many HBCUs were established with the assistance of the Freedman's Bureau (Roebuck & Murty, 1993). Other organizations that played a role in the development of HBCUs were Black churches, such as the American Missionary Association (AMA), Northern missionaries, and private philanthropists. Additionally, HBCUs were established with the promulgation of the Morrill Act of 1880. According to Brown (1999), this legislation spurred the establishment of dual, public land-grant institutions in 19 Southern and border states, such as Alabama, Arkansas, Mississippi, Delaware, Florida, Georgia, Kentucky, Louisiana, Maryland, Pennsylvania, South Carolina, Tennessee, Texas, Virginia, and West Virginia (Brown, 1999). Nineteen HBCUs resulted from this legislation. Although these educational institutions were called colleges and universities, many functioned as multilevel schools, providing secondary education, college preparation, and college level courses.

The curriculum of HBCUs was influenced by either the teachings of Booker T. Washington or W. E. B. Du Bois. Washington, a self-educated man, born in 1856, advocated that Blacks focus on industrial education and racial segregation to achieve in society, while Du Bois endorsed racial integration and broached the importance of a liberal arts education for Blacks (Allen & Jewel, 2002). Universities such as Hampton and Tuskegee focused on Washington's teachings, emphasizing basic academic competence, manual labor skill, and political accommodations that mirrored the South's racial code (Allen & Jewel, 2002). Most HBCUs that adopted Du Bois' teachings, focused on providing their students with a liberal arts education (Allen & Jewel, 2002). Generally, the decision to adopt one concept for the curriculum over another was not in the hands of Blacks, rather White-controlled state government, corporate philanthropists, and White-dominated agencies made such decisions (Allen & Jewel, 2002).

Allen and Jewel (2002) argued that "White philanthropy and missionary control of HBCUs remained an issue for Blacks colleges until the 1920s" (p. 246).

In 1896, the clause of separate but equal, stemming from *Plessey v. Ferguson* (1896), became the litmus test used to measure educational equality. Beginning in the 1930s, the National Association for the Advancement of Colored People (NAACP) used tactics to attack social, political, and educational inequality. The organization's focus on education was limited initially to higher education. The NAACP defense team successfully litigated cases, such as *Gaines v. University of Missouri Law School* (1938), *Sipuel v. Board of Regents* (1948), *Sweatt v. Painter* (1950), and *Mc Laurin v. University of Oklahoma* (1950) (Roebuck & Murty, 1993). Their legal emphasis in these cases was not to undermine the separate but equal clause resulting from *Plessy v. Ferguson*, but to force states to live up to the separate but equal clause (Patterson, 2001). The NAACP defense team turned its attention to attacking separate but equal in primary and secondary education in the early 1950s, resulting in the Supreme Court's ruling in *Brown v. Board of Education* (1954), which struck down "separate but equal" in elementary and secondary schools.

Large scale desegregation did not arrive in America's colleges and universities until President Lyndon B. Johnson signed the Civil Rights Act of 1964 (Brown, 1999; Palmer, Davis, & Gasman, 2011). The law granted the federal government the authority to advocate, through legislation, on behalf of individuals who were discriminated against. Specifically, Title VI of Civil Rights Act of 1964 curtailed spending federal funds in segregated schools and colleges (Brown, 1999).

One court case that shaped desegregation in higher education was *Adams v. Richardson* (1973). Brown (1999) posited that this case was brought because 10 states, which eventually included 19 Southern states, maintained segregated and discriminatory higher education systems. In July 1977, the federal court mandated that the Department of Health, Education, and Welfare devise guidelines for states with segregated systems when they were preparing desegregation plans for compliance with Title VI. The court also stipulated that states must attain racial diversity for faculty and students at both PWIs and HBCUs (Roebuck & Murty, 1993). The issue of collegiate desegregation reappeared in *United States v. Fordice* (1992). *Fordice* stemmed from Mississippi's efforts to continue de jure segregation in its public university system by maintaining universities segregated along racial lines. Thus, a group of citizens sued the governor of Mississippi for alleged racial discrimination in the state university system. The United States intervened on the basis that state officials failed to disassemble the dual system, which violated the Equal Protection Clause of the 14th Amendment and Title VI of the Civil Rights Act of 1964. In 1992, *Fordice* reached the Supreme Court (Brown, 1999).

The Court identified four policies traceable to the vestiges of de jure segregation (see Gasman et al., 2007). As such, the Supreme Court returned the

Fordice case to a federal district court in Mississippi and charged it with developing a new desegregation plan (Hebel, 2004). The court mandated Mississippi to pay for new academic programs, construction, and start an endowment for the state's HBCUs. This plan required Mississippi's three HBCUs to recruit and retain at least 10% of non-Black students for three consecutive years. Until such time, the universities would not be allowed to control their share of the principal of the new endowments (Hebel, 2004). The Office of Civil Rights (OCR) has applied *Fordice* to states such as Florida, Kentucky, Texas, Maryland, Pennsylvania, and Virginia, to spur desegregation in higher education (Palmer, Davis, & Gasman, 2011).

Due to these court cases and federal and legal initiatives (e.g., The Civil Rights Act of 1964), the total number of Blacks enrolled in HBCUs declined from 18.18% in 1980 to 13.70% in 1998 while the number of Blacks enrolled in other institutions of higher education grew from 80.82% in 1980 to 86.3% in 1998. In 2007, the number of Black students attending HBCUs further declined to 10.63% while 89.37% now attend other postsecondary institutions (Palmer & Wood, 2012). In addition to court cases and federal and legal initiatives, the Higher Education Act of 1965 also played a critical role in opening up higher education to more URMs by the creation of the basic education opportunity grants as well as other financial aid programs. Interestingly, this legislation included Title III—Strengthening Developing Institutions—which provides federal funding to institution characterized as "developing," such as HBCUs and non-HBCUs, for their survival and enhancement. Title III allows institutions, such as HBCUs to use this federal funding for curriculum improvement, student services, faculty improvement programs, administrative improvements, and faculty and student exchanges (Roebuck & Murty, 1993).

Indeed, while fewer Blacks are attending HBCUs, there has been an increase in other student populations at these institutions (Gasman, 2008). Specifically, HBCUs, especially public institutions, are more racially and ethnically diverse institutions now than they were a decade earlier. For example, according to statistics from the Thurgood Marshall College Fund (2008), White student enrollment at HBCUs stands at 15,820 or 8%, Latino enrollment is 4,332 or 2%, and Asian enrollment is 2,464 or 1%. Most interestingly, Latinos have increased their enrollment at HBCUs by 124% (Gasman, 2009). This diversity is reflective among faculty as well. Approximately 60% of the faculty at HBCUs are from Africa or the Caribbean, or they are African Americans: Whites account for 30%; and Latinos and Asians make up the remaining 10% (Gasman, 2009). Despite the diversity in student enrollment, the majority of HBCUs have predominant Black enrollments, while three HBCUs have majority White student enrollment: Lincoln University (Missouri), West Virginia State University, and Bluefield State University [West Virginia] (Lee, forthcoming).

Notwithstanding the change in HBCUs' student enrollment, the relevancy, importance, and contribution of HBCUs are unquestionable (Allen & Jewel,

2002; Palmer, 2010). Numerous researchers have emphasized the HBCUs' prominent role in educating Black students (Gasman, 2008; Palmer & Gasman, 2008). Indeed, while there are 103 HBCUs, research shows they enroll 16% and graduate 20% of Black undergraduates (Gasman et al., 2010; Harmon, 2012). Furthermore, Allen and colleagues reported that HBCUs awarded 20% of all first professional degrees to Black students (Allen, Jewell, Griffin, & Wolf, 2007). Research also indicates that the HBCU experience propels more Blacks to seek professional education beyond the bachelor's degree (Gasman, 2008).

Historical Overview of HSIs

Unlike HBCUs, which were founded to provide access to postsecondary education for Blacks because they were intentionally excluded from PWIs, the founding and classification of HSIs is a recent phenomenon (Gasman, 2008). In fact, according to Nelson Laird et al. (2007), HSIs were born out of the reauthorization of the Higher Education Act of 1992 and are classified as such if their enrollment of Latino students accounts for 25% or more of their undergraduate enrollment (Gasman, 2008). Conversely, if an institution's enrollment of Latino students drops below 25%, their HSI designation will be in jeopardy (Contreras et al., 2008). Thus, Gasman (2008) posits that the term *Hispanic serving institutions* is a misnomer. A more fitting term, she suggests is *Hispanic enrolling institutions*. Indeed, while the majority of HSIs have emerged recently due to shifting demographics, the availability of financial aid, and PWIs being more open to nontraditional populations, some institutions (e.g., Hostos Community College, New York; National Hispanic University, California, and Boricua College, New York) were established as a consequence of the Civil Rights Movement with the intent of providing education to Latino students (Gasman, 2008).

According to Harmon (2012), HSIs are the fastest growing MSI designations and they award more associate and bachelor's degrees to Latino students than other colleges combined. Contreras et al. (2008) notes that there are 242 HSIs in the United States and Puerto Rico, the majority of which are public 2-year colleges (Contreras et al., 2008; Harmon, 2012; Laden, 2004). Specifically, 129 HSIs in the United States and Puerto Rico are 2-year colleges and 113, with the majority being in Puerto Rico, are 4-year institutions (Contreras et al., 2008). Research indicates that a large number of HSIs are located in California, Florida, New Mexico, and Texas (Harmon, 2012). Indeed, given that the Latino population is growing at an exceptional rate, the number of HSIs will likely continue to grow (Gasman, 2008).

The growing in student enrollment among HSIs is closely tied to its federal funding. With the reauthorization of the Higher Education Act of 1998, HSIs were placed under Title V—"Developing Institutions." Under Title V, HSIs are eligible for federal funding from the U.S. Department of Education if they can prove that 50% or more of their Latino students fall below the poverty level restrictions per the U.S. Census (Gasman, 2008), are accredited and nonprofit institutions, and they enroll at least 25% of Latino undergraduate students (Contreras et al., 2008). HSIs can apply for Title V funding through an annual grant competition and they can use this funding on a variety of initiatives intended to better serve the needs of their students. Despite the fact that funding for HSIs has increased over the past decade, these institutions remain underfunded compared to their non-MSIs counterparts. Contreras et al. (2008) surmised that this is because many HSIs are 2-year institutions, which are an underfunded segment of postsecondary education.

While HSIs were not created to exclusively serve Latino students, except in Puerto Rico, many are located in communities where there is a high population of Latino students. As such, these institutions create vehicles to inform Latino students throughout the educational pipeline about resources, services, and information about higher education (S. Brown, Santiago, & Lopez, 2003). Although HSIs are relatively new to the landscape of higher education, some evidence suggests that faculty, administrators, and programs at these institutions positively enhance the success of Latino students (Dayton, Gonzalez-Vasquez, Martinez, & Plum, 2004; Nelson Laird et al., 2007). Specifically, Laden (2004) noted that HSIs offer a wide array of academic and social support programs aimed to enhance the retention and completion rates of Latino students.

Historical Overview of TCUs

Similar to HSIs, there is scant literature on TCUs. Gasman (2008) speculates that this is because most TCUs are remote, resource deprived 2-year colleges, lacking systematic research and little infrastructure. Nevertheless, research indicates that the Navajo Nation created the first Tribal college in 1968, now called Diné College, as a consequence of the Civil Rights Movements of the 1960s. This college aimed to provide culturally centered and affordable education to American Indian students. During the 1970s and 1980s, many more TCUs were established because "many Native Americans realized the importance of building their own institutions and self-governance" (Gasman, 2008, p. 24).

Under the Tribally Controlled College or University Assistance Act, TCUs are accredited institutions with an enrollment of 50% or more of American Indian students (Gasman, 2008). According to Guillory and Ward (2008), there are currently 30 tribally controlled colleges that serve more than 30,000 students and represent more than 250 tribes from the United States, Mexico, and Canada. Further, there are three federally chartered Tribal colleges, all of which are members of the American Indian Education Consortium (AIHEC), which was established in 1972 and provides a collective and unifying voice for TCUs. Specifically, this organization "provides leadership and influences public policy on American Indian higher education issues through advocacy, research, and program initiatives" (AIHEC, n.d.). While the majority of TCUs offer associate degrees, seven offer baccalaureate degrees, and two offer master's degrees (Guillory & Ward, 2008).

TCUs are located in states such as Montana, North and South Dakota, Minnesota, California, Washington, Michigan, Nebraska, Arizona, Wisconsin, New Mexico, and Kansas; they are located on reservations or on land that is tribally controlled (Gasman, 2008). Unlike most American colleges and universities, Tribal colleges have a more interactive relationship with the neighborhoods in which they are situated and are heavily service oriented in relation to their communities (Gasman, 2008). Aside from being heavily engaged in the communities where they are located, TCUs also provide a fundamental purpose to the American Indian populations they serve. Specifically, they provide education to Native Americans living on reservations that are geographically isolated. They also serve as a conduit through which Tribal cultures and missions are discovered, restored, shaped, and preserved. Finally, "they encourage and enhance economic development within the Tribal community" (Gasman, 2008, p. 26).

Like HBCUs, TCUs receive Title III funding under the Higher Education Act. Gasman (2008), however, notes that while this money had increased from $6 million in 2000 to $24 million in 2005, it is well below what is necessary for TCUs, which have few resources, insufficient facilities, and problems recruiting and retaining faculty (Guillory & Ward, 2008). Despite the deficiency in funding, the enrollment of TCUs has increased substantially. Indeed, Gasman (2008) noted that in 1982, student enrollment at TCUs stood at 2,100; however, by the fall of 2001, student enrollment had increased to 13,961, a 565% increase. Guillory and Ward (2008) supported the burgeoning growth in enrollment among TCUs. In fact, they declared that: "TCUs are quietly changing the educational and social topography of reservations. Indian students are flocking to TCUs in unprecedented numbers to begin and/or continue to pursue a postsecondary education" (p. 97). Indeed, according to Harmon (2012), TCUs currently enroll approximately 19% of all American Indians.

Historical Overview of AANAPISIs

AANAPISIs, the most recently designated MSI, have a relatively recent history compared to HBCUs, TCUs, and HSIs. According to Park and Teranishi (2008), AANAPISIs emerged in a series of stages. In response to the lack of information and data about Asian American and Pacific Islander (AAPI) student needs in education, and the recognition of the importance of linking AAPI community based organizations with the federal government, a 2001 report by the White House Initiative on Asian Americans and Pacific Islanders (WHIAAPI) recommended that there be a federal designation for Asian

Americans and Pacific Islanders (Park & Teranishi, 2008). Although there were a number of events that led up to the development of AANAPISIs, it was not until May 2002 (U.S. Congress, H.R. 4825) that Congressman Robert Underwood (D-Guam) formally proposed an amendment to the Higher Education Act of 1965. Underwood suggested authorization to provide funding for colleges and universities that served Asian Americans and Pacific Islanders (Park & Teranishi, 2008). This proposal sparked further action as H.R. 4825 was reintroduced in the House of Representatives and eventually in the Senate. The first reintroduction was as H.R. 333 by Congressman David Wu (D-OR) in 2003 and as H.R. 2616 in 2005 by Senators Barbara Boxer (D-CA) and Daniel Akaka (D-HI) as a Senate companion bill S. 2160, the Asian American and Pacific Islander Serving Institutions Act (Park & Teranishi, 2008).

In 2007, as part of the College Cost Reduction and Access Act of 2007, the AANAPISI federal program was instituted (National Commission, 2010). One of the intentions of this policy was to provide resources for higher education institutions that were already serving a large number of AAPI students. More specifically, higher education institutions that were designated as AANAPISIs had at least 10% of AAPI full-time enrolled college students, a minimum threshold of low income students, and lower than average cost expenditure per student to compete for a grant (National Commission, 2010, 2011). There are currently 52 institutions that have been designated as an AANAPIS. However, because AANAPISIs must compete for federal grant funding, only 15 have been awarded grant funding to date. The 15 institutions are located in eight states: California, Hawaii, Illinois, New York, Massachusetts, Maryland, Texas, and Washington as well as the U.S. territory, Guam. Although 4-year universities were awarded, the majority of the 15 designated institutions are public 2-year colleges. In addition, among the 15 institutions, the enrollment of AAPI students has ranged between 11.5% and 90.9% (National Commission, 2011). Because AANAPISIs are newly designated MSI institutions, data and educational outcomes are still limited; however, according to the National Commission on Asian American and Pacific Islander Research in Education the AANAPISIs that have been granted federal funding (2008–2010) have indicated useful descriptive statistics for higher education. For example, descriptive findings have helped address the concern that AAPI students from specific ethnic groups who enter these institutions are first generation college students, come from underserved high schools, and are underprepared for college level work due to socioeconomic status. AANAPISIs focus on three main areas (a) student services (b) curriculum and academic programs, and (c) resources and research (National Commission, 2011). The AANAPISI designation for higher education institutions acknowledges the challenges faced by AAPI students and increases the potential to provide services and resources for the well-being of AAPI students.

Conclusion

Though MSIs have diverse histories, these institutions have a common aim of racial uplift, providing quality and affordable education to URMs, and being supportive educational venues through which racial minorities are able to envision and realize their dreams. Although they serve different segments of the URM populations, their ability to promote college access and success among URMs in general and in STEM specifically is noteworthy. As noted, not all MSIs are successful in promoting student success, but a large percentage of them are (Clewell, de Cohen, & Tsui, 2010; Contreras et al., 2008; Gasman, 2010, 2012; Harmon, 2012; Museus et al., 2011; Perna et al., 2009; Stage et al., 2012). To this end, this edited volume discusses the significant role that MSIs play in the production of URMs in STEM and provides insight into institutional practices, policies, and programmatic strategies that have helped to advance the success of minority students in STEM at MSIs.

Indeed, this book will be an important resource for institutions concerned with meeting the clarion call by political and educational leaders, who assert that *more* must be done to increase the success of URMs in STEM. Student affairs professionals, faculty, and administrators could use the information herein to establish best practices on campus that will positively contribute to and enhance educational outcomes among URMs in STEM. Furthermore, institutional officials could emulate institutional policies and strategies from the discussions in the book to be more intentional about increasing the retention and persistence among URMs in STEM majors.

References

Adams v. Richardson, 351 f.2d 636 (D.C.Cir. 1972).

Adelman, C. (2006). *The toolbox revisited: Paths to degree completion from high school through college.* Washington, DC: Department of Education.

Allen, W. R., & Jewell, J. O. (2002). A backward glance forward: Past, present and future perspectives on historically Black colleges and universities. *Review of Higher Education, 25*, 241–261.

Allen, W. R., Jewell, J. O., Griffin, K. A., & Wolf, D. S. (2007). Historically Black colleges and universities: Honoring the past, engaging the present, touching the future. *Journal of Negro Education, 76*(3), 263–280.

American Indian Higher Education Consortium. (n.d.). Retrieved from http://www.aihec.org/about/historyMission.cfm

Brown v. Board of Education, 347 U.S. 483 (1954).

Brown, M. C. (1999). *The quest to define collegiate desegregation: Black colleges, Title VI compliance, and post-Adams litigation.* Westport, CT: Bergin & Garvey.

Brown, M. C. (2001). Collegiate desegregation and the public Black college: A new policy mandate. *Journal of Higher Education, 72*(1), 46–62.

Brown, S. E., Santiago, D., & Lopez, E. (2003). Latinos in higher education: Today and tomorrow. *Change, 35,* 40–46.

Cabrera, A., Colbeck, C., & Terenzini, P. (2001). Developing performance indicators for assessing classroom teaching practices and student learning: The case of engineering. *Research in Higher Education, 42*(3), 327–352.

Civil Rights Act of 1964 (Title VII), 42 U.S.C. 2000e et. seq. 29 C.F.R. 1600-1610.

Clewell, B., Cosentino de Cohen, C., & Tsui, L, (2010). Capacity building to diversity STEM: Realizing potential among HBCUs. Washington, DC: Urban Institute.

Cole, D., & Espinoza, A. (2008). Examining the academic success of Latino students in science, technology, engineering, and mathematics (STEM) majors. *Journal of College Student Development, 49*(4), 285–300.

Contreras, F., Bensimon, E., & Malcom, L. (2008). An equity-based accountability framework for Hispanic serving institutions. In M. Gasman, B. Baez, & C. S. V. Turner (Eds.), *Understanding minority serving institutions* (pp. 71–90). Albany, NY: SUNY Press.

Dayton, B., Gonzalez-Vasquez, N., Martinez, C. R., & Plum, C. (2004). Hispanic serving institutions through the eyes of students and administrators. *New Directions for Student Services, 105,* 29–39.

Dowd, A. C., Malcom, L. E., & Bensimon, E. M. (2009). *Benchmarking the success of Latino and Latina students in STEM to achieve national graduation goals.* Los Angeles, CA: University of Southern California Press.

Fergus, E. (2009). Understanding Latino students' schooling experiences: The relevance of skin color among Mexican and Puerto Rican high school students. *Teachers College Record, 111*(2), 339–375.

Fries-Britt, S., Burt, B., & Franklin, K. (2012). Establishing critical relationships: How Black males persist in physics at HBCUs. In R. T. Palmer & J. L. Wood (Eds.), *Black men in college: Implications for HBCUs and beyond* (pp. 71–88). New York: Routledge.

Gándara, P., & Contreras, F. (2009). *The Latino education crisis: The consequences of failed social policies.* Cambridge, MA: Harvard University Press.

Gasman, M. (2008). Minority-serving institutions: A historical backdrop. In M. Gasman, B. Baez, & C. S. V. Turner (Eds.), *Understanding minority-serving institutions* (pp. 18–27). Albany, NY: SUNY Press.

Gasman, M. (2009). Diversity at historically Black colleges and universities. Retrieved from http://diverseeducation.wordpress.com/2009/06/05/diversity-at-historically-black-colleges-and-universities/

Gasman, M. (2010). Bolstering African American success in the STEM fields. Retrieved from http://chronicle.com/blogs/innovations/

Gasman, M. (2012). Succeeding in STEM: Lessons from Black colleges. Retrieved from http://www.huffingtonpost.com/marybeth-gasman/black-colleges-education_b_1318328.html

Gasman, M., Baez, B., Drezner, N. D., Sedgwick, K., Tudico, C., & Schmid, J. M. (2007). Historically Black colleges and universities: Recent trends. *Academe, 93*(1), 69–78.

Gasman, M., Lundy-Wagner, V., Ransom, T., & Bowman, N. (2010). *Unearthing promise and potential: Our nation's historically Black colleges and universities* (ASHE Higher Education Report). San Francisco, CA: Jossey-Bass.

Grandy, J. (1988). Persistence in science of high-ability minority students: Results of a longitudinal study. *Journal of Higher Education, 69*(6), 589–620.

Guillory, J., & Ward, K. (2008). Tribal colleges and universities: Identity, invisibility, and current Issues. In M. Gasman, B. Baez, & C. S. V. Turner (Eds.), *Understanding minority-serving institutions* (pp. 91–110). Albany, NY: SUNY University Press.

Harmon, N. (2012). *The role of minority-serving institutions in national college competition goals: Institute of Higher Education Policy.* Washington, DC: Author.

Harper, S. R. (2009). Niggers no more: A critical race counternarrative on Black male student achievement at predominantly White colleges and universities. *International Journal of Qualitative Studies in Education, 22*(6), 697–712.

Harper, S. R., & Newman, C.B. (Eds.). (2010). *Students of color in STEM: New directions for institutional research.* San Francisco, CA: Jossey-Bass.

Hebel, S. (2004, October 29). Supreme Court clears way for settlement of college-desegregation case. *Chronicle of Higher Education,* A26–A26.

Hrabowski, F. A., & Maton, K. I. (1995). Enhancing the success of African American students in the sciences: Freshman year outcomes. *School of Science and Mathematics, 95*(1), 19–27.

Hurtado, S., Milem, J. F., Clayton-Pedersen, A. R., & Allen, W. R. (1999). *Enacting diverse learning environments: Improving the campus climate for racial/ethnic diversity in higher education* (ASHE-ERIC Higher Education Reports Series, Vol. 26, No. 8). San Francisco, CA: Jossey-Bass.

Kim, M. M., & Conrad, C. F. (2006). The impact of historically Black colleges and universities on the academic success of African American students. *Research in Higher Education, 47*(4), 399–427.

Institute of Higher Education Policy. (2009). *Diversifying the STEM pipeline: The model replication institutions program.* Washington, DC: Author.

Laden, B. V. (2004). Hispanic-serving institutions: What are they? Where are they? *Community College Journal of Research and Practice, 28*(3), 181–198.

Ladson-Billings, G. (1995). But that's just good teaching! The case for culturally relevant pedagogy. *Theory into Practice, 34*(3), 159–165.

Lee, J. M. (forthcoming). An examination of the participation of African American students in graduate education without public HBCUs. In R. T. Palmer, A. A. Hilton., & T. P. Fountaine (Eds.), *Black graduate education at historically Black colleges and universities: Trends, experiences, and outcomes.* London: Information Age Press.

Maton, K. I., & Hrabowski, F. A. (2004). Increasing the number of African American Ph.D.s in the sciences and engineering: A strengths-based approach. *American Psychologist, 59,* 629–654.

Maton, K. I., Hrabowski, F. A., & Ozdemir, M. (2007). Opening an African American STEM program to talented students of all races: Evaluation of the Meyerhoff scholars programs, 1991–2005. In G. Orfield, P. Marin, S. M. Flores, & L. Garces (Eds.), *Charting the future of college affirmative action: Legal victories, continuing attacks, and new research* (pp. 125–156). Los Angeles, CA: The Civil Rights Project at UCLA.

Maton, K. I., Hrabowski, F. A., & Schmitt, C. L. (2000). African American college students excelling in the sciences: College and postcollege outcome in the Meyerhoff Scholars Program. *Journal of Research in Science Teaching, 37*(7), 629–654.

McLaurin, v. Oklahoma State Regents, 339 U.S. 637 (1950).

Missouri ex rel. Gaines v. Canada, 305 U.S. 337 (1938).

Morrill Act of 1890, Ch. 841, 26 stat. 417

Museus, S. D., Palmer, R. T., Davis, R. J., & Maramba, D. C. (2011). *Racial and ethnic minority student's success in STEM education* (ASHE-Higher Education Report Series, Vol. 36, No. 6). San Francisco, CA: Jossey-Bass.

National Academies. (2010). *Expanding underrepresented minority participation: America's science and technology talent at the crossroads.* Washington, DC: Author.

National Commission on Asian American and Pacific Islander Research in Education. (2010). *Federal higher education policy priorities and the Asian American and Pacific Islander community.* New York: USA Funds.

National Commission on Asian American and Pacific Islander Research in Education. (2011). *The relevance of Asian Americans and Pacific Islanders in the college completion agenda.* New York: USA Funds.

Nelson Laird, T. F., Bridges, B. K., Morelon-Quainoo, C. L., Williams, J. M., & Holmes, M. S. (2007). African American and Hispanic students' engagement at minority serving and predominantly White institutions. *Journal of College Student Development, 48*(1), 39–56.

Newman, C. B. (2011). Engineering success: The role of faculty relationships with Black collegians. *The Journal of Women and Minorities in Science and Engineering, 17*(3), 193–209.

Oakes, J. (1990). Opportunities, achievement, and choice: Women and minority students in science and mathematics. *Review of Research in Education, 16*(2), 153–166.

Palmer, R. T. (2010). The perceived elimination of affirmative action and the strengthening of historically Black colleges and universities. *Journal of Black Studies, 40*(4), 762–776.

Palmer, R. T., Davis, R. J., & Gasman, M. (2011). A matter of diversity, equity and necessity: The tension between Maryland's higher education system and its historically Black institutions over the OCR agreement. *Journal of Negro Education, 80*(2), 121–133.

Palmer, R. T., Davis, R. J., & Hilton, A. A. (2009). Exploring challenges that threaten to impede the academic success of academically underprepared African American male collegians at an HBCU. *Journal of College Student Development, 50*(4), 429–445.

Palmer, R. T., Davis, R. J., & Thompson, T. (2010). Theory meets practice: HBCU initiatives that promote academic success among African Americans in STEM. *Journal of College Student Development, 51*(4), 440–443.

Palmer, R. T., & Gasman, M. (2008). "It takes a village to raise a child": The role of social capital in promoting academic success for African American men at a Black college. *Journal of College Student Development, 49*(1), 52–70.

Palmer, R. T., & Griffin, K. (2009). Desegregation policy and disparities in faculty salary and workload: Maryland's historically Black and predominantly White institutions. *Negro Educational Review, 60*(1–4), 7–21.

Palmer, R. T., Maramba, D. C., & Dancy, T. E. (2011). A qualitative investigation of factors promoting the retention and persistence of students of color in STEM. *Journal of Negro Education, 80*(4), 491–504.

Palmer, R. T., Maramba, D. C., & Holmes, L. S. (2011). A contemporary examination of factors promoting the academic success of minority students at a predominantly White university. *Journal of College Student Retention, 13*(3), 329–348.

Palmer, R. T., & Wood, J. L. (Eds.). (2012). *Black men in college: Implications for HBCUs and beyond.* New York: Routledge.

Park, J. J., & Teranishi, R. T. (2008). Asian American and Pacifica Islander serving institutions. In M. Gasman, B. Baez, & C. S. V. Turner (Eds.), *Understanding minority serving institutions* (pp. 111–126). Albany, NY: SUNY Press.

Patterson, J. T. (2001). *Brown v. Board of Education: A civil rights milestone and its troubled legacy.* New York: Oxford University Press.

Perna, L., Lundy-Wagner, V., Drezner, N. D., Gasman, M., Yoon, S., Bose, E., & Gary. S. (2009). The contribution of HBCUs to the preparation of African American women for STEM careers: A case study. *Research Higher Education, 50*(*1*), 1–23.

Plessy v. Ferguson, 163 U.S. 537 (1896).

Roebuck, J. B., & Murty, K. S. (1993). *Historically Black colleges and universities: Their place in American higher education.* Westport, CT: Praeger.

Seymour, E., & Hewitt, N. M. (1997). *Talking about leaving: Why undergraduates leave the sciences.* Oxford, England: Westview Press.

Sipuel v. Board of Regents, 332 U.S. 631 (1948).

Smith, W. A., Yosso, T. J., & Solórzano, D. G. (2007). Racial primes and Black misandry on historically White campuses: Toward critical race account ability in educational administration. *Educational Administration Quarterly, 43*(5), 559–585.

Solórzano, D. G., Ceja, M., & Yosso, T. J. (2000). Critical race theory, racial microaggressions, and campus racial climate: The experiences of African American college students. *Journal of Negro Education, 69*, 60–73.

Solórzano, D. G., & Yosso, T. J. (2002). A critical race counterstory of race, racism, and affirmative action. *Equity & Excellence in Education, 35*(2), 155–168.

Sweatt v. Painter, 339 U.S. 629 (1950).

Tate, F. W. (1995). Returning to the root: A cultural relevant approach to mathematics pedagogy. *Theory into Practice, 34*(3), 166–173.

Thurgood Marshall College Fund. (2007–2008). *Demographic report.* Retrieved from http://www.thurgoodmarshallfund.net/images/pdf/07-08-demographic-report-3-8.pdf

United States v. Fordice, 112 S. Ct. 2727(1992).

U.S. Census Bureau. (2008). An older and more diverse nation by mid-century. Retrieved from http://www.census.gov/PressRelease/www/releases/archives/population/012496.html.

2

MINORITY SERVING INSTITUTIONS AND STEM

Charting the Landscape

Frances K. Stage, Valerie C. Lundy-Wagner, and Ginelle John

Calls to increase the science, technology, engineering, and mathematics (STEM) pipeline have largely focused on improving postsecondary access to historically underrepresented students (Cook & Córdova, 2006; National Academy of Science [NAS], 2010). Stakeholders in higher education as well as those in other areas have pointed primarily toward student-level characteristics (e.g., precollege preparation, demography, attitudes, or behaviors) to identify disparities in STEM participation and success (Maple & Stage, 1991), but also to develop strategies for expanding access to STEM. This has coincided largely with the recognition that American colleges and universities serve an increasingly diverse population (Baum & Ma, 2007; Chang, Cerna, Han, & Saenz, 2008; Hurtado, Newman, Tran, & Chang, 2010). In fact, data show that between 1967 and 2007 the Asian and Latina/o undergraduate student populations increased from 2% to 7% and 4% to 11%, respectively (Snyder, Dillow, & Hoffman, 2009). Despite these and aggregate gains by historically underrepresented students in higher education, enrollment and completion in STEM specifically has not grown as fast. In fact, besides increases in STEM participation by Asian students, the enrollment and completion gains for other minorities in STEM have been less than impressive (National Science Foundation [NSF], Division of Science Resources Statistics, 2009).

While the number of undergraduates of color who initially choose STEM fields has grown, few students succeed and persist (Hurtado et al., 2007; Palmer, Davis & Hilton, 2009). Policymakers, government agencies, and foundations have supported research on minorities in STEM as well as programs to encourage students to persist in science and mathematics. However, trends in the numbers of students who go on to STEM careers is dismal. For example,

Native Americans, Blacks, and Hispanics (Latina/os) each comprise only 3% of all employed scientists and engineers (NSF, 2005). Additionally, students from those populations earn doctoral degrees at proportions that range from one quarter to one tenth of their proportion in the general population (Thurgood, Golladay, & Hill, 2006). Those percentages are dramatically lower for STEM doctorates; Blacks earned 3.5% and Hispanics 3.7% of all science doctorates and Native Americans earned 0.5% (NSF, 2005). Subsequent transition to the science and engineering labor force is lower. These data are often confounded by the inclusion of foreign nationals (Teranishi, 2007). In spite of that, some institutional contexts exist where underrepresented students are more likely to persist and complete bachelor's degrees in STEM fields.

Studies that focus on students' baccalaureate origins examine institutions as the unit of analysis, comparing them in terms of the success of their baccalaureate graduates (Stage & Hubbard, 2009; Wolf-Wendel, 1998). Those baccalaureate studies typically resulted in listings of particular institutions that were successful in producing relatively large numbers of STEM graduates who went on to succeed in science careers. Results from these studies have found that many historically Black colleges and universities (HBCUs) have graduated disproportionate percentages of underrepresented minority students who continue on to earn STEM doctorates (Hubbard & Stage, 2010; Solórzano, 1995; Stage, John, & Hubbard, 2011; Thurgood et al., 2006; Wolf-Wendell, 1998). Additionally, Hubbard and Stage (2009), in a national study of full-time faculty at predominately Black institutions, found that they preferred teaching undergraduates.

Many postsecondary stakeholders are familiar with HBCUs and their contributions to specifically African American STEM success (see Brown & Davis, 2001, Harper & Newman, 2010; Palmer, Davis, & Thompson, 2010; Perna et al., 2009; Solórzano, 1995). However, considerably less information exists on the STEM contribution of Tribal colleges and universities (TCUs), Hispanic serving institutions (HSIs), and the more recently established Asian American and Native American Pacific Islander serving institutions (AANAPISIs), all of which are classified as minority-serving institutions (MSIs; Gasman, Baez, & Turner, 2008; Li & Carroll, 2007; Museus, 2009; Teranishi, 2010). While each of these four MSI designations typically enrolled disproportionate percentages of a particular ethnic/racial group, more recent additions (i.e., HSIs and AANAPISIs) require both measures of race/ethnicity and socioeconomic status to determine eligibility for the designation. This is important, because it allows greater participation by students from low-income backgrounds and it allows greater attention to be paid to their educational needs (NAS, 2010; NSF, 2009; Ohland, Orr, Lundy-Wagner, Veenstra, & Long, 2012). However, despite this work on ethnicity/race and socioeconomic status in STEM, to date little work exists that specifically characterizes the MSI contribution to the underrepresented student STEM pipeline.

Background and Purpose

MSIs are a federally designated group of institutions that were classified based on legislation or the percentage of their minority and low-income enrollment (Gasman et al., 2008; Li & Carroll, 2007). MSIs represent a heterogeneous set of 2- and 4-year institutions, many with missions to serve historically underrepresented or economically disadvantaged students (Gasman, 2008; Stage, Conway, John, & Lundy-Wagner, 2011). HBCUs and TCUs were initially established to empower African American and Native American students, providing low-cost and virtually open access due to legal, social, or geographical limitations that prevented postsecondary access (Gasman, Lundy-Wagner, Ransom, & Bowman, 2010). However, HSIs and AANAPISIs are predominantly White institutions (PWIs) that enroll a significant proportion of underrepresented students including students from low-income backgrounds (Mercer & Stedman, 2008). While many of these institutions serve large proportions of Asian and Pacific Islander, African American, Latina/o, and Native American/Alaskan Native students, their establishment and evolution, as well as ongoing strategies for serving these populations varies (Dowd, Malcolm, & Bensimon, 2009; Gasman et al., 2008).

Nonetheless, the lack of research on the MSI contribution to STEM is problematic for at least four reasons. First, MSIs confer a significant proportion of underrepresented minority students' bachelor's degrees (Baum & Ma, 2007; Thurgood et al., 2006). It would be useful to learn about the productivity of these colleges and universities with regard to STEM degrees. Data on STEM productivity at MSIs could provide information about new ways of facilitating access to STEM bachelor degree programs for underrepresented minority populations (Li & Carroll, 2007). This may be especially helpful given the changing ethnic/racial composition of the undergraduate population. In addition, the lack of research on MSIs in aggregate groups prevents a comprehensive characterization of MSI successes and challenges to improving STEM access and equity (Harper & Newman, 2010).

Second, MSIs as a group often enroll students deemed academically underprepared, and thus provide disadvantaged students with pathways into STEM education and workforce. While calls to increase the composition of the STEM pipeline often focus on student characteristics like ethnicity/race or gender (NAS, 2010), some consider the postsecondary institutional context equally important for improving access to higher education in general (Hurtado, Carter, & Kardia, 1998), and to success in STEM in particular (e.g., Carmichael, Labat, Hunter, Privett, & Sevenair, 1993). Also, as primary, secondary, and remedial education programs continue to lose resources due to the financial crisis and retrenchment, so do those students most vulnerable to such policy changes, many of whom will likely end up at a MSI, if they choose postsecondary education.

Third, MSIs have a history of success in preparing underrepresented minority and low-income students in the STEM fields at the undergraduate and graduate levels. While many of the gains by African Americans and Latina/os in STEM come from students attending HBCUs or HSIs (Crisp, Nora, & Taggart, 2009; Perna et al., 2009; Solórzano, 1995), the other less frequently discussed MSIs, TCUs, and AANAPISIs may also play an important role in diversifying the undergraduate STEM pipeline. Building on work by numerous scholars about perspectives that challenge the deficit framework (e.g. Contreras, Malcom, & Bensimon, 2008; Dowd et al., 2009), this study examines the production of STEM degrees at all types of MSIs.

Fourth, most research on MSIs focuses on one particular institution or on one particular MSI designation (Gasman et al., 2008). In this chapter we characterize the contribution of each MSI type to the STEM pipeline disaggregated by racial/ethnic designation of the students. Given the sustained attention to improving the STEM pipeline by increasing underrepresented student participation and success, we contextualize the individual and aggregate MSI contribution to underrepresented STEM bachelor's degrees within the larger postsecondary system generally and specifically to capture their role in promoting STEM success.

This chapter fills a gap in the literature by reporting recent data on underrepresented undergraduate students' participation in STEM bachelor's degree programs at MSIs. This work contributes to the research on underrepresented students' access to and success in STEM but also to the growing body of work on MSIs. In particular, we add to the existing literature on the HBCU and HSI contributions to Black and Latina/o participation and success in STEM, as well as characterizing the TCU and AANAPISI contributions to STEM bachelor's degree recipients. The research question guiding this work is: What is the contribution of MSIs to minority earned STEM undergraduate degrees?

Methodology

To answer the research question we use two datasets sponsored by the Department of Education's National Center for Education Statistics (NCES). More specifically, we used the Integrated Postsecondary Educational Data System (IPEDS) and general tables at the Department of Education's National Center for Education Statistics (NCES). IPEDS data are collected annually from all U.S. postsecondary education institutions that participate in the federal student financial aid programs. IPEDS collects data in the following seven areas: enrollments, degree completion, institutional characteristics, tuition, financial aid, persistence, and finances.

We identified the 2008–2009 academic year as critical, given that it was the first year that AANAPISIs received their federal designation and monies as MSIs. Despite the fact that by 2011 there were 10 official MSI designations

(National Center for Education Statistics [NCES], 2011a), we focused our research on the four federal institutional designations that represent historically underrepresented minority ethnic and cultural groups. Using the NCES general tables, we identified a list of institutions with the AANAPISI and HSI designations for that year. The HBCU and TCU institutions are readily identifiable in the IPEDS dataset; these two designations are part of the "Frequently Used" variables on the institutional characteristics survey.

We then used the IPEDS completions survey to identify the number of completions by each institution for the 2008–2009 year (NCES, 2011b). We specifically used the "Postsecondary Awards in Science, Technology, Engineering, and Mathematics: 2008-09" completion records to get the actual numbers and percentages of STEM and non-STEM graduates from MSI and non-MSI institutions with data disaggregated by racial/ethnic group. That survey included the following academic programs as STEM: mathematics/statistics, natural sciences (agricultural, biological, and physical sciences), engineering/engineering technologies, and computer/information sciences. Once the completions data had been identified, we ran descriptive statistics to calculate the MSI and non-MSI contributions to STEM and non-STEM bachelor's degree programs overall, by both ethnicity/race and MSI designation.

The number of institutions included in our analysis was determined by whether or not institutions had reported data for the 2008–2009 academic year. These are the number of institutions in each of the four MSI designations: Asian American and Native American Pacific Islander-serving Institution (AANAPISI, n = 27); historically Black colleges and universities (HBCU, n = 99); Hispanic-serving institutions (HSIs, n = 29); and Tribal colleges and universities (TCUs, n = 32) (see Appendix A). Finally, possibly more institutions would have qualified for MSI status during the 2008–2009 academic year; however, for the HSI and AANAPISI designations, institutions must opt in, apply for, and receive federal funding. These qualifications likely limited the number of MSIs included in the following analysis, and contributes to conservative estimates of total MSIs' production of underrepresented minority STEM bachelor's degrees at these two types of institutions.

Results

These findings suggest that the four MSI designations under consideration played a significant role in the production of minority undergraduate degrees in STEM during the 2008–2009 academic year, both in the aggregate, and with respect to their individual ethnic/racial group designations. Table 2.1 presents a summary of STEM bachelor's degree production by ethnicity/race and MSI institution type, including the total number of STEM bachelor's degrees conferred and the percentages of students from various ethnic/racial groups graduated from each MSI type. Among the 9,965 STEM bachelor's degrees granted by AANAPISIs, HBCUs, HSIs, and TCUs during the 2008–2009 academic year in the aggregate, approximately 71% (7,078 of 9965) were earned by American Indian/Alaskan Native, Asian American, African American, and Latina/o undergraduates.

Table 2.1 also shows, as expected, that colleges within each MSI designation conferred a considerable proportion of its STEM bachelor's degrees to students of the related ethnic/racial group. For example, for Black or African Americans at MSIs, 86% of STEM bachelor's degrees were conferred at an HBCU. Similarly, TCUs conferred 63% of STEM degrees earned by Native Americans (63%) and AANAPISIs conferred 34% of STEM degrees earned by Asian Americans. However, for HSIs, only 6% of the STEM degrees awarded went to Hispanic or Latino/a graduates.

In addition, a wide variation existed in the percentage of each MSI designation conferring STEM bachelor's degrees. For example, while over 80% of HBCUs awarded STEM bachelor's degrees, that percentage is remarkably higher in comparison to the percentages for other MSIs, with only 41% of AANAPISIs, 24% of HSIs, and 9% of TCUs awarding STEM bachelor's degrees. In fact, the TCU contribution to MSI production of minority STEM bachelor's degrees was especially small. Many TCUs are 2-year colleges; among the 32 TCUs included, only three TCUs conferred STEM bachelor's degrees in 2008–2009.

Overall, MSIs were an important producer of STEM bachelor's degrees to students of all races and ethnicities, awarding nearly 10,000 in 2008–2009. However, the contribution of each designation varied considerably. HBCUs with 99 institutions awarded nearly half of the MSI bachelor's degrees. AANAPISIs (27 institutions) awarded over 40%, HSIs (29 institutions) nearly 10%, and TCUs (32 institutions) less than 1% in 2008–2009.

To better understand the MSI contribution to minority STEM bachelor's degrees, Table 2.2 presents a summary of non-STEM bachelor's degree production by ethnicity/race and MSI institution type for comparison. While underrepresented minority students earned 71% of MSI STEM bachelor's degrees, a smaller proportion of non-STEM MSI bachelor's degrees were awarded (67% or 38,848 of 58,261). Finally, about 15% of all bachelor's degrees earned at MSIs were STEM degrees. However, this varied across groups. For example, more than 22% of all bachelor's degrees earned at MSIs by Asian Pacific Islander students were STEM. However, for other designations the percentage was lower. About 15% of the MSI bachelor's degrees earned by African American students were STEM degrees. Similarly, corresponding percentages were Hispanic or Latino 12%, White 11%, and Native American 8%.

Table 2.3 presents a broader overview of the contribution MSIs play in the earning of a STEM bachelor's degree by underrepresented minority students. In fact, the data show that the percentage of Asian American, African American, and Latina/o students attending MSIs and earning STEM bachelor's degrees

TABLE 2.1 *STEM Bachelor's Degree Production by Ethnicity/Race and MSI Designation, 2008–2009*

STEM	American Indian or Alaskan Native		Asian/Native Hawaiian/Other Pacific Islander		Black or African American		Hispanic or Latina/o		White		Non-Residents		Other		Total
	#	%	#	%	#	%	#	%	#	%	#	%	#	%	*Total*
AANAPISIs n=27	35	0.812	1465	34	170	4	487	11	1400	32	291	7	465	11	4313
HBCUs n=99	4	0.082	92	2	4184	86	67	1	222	5	223	5	101	2	4893
HSIs n=29	4	0.533	73	10	25	3	467	6	134	18	18	2	30	4	751
TCUs n=32	5	63	0	0.0	0	0.0	0	0.0	3	38	0	0.0	0	0.0	8
Total n=187	48	0.482	1630	16	4379	44	1021	10	1759	18	532	5	596	6	9965

Note: During this academic year, there were 27 AANAPISIs, 11 of whom were granted STEM bachelor's degrees; 99 HBCUs, of whom were 80 granted STEM bachelor's degrees; 29 HSIs, of whom 7 granted STEM bachelor's degrees; and 32 TCUs, of whom 3 were granted STEM bachelor's degrees.

TABLE 2.2 Non-STEM Bachelor's Degree Production by Ethnicity/Race and MSI Designation, 2008–2009

Non-STEM	American Indian or Alaskan Native		Asian/Native Hawaiian/ Other Pacific Islander		Black or African American		Hispanic or Latina/o		White		Non-Residents		Other		Total
	#	%	#	%	#	%	#	%	#	%	#	%	#	%	
AANAPISIs n=27	279	1	5212	21	1424	6	4484	18	10395	41	762	3	2759	11	25315
HBCUs n=99	60	0.23	203	0.77	22829	86	357	1	2145	8	453	2	476	2	26523
HSIs n=29	33	0.53	385	6	736	12	2689	43	1855	30	72	1	453	7	6223
TCUs n=32	155	78	1	0.50	1	0.50	0	0.0	19	10	24	12	0	0.0	200
Total n=187	527	0.91	5801	10	24990	43	7530	13	14414	25	1311	2	3688	6	58261

Note: During this academic year, there were 27 AANAPISIS, 13 of whom were granted non-STEM bachelor's degrees; 99 HBCUs, of whom 85 were granted non-STEM bachelor's degrees; 29 HSIs, of whom 8 were granted non-STEM bachelor's degrees; and 32 TCUs, of whom 8 were granted non-STEM bachelor's degrees.

is considerably higher than for those same groups attending non-MSIs. For example, 44% of MSI STEM bachelor's degree recipients were African American whereas only 5% of non-MSI STEM bachelor's degrees were conferred to African American students. Although the difference for Asian, Latina/o, and Native American students is smaller, these results point to the contribution MSIs play in providing minority students with access to STEM and suggests the possibility of an academic climate at MSIs that is important in fostering success for underrepresented minority STEM majors.

By contrast, Table 2.4 presents a summary of the comparative contributions of MSIs and non-MSIs in conferring non-STEM bachelor's degrees. While 22% of the non-STEM bachelor's degrees conferred at non-MSIs are awarded to Asian, Black, Latina/o, and Native American students, 67% were awarded at MSIs. In fact, for each ethnic/racial group, a higher percentage of non-STEM bachelor's degrees were awarded to minorities at MSIs compared to non-MSIs. Specifically, 43% of Black, 13% of Latina/o, 10% of Asian, and nearly 1% of Native American non-STEM bachelor's degree recipients were conferred degrees from MSIs; whereas the numbers for non-MSIs are 8%, 8%, 5%, and 0.71%, respectively. From these tables we see that MSIs play an important and unique role in the production of underrepresented minorities in the STEM fields, but also non–STEM fields.

Discussion and Conclusion

Recent work focuses on specific types of MSIs and the role they play in underrepresented college student success (Contreras et al., 2008; Palmer et al., 2009). The research reported in this chapter focused on a national view of the role, in the aggregate, that MSIs play in the success of the undergraduate stem majors.

MSIs represent a relatively small number of the thousands of postsecondary education institutions in the United States, yet provide an environment for budding scholars, and particularly for underprepared students who seek STEM degrees. Given gaps in postsecondary access and success in STEM fields (NSF, 2009), MSIs can provide academically underprepared pathways into STEM. While calls to increase the pipeline often include attention to ethnicity/race (NAS, 2010), others have considered the institutional context an equally important consideration (e.g., Perna et al., 2009). Further, as K-12 and remedial education suffer economically, so will students most vulnerable to reforms (or the lack thereof), and many of them will likely end up at a MSI if they choose postsecondary education.

MSIs have a history of success in preparing underrepresented minority and low-income students in STEM and these results confirm that successful history, but scholars usually focus on HBCUs or HSIs. Here we learn that AANAPISIs and TCUs also play an important role in diversifying the undergraduate STEM pipeline demonstrated in the results described in this chapter. The percentages

TABLE 2.3 STEM Bachelor's Degree Production by Ethnicity/Race: MSIs vs. Non-MSI Designation, 2008–2009

STEM	American Indian or Alaskan Native		Asian/Native Hawaiian/ Other Pacific Islander		Black or African-American		Hispanic or Latina/o		White		Non-Residents		Other		Total
	#	%	#	%	#	%	#	%	#	%	#	%	#	%	
MSIs n=101	48	0.48	1630	16	4379	44	1021	10	1759	18	532	5	596	6	9965
Non-MSIs n=1662	1370	0.61	26017	11	11373	5	16572	7	148236	65	9635	4	13430	6	226633
Total n=1763	1418	0.60	27647	12	15752	7	17593	7	149995	63	10167	4	14026	6	236598

Note: During the academic year, 101 MSIs granted STEM bachelor's degrees and 1,662 non-MSIs granted STEM bachelor's degrees.

TABLE.2 4 Non-STEM Bachelor's Degree Production, by Ethnicity/Race: MSIs vs. Non-MSI Designation, 2008–2009

Non-STEM	American Indian or Alaskan Native		Asian/Native Hawaiian/ Other Pacific Islander		Black or African-American		Hispanic or Latina/o		White		Non-Residents		Other		Total
	#	%	#	%	#	%	#	%	#	%	#	%	#	%	
MSIs n=114	527	0.91	5801	10	24990	43	7530	13	14414	25	1311	2	3688	6	58261
Non-MSIs n=2294	9467	0.71	71846	5	105338	8	112668	8	905873	68	34509	3	86221	7	1325922
Total n=1408	9994	0.72	77647	6	130328	9	120198	9	920287	66	35820	3	89909	6	1384183

Note: During the academic year, 114 MSIs granted non-STEM bachelor's degrees and 2,294 non-MSIs granted non-STEM bachelor's degrees.

of students from underrepresented minority groups earning STEM bachelor's degrees at the four MSIs reported here by and large exceeded the percentages of students from the same minority groups earning STEM degrees at PWIs with one exception, Native Americans.

Native Americans students had the lowest rates of STEM participation and graduation relative to their percentage in the general population. This lack of participation can be due to a variety of factors. First, a history of low college going and graduation rates among Native Americans can mean lower socio-economic status and lack of cultural capital regarding access to and success in college. Second, a large proportion of the Native American population lives far from the location of MSIs and particularly HBCUs (the largest number of MSIs) that are located primarily in the Eastern United States. Third, many Native Americans students begin their education at small TCUs that may have a lack of funding for STEM related facilities and supplies. Fourth, the pre-college academic preparation for Native American students frequently differs from the Eurocentric type of education that typifies American colleges and universities and possibly presents transition problems for Native American students (Guillory & Ward, 2008; Ortiz & Boyer, 2003; Zolbrod, 2006). Finally, although relatively large numbers of Native Americans attend and succeed at Tribal colleges and universities, the number of those institutions is small and most of them are 2-year colleges.

Despite this, for many minority students, an education at an MSI provides an option for a STEM education at a campus that likely provides a more supportive cultural climate and that differs significantly from the climate of PWIs which tend to be large and impersonal (Carmichael et al., 1993; Hagedorn, Maxwell, & Hampton, 2002; Hurtado et al., 1998).

Finally the production of STEM bachelor's degrees remains low relative to underrepresented students' representation in the general population. This remains an important hurdle in expanding the STEM workforce; it is also critical for increasing doctoral degrees in STEM—another focus of stakeholders (NSF, 2009). In fact, studies focusing on the baccalaureate origins of minority doctoral degree recipients in STEM fields, found that many obtained their bachelor's degree at an MSI (Solórzano, 1995; Stage & Hubbard, 2009; Wolf-Wendel, 1998). Given that MSIs represent a relatively small number of postsecondary education institutions, our findings suggest they provide an important environment for underrepresented students seeking STEM undergraduate degrees and persisting into more advanced STEM graduate work or into industry.

This study supports existing literature on MSIs and the production of underrepresented undergraduates receiving STEM degrees. Findings suggest that the MSIs in this study not only produced a substantial number of minority STEM bachelor's degree recipients, but that STEM bachelor's degree production for designated MSIs and their respective ethnic/racial group were significant.

References

Baum, S., & Ma, J. (2007). *Education pays: The benefits of higher education for individuals and society.* New York: College Board.

Brown, M. C., & Davis, J. E. (2001). The historically Black college as social contract, social capital, and social equalizer. *Peabody Journal of Education, 76*(1), 31–49.

Carmichael, J. W., Labat, D. D., Hunter, J. T., Privett, J. A., & Sevenair, J. P. (1993). Minorities in the biological sciences: The Xavier success story and some implications. *BioScience, 43*(8), 564.

Chang, M. J., Cerna, O., Han, J., & Saenz, V. (2008). The contradictory roles of institutional status in retaining underrepresented minorities in biomedical and behavioral science majors. *Review of Higher Education, 31*(4), 433–464

Contreras, F., Malcom, L., & Bensimon, E. (2008). Hispanic serving institutions: Closeted identity and the production of equitable outcomes for Latino/a students. In M. Gasman, B. Baez, & C. S. Turner (Eds.), *Understanding minority-serving institutions* (pp. 71–90). Albany, NY: SUNY Press.

Cook, B. J., & Córdova, D. I. (2006). *Minorities in higher education: Twenty-second annual status report.* Washington, DC: American Council on Education.

Crisp, G., Nora, A., & Taggart, A. (2009). Student characteristics, pre-college, college, and environmental factors as predictors of majoring in and earning a STEM degree: An analysis of students attending a HSI. *American Educational Research Journal, 46*(4), 924–942.

Dowd, A. C., Malcom, L. E., & Bensimon, E. M. (2009). *Benchmarking the success of Latino and Latina students in STEM to achieve national graduation goals.* Los Angeles, CA: University of Southern California. Retrieved from http://cue.usc.edu/project-files/Dec_2009_NSF_Report_FINAL.pdf

Gasman, M. (2008). Minority-serving institutions: An historical backdrop. In M. Gasman, B. Baez, & C. Turner, (Eds.), *Understanding minority-serving institutions: New interdisciplinary perspectives* (pp. 18–27). Albany, NY: SUNY Press.

Gasman, M., Baez, B., & Turner, C. S. (Eds.). (2008). *Understanding minority-serving institutions: New interdisciplinary perspectives.* Albany, NY: SUNY Press.

Gasman, M., Lundy-Wagner, V., Ransom, T., & Bowman, N. (2010). *Unearthing promise and potential: Our nation's historically Black colleges and universities* (ASHE Higher Education Report, Vol., No. 5). San Francisco, CA: Jossey-Bass.

Guillory, J. P., & Ward, K. (2008).Tribal colleges and universities: Identity, invisibility, and current issues. In M. Gasman, B. Baez, & C. Turner (Eds.), *Understanding minority serving institutions: New interdisciplinary perspectives* (pp. 91–110). Albany, NY: SUNY Press.

Hagedorn, L. S., Maxwell, W., & Hampton, P. (2002). Correlates of retention for African American males in community colleges. *Journal of College Student Retention, 3*(3), 243–263.

Harper, S. R., & Newman, C. B. (Eds.). (2010). *Students of color in STEM* (New Directions for Institutional Research, No. 148). San Francisco, CA: Jossey-Bass.

Hubbard, S., & Stage, F. K. (2009). Attitudes, perceptions, and preferences of faculty at Hispanic Serving and predominantly Black institutions. *Journal of Higher Education, 80*(3), 270–289.

Hubbard S., & Stage, F. K. (2010). Identifying comprehensive public institutions that develop minority scientists. In S. Harper & C. Newman (Eds.), *Students of color in STEM* (New Directions for Institutional Research, No. 148, pp. 53–62). San Francisco, CA: Jossey-Bass.

Hurtado, S., Carter, D. F., & Kardia, D. (1998). The climate for diversity: Key issues for institutional self-study. In K. Bauer (Ed.), *Campus climate: Understanding the critical components of today's colleges and universities* (New Directions for Institutional Research, No. 98: pp. 53–63). San Francisco, CA: Jossey-Bass.

Hurtado, S., Eagan, M. E., Cabrera, N. L., Lin, M. H., Park, J., & Lopez, M. (2007). Training future scientists: Predicting first-year minority student participation in health science research. *Research in Higher Education, 49*(2), 126–152.

Hurtado, S., Newman, C. B., Tran, M. C., & Chang, M. J. (2010). Improving the rate of success for underrepresented racial minorities in STEM fields: Insights from a national project. In

S. Harper & C. Newman (Eds.), *Students of color in STEM* (New Directions for Institutional Research, No. 148, pp. 5–16). San Francisco, CA: Jossey-Bass.

Li, X., & Carroll, C.D. (2007). *Characteristics of minority-serving institutions and minority undergraduates enrolled in these institutions* (NCES 2008-156). Washington, DC: National Center for Education Statistics, Institute of Education Sciences, U.S. Department of Education.

Maple, S. A., & Stage, F. K. (1991) Influences on the choice of math/science majors by gender and ethnicity. *American Educational Research Journal, 28*(1), 37–60.

Mercer, C. J., & Stedman, J. B. (2008). Minority-serving institutions: Selected institutional and student characteristics. In M. Gasman, B. Baez, & C. Turner (Eds.), *Understanding minority-serving institutions* (pp. 28–42). Albany, NY: SUNY Press.

Museus, S. D. (2009). Deconstructing the model minority myth and how it contributes to the invisible minority reality in higher education research In S. D. Museus (Ed.), *Conducting research on Asian Americans in higher education* (New Directions for Institutional Research, No. 142, pp. 5–15). San Francisco, CA: Jossey-Bass.

National Academy of Sciences (NAS). (2005). *Rising above the gathering storm.* Washington, DC: National Academy Press.

National Academy of Sciences. Committee on Underrepresented Groups and the Expansion of the Science and Engineering Workforce Pipeline. (2010). *Expanding underrepresented minority participation: America's science and technology talent at the crossroads.* Washington, DC: National Academies Press. Retrieved from http://www.nap.edu/catalog/12984.html

National Center for Education Statistics. (2011a). List of postsecondary institutions enrolling populations with significant percentages of minority students. Retrieved from http://www2.ed.gov/about/offices/list/ocr/edlite-minorityinst.html

National Center for Education Statistics. (2011b). *Postsecondary awards in science, technology, engineering, and mathematics, by state: 2001 and 2009.* Web Tables, April 2011 (NCES 2009-226), Table 3. Retrieved from http://nces.ed.gov/pubs2011/2011226.pdf

National Science Foundation. (2005). *Women, minorities, and persons with disabilities in science and engineering: 2003.* Arlington, VA: National Science Foundation.

National Science Foundation. (2011). Award search. Retrieved from http://www.nsf.gov/awardsearch/progSearch

National Science Foundation, Division of Science Resources Statistics. (2009, January). *Women, minorities, and persons with disabilities in science and engineering: 2009* (NSF 09-305). Arlington, VA: Author. Retrieved from http://www.nsf.gov/statistics/wmpd/

Ohland, M. W., Orr, M. K., Lundy-Wagner, V., Veenstra, C. P., & Long, R. A. (2012). Viewing access and persistence through a socioeconomic lens. In C. Baillie, A. L. Pawley, & D. Riley (Eds.), *Engineering and social justice: In the university and beyond* (pp. 157-180). West Lafayette, IN: Purdue University Press.

Oritz, A. M., & Boyer, P. (2003). Student assessment in Tribal colleges. In M. C. Brown & J. E. Lane (Eds.), *Studying diverse institutions: Contexts, challenges, and considerations* (New Directions for Institutional Research, No. 118, pp. 41–49). San Francisco, CA: Jossey-Bass.

Palmer, R. T., Davis, R., & Hilton, A. (2009). Exploring challenges that threaten to impede the academic success of academically underprepared Black males at an HBCU. *Journal of College Student Development, 50*(4) 429–445.

Paulsen, M. B., & St. John, E. P. (2002). Social class and college costs: Examining the financial nexus between college choice and persistence. *Journal of Higher Education, 73,* 189–236.

Perna, L.W., Lundy-Wagner, V. C., Drezner, N. D., Gasman, M., Yoon, S., Bose, E., & Gary, S. (2009). The contribution of HBCUs to the preparation of African American women for STEM careers: A case study. *Research in Higher Education, 50*(1), 1–23.

Snyder, T. D., Dillow, S. A., & Hoffman, C. M. (2009). *Digest of education statistics 2008.* Washington DC: U.S. Department of Education.

Solórzano, D. (1995). The doctorate production and baccalaureate origins of African Americans in the sciences and engineering. *Journal of Negro Education, 64*(1), 15–32.

Stage, F. K., & Hubbard, S. (2008). Teaching Latino, African American, and Native American undergraduates: Faculty attitudes, conditions, and practices. In Gassman, M., Baez, B., &

Turner, C. S. (Eds.), *Understanding minority-serving institutions: New interdisciplinary perspectives* (pp. 237–256. Albany, NY: SUNY Press.

Stage, F. K., Conway, K. John, G., & Lundy-Wagner, V. (2011). Minority serving community colleges and the production of STEM associate degrees. Unpublished manuscript.

Stage, F. K., & Hubbard, S. M. (2009). Undergraduate institutions that foster women and minority scientists. *Journal of Women and Minorities in Science and Engineering, 15,* 77–91.

Stage, F. K., John, G., & Hubbard, S. (2011). Undergraduate institutions that foster Black scientists. In W. F. Tate & H. T. Frierson (Eds.), *Beyond stock stories and folktales: African Americans paths to STEM fields* (pp. 3–21). Bingley, England: Emerald Group.

Teranishi, R. T. (2007). Race, ethnicity, and higher education policy. In F. K. Stage (Ed.), *Answering critical questions with quantitative data* (New Directions for Institutional Research, No. 133, pp. 37–50). San Francisco, CA: Jossey-Bass.

Teranishi, R. T. (2010). *Asians in the ivory tower: Dilemmas of racial inequality in American higher education.* New York: Teachers College Press.

Thurgood, L., Golladay, M., & Hill, S. (2006). *U.S. doctorates in the 20th century.* Washington, DC: National Science Foundation.

Wolf-Wendel, L. E. (1998). Models of excellence: The baccalaureate origins of successful European American Women, African American women and Latinas. *Journal of Higher Education, 69*(2), 144–172.

Zolbrod, P. H. (2006). Talking circle: Reading and writing in a cross-cultural classroom. *Tribal College Journal of American Indian Higher Education, 17*(3), 22–23.

APPENDIX A

List of AANAPISIs, HBCUs, HSIs, and TCUs Used In This Study

AANAPISIs

* ★ California State University-Fresno
* ★ California State University-Long Beach
* ★ California State University-Sacramento
* ★ California State University-San Marcos
* ★ San Jose State University
* ★ University of California-Merced
* ★ University of Guam
  University of Hawaii Maui College
* ★ University of Hawaii at Hilo
* ★ University of Illinois at Chicago
* ★ Stony Brook University
* ★ Saint Martin's University
  Seattle Community College-South Campus

HBCUs

* ★ Alabama A & M University
* ★ Alabama State University
  Concordia College-Selma
* ★ Miles College

* Oakwood University
  Selma University
* Stillman College
* Talladega College
* Tuskegee University
  Arkansas Baptist College
* University of Arkansas at Pine Bluff
* Philander Smith College
* Delaware State University
* University of the District of Columbia
* Howard University
* Bethune-Cookman University
* Edward Waters College
* Florida Agricultural and Mechanical University
* Florida Memorial University
* Albany State University
* Clark Atlanta University
* Fort Valley State University
* Morehouse College
* Paine College
* Savannah State University
* Spelman College
* Kentucky State University
* Dillard University
* Grambling State University
* Southern University and A & M College
* Southern University at New Orleans
* Xavier University of Louisiana
* Bowie State University
* Coppin State University
* University of Maryland Eastern Shore
* Morgan State University
* Alcorn State University
* Jackson State University
* Mississippi Valley State University
* Rust College
* Tougaloo College
* Harris–Stowe State University
* Lincoln University
* Bennett College for Women
* Elizabeth City State University
* Fayetteville State University
* Johnson C Smith University
* Livingstone College

* North Carolina A & T State University
* North Carolina Central University
* Saint Augustine's College
* Shaw University
* Winston-Salem State University
* Central State University
* Wilberforce University
* Langston University
* Cheyney University of Pennsylvania
* Lincoln University of Pennsylvania
* Allen University
* Benedict College
* Claflin University
* Morris College
* South Carolina State University
* Voorhees College
* Fisk University
* Lane College
* Le Moyne-Owen College
* Tennessee State University
* Huston-Tillotson University
* Jarvis Christian College
* Paul Quinn College
* Prairie View A & M University
  Southwestern Christian College
* Texas College
* Texas Southern University
* Wiley College
* Hampton University
* Norfolk State University
* Saint Pauls College
  Virginia University of Lynchburg
* Virginia State University
* Virginia Union University
* Bluefield State College
* West Virginia State University
* University of the Virgin Islands

HSIs

* Universidad Del Este
* California State University-Bakersfield
  Carlos Albizu University-Miami Campus
* Our Lady of the Lake University-San Antonio

* ★ California State University–Dominguez Hills
* ★ Northeastern Illinois University
* ★ Universidad Politecnica de Puerto Rico
* ★ Eastern New Mexico University–Main Campus

TCUs

    Haskell Indian Nations University
* ★ Salish Kootenai College

    Institute of American Indian and Alaska Native Culture

    Sitting Bull College

    Turtle Mountain Community College
* ★ Oglala Lakota College
* ★ Sinte Gleska University

    Northwest Indian College

★denotes institutions that awarded STEM bachelor's degrees.

3

IMPACT OF INSTITUTIONAL CLIMATES OF MSIs AND THEIR ABILITY TO FOSTER SUCCESS FOR RACIAL AND ETHNIC MINORITY STUDENTS IN STEM

Terrell L. Strayhorn

Introduction

Increasing the number of racial and ethnic minority (REM) students who complete college degrees in highly technical or scientific majors such as science, technology, engineering, and math (STEM) is a national priority. Several trends lend support to this conclusion. First, federal agencies such as the National Science Foundation (NSF) have established new programs and areas through which to fund projects that aim to broaden participation for REMs in STEM fields. For instance, consider the recent Diversity in Engineering, Girls in Science and Engineering, Tribal College Pathways, and Research on Gender in Science and Engineering competitions within the Foundation (National Science Foundation, 2010). Second, federal organizations have adopted additional evaluation measures—what NSF calls merit review criteria (e.g., broader impact)—to assess the worth of a project or idea, based on its ability to foster the development of women or REMs in STEM fields. Both of these underscore the national importance of broadening participation of REMs in STEM fields.

Increasing the number of REMs in STEM fields is critical, especially given that science and engineering employment has grown nearly 40% in 10 years, while degree production in that area has lagged among women and REMs (Center for Institutional Data Exchange and Analysis, 2000). And despite some recent progress, women comprise 75% of BAs in psychology, but only 21% in engineering and computer science (National Science Board, 2006). REMs still represent a relatively small proportion of STEM BA degrees: 11% of degree recipients in math and computer science. Furthermore, REM women earn less than 5% of degrees in engineering (National Science Foundation, 2011). In light of these trends, the Sullivan Commission (2004) declared REMs "missing persons" in STEM fields.

Not only is it important to increase the number of REM undergraduates who major in STEM fields by building new or reinforcing existing pipelines (Jackson, 2007) or what I call "pathways" (Strayhorn, 2011) to such disciplines, but it is also imperative to foster the success of REMs in STEM fields to degree completion. Majoring in a field is of little value if the individual leaves college before completing the degree (Perna, 2005). And much of what we know about the economic and social benefits of a college education assumes that the maximum return on one's investment is earned after graduating from college (Thomas, 2000). Yet, national reports indicate that REMs are disproportionately represented among those who "stop out" of college for long periods of time, "change out" of STEM majors frequently, or "drop out" of college altogether (Seymour & Hewitt, 1997; Tinto, 1993; U.S. Department of Education, 2010). In fact, the NSF (2010) reported that only 24% of REMs who began as science majors completed a BA degree in science within 6 years of college entry compared to over 40% of White students.

REM Retention in STEM

REMs may leave STEM majors for several reasons. First, scholars have shown that some REMs may lack adequate preparation for college-level math and science courses, which typically serve as gatekeepers to STEM majors (Adelman, 1998; Strayhorn, 2011). Part of this is due to the fact that REMS are not always exposed to rigorous math and science courses in high school that are taught by qualified teachers, oftentimes reflecting the socioeconomic inequities that characterize segments of the K-12 education system (Bonous–Hammarth, 2000). Deficiencies in math can have long-term effects on those who aspire to study STEM because math is the basic language of science and engineering without which one is hardly prepared for the rigors of college-level work (Babco, 2003).

REMs also may leave STEM majors due to lack of interest or belonging in STEM, strong(-er) interest in another major, or difficulty applying STEM to solving practical problems (Cole & Espinoza, 2008; Strayhorn, 2009a, 2011). For instance, there is fairly consistent evidence that some REMs equate math and science with words (e.g., *boring, hard, nerd*) that have negative connotations, which, in turn, can lead to negative attitudes toward such subjects or scientists in general (May & Chubin, 2003; Sumrall, 1995). Additionally, I have found in previous studies that Black and Latino males can find STEM subject matter (e.g., water filtration formulas, wind turbine operations) too technical to apply to solving real-world problems; without clear understanding of its use, some students disengage from classroom instruction, avoid studying such material, or lose interest in the major altogether (Strayhorn, 2009a).

Encountering unsupportive, unwelcoming environments in STEM majors is another reason some REMs may leave such fields (Elliott & Shin, 2002; Grandy, 1998; Seymour, 1992; Strayhorn, 2009b, 2010b). The importance of campus climate has been documented in the literature for decades, although our initial understanding of its influence on student success in STEM fields came from studies of college women (e.g., Laanan, Starobin, Bruning, & Inkelas, 2007). Seymour and Hewitt (1997) conducted a series of studies and found that students might leave STEM fields and engineering specifically for nonacademic reasons such as: (a) belief that non-STEM careers offer greater intrinsic rewards, (b) loss of interest in STEM, (c) rejection of the lifestyle associated with STEM careers, and (d) negative perceptions of science environments. In my own work, I have found that REMs report obstacles to their success in STEM such as racism, prejudice, social isolation, and insensitivity to the needs and interests of minorities (Strayhorn, 2009b). Similar results have been reported elsewhere, noting that REMs in STEM may encounter racial microaggressions, everyday occurrences of prejudice and racism that may go unnoticed yet hinder students' willingness to seek help or support in the face of problems (Thiry, Lauren, & Hunter, 2011).

While we know a fair deal about reasons REMs may leave STEM majors in general, we know comparatively little about the role that campus climate plays in promoting or inhibiting REMs' success in STEM fields at the undergraduate level. The weight of empirical evidence clearly indicates, however, that minority-serving institutions (MSIs) serve as major providers of highly skilled REM graduates in STEM and related fields (May & Chubin, 2003). For instance, in 2010, nine of the top 10 producers of Blacks who later earned a PhD were historically Black colleges and universities (HBCUs), one type of MSI; these findings reflect those reported elsewhere (Perna et al., 2009). Additionally, seven of the top 10 producers of Blacks in engineering were HBCUs including North Carolina A&T State University. There are other accolades for HBCUs including Xavier University which ranks in first place nationally in placing Blacks into medical school and producing Blacks in physical sciences. Although HBCUs represent only 3% of higher education institutions in this country, they educate over 15% of all Black students; a growing share of White, low-income, and veteran students; and still produce large shares of Black political leaders, federal judges, doctors, and scientists (Strayhorn, 2008).

What We Know About HBCUs

Research on HBCUs suggests several major conclusions that relate to the focus of this chapter. First, HBCUs have long accommodated the educational needs of Blacks in the United States, and thus reflect an abiding commitment to the education of historically underserved populations (Gasman, 2008). HBCUs educated freed slaves after the Civil War and awarded approximately 80% of all BA degrees to Blacks even as late as 1964.

Second, HBCUs offer educational opportunities to historically underserved groups and have been successful in providing remedial programs for certain students such as Black men (Palmer & Gasman, 2008; Palmer & Strayhorn, 2008). To this point, Garibaldi (1991) explained:

> Historically Black colleges maximize … students' potential by providing small classes, regular academic advising by faculty, small group tutoring by peers and instructors, exposure to role models (faculty and alumni), formal opportunities for remedial assistance in the basic skills, and professional and academic internships at businesses and large research universities in their chosen field during the summer.
>
> *(p. 103)*

Third, HBCUs have environments that are more welcoming and supportive than predominantly White institutions (PWIs), although they do so lacking resources compared to their PWI counterparts (Kim & Conrad, 2006). HBCUs also tend to operate on a familylike model where faculty members and administrators act as surrogate parents for students, caring deeply about their academic and personal success and their personal well-being, while holding high aspirations about their future success (Hirt, Strayhorn, Amelink, & Bennett, 2006). This approach can engender a sense of belonging for students, which is contrasted with the unwelcoming, unsupportive, and alienating environment that many Black students find at PWIs (Allen, 1992; Fries-Britt & Turner, 2002). So, if we know anything at all from the literature on HBCUs, we know that they provide Black students with safe, affirming educational climates or environments in which to learn and pursue their academic interests (e.g., Allen, 1992). Still, the extant literature is virtually silent on the role that campus climate plays in the success of REMs in STEM fields at HBCUs. This is the gap addressed by the present chapter.

Purpose

The purpose of this chapter is to identify aspects of the campus climate that affect REMs' success in STEM at HBCUs, explain the role that such factors play in their success, and identify ways to foster REMs' success in STEM at MSIs through improved educational practices and policies. For the purposes of this chapter, campus climate is defined as individuals' perceptions of current patterns of beliefs and behaviors that shape their experiences on campus. There are four dimensions to campus climate: institutional history, structural diversity, psychological climate, and behavioral climate (Hurtado, Milem, Clayton-Perderson & Allen, 1998). Indeed, the term *campus climate* refers to "students' perceptions of their experiences both in and out of the classroom" (Woodard &

Sims, 2000, p. 540). Assuming this definition, I draw upon both quantitative and qualitative data from REM undergraduates majoring in STEM fields at HBCUs to achieve the objectives stated. In the next section, I describe the studies that informed this chapter and proceed to highlight several major findings.

The Studies

I was interested in describing the role that campus climate plays on REMs' success in STEM fields at HBCUs, so I drew upon data from several recent projects to study this topic. Quantitative data came from a multi-institutional survey sample, while qualitative data came from a narrative inquiry (Strayhorn, 2011).[1] In consonance with this methodological approach, I focused on the richness of the stories told and retrospective meaning-making from students regarding their experiences (Clandinin & Connelly, 2000).

Data were collected in one of two ways. First, an electronic survey was used to collect information about participants' backgrounds, academic preparation, opinions of college life, and experiences in STEM. Second, semistructured interviews were conducted with willing participants to probe survey results as well as "critical cues," or topics that arose during the interview that seemed to relate to the study's objectives (Kvale, 1996); examples of critical cues range from successes to failures, to name a few. Most interviews were conducted face-to-face individually or via focus groups. The use of focus groups not only afforded the researcher an opportunity to speak directly with participants in-depth about their experiences but also allowed participants to react to, reflect upon, and respond to their peers about shared experiences as well as differences (Krueger & Casey, 2000). Where circumstances or distance made this difficult, interviews were conducted via phone or computer (i.e., Skype) using appropriate recording equipment. For more information, see Strayhorn (2011).

Data analysis for this chapter proceeded in three stages. First, survey data were prepared for analysis by removing or replacing missing values, creating composites, or calculating scales where necessary. Survey respondents were sorted into categories: (a) achievers and nonachievers (based on grades) and (b) persisters and nonpersisters. I used descriptive and multivariate techniques to measure differences among these groups in terms of campus climate factors.

Qualitative data were analyzed using the constant comparison method described by Glaser and Strauss (1999), given that these studies could lead to a new or revised grounded theory of REMs' success in STEM. Specifically, I read and reread each transcript making "marginal remarks" (Miles & Huberman, 1994) about participants' comments regarding their experiences in STEM and identified an initial set of codes using a form of open coding. Then, data were reanalyzed using axial coding to determine whether different words or phrases could be combined or collapsed into similar categories (e.g., belonging and community). I also eliminated codes that did not prove significant across multiple participants. In the final stage, three major themes were identified that will be described in the next section.

Major Findings

Survey respondents varied in terms of their academic performance in STEM, with undergraduate GPAs ranging from 1.2 to 4.0. After sorting participants into two groups (i.e., achievers with GPAs > 2.0 and nonachievers with GPAs < 2.0), I found statistical differences in their perceptions of campus climate. For instance, REM "achievers" in STEM rated the campus environment as more welcoming than their "nonachiever" counterparts. Similarly, achievers reported slightly more frequent interactions than nonachievers with those whose racial backgrounds differed from their own. Conversely, nonachievers tended to rate the campus as more "cold and uncaring" than their achiever counterparts. Interestingly, nonachievers scored higher than achievers on "classroom sizes are so large that I feel like just one in a number," indicating that REMs who felt this way tended to earn low grades and vice versa.

Survey respondents also varied in terms of their persistence within a STEM major, with 78% of the sample persisting and 22% changing to a non–STEM major during their undergraduate career. Persisters and nonpersisters differed significantly on three survey items: "University seems like a cold, uncaring place"; "Class sizes are so large that I feel like just one in a number"; and "the campus environment is welcoming to me." Those who perceived the campus as a cold, uncaring place with class sizes too large to feel important were more likely to change their major. On the other hand, REMs who felt the campus was welcoming tended to persist in their major. Table 3.2 presents a summary of these results.

In light of these important findings, interviews were conducted to understand further the specific role of campus climate in promoting the success of REMs in STEM fields at HBCUs. Specifically, questions were designed to tap aspects of class size, friendliness of faculty members and peers, as well as

TABLE 3.1 Group Means: REM STEM Students' at HBCUs

Survey item	Achievers M(SD)	Non-Achievers M(SD)
University seems like a cold, uncaring place	2.63 (1.59)	2.94 (1.56)
Class size is too large	3.36 (1.64)	3.57 (1.83)★
Campus environment is welcoming	5.06 (1.37)★	4.57 (1.65)
Interactions with different races	2.77 (0.95)	2.67 (1.03)
Interactions with different religions	2.73 (0.95)	2.81 (0.92)
Interactions with different political	3.03 (0.95)	2.94 (0.99)

★ $p < 0.05$.

TABLE 3.2 Group Means: REM STEM Students' at HBCUs

Survey item	Persisters M (SD)	Non-persisters M (SD)
University seems like a cold, uncaring place	2.49 (1.50)	3.25 (1.73)★
Class size is too large	3.28 (1.60)	3.74 (1.79)★
Campus environment is welcoming	5.15 (1.33)★	4.55 (1.51)
Interactions with different races	2.65 (0.95)	2.79 (0.96)
Interactions with different religions	2.75 (0.94)	2.70 (0.93)
Interactions with different political	3.01 (0.96)	3.06 (0.88)

★ $p < 0.05$.

particular dimensions of the academic department (e.g., interpersonal relations). Three themes were identified using a version of the constant comparison method of analysis: "One in a number," "We are family," and "Engagement with Everyone." Illustrative quotes are used to demonstrate the meaning and significance of each theme.

One in a Number: Class Size Matters

Participants described in sufficient detail how they experienced STEM contexts on campus; STEM contexts included classrooms, laboratories, study groups, and, on one campus, a living-learning community. Specifically, REMs at the HBCUs in this study shared how they felt like "one in a number" in classes that were too large for them to feel recognized, noticed, or otherwise "special." Conversely, those who were performing well in STEM and felt confident in their skills to succeed described how they benefited from meaningful interactions with faculty members in smaller class settings or lab demonstrations. Consider the following quotes that reflect this point:

> Part of my trouble is that I don't really feel connected yet. I don't really feel like I matter so it's hard to care about the subject. I guess I have to [do it] though because it's my [academic] major. The intro[ductory] classes are just so large, you don't really stick out … you just sort of blend in and it's easy to fall behind.
>
> A lot of my friends say they have really big classes at other schools. Here the classes are like adequately small and that makes it easier to get to know the professor and ask questions. Like it's pretty typical to be able to reach the teacher after class and they call and check up on you when you're not there in class. So then I guess I'm like motivated to work hard because I know that they'll care if I don't (laughing).

So, while some REMs at HBCUs complain about large class sizes in STEM and, thus, lack a sense of belonging in their major, others call attention to the benefits of smaller class sizes such as getting to know one's instructors, developing a sense of belonging in STEM, and feeling compelled to study, which, in turn, promotes REMs' success in such demanding fields.

We Are Family: Faculty and Staff Support at HBCUs

Over half of all participants alluded to the idea of "family" at some point in their interview, reflecting the nature of relationships with faculty and staff members at HBCUs. For instance, Jessica, a biology major (math minor) commented: "It's like we're family ... you can tell they really, really care about us and go out of their way to [help] us." Close analysis of the interview data reveal the various ways in which HBCU faculty and staff serve as surrogate family members or what I call "fictive kin"—that is, nonbiological familial relationships with individuals who are not related by blood, yet provide much-needed forms of support (Karner, 1998). Consider the following quote that reflects the essence of comments shared by other participants:

> Dr. Trehern is not just a professor; he's a true mentor ... someone you can depend on. He's really gone out of his way to help me find scholarships, enter design competitions, access internships that will help me if and when I decide to go to graduate school. And there was this one time he coached me on how to approach a White professor about my grade in his class.
>
> *(Zeek, electrical and computer engineering major)*

Recalling the various ways in which HBCU faculty and staff "go beyond the call of duty" to support students also helped them to articulate *how* such support enabled their success in STEM. For instance, Zeek went on to explain how Dr. Trehern's advice empowered him to respectfully approach his professor about the grade, which led him to change the grade and kept Zeek from academic probation. Other participants spoke extensively about faculty members who were willing to meet with them at night or on the weekends to discuss course content, answer their questions prior to exams, and offer advice about personal or professional matters. One participant summed it up nicely when she said: "We're not just students to them ... we're like family and you know how family members look out for each other." That HBCU faculty and staff went out of their way—or beyond the "call of duty"—to provide various forms of personal and academic support; what some refer to as an "ethic of care," seemed to promote REMs' success in STEM majors.

Engagement with Everyone: Supportive Departmental Culture

Not only did participants describe the nature of their relationships with STEM faculty and staff at HBCUs as supportive and "familylike," but they also stressed the importance of a supportive departmental culture or climate. Supportive departmental climates were characterized by high and clear expectations of students, collegial relationships among faculty members, and opportunities for students to engage others (i.e., faculty, staff, peers) in educationally productive ways. Meaningful opportunities for engagement ranged from "brown bag" luncheon seminars to service-learning projects, from group-based field experiences to professional conferences and seminars, to name a few. Here two participants share their perspective on such experiences:

> I'm in a major where, of course, I am like the only person of color in most classes and labs. It was sort of like that in my high school—not the school but the advanced courses. I was the only little speck in the room. But, being the only computer science major means that I often have to "find" a team for group projects while others naturally gravitate to each other.
>
> I think it really helps to get to know a lot of different people in your department. Like in environmental [engineering] we had like an orientation to welcome us to our program in our first year and that's where you got to learn a lot about what you'll be doing as a major. Then, sometimes professors have a gathering at their house or at the Applebee's near [said university] ... so that brings the social aspect. I think that really makes a difference when you have many ways to fit in.

Engaging faculty, staff, and peers in a supportive departmental culture offered REMs in STEM at HBCUs multiple forms of support, clarified what's expected of them, and nurtured their sense of belonging in the major, which, in turn, promoted their academic success. The next section discusses these findings in the context of previous literature and highlights important recommendation for educational practice.

Discussion

Findings from the studies that informed this chapter suggest several conclusions. First, campus climate is important in promoting the success of REMs in STEM at HBCUs. It will be recalled that REMs who performed well academically and who persisted in their major tended to perceive the campus climate as welcoming rather than "cold and uncaring" or "too large" for them to feel significant. These findings not only substantiate prior claims about the influence of climate on student outcomes (Grandy, 1998; Hurtado, 1992; Seymour, 1992), but also extend our current understanding by demonstrating that campus climate plays a critical role in promoting the success of REMs in STEM fields at HBCUs specifically.

It is also true that REMs who persisted in their STEM major at HBCUs differed from nonpersisters in their perceptions of campus climate, as well as the frequency with which they engaged individuals whose racial backgrounds differed from their own. This finding relates to a long line of research on the educational benefits of cross-racial interactions in college (Hurtado & Carter, 1997; Strayhorn, 2010a; Wathington, 2004), but again adds to our collective understanding by demonstrating that campus climate perceptions and frequent interactions with diverse others may distinguish REM "persisters" in STEM at HBCUs from nonpersisters.

Qualitative data not only lend support to the statistical findings based on the survey study, but also clarify the specific ways in which HBCU faculty, staff, and departmental cultures promote the success of REMs in STEM. For instance, participants stressed the importance of small(-er) class sizes and more intimate STEM settings (e.g., lab, study group) where they could feel "special," cared about, and where their contributions were recognized. Another important point is that participants in my studies shared how HBCU faculty and staff members fill "familylike" roles and provide important forms of academic and personal support (e.g., tutelage, advice, financial assistance). Sharing nonbiological, yet kinlike, ties with HBCU faculty and staff signaled to students that they matter, they're cared about, and their success is important to others.

In many ways, what participants talked about during the interviews alluded to issues of mattering and a sense of belonging, which I address in detail elsewhere (Strayhorn, 2012). Specifically, I argue that belonging is a basic human need that has the power to motivate and inspire human behavior. Satisfaction of one's need to belong yields positive outcomes such as enhanced self-esteem, academic achievement, persistence in college, and even happiness in life. Findings presented in this chapter lend additional support to my theoretical claims; REMs in STEM at HBCUs who feel a sense of belonging on campus and within their major do well academically.

Findings presented in this chapter strongly suggest several implications for practice and policy. For instance, STEM faculty and academic leaders (e.g., department heads) at HBCUs might consider the results about cross-racial interactions when recruiting new students and planning activities for their majors. Establishing formal mechanisms through which students can interact frequently and purposively may promote REMs' success in STEM; examples of such mechanisms include service-learning projects, lab demonstrations, undergraduate research experiences, and living-learning communities.

Several findings point to the importance of mattering or sense of belonging in STEM students' success at HBCUs. HBCU faculty members might develop additional ways to signal to students that they matter and that others are concerned about their success. For instance, faculty might use electronic mail or telephone to check up on students, as described by my participants. Alternatively, faculty might meet with students regularly to discuss their progress in STEM courses, plans for the future, and any personal problems that might detract from their studies.

Academic advisors and counselors at HBCUs who are in routine contact with students might use these findings in their work with REMs in STEM. Specifically, advisors can use their time to offer advice to students on academic and personal matters, to explain academic policies and procedures (e.g., what's expected of chemistry majors), and to share information about the various ways in which students can engage in educationally purposeful activities with faculty, staff, and peers. All of these are likely to nurture students' interest in STEM, sustain their expectation of completing a STEM degree, and affirm their sense of belonging, which, in turn promotes their success in STEM, which is a matter of national priority.

Note

1   Data were drawn from the author's larger research program titled, "Investigating the Critical Junctures: Strategies that Broaden Minority Participation in STEM Fields," which is funded by the NSF.

References

Adelman, C. (1998). *Women and men of the engineering path: A model for analyses of undergraduate careers.* Washington, DC: Office of Educational Research and Improvement, U.S. Department of Education.

Allen, W. (1992). The color of success: African American college student outcomes at predominantly White and historically Black public colleges and universities. *Harvard Educational Review, 62*(1), 26–44.

Babco, E. L. (2003). *Trends in African American and Native American participation in STEM higher education.* Washington, DC: Commission on Professionals in Science and Technology.

Bonous-Hammarth, M. (2000). Pathways to success: Affirming opportunities for science, mathematics, and engineering majors. *Journal of Negro Education, 69*(1–2), 92–111.

Center for Institutional Data Exchange and Analysis. (2000). *1999–2000 Science, math, engineering, and technology (SMET) retention report.* Norman: University of Oklahoma.

Clandinin, D. J., & Connelly, F. M. (2000). *Narrative inquiry: Experience and story in qualitative research.* San Francisco, CA: Jossey-Bass.

Cole, D., & Espinoza, A. (2008). Examining the academic success of Latino students in science, technology, engineering and mathematics (STEM) majors. *Journal of College Student Development, 49*(4), 285–300.

Elliott, K. M., & Shin, D. (2002). Student satisfaction: An alternative approach to assessing this important concept. *Journal of Higher Education Policy and Management, 24*, 197–209.

Fries-Britt, S. L., & Turner, B. (2002). Uneven stories: Successful Black collegians at Black and White campuses. *Review of Higher Education, 25*(3), 315–330.

Garibaldi, A. (1991). The role of historically Black colleges in facilitating resilience among African-American students. *Education and Urban Society, 24*(1), 103–112.

Gasman, M. (2008). Minority-serving institutions: A historical backdrop. In M. Gasman, B. Baez, & C. S. V. Turner (Eds.), *Understanding minority-serving institutions* (pp. 18–27). Albany, NY: SUNY Press.

Glaser, B. G., & Strauss, A. L. (1999). *The discovery of grounded theory: Strategies for qualitative research.* New York: Aldine De Gruyter.

Grandy, J. (1998). Persistence in science of high-ability minority students: Results of a longitudinal study. *Journal of Higher Education, 69*(6), 589–620.

Hirt, J. B., Amelink, C. T., Bennett, B. R., & Strayhorn, T. L. (2008). A system of othermothering: Relationships between student affairs administrators and students at historically Black colleges and universities. *The NASPA Journal, 45*(2), 210–236.

Hirt, J. B., Strayhorn, T. L., Amelink, C. T., & Bennett, B. R. (2006). The nature of student affairs work at historically Black colleges and universities. *Journal of College Student Development, 47*(6), 661–676.

Hurtado, S. (1992). Campus racial climates: Contexts for conflicts. *Journal of Higher Education, 63*(5), 539–569.

Hurtado, S., & Carter, D. F. (1997). Effects of college transition and perceptions of campus racial climate on Latino college students' sense of belonging. *Sociology of Education, 70*(4), 324–345.

Hurtado, S., Milem, J. F., Clayton-Pedersen, A., & Allen, W. R. (1998). Enhancing campus climates for racial/ethnic diversity: Educational policy and practice. *The Review of Higher Education, 21,* 279–302.

Jackson, J. F. L. (2007). Introduction: A systematic analysis of the African American educational pipeline to inform research, policy, and practice. In J. F. L. Jackson (Ed.), *Strengthening the African American educational pipeline: Informing research, policy, and practice* (pp. 1–14). Albany, NY: SUNY Press.

Karner, T. X. (1998). Professional caring: Homecare workers as fictive kin. *Journal of Aging Studies, 12*(1), 69–82.

Kim, M. M., & Conrad, C. F. (2006). The impact of historically Black colleges and universities on the academic success of African American students. *Research in Higher Education, 47*(4), 399–427.

Krueger, R. A., & Casey, M. A. (2000). *Focus groups: A practical guide for applied research* (3rd ed.). Thousand Oaks, CA: Sage.

Kvale, S. (1996). *InterViews: An introduction to qualitative research interviewing.* Thousand Oaks, CA: Sage.

Laanan, F. S., Starobin, S., Bruning, M., & Inkelas, K. K. (2007). *Broadening participation among women in STEM fields: Research, policy, and practice in higher education and beyond.* Paper presented at the annual meeting of the Association for the Study of Higher Education.

May, G. S., & Chubin, D. E. (2003). A retrospective on undergraduate engineering success for underrepresented minority students. *Journal of Engineering Education, 92*(1), 27–39.

Miles, M., & Huberman, A. (1994). *An expanded sourcebook: Qualitative data analysis* (2nd ed.). Thousand Oaks, CA: Sage.

National Science Board. (2006). *Science and engineering indicators 2006* (2 vols.). Arlington, VA: National Science Foundation.

National Science Foundation. (2010). *NSF mission, NSF in a changing world: The National Science Foundation's strategic plan.* Retrieved from http://www.nsf.gov/nsf/nsfpubs/straplan/mission.htm

National Science Foundation, Division of Science Resources Statistics. (2011). *Women, minorities, and persons with disabilities in science and engineering: 2011* (No. Special Report NSF 11-309). Arlington, VA: Author.

Palmer, R. T., & Gasman, M. B. (2008). "It takes a village to raise a child": The role of social capital in promoting academic success of African American men at a Black college. *Journal of College Student Development, 49*(1), 52–70.

Palmer, R. T., & Strayhorn, T. L. (2008). Mastering one's own fate: Non-cognitive factors associated with the success of African American males at an HBCU. *National Association of Student Affairs Professionals Journal, 11*(1), 126–143.

Perna, L. W. (2005). The benefits of higher education: Sex, racial/ethnic and socioeconomic group differences. *The Review of Higher Education, 29*(1), 23–52.

Perna, L. W., Lundy-Wagner, V., Drezner, N., Gasman, M. B., Yoon, S., & Bose, E. (2009). The contribution of HBCUs to the preparation of African American women for STEM careers: A case study. *Research in Higher Education, 50*(1), 1–23.

Seymour, E. (1992, February). "The Problem Iceberg" in science, mathematics, and engineering education: Student explanations for high attrition rates. *Journal of College Science Teaching, 21*(4), 230–238.

Seymour, E., & Hewitt, N. M. (1997). *Talking about leaving: Why undergraduates leave the sciences.* Boulder, CO: Westview Press.

Strayhorn, T. L. (2008). Influences on labor market outcomes of African American college graduates: A national study. *The Journal of Higher Education, 79*(1), 29–57.

Strayhorn, T. L. (2009a). The absence of African American men in higher education and veterinary medicine. *Journal of Veterinary Medical Education, 36*(4), 351–358.

Strayhorn, T. L. (2009b, October). *Academic and social barriers to Black and Latino male collegians in engineering.* Paper presented at the 39th Annual Frontiers in Education (FIE) Conference, San Antonio, TX.

Strayhorn, T. L. (2010a). The influence of diversity on learning outcomes among African American college students: Measuring sex differences. *Journal of Student Affairs Research and Practice, 47*(3), 343–366.

Strayhorn, T. L. (2010b). *Social barriers and supports to underrepresented minorities' success in STEM fields.* Paper presented at the Frontiers in Education (FIE) Conference, Washington, DC.

Strayhorn, T. L. (2011). Sense of belonging and African American student success in STEM: Comparative insights between men and women. In H. T. Frierson, Jr. & W. F. Tate (Eds.), *Beyond stock stories and folktales: African Americans' paths to STEM fields* (pp. 213–226). New Milford, CT: Emerald Books.

Strayhorn, T. L. (2012). *College students' sense of belonging: A key to educational success.* New York: Routledge.

Sullivan Commission. (2004). *Missing persons: Minorities in the health professions.* Retrieved from http://www.sullivancommision.org

Sumrall, W. J. (1995). Reasons for the perceived images of scientists by race and gender of students in grades 1–7. *School Science and Mathematics, 95*(2), 83–90.

Thiry, H., Lauren, S. L., & Hunter, A. B. (2011). What experiences help students become scientists: A comparative study of research and other sources of personal and professional gains for STEM undergraduates. *Journal of Higher Education, 82*(4), 357–388.

Thomas, S. L. (2000). Deferred costs and economic returns to college major, quality, and performance. *Research in Higher Education, 41*(3), 281–313.

Tinto, V. (1993). *Leaving college: Rethinking the causes and cures of student attrition* (2nd ed.). Chicago, IL: University of Chicago Press.

U.S. Department of Education, National Center for Education Statistics. (2010). *The condition of education 2010* (NCES Report No. 2010-081). Washington, DC: U.S. Government Printing Office.

Wathington, H. D. (2004). In search of the beloved community: Understanding the dynamics of student interaction across racial and ethnic communities. *Dissertation Abstracts International, 65*(06A), 2120.

Woodard, V. S., & Sims, J. M. (2000). Programmatic approaches to improving campus climate. *NASPA Journal, 37*(4), 539–552.

4

ENGINEERING THE ACADEMIC SUCCESS OF RACIAL AND ETHNIC MINORITY STUDENTS AT MINORITY SERVING INSTITUTIONS VIA STUDENT–FACULTY INTERACTIONS AND MENTORING

Darnell Cole and Araceli Espinoza

Over the last two decades, the total number of minority serving institutions (MSI) have increased, due primarily to the growth of Hispanic serving institutions (HSIs; Li & Carroll, 2007). In 1990, about 137 institutions were identified as HSIs; by 2006 this figure had increased to approximately 268 institutions (Hispanic Association of Colleges and Universities [HACU], 2008). The increase in student enrollment at MSIs is also primarily attributed to HSIs. In 2004, HSIs enrolled the largest proportion of racial ethnic minority students (27%), followed by historically Black colleges and universities (HBCUs, 5%) and Tribal colleges and universities (TCUs, 1%; Li, 2007). In fact, in addition to enrolling approximately one-half of all Latino undergraduate students in 2004, HSIs were also responsible for 19%, 13%, and 11% of the total enrollment of Asian American, American Indian, and African American students, respectively (Li, 2007). The contribution made by HSIs to the undergraduate education of American Indians and African Americans was comparable to that made by TCUs (16%), and HBCUs (12%), respectively (Li, 2007).

The contribution of MSIs in conferring bachelor's degrees on racial or ethnic minority students is noteworthy. For instance, in 2000, HSIs were responsible for 39% of all bachelor's degrees awarded (Stearns, Watanabe, & Snyder, 2002). The number of bachelor's degrees awarded by HSIs rose 26% between 1991–1992 and 1999–2000, while the number of bachelor's degrees awarded by all U.S. institutions rose by only 9% (Stearns et al., 2002). In 2001, HBCUs were responsible for 21.5% of the bachelor's degrees earned by African American students (Provasnik, Shafer, & Snyder, 2004). At TCUs, during the 2006–2007 academic year, there were 2,262 graduates (American Indian Higher Education Consortium [AIHEC], 2009); the majority of graduates earned an associate's degree (1,544, 68.3%); followed by a certificate (536, 23.7%); bachelor's degree

(149, 6.6%); an apprenticeship and diploma (21, 0.9%), and a master's degree (12, 0.5%; AIHEC, 2009).

In fields traditionally considered rigorous, such as science, technology, engineering, and mathematics (STEM), HBCUs have played and continue to play an important role in educating and producing African American baccalaureates in STEM fields. In the 1970s, most African American scientists received their bachelor's degree from an HBCU (Trent & Hill, 1994) and as recently as 2001, many of the top baccalaureate-origin institutions of African American science doctorate recipients were HBCUs, including Howard, Spelman, Hampton, Morehouse, and North Carolina A&T (Chubin, May, & Babco, 2005). In 2004, HBCUs were responsible for 23.3% of bachelor's degrees in science and engineering conferred on African American students (National Science Foundation [NSF], 2007).

Similarly, HSIs are responsible for producing a notable number of science and engineering bachelor's degrees. In 2004, across all 4-year institutions, 28,321 bachelor's degrees in science and engineering were awarded to Latino students (NSF, 2007). Of those awarded, 33.5% (i.e. 9,494 of 28,321) were earned by Latino students who attended an HSI (NSF, 2007). Despite the educational contributions made by MSIs to the number of baccalaureate degree holders in STEM fields (Crisp, Nora & Taggart, 2009), the value and quality of these institutions are still questioned (Allen, 1992; Kim & Conrad, 2006; Palmer & Gasman, 2008). Gasman (2010), for instance, cites eight unique occurrences among HBCUs where poor leadership, violations of academic freedom, and the unilateral firing of tenured faculty raise questions regarding institutional quality, at least among a few select MSIs. The criticisms most often cited regarding the quality of MSIs, however, are issues related to institutional selectivity and academic quality, in that many MSIs have nonselective or minimally selective admissions policies (Baez, Gasman, & Turner, 2008).

In their book *Crossing the Finish Line,* Bowen, Chingos, and McPherson (2009) indicate that "undermatched" students (i.e. first generation, low-income students who bring significantly higher SAT/ACT scores than the institutional SAT/ACT average of their peers) take longer "to complete their program" (p. 108) and are even less likely to finish; "this phenomenon is particularly likely for female students at [HBCUs]" (p. 103). Chang, Cerna, Han, and Sàenz (2008) concur, in that there are important mismatch issues for underrepresented minority (URM) students in STEM fields; but Chang et al. (2008) also argue that such mismatches are more likely to occur among highly selective institutions where weeding out students is the norm in highly competitive environments that dictate whether even the most "well matched and highly qualified students … will actually 'make the cut'" (pp. 454–455). These competitive college environments also promote a peer culture where only a few are likely to succeed and where faculty focus little attention on teaching (Chang et al., 2008). It is within this context of campus climate, student–faculty interactions, and structured mentoring programs that we examine the degree attainment of students in STEM majors at MSIs. The research questions that guide this study are:

1. To what extent does campus climate affect the degree attainment of students in the STEM fields attending MSIs?
2. To what extent do student–faculty interactions and structured mentoring programs affect the degree attainment of students in the STEM fields who are attending MSIs?

Campus Climate

In order to understand the college experience of African American and Latino students across institutions, it is necessary to understand how they perceive and interpret the campus climate and their interpersonal interactions (Outcalt & Skewes-Cox, 2002). Specifically, it is important to understand the cultural factors within the college environment that influence how African American and Latino students experience college. Gloria and Robinson Kurpius (1996) refer to the fit between an individual's values and the values of the environment in which they operate as cultural congruity. A lack of fit or cultural congruity between students and the institution can result in a less favorable college experience and negatively affect the academic persistence of underrepresented racial ethnic minority (URM) students (Gloria, Robinson Kurpius, Hamilton, & Willson, 1999).

For URM students, encounters with discrimination and an unwelcoming or hostile learning environment within the university context results in lower levels of cultural congruity and a poor perception of the university environment (Gloria, Castellanos, Lopez, & Rosales, 2005; Gloria, Hird, & Navarro, 2001). A poor perception of the university environment can in turn produce cultural alienation and isolation for URM students within their academic context (Gloria & Rodriguez, 2000); although such findings are typically reported among URM students attending predominantly White institutions (PWIs). How URM students perceive their university context is also a product of the type of support they receive. Social support from faculty, administrators, or same-race peers within the college environment positively affects African American and Latino students' adjustment and comfort on campus (Chang et al., 2008; Gloria, Hird, & Navarro, 2001; Gloria & Robinson Kurpius, 1996; Gloria, Robinson Kurpius, Hamilton, et al., 1999; Hurtado, Newman, Tran, & Chang, 2010). This is particularly true for Latino students majoring in academically rigorous fields like STEM (Cole & Espinoza, 2008). Hurtado et al. (2007) report that URM students in the biomedical and behavioral sciences who perceive a hostile racial climate or highly competitive environment are less likely to feel successful at managing their academic environment. Unlike their URM counterparts, White and some Asian students are not hindered by a competitive environment or hostile racial climate (Hurtado et al., 2007). Similarly, support from and interactions with faculty members are particularly important factors in the academic success of URMs in STEM fields (Bonous-Hammarth, 2000; Cole & Espinoza, 2008; Grandy, 1998; Leslie, McClure, & Oaxaca, 1998). Such student–faculty interactions usually form the basis for establishing more meaningful mentoring relationships that occur between students and faculty, which have the potential to significantly influence academic success, retention, and persistence of URM students in STEM (Landefeld, 2009).

Structured Mentoring Programs and Student–Faculty Interactions

Mentoring is an institution strategy often used to increase academic success and persistence, yet remains an underexamined area that influences URM students in STEM fields, (Blake-Beard, Bayne, Crosby, & Muller, 2011; Girves, Zepeda, & Gwathmey, 2005). Mentoring, according to Blackwell (1989), is defined as "a process by which a person of superior rank, special achievements, and prestige instruct[s], counsel[s], guide[s], and facilitate[s] the intellectual and/or career development of protégés" (p. 9). This definition suggests that mentoring between faculty and students is not unidirectional and is more than role modeling such that there is an awareness and active engagement between faculty and students (Lee, 1999). Mentoring can occur in many ways, one-on-one, as a group, or as part of an educational program. The informal relationship, initiated by either the student or faculty member, is voluntary and often unstructured, while formal mentoring relationships are usually "deliberate, intentional, planned, and structured" (Lee, 1999, p. 32). In either case, however, formal or informal mentoring has the potential to impact URM students' academic success and persistence (Strayhorn & Saddler, 2008).

There are several structured programs that have mentoring functions or have embedded mentoring elements. There are programs such as the Ronald E. McNair Post-Baccalaureate Achievement Program for those interested in graduate school; the Louis Stokes Alliance for Minority Participation Program (LSAMP) for students in STEM fields; the Summer Research Opportunity Program (SROP) to gain disciplinary based research experience; Women in Science and Engineering (WISE) initiative; and many other such national and institution-specific programs (Girves et al., 2005). Girves et al. (2005) argues that these and other similar programs have grown among postsecondary institutions, yet have had a differential effect on URM students' degree completion. That is, when these programs are "small, isolated, and not centrally located within the administrative structure" (p. 458) they have little systematic impact on academic success as measured by degree completion. Large, federally funded programs tend to produce greater effects on overall degree completion, and this is particularly so in STEM fields (Girves et al., 2005). As is the case with LSAMP, a large federally funded program, students' shared sense of community, mentorship, and academic support activities were among the primary reasons for the success of these students (Girves et al., 2005). Hurtado et al. (2010) assert that, regardless of program size, structured programs provide research opportunities that contribute to persistence; yet, the long-term effects of structured programs on outcomes such as degree completion are unclear.

With regard to student–faculty interactions, not structured by an educational program, URM students are better equipped to succeed in STEM fields with support from faculty members (Bonous-Hammarth, 2000; Leslie et al., 1998). According to Grandy (1998), one of the most important indicators of persistence for URM students in STEM fields is the support they receive from faculty during college. Support is related to science ambition, attitudes, enjoyment, and willingness to make a career commitment (Grandy, 1998). Cole and Espinoza (2008) indicate that faculty support and encouragement positively influences the grade point average (GPA) of Latino students in STEM. URM students in science and engineering, who perform well academically (i.e. GPA) and persist toward graduation, typically highlight the role of a faculty member as instrumental to their degree attainment (Leslie et al., 1998). Chang et al. (2008), however, found that participating in an academic support program for URM and receiving negative feedback about academic work had no statistically significant effect on the persistence of URMs in biological, biomedical, or behavioral science majors after their first year of college. In fact, URMs in these majors were less likely to persist if they received advice about their educational program from a professor. For the purpose of this chapter, student–faculty interactions and participation in structured educational programs are explored for their effect on students' degree completion in STEM fields at MSIs.

Theoretical and Conceptual Background

Campus climate theory forms the primary theoretical grounding for the analysis of this study. Hurtado, Milem, Clayton-Pedersen, and Allen (1998) define campus climate through four interconnected dimensions: (a) the institution's historical legacy of inclusion or exclusion of various racial/ethnic groups, (b) its structural diversity in terms of numerical representation of various racial/ethnic groups, (c) the psychological climate of perceptions and attitudes between and among groups, and (d) the behavioral climate dimension, characterized by intergroup relations on campus. Dimensions (a) and (b) support the type of institutions chosen as the focal points of the analysis conducted in this chapter: HBCUs and HSIs. While HBCUs were designed to serve African Americans and HSIs, in most cases they have become Hispanic serving through demographic changes, and it is expected that these institutions have established campus climates more reflective of their underrepresented student populations; although, HSIs are still likely to serve significant numbers of White and Asian students (Baez et al., 2008; Chang et al., 2008).

The psychological dimension focuses on how URM students' view their relationship with peers and faculty (Hurtado et al., 1998). For instance, Ancis, Sedlacek, and Mohr (2000) indicate that URM students attending PWIs report incidents of racial prejudice in the form of unfair treatment from peers, faculty, and teaching assistants. Individual perceptions of the campus climate, particularly among MSIs, are important because they are reportedly more supportive of URMs when compared to PWIs and are positively related to learning outcomes like GPA and persistence; these findings are also true of URMs in STEM fields (Chang et al., 2008; Rankin & Reason, 2005). The behavioral climate dimension suggests that individual interpretations of an institution's climate can also be discerned by how individuals interact with peers and faculty (i.e., structured mentoring program or student–faculty relationships) with regard to how involved they are on campus (Hurtado et al., 1998). Laird, Morelon-Quainoo, Williams, and Holmes (2007) indicate that a positive perception of the campus produces a higher level of campus engagement (Laird et al., 2007). As such, campus climate is used to determine how students with STEM majors at HBCUs and HSIs interpret their college environment, how they perceive and interact with peers and faculty within the academic milieu of campus, and in turn how their college experiences are related to their academic success as measured by the number of degrees obtained by 2001.

Data and Analytical Methods

Data and Sample

Our interest was to consider the number of degrees attained by students attending MSIs, with particular interest in students majoring in STEM fields; as such, the Beginning Postsecondary Student Longitudinal Study (BPS: 96/98/01) dataset was obtained and chosen to address the research questions. The 1996 to 2001 cohort of BPS data, included 12,100 first-year students from 973 institutions and was representative of all first-time beginning students completing the 1996 National Postsecondary Student Aid Study (NPSAS; for comprehensive explanations of the sampling and response rate information, see Wine et al., 2002). The sample for this longitudinal study was N = 174 students attending either a 2-year or 4-year (HBCU) or an institution where Latino students (Hispanics) represented 25% or more of the student body (i.e., a characteristic used to define the federal government's designation of HSIs; see Integrated Postsecondary Education Data System [IPEDS] Glossary, n.d.). Because no data were available for students attending TCUs, it was not possible to include TCUs in the analysis.

When using large-scale secondary data with complex samples, Heck and Thomas (2000) recommend using a design-based approach that uses parameters estimated by the NCES longitudinal probability weight (B01LWT1). The purpose of the weight was to adjust for unequal probabilities of selection in the sample design (Heck &Thomas, 2000), as well as students' participation in each iteration of the data collection process. That is, without a sampling weight there was no account for oversampling (i.e., unequal probability of selection) within and across strata and the sample was not representative of the target population, which results in incorrect estimates (Heck & Thomas, 2000). Because the BPS does include a weight, unequal probabilities in the selection of the sample design were considered (Heck & Thomas, 2000); yet, this sampling weight was not designed specifically for students attending MSIs and thus, only accounted for the sample distribution for the longitudinal data collection process from which this selection of data was extracted.

Measures

The dependent variable was coded as an ordinal variable measuring the number of degrees attained by 2001 which was obtained on the 2001 BPS follow-up. To identify the independent variables, prior empirical research on MSIs, campus climate, student–faculty interactions/structured mentoring programs, and URM in STEM fields was used to support variable selection. From the research, it was determined that the number of degrees completed is a function of gender (Bowen et al., 2009), race/ethnicity (Bowen et al., 2009; Chang et al., 2008; Cole & Espinoza, 2008), parental level of education (Bowen et al., 2009), STEM majors (Hurtado et al., 2007), campus climate (Hurtado et al., 2007), and student–faculty interactions/structured mentoring programs (Chang et al., 2008; Cole & Espinoza, 2008).

Of the 12 independent variables, 4 described student characteristics, educational preparation of students' parents, and college major. These included: (a) gender, (b) parents' level of education, (c) race, and (d) college major. Each of these variables was collected in 1996, except for college major, which was collected in 2001. Three independent variables were used to represent the educational environment; they were: (a) climate–academic integration, (b) satisfaction with instructor teaching ability, and (c) satisfaction with campus climate. The remaining five variables were: (a) how often did you have social contact with faculty (collected from the 1996 data); (b) how often did you talk with faculty about academic matters, outside of class time (1998 data); (c) how often did you participate in a cooperative education program, internship, or apprenticeship during 1995–1996 (1998 data); (d) is/was your job as a/an work study position, an internship, a coeducational program (co-op) placement, or none of these (2001 data), and (e) did you participate in a cooperative education program, paid internship, apprenticeship, or assistantship during the last term you were enrolled (2001 data).

Analyses

Descriptive, correlation, and Ordinary Least Squares (OLS) regression analyses were conducted. The descriptive data provided information for each variable about the category of interest and its mean and standard deviation. A correlation matrix was conducted to determine the extent to which independent variables overlap and created collinearity issues in their potential contribution within the regression model. While considering the clustering effects of individual students nested within institutions, chi-square and intraclass correlations were used to determine whether OLS regression analyses or multilevel regression analyses would provide more accurate estimates of standard error. OLS regression analyses were used to examine the number of degrees attained for students attending MSIs. An OLS regression analysis of students attending MSIs was conducted to determine the impact of structured mentoring programs and student–faculty interactions on students' degree attainment. A variety of diagnostics have been conducted, including multicollinearity and in the final analysis the index did not exceed 30.

Limitations

There were two main limitations to consider for this study. While the NCES BPS has an appropriate weight (B01LWT1) to approximate the sample selection and participation at each point of data collection, the analytic sample was relatively small and was not representative of all students specifically attending MSIs; thus, limiting the number of predictors used to construct our model and the generalizability of our findings across all students attending MSIs. Second, three of the independent variables which serve as proxies for student participation in structured mentoring programs offered little information on the nature of the program, particularly regarding mentorship. There were a few measurement issues, where students indicated that they "didn't know" or were unsure about their participation in structured mentoring programs. As such, caution is recommended when interpreting the findings of this study.

Results

The descriptive statistics suggested that only two students during their first year of college participated in cooperative programs. A few more students, however, were involved in work study internships, cooperative education programs, and apprenticeships in 1998 (n = 6) and 2001 (n = 12). While more than three-quarters (77.6%) reported having frequent conversations with faculty outside of class about academic issues, only a little over half (54.6%) reported having had social contact with faculty. In 1998, when reflecting back on their first year of college in 1995–1996, almost all students indicated that they were satisfied with the campus climate (90.8%) and with their instructors' ability to teach (89.7%). A little more than a third (36.6%) of students indicated that they were well integrated into the academic milieu of campus life.

The regression models represented approximately 19.3% of the variance for the number of degrees attained in 2001, over a 6-year period. College experience variables were significant in explaining students' degree attainment (changed in $R^2 = .137$), but this was particularly true for students' satisfaction with campus climate, academic integration, and student–faculty interactions (changed in $R^2 = .125$).

The regression analysis indicated that campus climate ($\beta = .144$, $p < .05$) and academic integration ($\beta = -.260$, $p < .05$) were the only significant college climate indicators related to the number of degrees attained, only one of which was positive. In terms of student–faculty interactions, both frequency in which students talked with faculty outside of the classroom about academic issues ($\beta = .246$, $p < .01$) and having had social contact with faculty ($\beta = .369$, $p < .001$) were significant and positive in their influence on degree attainment.

With regard to student characteristics, parents educational level ($\beta = .193$, $p < .01$) and students majoring in STEM fields ($\beta = -.151$, $p < .05$) were significant; albeit, URM students majoring in STEM fields were less likely to earn their degree when compared to non-STEM majors. Gender and race were not significant. In earlier regression models, where level of institution (4-year and 2-year) was considered, whether a student attended a 2-year (25.3%) or 4-year college (74.7%) was not a statistically significant indicator in this model.

Discussion and Conclusion

Three major conclusions can be drawn from the analyses in this study. First, the regression model was effective in explaining about one fifth of the variance of students' academic success as measured by the number of degrees students obtained at MSIs over a 6-year period. Consistent with prior research, students whose parents have at least a baccalaureate degree were more likely to complete their 2-year or 4-year degree. Interestingly, students in STEM majors were less likely to obtain their degree. Although this finding is not new, particularly among PWIs, it confirms that degree completion can be difficult, even among students attending MSIs in STEM fields, when it is compared against non-STEM students also attending MSIs. Overall, this regression model was not particularly robust in explaining the number of degrees obtained; yet, several college experience variables were identified as useful predictors such that the change in R^2 moved from .058 to .193 once the college experience variables were added to the regression model.

Second, campus climate activities were significant predictors for the number of degrees that students attained. Prior research, for instance, has indicated that students' participation in activities involving student organizations and ethnic-specific events at PWIs can serve as negative predictors for URM students' academic performance in STEM majors (Cole & Espinoza, 2008). According to Cole and Espinoza (2008), this negative relationship likely occurs either as a result of "time on task" (i.e., the amount of time students devote to social activities reduces the available time devoted to academic activities) or because these activities serve as a social outlet needed to counter the academic pressures that students experience within academically rigorous STEM majors. Within the context of the current study, such experiences at MSIs include social and academic involvement, which are typically considered to have a positive contribution to the campus environment that, in turn positively affects students' ethnic identity, quality of college experience, and retention. Yet, academic integration appears to negatively affect students' degree attainment, whereas students' perceptions of campus climate have a positive effect. Further research is needed to determine whether the same rationale offered by Cole and Espinoza (2008) for students attending PWIs can also be applied to students who are attending MSIs.

Finally, student–faculty interactions seem to be the most important part of the college experience affecting the number of degrees students obtain at MSIs. As such, the role of faculty contact and the nature of their interactions with students can significantly enhance students' academic success. Much of the research supports this finding, with some notable exceptions. Chang et al. (2008), for instance, reports that receiving advice about educational programs from a professor negatively impact students' persistence in biological, biomedical, and behavioral science majors. Chang et al. (2008) also reports that there were no significant influences on persistence in these majors that derived from students' participation in an academic support program for URMs. Similarly, in the current study, students' participation in structured mentoring programs as measured by cooperative programs, internships, and apprenticeships were not significant to the number of degrees students attain; while similar to Chang et al.'s (2008) research, this finding may reflect how these variables are measured in the current study, as well as the lack of students' participation in them.

In conclusion, there is a need to enhance students' degree completion rates in STEM fields at MSIs. To do so, there is a need to conduct further studies that explore how students spend their time in social and academic activities at MSIs. Student–faculty interactions, in most cases, are likely to offer opportunities that significantly enhance degree completion. Although similar evidence supports the impact of structured mentoring programs on degree attainment, the data in the current study were inadequate to effectively address this issue and as such, more research is required.

References

Allen, W. R. (1992). The color of success: African American college student outcomes at predominantly White and historically Black colleges and universities. *Harvard Educational Review, 62*(1), 26–44.

American Indian Higher Education Consortium. (2009). *AIHEC AIMS fact book 2007: Tribal colleges and universities report.* Retrieved from http://www.aihec.org/resources/documents/AIHEC_AIMS_FactBook2007.pdf

Ancis, J. R., Sedlacek, W. E., & Mohr, J. J. (2000). Student perceptions of campus cultural climate by race. *Journal of Counseling and Counseling Development, 78,*180–185.

Baez, B., Gasman, M., & Turner, C.S.V. (2008). On minority-serving institutions. In M. Gasman, B. Baez, & C. S. V. Turner (Eds.), *Understanding minority-serving institutions* (pp. 3–17). Albany, NY: SUNY Press.

Blackwell, J. (1989). Mentoring: An action strategy for increasing minority faculty *Academe, 75*(5), 8–14.

Blake-Beard, S., Bayne, M. Crosby, F., & Muller, C. (2011). Matching by race and gender in mentoring relationships: Keeping our eyes on the prize. *Journal of Social Issues, 67*(3), 622–643.

Bonous-Hammarth, M. (2000). Pathways to success: Affirming opportunities for science, mathematics, and engineering majors. *Journal of Negro Education, 69*(1/2), 92–111.

Bowen, W. G., Chingos, M. M., & McPherson, M. S. (2009). *Crossing the finish line: Completing college at America's public universities.* Princeton, NJ: Princeton University Press.

Chang, M. J., Cerna, O., Han, J., & Sàenz, V. (2008). The contradictory roles of institutional status in retaining underrepresented minorities in biomedical and behavioral science majors. *Review of Higher Education, 31*(4), 433–464.

Chubin, D. E., May, G. S., & Babco, E. L. (2005). Diversifying the engineering workforce. *Journal of Engineering Education, 94*(1), 73–86.

Cole, D., & Espinoza, A. (2008). Examining the academic success of Latino students in science, technology, engineering and mathematics majors. *Journal of College Student Development 49*(4), 285–300.

Cole, D., & Espinoza, A. (2009). When gender is considered: Racial ethnic minority students in STEM majors. *Journal of Women and Minorities in Science and Engineering, 15*(3), 263–277.

Crisp, G., Nora, A., & Taggart, A. (2009). Student characteristics, pre-college, college, and environmental factors as predictors of majoring in and earning a STEM degree: An analysis of students attending a Hispanic serving institution. *American Educational Research Journal, 46*(4), 924–942.

Gasman, M. (2010). A growing tradition? *Nonprofit Management and Leadership, 21,* 121–138.

Girves, J., Zepeda, Y., & Gwathmey, J. (2005). Mentoring in a post-affirmative action world. *Journal of Social Issues, 61*(3), 449–479.

Gloria, A. M., Castellanos, J., Lopez, A. G., & Rosales, R. (2005). An examination of the academic non-persistence decisions of Latino undergraduates. *Hispanic Journal of Behavioral Sciences, 27*(2), 202–223.

Gloria, A. M., Hird, J. S., & Navarro, R. L. (2001). Relationships of cultural congruity and perception of the university environment to help-seeking attitudes by sociorace and gender. *Journal of College Student Development, 42*(6), 545–562.

Gloria, A. M., & Robinson Kurpius, S. E. (1996). The validation of the cultural congruity scale and the university environment scale with Chicano/a students. *Hispanic Journal of Behavioral Science, 18,* 533–550.

Gloria, A. M., Robinson Kurpius, S. E., Hamilton, K. D., & Willson, M. S. (1999). African American students' persistence at a predominately White university: Influences of social support, university comfort, and self-beliefs. *Journal of College Student Development, 40*(3), 257–268.

Gloria, A. M., & Rodriguez, E. R. (2000). Counseling Latino university students: Psychosiocultural issues for consideration. *Journal of Counseling and Development, 78*(2), 145–154.

Grandy, J. (1998). Persistence in science of high-ability minority students: Results of a longitudinal study. *Journal of Higher Education, 69*(6), 589–620.

Heck, R., & Thomas, S. (2000). *An introduction to multilevel modeling techniques*. Mahwah, NJ: Erlbaum.

Hispanic Association of Colleges and Universities (HACU). (2008). *Membership advisory*. Retrieved from http://www.hacu.net/hacu/MA_HEA_reauthorized.asp?SnID=406967444

Hurtado, S., Han, J. C., Sáenz, V. B., Espinosa, L. L., Cabrera, N. L., & Cerna, O. S. (2007). Predicting transition and adjustment to college: Biomedical and behavioral science aspirants' and minority students' first year of college. *Research in Higher Education, 48*(7), 841–887.

Hurtado, S., Milem, J. F., Clayton-Pedersen, A. R., & Allen, W. R. (1998). Enhancing campus climates for racial/ethnic diversity: Educational policy and practice. *Review of Higher Education, 21*(3), 279–302.

Hurtado, S., Newman, C. B., Tran, M. C., & Chang, M. J. (2010). Improving the rate of success for underrepresented racial minorities in STEM fields: Insights from a national project. In S. Harper & C. Newman (Eds.), *Students of color in STEM. New Directions for Institutional Research* (No.148, pp. 5–16). San Francisco: Jossey-Bass.

Integrated Postsecondary Education Data System (IPEDS). (n.d.). Glossary. Retrieved from http://nces.ed.gov/ipeds/glossary/?charindex=H.

Kim, M. M., & Conrad, C.F. (2006). The impact of historically Black colleges and universities on the academic success of African-American Students. *Research in Higher Education, 47*(4), 399–427.

Laird, T. F. N., Bridges, B. K., Morelon-Quainoo, C. L., Williams, J. M., & Holmes, M. S. (2007). African American and Hispanic student engagement at minority serving and predominately White institutions. *Journal of College Student Development, 48*(1), 39–56.

Landefeld, T. (2009). *Mentoring in academia and industry: Vol. 4. Mentoring and diversity: Tips for students and professionals for developing and maintaining a diverse scientific community*. New York: Springer.

Lee, W. Y. (1999). Striving toward effective retention: The effect of race on mentoring African American students. *Peabody Journal of Education, 74*(2), 27–43.

Leslie, L. L., McClure, G. T., & Oaxaca, R. L. (1998). Women and minorities in science and engineering: A life sequence analysis. *Journal of Higher Education, 69*(3), 239–276.

Li, X., & Carroll, C.D. (2007). *Characteristics of minority-serving institutions and minority undergraduates enrolled in these institutions* (NCES 2008-156). National Center for Education Statistics, Institute of Education Sciences, U.S. Department of Education. Washington, DC.

National Science Foundation. (2007). *Women, minorities, and persons with disabilities in science and engineering* (NSF 07-315). Arlington, VA: Author.

Outcalt, C. L., & Skewes-Cox, T. E. (2002). Involvement, interaction, and satisfaction: The human environment at HBCUs. *Review of Higher Education, 25*(3), 331–347.

Palmer, R. T., & Gasman, M. (2008). 'It takes a village to raise a child': Social capital and academic success at historically Black colleges and universities. *Journal of College Student Development 49*(1), 52-70.

Provasnik, P., Shafer, L. L., & Snyder, T. D. (2004). *Historically Black colleges and universities, 1976–2001* (NCES Rep. No. 2004-062) Washington, DC: National Center for Education Statistics.

Rankin, S. R., & Reason, R. D. (2005). Differing perceptions: How students of color and White students perceive campus climate for underrepresented groups. *Journal of College Student Development, 46*(1), 43–61.

Stearns, C., Watanabe, S., & Snyder, T. D. (2002). *Hispanic serving institutions: Statistical trends from 1990 to 1999* (NCES Publication No. 2002-051). Washington, DC: National Center for Education Statistics, U.S. Department of Education.

Strayhorn, T. L., & Saddler, T. N. (2009). Gender difference in the influence of faculty-student mentoring relationships on satisfaction with college among African Americans. *Journal of African American Studies, 13*(4), 476–493.

Trent, W., & Hill, J. (1994). The contributions of historically Black colleges and universities to the production of African American scientists and engineers. In W. Pearson & A. Fechter (Eds.), *Who will do science? Educating the next generation* (pp. 68–80). Baltimore, MD: Johns Hopkins University.

Wine, J. S., Hever, R. E., Wheeless, S. C., Francis, T. L., Franklin, J. W., & Dudley, K. M. (2002). *Beginning postsecondary students longitudinal study: 1996-2001 (BPS, 96/01) methodology report* (NCES Report No. 2002-171). Washington, DC: Office of Educational Research and Improvement, U.S. Department of Education.

5

MODEL PROGRAMS FOR STEM STUDENT SUCCESS AT MINORITY SERVING TWO-YEAR COLLEGES

Soko S. Starobin, Dimitra Jackson, and Frankie Santos Laanan

The United States is facing serious competition regarding preparation for science, technology, engineering, and mathematics (STEM). Individuals with significant math and science preparation are essential to the economic growth of the United States. Within the last 6 decades, the number of workers in science and engineering (S&E) occupations had grown from about 182,000 to 5.5 million by 2007 (National Science Foundation, Division of Science Resources Statistics [NSF, DSRS], 2011). This represents an average annual growth rate of 6.2% for the total workforce over the age of 18 during this period. It is anticipated that the market for S&E jobs will continue to increase and that by 2016, the total employment occupations that the National Science Foundation classifies as S&E will be more than double the overall growth rate for all jobs (NSF, DSRS, 2011).

In addition to the need for more individuals to be competent in math and science, there is an urgent need to ensure that in particular, historically underrepresented populations, including women and underrepresented minorities (URMs), be equipped to assume the increasing number of S&E jobs. The focus on increasing women and people of color in STEM areas emerges from several factors that include a projection that minorities will represent about half of the resident U.S. population by 2050 (NSF, DSRS, 2011. As the nation seeks to establish a more ethnically diverse and global knowledge-based economy (Li, 2007), the nation must ensure that women and URMs are prepared so that they can compete in an ever-changing STEM workforce. Even with these projections and the national awareness of STEM education and preparation, too few women and URMs are pursuing bachelor's degrees in STEM areas.

The literature is very explicit regarding the role of 2-year institutions in general and 2-year minority serving institutions (MSIs) in STEM education and preparation. Community colleges and MSIs have been identified as essential pathways for women and URMs in pursuit of STEM degrees. Overall, between 2001 and 2007 more than 50% of all S&E bachelor degree recipients attended a community college at some point in their educational career (Li, 2007). More specifically, while 78% of students graduated with an associate's degree in a STEM field in 2007, only 50% of bachelor's degree recipients received a degree in a STEM area in this same year (NSF, DSRS, 2011). These statistics indicate that the majority of our talented women and URMs will enter our universities by way of the community college. In 2007, 54.7% of females, as compared to 44.4% of males, had attended a community college prior to obtaining their bachelor's degree in a STEM area. The same remains true for individuals of color. In 2007, more than half of American Indian/Alaska Native, Blacks, and Hispanics had attended a community college prior to obtaining their 4-year college degree in a STEM area (Mooney & Foley, 2011).

MSIs, which are "classified as minority-serving based on either one of two *separate* criteria: legislation or the percentage of minority student enrollment" (Li, 2007, p. iv), are institutions whose primary mission is to educate URM populations, such as African Americans, American Indians/Alaska Native, Asians, and Hispanics. Based on the fall 2004 institutional data (Li, 2007), there were 3,935 degree-granting Title IV postsecondary institutions. Among these institutions, 1,254 (41.9%) were reported as MSIs, and public 2-year institutions represented 30.1% (or 377) of the MSIs. With regard to the minority undergraduate enrollment and its percentage distributions, approximately 4.7 million minority undergraduate students enrolled in postsecondary institutions in fall 2004. More than 2.7 million minority undergraduate students enrolled in MSIs, and more than a majority (54.9%) enrolled in public 2-year institutions (Li, 2007). For the purposes of this study, we focus on 2-year public MSIs because they serve substantial proportions of minority students (the criteria for MSI status being 25% of the student body belonging to a specific minority group or the majority of enrollment being minority students) but do not have legal status as a historically Black college and university (HBCU) or as a Tribal college or university (TCU; Li, 2007).

Women and Underrepresented Minority Students (URMs) in STEM

Two-year MSIs have served a significant role in increasing the representation of women and individuals of color in STEM areas, but a lack of representation of these groups in the STEM pipeline remains a critical national concern (Blickenstaff, 2005; Landefeld, 2009). Although women are pursuing college degrees and comprise more than half of college graduates overall, they still remain an undertapped resource in STEM. Several studies have been conducted to investigate the disparities that exist between women and men in terms of STEM.

The disparities range from gender differences in access to STEM-related activities to academic performance measured by grade point average (GPA). Additionally, the underrepresentation of ethnic minorities, including African Americans, Native Americans, Hispanics, and Pacific Islanders, in STEM areas has "been an issue for many decades and has been exhibited at all levels of the educational pathway" (Landefeld, 2009, p. 19). Studies highlight several factors that impact this underrepresentation. The factors range from a shortage of mentors and advisors to a lack of financial assistance to the institutions (Landefeld, 2009). The United States is becoming more racially and ethnically diverse and is in need of equally prepared women and URM populations in STEM areas to ensure that a "diversity of perspectives in the search for knowledge and solutions to human problems" are available to aid in "the ability to see questions and answers from many perspectives [which] will help make scientific explanations more robust and complete" (Blickenstaff, 2005, p. 383). While there have been some gains, the aforementioned populations in STEM fields still do not represent the racial and ethnic percentage of the U.S. population.

Role of Community Colleges and Two-Year MSIs in Educational Pathway

Community colleges and MSIs have been identified as avenues for fostering STEM aspirations among bachelor's degree seeking individuals, especially among women (Berger & Malaney, 2003) and URMs (Landefeld, 2009). Over the last few decades, community colleges have facilitated the increase of female and minority representations in STEM fields (Brazziel & Brazziel 1994; Quimbita 1991; Starobin, 2004; Starobin & Laanan, 2005).

As previously mentioned, among the many roles of community colleges is the transfer function (Cohen & Brawer, 2003), which allows students to transfer to a 4-year institution to complete the bachelor's degree (Laanan, 1998; Townsend & Wilson, 2006). Use of the transfer function is becoming increasingly common for several reasons. According to the NSF 2008 National Survey of Recent College Graduates (NSRCG), Tsapogas (2004), who analyzed the data from the National Survey of Recent College Graduates (NSRCG), and the Committee on Prospering in the Global Economy of the 21st Century (2005), found among the reasons that students attend community colleges, are to complete credits for a bachelor's degree, financial reasons (e.g., cost of a 4-year school), and to gain skills or knowledge that will enable them to be successful in a 4-year college (Mooney & Foley, 2011). To date, at least one out of every five community college students transfers to a 4-year institution (Eggleston & Laanan, 2001). Moreover, more than half of all recipients of STEM bachelor's degrees attended a community college at some point (Mooney & Foley, 2011). The current Obama Administration has noted that community colleges need to produce 5 million more graduates by 2020. The Lumina Foundation notes that "about one-third of all American students of color are educated at MSIs, which translates into almost 2.3 million students" (Landefeld, 2009, p. 23). Thus, MSIs educate the majority of our URM population. Li (2007) suggests that between 1984 and 2004, the total minority enrollment in MSIs (Hispanics, Asians, American Indians, and Blacks) had increased by 146%. Further, it is noteworthy that for both 2-year Asian and 2-year Hispanic serving MSIs higher 3-year graduation rates have been reported than for 2-year non-MSIs (36% versus 25%, and 27% versus 25%, respectively; Li, 2007). Consequently, these particular institutions can assist in increasing the representation of URMs in 4-year colleges and ultimately in STEM areas. A closer look at MSIs is necessary, given their critical role in serving as a pathway for women and students of color in accessing not only higher education in general but STEM in particular.

Factors that Influence Governance and Structure for Student Success

In order to understand the preparedness level and provision of effective resources for the particular population of URMs, it is crucial to examine practices at 2-year MSIs. The literature draws attention to effective practices with this population that include the impact of mentors and role models, the need for sufficient resources, and the effectiveness of student services.

Mentors and Role Models

The role of faculty as effective mentors is an essential determinant of whether a student chooses to pursue a degree in a STEM area. Landefeld (2009) asserts that the lack of mentors is one of the reasons why "women and individuals from underserved and often underprivileged groups, such as Blacks, Hispanics, Native Americans, and Pacific Islanders, are grossly under-represented in the sciences" (p. 2). Additional research asserts that gender differences regarding STEM areas of study and self-confidence in these areas are related to formal and informal student–faculty interactions (Seymour, 1995; Stage & Kloosterman, 1995). Moreover, a study conducted by Jackson (2010), which focused on the academic and social transition of community college transfer students, found that the role of a mentor was essential in their decision to persist in a STEM area.

Financial Resources

In addition to faculty interaction and the role of mentors, funding for MSIs is essential in ensuring that students from these institutions are able to compete academically. The lack of available funding to MSIs creates challenges in providing current resources to ensure that women and historically underrepresented populations are competent in STEM areas. The funding that is at the disposal of MSIs is very different from the amount available at predominantly White institutions (PWIs). "In direct comparison and contrast to funding at MSIs, many of the PWIs are research institutions and, as such, have access to many more financial resources" (Landefeld, 2009, p. 23). This challenge creates opportunities for 2-year community colleges and 2-year MSIs to form collaborations and partnerships with universities for the sharing of resources and knowledge.

Student Services

Retention literature continues to support academic engagement and involvement in the academic environment as particularly important for students of color (Merisotis & Kee, 2006). Summer bridge programs have been identified as effective ways to spark interest in STEM careers. Learning communities have been documented as increasing both interest and retention among targeted groups, such as academically underprepared students, URMs, women, and students of color (Lenning & Ebbers, 1999). Learning communities assist in building a community of learners among individuals with similar interests and allow students to engage more and have increased interaction with faculty (Smith, MacGregor, Matthews, & Gabelnick, 2004). Exemplary models of practices assist us in identifying ways to effectively retain URMs in the STEM pipeline.

Case Study of Model Programs

This chapter portrays two model programs at 2-year public institutions (with high percentages of ethnically diverse student populations) that are assisting women to pursue STEM majors at 2-year MSIs. The purposes of this case study were to: (a) describe characteristics of model programs that assist females in navigating their STEM educational experiences; (b) ascertain how female students negotiate their academic and personal experiences in their STEM education programs; and (c) identify common threads between two programs in assisting females with success in the STEM pipeline. To guide a selection process of two model programs for this case study, recommendations from the Cross Roads (National Academy of Sciences, 2010) were reviewed. In the section of the journey beyond the crossroads, special program characteristics, such as (a) a summer bridge program and (b) academic support and social integration were noted as critical elements for student success, specifically among URMs in STEM fields. We selected two model programs that included these critical elements.

The first program, at San Diego City College, California, offers a unique summer bridge academy, which provides a "head start" for students who intend to major in a STEM field. The second program, at Highline Community College,

Washington, provides a learning environment that emphasizes academic support and fosters social integration for students in a pre-engineering program. Guided group interviews were conducted in summer 2011 and spring 2007 at San Diego City College and Highline Community College, respectively. Data from the guided group interviews were tape recorded and transcribed. The researchers reviewed and coded the transcripts to identify recurring themes and opinions. In addition to the data from the guided group interviews, notes from the program sessions, printed artifacts, such as program brochures, and session handouts were used for document analysis. Visual artifacts, such as program websites, photographs of program sessions and events were also utilized to better understand the contextual background of the program as well as the organizational culture at departmental and institutional levels.

Summer Academy and STEM Success Culture

As a member of the San Diego Mathematics, Engineering, and Science Achievement (MESA) Program since 2001, San Diego City College has served as a leading community college partner to enhance a statewide intersegmental regional collaboration in mathematics, engineering, and science education for economically disadvantaged and underrepresented student populations. San Diego City College is a designated Hispanic serving institution, with 38% Latino enrollment in the fall of 2010 (Integrated Postsecondary Education Data System [IPEDS], 2010a). The City College MESA Program offers academic support and a transfer program, which creates a *culture of success* using a *language of success* to enable students to take responsibility for their learning and academic success. In 2011, the City College MESA Program developed an Academy for STEM Success, which is a 3-day on-campus summer bridge program for incoming high school graduates, designed to teach them about the *culture of success*, study skills, and provide them with the opportunity to meet student mentors, faculty, administrators, and role models from business and industry in STEM. Two Academy sessions were designed exclusively for female and male groups.

Participants were recruited from high schools that are feeder schools for San Diego City College. To meet the objectives of the San Diego MESA Program, a special effort was made to invite URMs and women to the academy. For this case study, the Academy for STEM Success for the female group was examined.

Pre-Engineering Program at Highline Community College

Highline Community College (HCC) has been a member institution of the Mathematics Engineering Science Achievement (MESA) Washington and the MESA Community College Partnership (MCCP). MCCP is a NSF-funded program (formally known as Northwest Engineering Talent Expansion

Partnership) that is designed to increase the number of URMs and women in engineering who intend to transfer to 4-year colleges. Located in a suburb of Seattle, HCC enrolled a diverse student population (including, 14.8% Asian, 11.4% Black or African American, 6.5% Hispanic/Latino) and approximately 60% female students in fall 2010 (IPEDS, 2010b). It is critical for our case study that we recognize an underestimated enrollment statistic reported to the National Center for Education Statistics. In addition to the percentages of student populations mentioned above, 6.0% of students identified as two or more races and 12.5% as race/ethnicity unknown. With a funding support from the MCCP, a dedicated classroom space for academic and social activities is available for students in the pre-engineering program that offers courses equivalent to (that can be transferred as) the first 2 years of an engineering degree program at a 4-year university. Tutoring service, informal communication with a faculty advisor, participation in the annual Human Powered Paper Vehicle (HPPV) competition are examples that connect academic support and social interaction among peers, mentors, faculty, and support staff.

Examining Negotiation for Success: STEM Student Success Literacy Framework

To examine how female students negotiate their academic and personal experiences, we used a STEM Student Success Literacy framework proposed by Starobin (2010) to interpret our findings. Further, we perceive that the literacy comprises an intertwined relationship among three factors, (a) self-efficacy, (b) social capital, and (c) transfer knowledge that help female students understand and believe in their ability to successfully transfer from a 2-year to a 4-year postsecondary institution. STEM Student Success Literacy is based on the ground theories from previous studies on women in STEM fields. A plethora of literature documents a negative learning culture and environment in STEM fields for female students at 4-year research institutions (Lovitts, 2001; Sax, 1994; Seymour & Hewitt, 1997). In a study of engineering students at highly ranked West Coast research universities, Vogt, Hocevar, and Hagedorn (2007) assert that female students reported greater discrimination. Furthermore, this study used a critical Roth and Barton's (2004) social lens whereby they proposed to redefine the traditional meaning of scientific literacy by arguing that (unlike the traditional definition of the term) science literacy is a property of collective experiences and a social phenomenon irreducible to individual characteristics. Roth and Barton's (2004) perspective enabled the researchers to conceive of the STEM student as emerging into success literacy in a nested social process, in which each student's academic and social experiences are influenced by different levels of institutional and organizational units, such as classroom, program area, department, and college. Guided by the framework, the analysis of this case study focuses on how URMs and female students who participated in two model programs navigated their academic and social experiences at a community college, specifically looking at identifying key factors that positively influenced their self-concept, social capital, and transfer knowledge. While this chapter reviewed literature on both URMs and females, the subsequent part of this chapter will only focus on female STEM students.

Common Threads in the Model Programs

There are three common threads that emerged from the reflections and self-examinations on academic and social experiences among the female students who participated in the model programs in the selected MSIs. Three common threads are: (a) momentum of success literacy; (b) division of labor; and (c) emergence of success literacy. Additionally, we found that events and practices that are associated with these three common threads occur continuously and simultaneously. Though there was a developmental order for key events and practices to take place (e.g., one event leads to the next sequential event, etc.) within each common thread, most of the events and practices seemed to be materialized by virtue of the intuitive and holistic nature of student development and growth, especially for these female students.

Momentum of Success Literacy

One of the repeated comments from the group interview participants from both programs was that there was a moment of affirmation when they felt they could study and then build a career in a STEM field. This momentum of success literacy (that they can be successful in academics and career) changed the ways in which these students perceived themselves. One student stated, "Coming into the program, I was not really sure about what I wanted to do. At home I did not get the support, like 'Yeah, you can do it. You can be an engineer, you can be a doctor, you can be ...' and now after the third day, I feel like I can do it, and I am determined and I know what I want to do." A female student in a pre-engineering program reflected on her momentum and wished it had come much earlier: "I just wish someone had planted the seed and mentioned that you know, engineering is possible, and you can do this ... just that little statement just like changed my world basically."

Another notable momentum of success literacy helped the female students to discuss their own stereotypes and fears about studying STEM fields. Through study group and tutoring services, a student in a pre-engineering program began to describe her experiences with mathematics. She stated, "It is a skill that you have to learn...it is not ooh math, it is just a skill that you have to learn and there are ways to get around it." A summer bridge program participant also overcame her fear after learning about a *culture of success* with a *language of success*. She asserted, "It made me realize that I can work smarter [and not harder] and I have a growth mind-set, and not a fixed mind-set. You grow by learning." The researchers recognized that remembrances of each momentum contributed to the development of self-confidence in studying and pursuing a career in STEM fields for these students. In addition, at each momentum, a student had a sense of validation that they could be successful academically and socially in STEM fields.

Division of Labor: Governance and Structure for Success

Based on the findings from the group interview, it is evident that both 2-year institutions have governance and structure to develop and sustain their respective programs to support their students. In other words, there is a systematic division of labor to provide factors that are unique to assist traditionally underrepresented students in STEM fields. The factors included mentoring, financial resources, and student services. After participating in the summer bridge program, the female students began to see themselves in an academic discipline. One student expressed it this way: "The experience, what it means to me is I feel that I am part of this school now." Another female reflected on her experience and stated: "We were talking to either mentors or professors that came in, or people who have been in school for a long time with doctorate degrees, so it was very helpful to have their input" so as to be able to visualize herself studying a STEM discipline and being on campus. One student affirmed that, "Oh yeah, I want to be a math teacher, but now that I see where everybody is coming from, and careers, I feel like it is really determined what I really want to be now." Seeing role models who navigated the educational pathway in STEM fields, these students also gained their transfer knowledge (moving from 2-year to 4-year institutions) to pursue a STEM baccalaureate degree and beyond.

Student services, such as the San Diego MESA Program at the City College, can also provide governance and structure that facilitate student success. A female participant recognized the role of the San Diego MESA Program and stated, "I know that now I have a group of sisters at the MESA and I could just go in there and I know everybody there, say hi to them and go to my class and expand my horizon, you know, get out of my comfort zone." At Highline Community College, participation in the annual Human Powered Paper Vehicle (HPPV) competition connects academic experiences and social interaction among peers outside of the classroom. One student reflected on her experience in the preparation process for the competition and asserted, "It really bonded us together because we had to fight through this thing [development of the HPPV], and it really made me step up and be a leader because before that I was kinda like just going along with them and doing what they wanted and stuff like that ... I can do this, I can lead and so it was just really we've now gone off into our engineering love." It was clear that the out of classroom experiences provided through the student services were as important as in-classroom experiences for these students to feel a sense of belonging and develop their self-confidence in studying a STEM field.

Emergence of Success Literacy: A Nested Social Practice

There are several characteristics that formed an emergence of STEM student success literacy at these two institutions. We observed less presence of the characteristics of the traditional STEM academic culture known at 4-year research institutions (e.g., competitive, bureaucratic, hierarchical) and more of the academic and social environments that reflect their students' background and the uniqueness of the surrounding communities regarding their cultural and life style diversities. For instance, many females in the summer bridge program were first generation college students, and only a few of them received support from their family for doing what was necessary to obtain a degree and build a career in the STEM field. Even those who received parental support still needed to search for information about studying and working in the STEM field. One female participant explained, "At home my parents also want me to become someone, like a doctor. They just tell me to go and do it, but they don't tell me the steps. They don't know what it takes to get there, but thanks to the people who were there, what they said about their lives, I know more about the field that I am going into." A peer concurs with her and states, "Knowing that they [mentors] come from where we come from, and how their situation was is how our situation is, I can relate to them." This example implies that the partnership between the program and business/industry and the interaction between professional mentors and students can fill a knowledge gap that exists in many of the parents of first generation college students who would like to see their children succeed in their chosen field, but lack the background to provide them with the essential basic information.

Conclusions

The findings from the group interview revealed three common threads in the aforementioned model programs. Utilization of the STEM student success literacy framework further assisted the researchers to deeply understand how these traditionally underrepresented female students negotiated their academic and social experiences at public 2-year institutions that serve ethnically and culturally diverse student populations. It was evident to the researchers that there was a momentum to students' success literacy, and that the first boost to student self-confidence in studying in a STEM field should arrive at the very beginning of their academic experience. Additionally, such momentum should be provided in different contexts, such as in and out of classroom experiences and at different levels (e.g., from peer mentors, student support service staff, faculty, and professional career mentors).

Further, remarks from the female students in the group interviews clearly justify the need for a partnership that facilitates the emergence of STEM student success literacy. This emergence, which we understood as being a nested social practice, provides opportunities for traditionally underrepresented students to recognize, self-actualize, and more importantly gain their social capital that relates to information and knowledge about studying a STEM field at a post-secondary institution as well as pursuing and building a career in a STEM field. It is critical for female students to interact through the model programs with student mentors and professionals who share the same background with regard to gender, ethnicity, culture, and family.

Recommendations for Practice, Policy, and Future Research

Financial resources from institutions as well as external agencies are critical for development, implementation, and sustainability of the model programs that assist URMs and female students to have positive academic and social experiences in STEM education. The findings suggest that it is imperative that each institution share both financial resources and human capacity to maximize support services for students. Furthermore, external government agencies, such as the National Science Foundation, and state departments of education can provide financial resources for 2-year MSIs to develop programs, services, and partnerships with business and industry. As a program matures through successful employment among graduates of STEM programs, business and industry can provide additional funding to sustain the necessary quality of academic programs to meet the demands of the STEM workforce.

With regard to policy implications, findings from this study assert that a strong partnership among institutions from all educational sectors (e.g., high school, 2- and 4-year postsecondary institutions) is key in creating a seamless academic experience for URM and female students to navigate their STEM education. It is noteworthy that the two model programs discussed in this chapter are located in states (California and Washington) that have state policy regarding transfer and articulation of courses between and among 2- to 4-year institutions. Such state policy guides postsecondary institutions to develop transfer agreements, utilize common course numbers, and implement other practices that encourage students to transfer from 2- to 4-year institutions. It implies that a synergy between institutional policy and state policy should be created for these model programs to sustain their successful practices. Perhaps continuous assessment and evaluation of academic and support programs will strengthen the synergy between institutional and state policy.

Recommendations for future research are to articulate other model programs to assist URM and female students pursuing a STEM degree at 2-year MSIs and to continue to examine common threads across model programs. This study introduced a utilization of a STEM student success literacy framework to identify common threads at different institutions. The framework may provide a guideline for other MSIs to conduct program assessment and evaluation. Furthermore, an application of both quantitative and qualitative research inquiries is suggested to facilitate the program assessment and evaluation processes.

References

Berger, J. B., & Malaney, G. D. (2003). Assessing the transition of transfer students from community colleges to a university. *NASPA Journal, 40*(4), 1–23.

Blickenstaff, J. C. (2005). Women and science careers: Leaky pipeline or gender filter? *Gender and Education, 17*(4), 369–386.

Brazziel, W. F., & Brazziel, M. E. (1994). "Minority Science and Engineering Doctorate Recipients with Junior and Community College Backgrounds." *Community College Journal of Research and Practice, 18*(1), 71–80

Cohen, A. M., & Brawer, F. (2003). The American community college. San Francisco: Jossey-Bass.

Committee on Prospering in the Global Economy of the 21st Century. (2005). *Rising above the gathering storm: Energizing and employing America for a brighter economic future.* Washington, DC: National Academies Press.

Eggleston, L. E., & Laanan, F. S. (2001). Making the transition to the senior institution. *New Directions for Community Colleges, 30,* 87-98.

Integrated Postsecondary Education Data System (IPEDS). (2010a). San Diego City College. Retrieved from http://nces.ed.gov/globallocator/col_info_popup.asp?ID=122339

Integrated Postsecondary Education Data System (IPEDS). (2010b). Highline Community College. Retrieved from http://nces.ed.gov/globallocator/col_info_popup.asp?ID=235431

Jackson, D. L. (2010). *Transfer students in STEM majors: Gender differences in the socialization factors that influence academic and social adjustment.* (Unpublished doctoral dissertation). Educational Leadership and Policy Studies, Iowa State University, Ames.

Laanan, F. S. (1998). Descriptive analysis of students' post-college earnings from California community colleges. In J. R. Sanchez & F. S. Laanan (Eds.), *Determining the economic benefits of attending community college* (New Directions for Community Colleges, No. 104, pp. 77–87). San Francisco, CA: Jossey-Bass.

Landefeld, T. (2009). *Mentoring in academia and industry: Vol. 4. Mentoring and diversity: Tips for students and professionals for developing and maintaining a diverse scientific community.* New York: Springer.

Lenning, O. T., & Ebbers, L. H. (1999). *The powerful potential of learning communities: I. Improving education for the future* (ASHE-ERIC Higher Education Report, Vol. 26, No. 6). Washington DC: ERIC Clearinghouse on Higher Education. http://www.eriche.org/reports

Li, X. (2007). *Characteristics of minority-serving institutions and minority undergraduates enrolled in these institutions* (NCES 2008-156). Washington, DC: National Center for Education Statistics, Institute of Education Sciences, U.S. Department of Education.

Lovitts, E. B. (2001). *Leaving the ivory tower: The cases and consequences of departure from doctoral study.* New York: Rowman & Littlefield.

Merisotis, J.P. and Kee, A.M. 2006. "A model of success: The Model Institutions for Excellence Program's decade of leadership in STEM education." *Journal of Hispanic Higher Education. 5,* 288–308.

Mooney, G. M., & Foley, D. J. (2011, July). *Community colleges: Playing an important role in the education of science, engineering, and health graduates* (Info Brief NSF 11-317). Arlington, VA: National Science Foundation. http://www.nsf.gov/statistics/infbrief/nsf11317/nsf11317.pdf

National Academy of Sciences. (2010). *Rising above the gathering storm, revisited: Rapidly approaching category 5.* Washington, DC: National Academy of Sciences. National Academy of Engineering, and Institute of Medicine.

National Science Foundation, Division of Science Resources Statistics. Directorate for Social, Behavioral, and Economic Sciences. (2011). *Women, minorities, and persons with disabilities in science and engineering.* Arlington, VA: National Science Foundation. Retrieved from http://www.nsf.gov/statistics/wmpd/pdf/wmpd2011.pdf

National Science Foundation, National Center for Science and Engineering Statistics. (2011). *Science and engineering degrees: 1966–2008. Detailed statistical tables* (NSF 11-316). Arlington, VA: National Science Foundation. Retrieved from http://www.nsf.gov/statistics/nsf11316/.

Quimbita, G. (1991). Preparing women and minorities for careers in math and science: The role of community colleges (ERIC Document Reproduction Service No. ED 333 943).

Roth, W. M., & Barton, A .C. (2004). *Rethinking scientific literacy (Critical social thought)*. New York: Routledge Falmer.

Sax, L. J. (1994a). Mathematical self-concept: How college reinforces the gender gap. *Research in Higher Education, 35*(2), 141–166.

Seymour, E. (1995). The loss of women from science, mathematics, and engineering undergraduate majors: An explanatory account. *Science Education, 79*(4), 437–473.

Seymour, E., & Hewitt, N.M. (1997). *Talking about leaving: Why undergraduates leave the sciences.* Boulder, CO: Westview Press.

Smith, B. L., MacGregor, J., Matthews, R. S., & Gabelnick, F. (2004). *Learning communities: Reforming undergraduate education.* San Francisco, CA: Wiley.

Stage, F. K., & Kloosterman, P. (1995). Gender, beliefs, and achievement in remedial college-level mathematics. *Journal of Higher Education, 66,* 294-311.

Starobin, S. S. (2004). *Gender differences in college choice, aspirations, and self-concept among community college students in science, mathematics, and engineering* (Unpublished doctoral dissertation). Denton: University of North Texas.

Starobin, S. S. (2010). *Opening doors for marginalized students: A framework for understanding STEM student success literacy in community colleges.* Paper presented at the Council for the Study of Community Colleges, 52nd Annual Conference. Seattle, WA.

Starobin, S. S., & Laanan, F. S. (2005). Influence of pre-college experience on self-concept among community college students in science and engineering. *Journal of Women and Minorities in Science and Engineering, 11*(3), 209–230.

Townsend, B. K., & Wilson, K. B. (2006). "A hand hold for a little bit": Factors facilitating the success of community college transfer students to a large research university. *Journal of College Student Development, 47*(4), 439-456.

Tsapogas, J. (2004). *The role of community colleges in the education of recent science and engineering graduates.* Washington, DC: National Science Foundation.

Vogt, C. M., Hocevar, D., & Hagedorn, L. S. (2007). A social cognitive construct validation: Determining women's and men's success in engineering programs. *Journal of Higher Education, 78*(3), 337–364.

6

TEACHING TO TEACH

African American Faculty, HBCUs, and Critical Pedagogy

Roland W. Mitchell, T. Elon Dancy II, Dana Hart, and Berlisha Morton

The establishment of the U.S. higher education system predates the founding of the nation itself. With Harvard College as its first chartered corporation and educational enterprise in 1636 (Thelin, 2004), U.S. higher education maintains a rich legacy of promoting knowledge and innovative thinking. Subsequently, U.S. higher education is often characterized as the envy of the world and a symbol of prosperity that intrinsically creates limitless opportunities for personal growth and development. However, both historical and current educational trends provide several illustrations that this characterization is truer for some U.S citizens than for others. Access and participation has consistently remained a hallmark of a privileged, White patriarchal class, where women and people of color were largely excluded from the enterprise. In fact, where U.S. higher education is concerned, race has been largely subordinated to an identity framed around pervasive practices of ethnocentrism, cultural elitism, and discrimination (Anderson, 1998; Watkins, 2001). It is through this racial oppression that historically Black colleges and universities (HBCUs) emerged, and from their foundation to the present, these institutions have continued to defend and define their existence. Understanding this story of how HBCUs developed to promote new educational, social, and economic opportunities for African Americans is critical in shaping a redefined perspective about American higher education.

HBCUs are an indispensable part of what makes the United States an intellectual and cultural world leader and its postsecondary system the envy of the world. Unfortunately, tightening financial constraints and conservative backlash against advances by communities of color in the post-Civil Rights era has led the United States to undervalue HBCUs. Thus, questions regarding the relevance of these institutions are directly informed by the still unresolved and tumultuous relationship between race and educational equity in America (Samuels, 2004; Wallenstein, 2008; Watkins, Lewis, & Chou 2001). Problematically, HBCUs are seen as a balm for soothing the wrongs perpetrated on African Americans prior to *Brown v. Board of Education* (1954). Notwithstanding, this chapter seizes an opportunity to meditate on the contributions HBCUs afford the nation today.

The chapter explores the range of contributions associated with the pedagogically meaningful knowledge inherent in the systematic inquiry, scholarly dissemination, and pedagogical practices of educators who learned to teach at HBCUs. In this effort, we drew upon the scholarship of teaching and learning (SoTL) literature which focuses on "the knowing that comes from doing" (Dewey, 1934) that can only be acquired from teaching. Additional attention is paid to the ways that teachers impart their subject matter/disciplinary knowledge to students. Consequently, this chapter is situated beyond the nearly 60-year morass concerning the relevance and continued necessity of historically Black colleges and universities for the 21st century.

The overarching theoretical framework of the chapter is informed by oppositional social theories and specifically the philosophy of W. E. B. Du Bois (1903/1999), sociologist Patricia Hill-Collins (1986, 1998), and educator Lisa Delpit (2002). Du Bois (1903/1999) in particular, as a preeminent expert, product, and critic of Black education and social life, highlights the importance of the influence of Black thought on American thought. Subsequently, his work is foundational for understanding the unique pedagogical knowledge emanating from HBCU classrooms. We conclude the chapter by illustrating the rich and educationally useful insight gleaned by African American teachers who learned the craft of teaching in historically Black college settings.

The Brokering of HBCUs: Past and Present Perspectives

Prior to the end of the Civil War, there was no real system for educating Blacks, which led to the common interpretation that Black education is exclusively the product of Northern White school marms, patrician class industrialists, or radical White Southerners. Clearly, the contribution of the fore-referenced groups or the post-Emancipation Proclamation date is justifiable; but, as our aim is to reenvision and more correctly describe the contributions of HBCUs, we offer a counter origin tale and starting date. It is our belief that Black education was established by Blacks prior to the end of slavery. And we further believe that the desire to attribute the lion's share of the success at establishing Black education to liberal Whites, in and of itself, is directly related to questions today about the viability of HBCUs and Black self-determination in 21st century America (Anderson, 1998; Mitchell, 2010; Watkins, 2001).

A critical rereading of the commonly accepted history of Black education reveals that Sabbath Schools sprang up across the South, during and after the

Civil War, and in effect are the early forebears of Black educational self-determination, social uplift, and most importantly for our work, HBCUs. Numbering more than 1,000 and primarily established and run by and for formerly enslaved African Americans, these church sponsored schools functioned in the evenings and on weekends and provided basic literacy and religious instruction to those who were unable to attend weekday schools (Span, 2009). History has, for the most part, overlooked Sabbath Schools in favor of the narrative of White Northerners coming to the South and subsequently establishing schools for Blacks. However, for each narrative of Black educational success as a result of White "do-gooders," or industrialists, there is an equally valid narrative of Black educational success as a result of Black self-determination. The Black community expended a tremendous amount of resources that, in the end, played a significant role in raising the African American literacy rate from approximately 6% at the close of the Civil War to nearly 77% by the 1930s (Anderson, 1998).

As emancipation occurred and a segment of the White population became actively engaged in the work of supporting Black education, Sabbath Schools were either closed or fell under White supervision. In many ways the eventual closure and subsequent erasure from history of Sabbath Schools mirrors the fate of African American controlled schools, school boards, and teacher organizations at the conclusion of *Brown* (Siddle-Walker, 2001). In both instances, White financial support was gained at the expense of Black control and as educational historian William Watkins asserts, allowed Whites to effectively serve as the Architects of Black Education.

Clearly, Sabbath Schools were not colleges; however, by situating these schools within the broader lineage of Black education, a more critical vantage is provided for understanding the history of Black education as opposed to simply lumping in the founding of colleges for African Americans with the 1636 establishment of Harvard College and American higher education in general. In fact, the tie that binds these two disparate yet distinctly American histories of U.S. higher education was that where pioneering U.S. colleges (e.g., Harvard, Yale, Princeton, Dartmouth) were initially established to educate the heathen population of the New World (Wright, 1988), HBCUs were founded in a similar vein to cultivate a civilized class out of the newly emancipated whose humanity and more importantly educability was in question. Consequently, the linkage between ethnocentrism/White supremacy and higher education is as American as "Apple Pie."

Black higher education in the United States developed primarily within a system of private liberal arts colleges (Anderson, 1988). While most of these colleges emerged in the Southern states after the end of the Civil War in 1865, a few Black colleges existed during the antebellum period, including Cheney State University and Lincoln University in Pennsylvania and Wilberforce in Ohio (Brooks, Starks, & Brooks, 2011). The Reconstruction era delivered new iterations and developments in educational attainment for African Americans, where having been prohibited from acquiring even the most basic education throughout their enslavement, many freedmen and women expressed a strong desire to learn, develop, and attain new opportunities (Brown, Ricard, & Donahoo, 2004). The federal government, through the Freedman's Bureau, and denominational groups and local communities began establishing Black colleges as early as 1865 (Gasman & Tudico, 2008). Northern missionaries, such as the American Baptist Home Missionary Society and the American Missionary Association, also helped in this effort. Guided by a sense of democratic idealism, these "Yankee" missionaries suggested the freed people had the right to public education and to political and civic equality (Anderson, 1988). Yet, this benevolence also framed their self-interest and racism, manifested in the specific goals in establishing Black higher education as a way to convert formerly enslaved people to their brand of Christianity (Gasman & Tudico, 2008).

During Reconstruction, Black religious denominations also founded colleges in Georgia, Texas, and South Carolina. These institutions were established by African Americans for African Americans and relied less on White support, which created opportunities to design their own curricula (Anderson, 2008). We will elaborate more on the importance of these institutions in the following section. In spite of conflicting motivations, these coordinating forces (Black churches/community, White industrialists, and the federal government) helped to establish and charter more than 200 Black colleges between 1865 and 1890 (Brown & Davis, 2001), over two centuries after the founding of Harvard College. The federal 1890 Land Grant legislation further promoted state higher education across much of the South into the 20th century. These colleges and universities were in name only, however, and their overall composition and survival depended on corporate philanthropic foundations and wealthy individuals (Watkins, 2001). As Anderson (1988) suggests:

> Northern white industrialists, beginning with the establishment of the Peabody Education Fund in 1867, saw universal schooling in much the same way as did southern white industrialists—as a means to make Black southerners an efficient laboring force of the South and to prepare them for a fairly definite caste system. It was mainly through their differences with the southern white planters that northern white industrialists gained their reputations as liberal reformers and were perceived as promoting in the South more just race relations.
>
> *(p. 280)*

These disparate sources sought to repress and shape Black higher education in ways that contradicted African American's overall interests in intellectual development (Anderson, 1988; Watkins, 2001). Thus, a distinctly different form of higher education emerged to ensure separate and unequal conditions and opportunities for African Americans. This pattern led to a dual system of higher education across much of the South, which solidified the status and place of HBCUs (Brown, 2001).

Despite a contested and race brokered educational model, HBCUs have presented an ability to offer African Americans opportunities to excel in social, political, and economic arenas (Mitchell & Mitchell, 2008; Palmer & Gasman, 2008; Palmer & Wood, 2012). Historically, these institutions have maintained a spirit of promoting community and racial uplift, and cultivating racial identity and scholarly achievement (Brown & Davis, 2001). Roebuck and Murty (1993) contend that HBCUs, unlike predominantly White institutions (PWIs) are "united in [a] mission to meet educational and emotional needs of Black students … and stress preparation for student leadership and service roles in the community" (p. 10). They remain a significant home for Black faculty and make enormous contributions to public life in the United States despite their history of racial discrimination, isolation, and economic disadvantage (Drewry & Doermann, 2001).

Today, HBCUs comprise only 3% of the nation's postsecondary institutions, a total of 103 public and private colleges and universities (National Center for Education Statistics, 2006). Yet, more than 20% of all African Americans who have graduated from college have attended one (Minor, 2008). They have graduated the nation's African American educators, doctors, lawyers, and scientists (Gasman & Tudico, 2008; Palmer & Gasman, 2008; Palmer & Wood, 2012), and of the top 10 colleges that graduate African American PhD candidates, nine are HBCUs (American Association of University Professors [AAUP], 2007). And in our current dialogue about education policy and practice, President Barack Obama mandated that the United States will have the highest proportion of college graduates in the world by the year 2020, suggesting this cannot be accomplished without the presence and active support of HBCUs; for they are "catalysts of change … and the cradles of opportunity where each generation inherits the American Dream" (Obama, 2010). Consequently, President Obama has called for $98 million in new funding for HBCUs, including a commitment of $850 million over 10 years, by extending the 30-year-old White House Initiative on HBCUs (Obama, 2010). To complement this goal, the Department of Education will also call for a more "explicit and re-imagined partnership" with the private sector to strengthen the capacity of HBCUs and shift the narrative from an appeal "centered on the need for corrective contributions to an appeal centered on creative investment" (Duncan, 2010).

The constant focus on survival or the continued utility of HBCUs is a racially coded and generally unproductive line of conversation. For example, questions about the need for religious institutions like Notre Dame or Pepperdine or women's institutions like Vassar or Wellesley is rarely raised. Even if one chooses to focus specifically on race and education, Southern universities like the University of Alabama (founded in Tuscaloosa, Alabama in 1831) are just as much a part of the legacy of America's segregationist past as HBCUs in the region like Alabama State University (founded in Montgomery, Alabama in 1867). However, questions about the relevance, utility, or continued existences of the University of Alabama to the people of the region seem bizarre.

So how is Alabama State University any more or less a product of Jim Crow than its older historically White sister institution? Both are deeply entrenched in the legacy of White supremacy but only one, the University of Alabama, is afforded a positive, and might we add an ahistorical reading. The other Alabama State is represented as a noxious remnant of America's post-*Brown* growing pangs and is now in danger of being erased in the desire for America to continue its peculiar national innocence. Therefore, if race is the defining characteristic between the two, we set out to turn this racially coded question— Do we still need HBCUs?—on its head through scholarly analysis of HBCU pedagogy. The remaining portions of the paper highlight the pedagogic value associated with learning to teach in institutions that, as a result of never practicing race-based discrimination, may very well be the true forbearers of the democracy that the nation's forefathers stridently championed in their rhetoric but never put into practice.

Understanding HBCUs through the Scholarship of Teaching: Reflections from the Field

We have spent an inordinate amount of time as researchers of HBCU classrooms, African American faculty, and minority-student outcomes, considering specifically what unique contributions HBCU faculty add to the American postsecondary educational system. The first author has discovered unique racialized consciousnesses in African American professors who received bachelor degrees from HBCUs, taught at HBCUs, and were employed by PWIs. The second author has noted a similar presence among educators of color who have likely graduated from HBCUs (Dancy & Brown, 2011). In addition, we have decades worth of observations and participation on HBCU campuses. From these experiences, we locate the dynamic impact that pedagogy in HBCUs has on students, particularly those who enter the teaching professions. Broadly, we have found that educators who spend time learning to teach at an HBCU hold indispensable insights for building pedagogically meaningful relationships among teachers, students, content, communities, and institutions. In this section, we highlight more specific areas of impact.

First, we note that a common theme across their research indicates that the more attentive professors regard issues of professional socialization among disciplinary communities (i.e., STEM), the larger collegiate community in general, and the better the engagement with students. Not surprisingly, this line of inquiry benefits African Americans and students from historically marginalized communities. But most importantly, common parlance among seasoned teachers contends that the core of good teaching involves building pedagogically meaningful relationships with students. The best approaches to teaching are good for all students regardless of race, gender, faith, or numerous other socio-cultural factors. Moreover, effective teachers foster dialogical relationships in their classrooms where they move from being a teacher of a specific subject matter, to being a student of their pupils' indigenous communities in ways that allow them to draw on understandings that are familiar to their students as a means to introduce new ideas.

The problem, however, is that teaching is a laborious task, regardless of the level or environment in which it is practiced. Lacking the time, inclination, or support to document and analyze their work, some of the best moments of teaching are overlooked. As each new teacher arrives in a college classroom he or she is challenged to teach conventionally. After time spent observing this phenomenon of precious understandings being lost and in the case of HBCUs, actually overlooked, we find that the scholarship of teaching literature (SoTL) is a useful frame for understanding the talented pedagogy in HBCUs.

Forwarded most visibly by the Carnegie Institute for the Advancement of Teaching and Learning, "the scholarship of teaching and learning" seeks to document, critically review, and publish professors' practical knowledge about teaching in their disciplines (Hutchings & Shulman, 2000). Mary Huber and Sherwyn Morreale (2002) define the SoTL as being concerned with an invitation to mainstream faculty to treat teaching as a form of inquiry into student learning, to share research and inquiry with colleagues, and to critique and build on one another's work. This critical analysis of professors' teaching seeks to envision the ways that pedagogy is improved when teachers look closely at their own teaching practice and share their findings with their colleagues.

This inquiry into pedagogy has implications for the examination of higher education teaching practices in all disciplines and in institutions of all kinds from community colleges to elite research universities and HBCUs specifically. Situating our past research within the SoTL movement affords an analysis of teaching at the intersection of the discipline and the experiences that the students and the teachers bring to the classroom. This enables an examination of the discourse of the discipline, teachers, or students, all of which may function well in specific contexts, but also the relationship among the three as viewed through the teachers' practice.

Our inquiry suggests that the ongoing question of the relevance of HBCUs influences the ways HBCU professors think about their teaching, their students, and their disciplines. Further, where traditionally SoTL researchers have raised questions about the ways in which disciplinary styles of thought and inquiry influence teaching and learning and the nature and roles of interdisciplinary exchange, our research adds to this conversation—an analysis of how all of these pedagogical and disciplinary issues are mediated by the historically and communally founded discourses that shape student and teacher experiences of higher education in HBCU settings. Hence, despite the SoTL's obvious contributions to our research—the valuing of lived experience and attention to disciplinary knowledge—the SoTL research, with the exception of some instances (Mitchell & Lee, 2006; Rosiek, 2003; Sconiers & Rosiek, 2000), has undertheorized the influence of sociocultural factors on the pedagogical knowledge that teachers utilize to engage their students.

When viewed through a SoTL lens, the establishment of Black education and self-determination demands seeing the passionate, experientially based approaches to teaching that African American teachers in Sabbath Schools brought to their classrooms postenslavement. These encounters pushed a subjugated knowledge as well as the skill to use this consciousness in pedagogically meaningful ways that diverged greatly from dedicated yet experientially different White crusaders for 19th century Black education.

Second, HBCU faculty demonstrate a knowledge we term *pedagogical double-consciousness* (PDC). PDC affords appreciation for the infinite variations of experiences, lived histories, or subject positions made available to students (Malewski, 2010) and faculty associated with HBCUs. And as the following section illustrates, past and ongoing research supports that PDC is a product of epistemic and subsequently ontological claims that uniquely result from learning to teach in institutions and to students who did not quite fit the mold of the traditional American college and college student.

Pedagogical Double Consciousness

The writings of W. E. B. DuBois, Patricia Hill-Collins, and Lisa Delpit significantly inform the term *pedagogical double consciousness* as a training tool for teaching in HBCU settings. This nuanced knowledge derives from historically oppressed minority groups grappling with the tensions between assimilation and cultural subordination. Social theories emerging from or on behalf of such historically oppressed groups investigate ways to escape from, survive in, or oppose prevailing social and economic injustices (Hill-Collins, 1998). Examples of this can be found in the Civil Rights movement of the 1960s as well as its precursors such as the Abolitionist movements of the 19th century, Pan-Africanism globally, and Sabbath Schools.

Du Bois (1903/1999) described the type of knowledge that this study seeks to document in the practice of HBCU faculty as a "dual consciousness" which, at the turn of the 20th century, he applied to the vision afforded African Americans struggling in a racist society. Commenting on this type of insight Du Bois (1903/1999) wrote:

> [T]he Negro is a sort of seventh son, born with a veil, and gifted with second-sight in this American world.... One ever feels his two-ness,—an American, a Negro; two souls, two thoughts, two unreconciled strivings; two warring ideals in one dark body, whose dogged strength alone keeps it from being torn asunder. The history of the American Negro is the

history of this strife,—the longing to attain self-conscious manhood, to merge his double self into a better and truer self.

(pp. 8–9)

Building on Du Bois's (1903/1999) insight and on 20th century feminist writing, Patricia Hill-Collins (1986) coined the phrase "outsiders within" to describe the usefulness of double consciousness in majority-dominated structures, like higher education. In *Fighting Words: Black Women and the Search for Justice* (1998), Hill-Collins outlined possibilities that can occur through outsider-within ways of knowing:

> Theorizing from outsider-within locations reflects the multiplicity of being on the margins within intersecting systems of race, class, gender, sexual, and national oppression, even as such theory remains grounded in and attentive to real differences in power. This, to me, is what distinguishes oppositional knowledges developed in outsider-within locations *both* from elite knowledges (social theory developed from within systems of power such as whiteness, maleness, heterosexuality, class privilege, or citizenship) *and* from knowledge developed in oppositional locations where groups resist only *one* form of oppression (e.g., a patriarchal Black cultural nationalism, a racist feminism, or a raceless, genderless class analysis). In other words, theorizing from outsider-within locations can produce distinctive oppositional knowledges that embrace multiplicity yet remain cognizant of power.
>
> *(p. 8)*

Du Bois (1903/1999) refers to a gift of "second-sight" that people of African descent possess in America. Hill-Collins (1998) spoke to the usefulness of Du Bois's (1903/1999) concept of second-sight by suggesting that through the development of "oppositional knowledges," an intimate understanding and ability to critique a system of meaning is acquired. Du Bois (1903/1999) wrote of this understanding as being crucial for both America in general and Black America in particular, believing that American citizens of African descent have something valuable to offer America and the world just as America has something valuable to offer people of African descent. Hill-Collins (1998) saw that value as the emergence of a type of understanding that resists White supremacy as well as (heterosexism, classism, sexism, ableism, etc.) through the development of a type of knowledge that is keenly aware of anomalies that exist in power relations that can resist and respond to a multiplicity of oppressions. Consequently, where Dubois (1903) theorized the development and content of this type of insight, Hill-Collins (1998) theorized its use and constructive possibilities.

Hill-Collins (1998) and Dubois (1903/1999) offered that this vision or perceptiveness is the product of being socialized as members of a marginalized community that has struggled to gain partial access to the dominant community. The underlying aspect of both Dubois's (1903/1999) and Hill-Collins's (1998) thought that is germane to our inquiry into the teaching of HBCU faculty is their discussion of how the experience of living in two worlds produces a type of understanding that may not be as readily available to individuals who primarily reside in either the dominant or subjugated groups.

Lisa Delpit (2002) provides a valuable illustration of this type of understanding in her book, *The Skin That We Speak* (2002). Delpit (2002) discusses the multiplicity of emotions that she faced when she decided to move her daughter from a highly regarded majority private school to attend a start-up charter school with a 98% African American student population. As her daughter began to acquire new speech patterns that differed from the Standard English that she was initially socialized with, Delpit (2002) commented:

> While my head looked on in awe at how my child could so magically acquire a second language form, at how brilliant her mind was to be able to adapt so readily to new circumstances, my heart lurched at some unexamined fear because she had done so.... If it is so easy for my child to "pick up" at school a new language, then what was preventing the millions of African American children whose home language was different from the school's from acquiring the dialect of Standard English?
>
> *(p. 34)*

Through this example, Delpit (2002) highlights the type of knowledge that DuBois (1903) and Hill-Collins (1986) referenced. Delpit (2002) had the ability to see this acquisition of new linguistic competency as an asset and a sign of brilliance where others without this type of oppositional knowledge may simply consider this new language acquisition a deficiency that needs to be addressed. Further, Delpit (2002) observed the flexibility in thinking that her daughter had effortlessly performed and through her recognition of her daughter's cognitive acumen she demonstrated the pedagogical value of the double consciousness that Du Bois (1903/1999) and Hill-Collins (1986) discussed.

This ability to move from the micro- to the macrolevels of explanation concerning the potential of an African American student is a product of having multiple narratives to draw upon in attempting to understand African American student behavior, intellectual development, and competence. This way of thinking about teaching, and particularly about what students from nonmajority backgrounds bring to the classroom, is essential for being able to improve pedagogy and an integral part of the type of knowledge (pedagogical double consciousness) in the practice of professors who learn to teach in HBCUs. Lacking PDC, an unsophisticated teaching staff can conclude that some students of color have no interest in and no talent for learning. Conversely, educators equipped with PDC conceptualize the types of understandings and skills that their students bring to the classroom as a starting point for further learning.

Purposeful Practices: Discussion and Conclusions

There arguably remains a unique insight that guides the practice of African American professors when they encounter majority culture. This insight is directly related to the time they spent in HBCUs (Mitchell, forthcoming; Mitchell & Edwards, 2010). Across past and forthcoming studies, we note the ways that HBCUs influence their graduates' pedagogical practices. Common themes include a strong sense of conviction and purpose directly connecting faculty teaching, pedagogical relationships, and overall expectations for students. We additionally recall the ways our past study participants' explicit use of phrases like service, ethics, success, and validation of Black students in an environment where a pervasive sense of nihilism, failure, and cultural inferiority is often attributed to African Americans. Additionally, we note how participants attributed this disposition to the utility of Black brilliance, cultivated in Black communal spaces, as a direct reflection of the utility of the learning that occurs in HBCUs.

As previously mentioned, the SoTL literature values the tacit insights about teaching and learning that teachers acquire through the act of teaching. While we have found this aspect of the literature extremely useful, the aspect of the SoTL that our past study participants challenge was the adherence to disciplinarity that is a central tenet of SoTL research. Participants in our studies considered the division of knowledge associated with disciplinarity a part of the ways that specific knowledge and ontologies (ways of knowing and being) are validated over others. And historically this means that non-European knowledge systems have been marginalized (Laible, 2000; Mayuzumi, 2009; Minhha, 1989; Ng-A-Fook, 2007).

Appropriately, common discourses about HBCU classrooms are consistent with fostering safe, engaging climates for students. The literature also finds these contexts accompanied with communal peer groups and even out-of-class support. Further, such social benefits largely involve encouragement and motivation which students find was important to constructions of self-efficacy and reinforced decisions to persist in their disciplines (i.e., science, technology, engineering, and mathematics [STEM]; Palmer, Maramba, & Dancy, 2011). However, in this chapter, we reflect on our research in HBCU classrooms and find that, beyond a surface of engagement, African American faculty and HBCU students understand the practice of teaching as capable of shaping historical conditions. The opening counternarrative about the establishment of Black education recalibrates the discussion of the legacy of HBCUs within the broader discussion of U.S. higher education. Given the unique history of race, nation, and education, HBCUs represent both the best our nation has to offer and the greatest challenges we have ahead.

When reflecting on our research, we find African American professors within HBCUs to be living representatives of insights and understandings that improve teaching for *all* students (not simply African Americans). To be sure, this would not be possible were there no HBCUs. By conducting inquiry into HBCU teaching, we understand both teacher knowledge and practice as constituted by broad cultural discourses. Mining that knowledge is consistent with the SoTL model and the subsequent understanding of pedagogical double consciousness as an instrument for enabling emancipatory action through social criticism on the part of Black teachers in majority White settings.

It appears that HBCUs work to nurture pedagogical double consciousness which, in turn, provides a sense of clarity about African American professors' hypervisibility in historically White spaces. Thus, African American professors who are HBCU graduates are likely familiar with the history of segregated schooling in a general sense as well as in the specific institution for which they were employed. They are also uniquely sensitive to the varying ways that they are perceived by both their White and Black students and colleagues. The ability to conceptualize the power dynamics within the environments in which they function is an essential building block for establishing more engaged and socially just approaches to teaching.

The twoness we note in our appeal to outsider social theories represents the possibility of exploring new ideas that could not exist in an exclusively Black or White context. Namely, this requires recognition that, from the very onset of African American faculty employment at PWIs, they are not simply viewed as individuals but representative of entire communities that had traditionally been excluded. As a result, teaching in a space that has traditionally blocked access or devalued the insights of communities of color provides a critical lens that challenges a nation to live up to the lofty ideals espoused over the last 400 years.

References

American Association of University Professors (AAUP). (2007). *Historically black colleges and universities: Recent trends. Retrieved from* http://www.aaup.org/AAUP/comm/rep/HBCUTrends.htm

Anderson, J. (1988). *The education of Blacks in the South 1860–1935.* Chapel Hill, NC: University of North Carolina Press.

Baker, R. S. (2001). The paradoxes of desegregation: Race, class, and education, 1935–1975. *American Journal of Education, 109*(3), 320–343.

Brooks, E. F., Starks, G. L., & Brooks. F. E. (2011). *Historically Black colleges and universities: An encyclopedia.* Santa Barbara, CA: ABC-CLIO.

Brown v. Board of Education, 347 U.S. 483 (1954).

Brown, M. C. (2001). Collegiate desegregation and the public Black college. *Journal of Higher Education, 72*(1) 46–62.

Brown, M. C., & Davis, J. E. (2001). The historically Black college as social contract, social capital, and social equalizer. *Peabody Journal of Education, 76*(1), 31–49.

Brown, M. C., Donahoo, S., & Bertrand, R. D. (2001). The Black college and the quest for educational opportunity. *Urban Education, 36,* 553–571.

Brown, M. C., Ricard, R. B., & Donahoo, S. (2004). The changing role of historically Black colleges and universities: Vistas on dual missions, desegregation, and diversity. In M. C. Brown

& K. Freeman (Eds.), *Black colleges: New perspectives on policy and practice* (pp. 3–28). Westport, CT: Praeger.

Dancy, T. E., & Brown, M. C. (2011). The mentoring and induction of educators of color: Addressing impostor syndrome in academe. *Journal of School Leadership, 21*(4), 607–634.

Delpit, L. (2002). No kinda sense. In L. Delpit & J. K. D. Kilgour (Eds.), *The skin that we speak: Thoughts on language and culture in the classroom* (pp. 31–48). New York: New Press.

Drewry, H. N., & Doermann, H. (2001). *Stand and prosper: Private Black colleges and their students.* Princeton, NJ: Princeton University Press.

Dewey, J. (1934). *Art as experience.* New York: Perigee Books.

Du Bois, W. E. B. (1999). *The souls of Black folk.* New York: Bartleby. (Original work published 1903)

Duncan, A. (2010). *Changing the HBCU narrative: From corrective action to creative investment.* Keynote address at the HBCU Symposium at the North Carolina Central University Centennial, Durham, NC.

Gasman, M., & Tudico, C. L. (2008). *Historically Black colleges and universities: Triumphs, troubles, and taboos.* New York: Palgrave Macmillan.

Hill-Collins, P. (1986). Learning from the outsiders within: The sociological significance of Black feminist thought. *Social Problems 33*(6), 14–32.

Hill-Collins, P. (1998). *Fighting words: Black women & the search for justice.* Minneapolis, MN: University of Minnesota Press.

Huber, M., & Morrael, S. (2002). *Situating the scholarship of teaching and learning: A cross disciplinary conversation.* Retrieved from www.carnagiefoundation.org/elibrary/docs/situating.htm

Hutchings, P., & Shulman, L. (1999). The scholarship of teaching: New elaborations, new developments. *Change,* 11–15.

Laible, J. C. (2000). A loving epistemology: What I hold critical in my life, faith and profession. *Qualitative Studies in Education, 13*(6), 683–692.

Malewski, E. (2010). *Curriculum studies handbook: The next movement.* New York: Routledge.

Mayuzumi, K. (2009). Unfolding possibilities through a decolonizing project: Indigenous knowledges and rural Japanese women. *International Journal of Qualitative Studies in Education, 22*(5), 507–526.

Minh-ha, T. (1989). *Woman native other.* Bloomington: Indiana University Press.

Minor, J. T. (2008). *Contemporary HBCUs: Considering institutional capacity and state priorities. A research report.* East Lansing: Michigan State University, College of Education, Department of Educational Administration.

Mitchell, R. (2010). The African American church, education and self-determination. *Journal of Negro Education, 79*(3), 202–205.

Mitchell, R. (forthcoming). *Racing higher education: Representations and refractions of race in college classrooms.* Charlotte: NC Information Age Press.

Mitchell, R., & Edwards, K. (2010). Power, privilege, and pedagogy: College classrooms as sites to learn racial equity. In T. Elon Dancy (Ed.), *Managing diversity: (Re)Visioning equity on college campuses* (pp. 45–69). Charlotte, NC: Information Age Press.

Mitchell, R., & Lee, T. (2006). Ain't I a woman: An inquiry into the experiential dimensions of teachers' practical knowledge through the experiences of African American female academics. *International Journal of Learning, 13*(7), 97–104.

Mitchell, R., & Mitchell, R. L. (2008). History and education mining the gap: Historically Black colleges as centers of excellence for engaging disparities in race and wealth. In B. Moran (Ed.), *Race and wealth disparities* (pp. 82–109). New York: University Press of America.

National Center for Education Statistics. (2006). *Economic impact of the nation's historically Black colleges and universities: Technical report* (DOE Publication No. NCES 2007-178). Washington, DC: U.S. Department of Education.

Ng-A-Fook, N. (2007). *An indigenous curriculum of place: The United Houma Nation's contentious relationship with Louisiana's educational institutions* (Vol. 25). New York: Lang.

Obama, B. (2010, February 26). *Speech*. The White House initiative on historically Black colleges and universities. White House, Washington, DC.

Palmer, R. T., & Gasman, M. (2008). "It takes a village to raise a child": The role of social capital in promoting academic success for African American men at a Black college. *Journal of College Student Development 49*(1), 52–70.

Palmer, R. T., Maramba, D. C., & Dancy, T. E. (2011). A qualitative investigation of factors promoting the retention and persistence of students of color in STEM. *Journal of Negro Education, 80*(4), 491–504.

Palmer, R. T., & Wood, J. L. (2012). *Black men in college: Implications for HBCUs and beyond.* New York: Routledge.

Roebuck, J. B., & K. S. Murty. 1993. *Historically black colleges and universities: Their place in American higher education.* Westport, CT: Praeger.

Rosiek, J. (2003). Emotional scaffolding: An exploration of teacher knowledge at the intersection of student emotion and subject matter content. *Journal of Teacher Education, 54*(5), 399–412.

Samuels, A. (2004). *Is separate unequal? Black colleges and the challange to desegregation.* Lawrence, KY: University Press of Kansas.

Sconiers, Z., & Rosiek, J. (2000). Historical perspectives as an element of teacher knowledge: A sonata-form case study of equity issues in a chemistry classroom. *Harvard Educational Review, 70*(3), 370–404.

Siddle-Walker, V. (2001). African-American teaching in the south: 1940–1960. *American Educational Research Journal, 38*(4), 751–779.

Span, C. (2009). *From cotton field to schoolhouse: African American education in Mississippi, 1862–1875.* Chapel Hill: The University of North Carolina Press.

Thelin, J. (2004). *The history of American education.* Baltimore, MD: Johns Hopkins University Press.

Wallenstein, P. (2008). *Higher education and the civil rights movement,* Gainesville, FL: University of Florida Press.

Watkins, W. (2001). *The White architects of Black education: Ideology and power in America, 1865–1954.* New York: Teachers College Press.

Watkins, W., Lewis, J., & Chou, V. (2001). *Race and education: The roles of history and society in education of African American Students.* Needham Heights, MA: Allyn & Bacon.

Wright, B. (1988). For the children of infidels?: American Indian education in the colonial colleges. *American Indian Culture and Research Journal, 12*(3), 1–14.

7

SUPPORTING THE DREAM

The Role of Faculty Members at Historically Black Colleges and Universities in Promoting STEM PhD Education

Shannon Gray

The intention of historically Black colleges and universities (HBCUs) has been to open educational doors and to create career pathways for a group of people marginalized by U.S. educational institutions. Black colleges are pivotal in educating Black students in science, technology, engineering, and mathematics (STEM) (Pearson & Fecher, 1994; Perna et al., 2009). According to Mullen (2001), STEM majors are highly concentrated at the most selective institutions, but Blacks represent a small proportion of students attending those schools, leaving a considerable number of Blacks to be educated in science and mathematics at less selective institutions. HBCUs outnumber predominantly White institutions (PWIs) in awarding degrees to Black students in most STEM disciplines (Perna et al., 2009; Southern Education Foundation [SEF], 2005). Likewise, HBCU students have higher degree aspirations than Black students at PWIs (Kim & Conrad, 2006; Perna et al., 2009; SEF, 2005; Wenglinsky, 1996). In fact, HBCUs have been shown to increase the educational aspirations of their students in most academic disciplines (Kim & Conrad, 2006; Pascarella, Wolniak, Pierson, & Flowers, 2004; Wenglinsky, 1997), resulting in Black colleges producing the majority of Black students who pursue doctoral degrees (SEF, 2005).

The dearth of Blacks pursuing PhDs in STEM has monumental consequences. The United States is poised to lose its position as the preeminent global technological leader due to a diminishing supply of trained domestic scientists, mathematicians, and engineers (American Association for the Advancement of Science, 2001; Anderson & Kim, 2006; Babco, 2003; Hurtado et al., 2009; SEF, 2005). To reverse this trend, STEM educators must recognize the talent that exists among Black students and other minority groups currently not participating in scientific or technological fields in substantial numbers (Committee on

Equal Opportunity in Science and Engineering, 2006; Hurtado, Cabrera, Lin, Arellano, & Espinosa, 2009; Leggon & Pearson, 1997). This talent pool must be cultivated and sustained to ensure a consistent inward flow of Black students in the STEM educational pipeline. Unfortunately, the flow of Black students in the science pipeline is most often outward, with Black students choosing to pursue other academic disciplines (Bonous-Hammarth, 2001; Goodchild, 2004; Oakes, 1990; Pearson & Fecher, 1994).

According to the National Center for Educational Statistics (2008), only 2% of STEM doctoral degrees were earned by Black students. The lack of Black students choosing to pursue majors and careers in science and technology at the undergraduate level is partly due to insufficient academic opportunities within STEM and ineffective academic and career counseling (Atwater, 2000; Jibrell, 1990; Ladson-Billings, 1997; Lewis & Collins, 2001).

Black students' absence within STEM fields at the baccalaureate level occurs because they have fewer opportunities to interact with science both inside and outside of school compared to their White counterparts (Oakes, 1990). According to Oakes (1990), Black students respond with increased interest and participation in STEM fields, similar to their White counterparts, when exposed to science and mathematics at equal levels. An early introduction to STEM fields allows Black students to realize the possibility of pursuing academic work and careers in those disciplines (Jones, 1997).

Significance of Study

Within STEM, Blacks are underrepresented in both industry and academia (Lewis & Collins, 2001). There has been extensive examination into the absence of substantial numbers of Blacks in STEM (Atwater, 2000; Jibrell, 1990; Ladson-Billings, 1997; Lewis & Collins, 2001; Oakes, 1990; O'Brien, Martinez-Pons, & Kopala, 1999). Likewise, a large body of literature focuses on the environmental factors of HBCUs (Allen & Jewell, 2002; Brown, Donahoo, & Bertrand, 2001; Fries-Britt & Turner, 2002; Outcalt & Skewes-Cox, 2002); however, most researchers focus on the broad implications of the HBCU environment and what makes it successful. There are very few studies that examine the role of faculty at HBCUs in Black students' retention in STEM disciplines at the undergraduate level and their progression to doctoral STEM programs. This study investigates the impact of faculty at HBCUs and their role in encouraging Black students to pursue STEM disciplines at the PhD level.

Literature Review

Blacks are an underrepresented group in professions that are based in the sciences and mathematics (Lewis & Collins, 2001). There are numerous factors that have contributed to the scarcity of Black scientists and mathematicians.

Increasing the number of Black students in the STEM pipeline depends on persuading them that they can succeed in STEM majors and careers. A Black student's decision to pursue a STEM field is strongly influenced by having other Blacks as role models within these disciplines as teachers, professors, and professionals (Jones, 1997; Perna et al., 2009). A student's access and connection to role models are integral to developing his or her vocational self-concept (Bowman & Tinsley,1991).

Role models have the ability to encourage Black students as they progress through the science and mathematics pipeline. They offer expertise and past experience regarding Black students' "perceived goal blockage" (Bowman & Tinsley, 1991, p.1) and how they are able to navigate through academia to avoid the potentially negative results of succumbing to those assumed threats that may derail their academic plans in STEM. Lewis (2003) argues that there is no clear evidence that supports the notion that Black students choose to pursue or persist in the science pipeline due to the influence of role models. However, this directly conflicts with many other findings regarding the interest, pursuit, and persistence of Black students in STEM fields (Atwater, 2000; Bonous-Hammarth, 2001; Bowman et al., 1991; Guiffrida, 2005; Hall & Post-Kammer, 1987; Hubbard & Stage, 2009; Palmer, Davis, & Maramba, 2010; Tobias, 1992), all of which state the importance of role models for Black students' engagement at an institution or in STEM.

Although many faculty members accept the idea that few students, both White and non-White, will perform well in STEM disciplines (Seymour & Hewitt, 1997), the performance expected of Black students, especially in STEM fields, is marginal at best. A common misconception on the part of faculty is that Black students are not motivated to perform as well as other groups (Treisman, 1992). Educators and parents will often insinuate that subjects and careers grounded in mathematics and science are meant for White males, thereby decreasing performance expectation for students that do not fit the specific demographic (Hrabrowski, 2003). Additionally, these lowered expectations often result in reduced opportunities for Black student exposure to STEM disciplines in practical ways (Russell & Atwater, 2005), such as increased laboratory experiences and STEM focused internships. Success and persistence in science and mathematics are fundamentally linked to high performance expectations during the early years of a student's college education (Summers & Hrabowski, 2006).

Faculty members at HBCUs have a high level of expectation for their students in STEM courses, as well as demonstrating confidence in their students' ability to perform at satisfactory levels academically within STEM disciplines (Hurtado et al., 2008; Palmer et al., 2010; Perna et al., 2009). This expectation manifests itself in numerous ways. Most notable is HBCUs' tendency to deviate from a weed-out model in regard to science and mathematics curricula (Hurtado et al., 2009). According to Seymour and Hewitt (1997), weed-out courses disproportionately target minority and female students. Likewise, weed-out courses, which typically focus on classes at the introductory level, are more apt to identify precollege preparation rather than assess students' science and mathematics ability or STEM disposition at the collegiate level (Hurtado et al., 2009). Instead, at most HBCUs, an ethos of encouragement and support permeates the campus, and STEM departments in particular (Hurtado et al., 2008; Palmer et al., 2010; Perna et al., 2009; Seymour & Hewitt, 1997).

Students need to be encouraged by instructors, institutions, and parents (Hrabowski, 2003; Russell & Atwater, 2005; Treisman, 1992). Instructors are pivotal in Black students' perseverance in the STEM pipeline. Professors possess the ability to positively affect a student's achievement and attitude towards mathematics and science (Palmer et al., 2010; Perna et al., 2009; M. Russell & Atwater, 2005). Positive instructor relationships with students enhance teachers' expectations, which results in increased student motivation and self-concept of ability (Hubbard & Stage, 2009; M. Russell & Atwater, 2005).

The opportunity to participate in undergraduate research is one of the most relevant forms of encouragement provided to undergraduate students. Exposure to undergraduate research allows the opportunity for students to learn through practical experience (Hunter, Laursen, & Seymour, 2007; Maton, Hrabowski, & Schmitt, 2000; Myers & Pavel, 2011). Additionally, it affords these students the ability to improve their cognitive skills, advances the continuation of STEM study, increases the probability of pursuing graduate degrees in mathematics and science, and offers them insight in performing science professionally (Hunter et al., 2007; Hurtado et al., 2009; Perna et al., 2009). The practical extension of what students learn in the STEM classroom increases confidence in ability, as well as increasing their self-expectation of advanced studies in STEM (Hunter et al., 2007; Russell, Hancock, & McCollough, 2007).

Practical STEM experience is critically important for minority students. It lessens their feeling of marginalization as they become initiated into the science community (Hunter et al., 2006). Additionally, it permits these students to contribute to the field in meaningful ways. Hunter et al. (2006) state that these experiences allow students to become accustomed to the norms of science and science professionals, as well as introduce the students to what it means to be a scientist. In essence, Black students are able to see how science and mathematics affect their daily lives and existence. These students are able to validate their interest in STEM and form an identity as part of the science community (Hunter et al., 2006), as well as increase their inclination to pursue graduate STEM degrees (Myers & Pavel, 2011).

The environment created at Black colleges enhances the probability of their students performing well academically due to increased interaction with faculty members, the absence of negative preconceived notions of Black student academic ability, and the presence of positive evaluation of Black student performance (Cokley, 2000). Carter (1999) argues this is largely due to faculty encouragement. Black students' ability to form salient relationships with faculty members offers students an opportunity to broaden their knowledge about graduate school options (Carter, 1999; Perna et al., 2009). In spite of greater educational resources at PWIs, an increased number of students attending HBCUs report engagement in faculty research projects compared to Blacks attending PWIs (Kim & Conrad, 2006). HBCUs create an environment that fosters this interaction, as well as persistence (Carter, 1999), largely due to faculty accessibility.

Accessibility is a pertinent factor in increasing Black students' academic and social engagement (Guiffrida, 2005; Latiker, 2003; Palmer et al., 2010; Perna et al., 2009). Faculty and staff provide individualized attention leading many HBCU students to describe their campus atmosphere as being reminiscent of family; this experience is often absent for Black students attending PWIs (Fries-Britt & Turner, 2002). Black colleges realize the necessity for faculty to be available and open in regard to creating meaningful relationships with students (Palmer & Gasman, 2008; Palmer et al., 2010; Perna et al., 2009). This is pivotal because intentional interactions and relationships between students and faculty are more meaningful for Black collegians (Kim & Conrad, 2006). It allows students a safe environment to take risks that are pertinent to academic and intellectual growth (Allen, 1992). In sum, the combination of faculty encouragement, an opportunity to be exposed to STEM, and meaningful interaction with science through undergraduate research projects and programs, as well as having faculty available as role models and coaches, ultimately assist in HBCUs developing a cadre of future Black STEM professionals.

Conceptual Framework

I will use both possible selves and socialization theory, as the conceptual framework for this study. Possible selves are defined as "the future-oriented component of the self-schema, are viewed as the components critical for putting the self into action. These selves are derived from past experience and from the positive and negative prototypes and images individuals are urged to attain and want to avoid, respectively" (Oyserman, Gant, & Ager, 1995, p. 1217). The development of a possible self occurs as a two-part process, "(a) construction of possible selves and (b) successful achievement or avoidance of constructed possible selves" (Pizzolato, 2006, p. 58).

Images students formulate as their possible selves are pivotal in motivating their actions (Oyserman, Terry, & Bybee, 2002) toward realizing positive goals and evading negative archetypes. The development of possible selves is an individual and personal process (Markus & Nurius, 1986), which involves not only the ambition of the student, but also considers the students' interaction with their environment (Pizzolato, 2007).

Students with scholastically oriented possible selves improve academic performance, self-esteem, and well-being (Oyserman, Bybee, & Terry, 2006; Oyserman, Terry, & Bybee, 2002). In addition, there is a need for students to observe role models when constructing possible selves for two reasons. According to Oyserman, Gant, and Ager (1995), role models primarily provide the assurance that students' prospects of what they want to become are indeed obtainable. Second, role models serve as a resource for imparting experiences and competencies necessary to achieve the students' future selves. The importance of forming relationships for Black students (Sedlacek, 2004), as well as their need to connect the relevance of their chosen major and career to the reality of their daily lives (Hunter et al., 2007) amplifies the need for role models as students develop and confirm their future selves. When students had the possible selves they had envisioned for themselves reaffirmed, they "retain[ed] or appropriately revised their goals ... in a way that solidified for them their motivation for proceeding and the modifications they needed to make to best support their own future successes" (Pizzolato, 2007, p. 218). Possible selves reiterate the ownership students possess in preparing and accomplishing their future goals.

Whereas possible selves captures the intrinsic motivations of students, it fails to encapsulate students' socialization into the fields of science and mathematics. Therefore, this study will also employ the use of socialization theory as a means of analysis. Socialization is defined as "the process by which newcomers learn the encoded systems of behavior specific to their area of expertise and the system of meanings and values attached to these behaviors" (Taylor & Antony, 2000, p. 186). Early career socialization and mentoring is necessary for minorities and women to provide them with knowledge acquisition, meaningful research, normative behavior, and exposure to research (Crawford, Suarez-Balcazar, Reich, Figert, & Nyden, 1996; Gasman, Lundy-Wagner, & Vultaggio, 2009). The core elements of socialization include: knowledge acquisition, investment, and involvement. Additionally, the stages of socialization are: anticipatory, formal, informal, and involvement (Weidman, Twale, & Stein, 2001).

According to Weidman et al. (2001), the process of socialization is both uniform and personal. Some experiences are common and held by all students, while others are personal and add an individualized dimension to the educational process. Regardless of the type of experience, "Each step along the journey has particular significance, becomes key rites of passage, or adds important people and information to the mix" (Weidman et al., 2001, p. 5). It is these processes that allow students to become accustomed to and accepted into the culture of science.

Weidman et al. (2001) state that the entire process of socialization has an ultimate goal of professionalization. Additionally, each step moves students closer to professional maturity ending in the student prepared to participate in the professional realm of his or her field. The process of socialization has been shown to be difficult for minority students due to a lack of exposure to research opportunities; ineffective precollege and college mentoring, as well as inadequate career and graduate school guidance (Gasman et al., 2009; Ulloa & Herrera, 2006). Appropriate socialization allows Black, as well as all other students' entrance into their professional field.

Methodology

Methodological Approach

The methodological approach used in this study was portraiture; that is, it focuses on capturing the research participants' understanding from an outsider's point of view (Lawrence-Lightfoot & Davis, 1997). Portraiture is a research method "that blurs the boundaries of aesthetics and empiricism in an effort to capture the complexity, dynamics, and subtlety of human experience and organizational life" (Lawrence-Lightfoot & Davis, 1997, p. xvi). It does so by illustrating the interaction of values, personality, and structure, as well as documenting human behavior and experience within a particular context (Lawrence-Lightfoot & Davis, 1997).

Lawrence-Lightfoot and Davis (1997) state that the context of an experience is "rich in cues about how the actors or subjects negotiate and understand their experiences" (p. 12). Likewise, it is important for the researcher and reader to understand that context is not static, "Context is a dynamic framework, changing and evolving, shaping and being shaped" (Lawrence-Lightfoot & Davis, 1997, p. 59). Portraiture provided an opportunity to explore the wholeness and essence of the Black college experience and provided participants with the opportunity through our conversations to explain their sense making of the faculty–student relationships that exist at Black colleges (Lawrence-Lightfoot & Davis, 1997). All data collected resulted from individual interviews with research participants.

Research Participants

Three of the four participants in this study were current Black doctoral students in biomedical science who had also earned a STEM baccalaureate degree from one of the following institutions: Dillard University, Hampton University, or North Carolina Agricultural and Technical State University (North Carolina A&T) at the time of the interview. The fourth participant was a first year postdoctoral student who earned his STEM baccalaureate degree from Xavier University of Louisiana. All were doctoral students from the University of Pennsylvania.

Sampling

The sampling method used to identify participants was criterion based, which ensured that all participants were alumni of HBCUs and could effectively communicate the experiences of a Black student attending one of these institutions. Participants were identified through the use of a personal contact associated with the University of Pennsylvania's Black Graduate and Professional Students Assembly (BGAPSA). For this study, I interviewed four individuals.

Data Collection

I interviewed each participant on three separate occasions for approximately 60 minutes. The interviews were semistructured using primarily open-ended questions. I aimed to provide enough flexibility to allow participants to describe situations that continued to capture the essence of their experiences, but were outside of the reach of questions asked.

Limitations

Despite the rigor of this study, a number of possible limitations remain with the findings. First, I am using one source of data, personal interviews. The lack of multiple sources prevents the process of triangulation—verifying data obtained from one source against those from another to substantiate information acquired (Heck, 2006). However, the nature of my research questions and the design of my study support the use of interviews as the sole source of data collection and does not lend itself to additional collection methods.

A second limitation is a reliance on participants' self-reported data. Portraiture depends on participants to discuss and offer insight into the meaning of themes being investigated (Lawrence-Lightfoot & Davis, 1997). It is important that my data are deemed credible to minimize this limitation (Heck, 2006). This was largely done through a process of member checking—asking research participants to authenticate the interpretation of their statements (Heck, 2006; Maxwell, 1998). A third limitation is transferability. It is important to realize in qualitative data that reliability and generalizability have limited applicability; instead the focus is on credibility (Toma, 2006).

Emergent Themes/Findings

Although the undergraduate experiences of each participant varied widely, all participants lauded the relationships they had with faculty members at their respective institutions. Participants provided numerous examples of how instructors at their respective HBCUs demonstrated encouragement regarding the student's pursuit of a STEM degree; exposure to science through undergraduate research; and the accessibility of faculty at their institution, which allowed instructors to offer both career and academic guidance, as well as serve as role models.

The majority of the participants stated that one of the most rewarding experiences of attending an HBCU was their interactions and relationships with faculty members. One participant shared:

> I felt the thing I liked most about going there [Dillard University] was that I had a close relationship with my professors. I still talk to some of them...I don't think that is something I could have had at a majority institution.
>
> *(Dillard University Alumna)*

Likewise, all of the participants described professors as accessible and concerned with their academic performance. For example, a North Carolina A&T alumnus stated, "You weren't just a number. I could go to their office [faculty members] or just talk and they were genuinely interested in you and cared about you as a person...." This sentiment was echoed by another participant as well,

> they [professors] cared whether or not we were grasping the concepts and they wanted to know whether or not they were communicating the concepts effectively ... chemistry classes, because there were only six of us in most of our classes, the teachers wanted us to be more engaged.... And if people didn't have questions, that's when they were usually like, "I don't believe you don't have any questions, so I'm just going to see how much you know."
>
> *(Hampton University Alumna)*

Often the relationship developed between students and faculty members at these institutions became stronger through the advocacy and nurturing students received from their instructors. Participants were inspired to persist in STEM fields at the undergraduate level and to pursue STEM degrees at the doctoral level.

> [T]eachers can tell when they have a certain type of student and they try to foster them ... they [faculty members] always instilled in us that you can do anything you want to do. Don't let obstacles or anything stand in your way.... They really empower you.
>
> *(North Carolina A& T Alumnus)*

A Hampton alumna shared,

> the chemistry department focused on encouraging students to obtain PhDs in their field, the chemistry department was like, "Well, maybe consider doing research. Do a summer program in research.... Why don't you have a long-term research project?"

HBCUs seem to foster an environment that reinforces the expectation that faculty members will teach and counsel their students. A Dillard University alumna credits the university with creating an ethos of teaching and mentoring for faculty members, "[At Dillard] The professor has to love to, and want to have that relationship with their students." Similarly, a Xavier University alumnus described valuable relationships with faculty members: "[T]hey were always there to help. That's something they [Xavier University] probably preach to their faculty." Through interviews with participants it is evident that intentional interactions with faculty members compelled these students to persist in the STEM educational pipeline. Likewise, these students' academic success and exposure to science were also assisted by instructors' availability and willingness to serve as guides. All students confirmed their instructors' accessibility and the professors' innate dedication to the academic success of their students. A Hampton University alumna shared a story regarding a need for additional assistance in physical chemistry,

> I'm remembering one thing in particular in physical chemistry—I was able to go and talk to my professor during his office hours and say, "I don't understand this concept. Can you please explain it to me?" And then he would explain it to me and ask, "You got it now?" and usually I would.

Faculty members acted as role models for each of these students and provided them with motivation directly through conversation; and indirectly through observation and the status they achieved by earning their PhD in a STEM field. An Xavier University alumnus stated, "I think the benefit of being at a Black school overall was just seeing people that looked like you coming from the background of being successful, and looking to them as authority figures." A North Carolina A&T alumnus shared a comparable sentiment. He believes a contributing factor to his persistence in STEM was observing the accomplishments of his professors, "just looking at them in their careers and things they've done and just seeing that they were able to go through … I saw people who had nice careers and who had excelled in science."

The encouragement received by faculty members regarding the students' capacity to become future scientists, as well as the faculty members serving as role models, resulted in all of the participants being exposed to STEM in practical ways through engagement in undergraduate research programs. All of the students participated in one or more of the following research programs: the Louis Stokes Alliance for Minority Participation (LS-AMP), Minority Access to Research Careers (MARC), McNair Program or the Minority International Research Training (MIRT) programs, which are federally funded programs aimed at increasing the number of minority students pursuing careers in STEM fields.

Each student asserted that his or her exposure to STEM was increased in functional and intentional ways by affiliation with these programs, and by the accompanying summer internships. The benefits were invaluable as a student at an HBCU, which are often known for their lack of updated facilities due to fewer resources than their historically White counterparts. For instance, a Dillard University alumna stated: "I had the opportunity to experience whatever a lab was because of the internships, but before that I didn't realize how much our [Dillard University] labs were lacking." Echoing the same notion, a Xavier University alumnus shared: "these programs were complements to the education I received at Xavier ... I learned a lot and came back [to Xavier] knowing what I wanted to do, what I needed to do, and how I was going to do it."

Encouragement from faculty members at their home institution persuaded all of the students to participate in the Research Experience for Undergraduates (REU) Program that supports active research participation by undergraduate students in any of the areas of research funded by the National Science Foundation (Research Experiences for Undergraduates, n.d.). Three of the four students engaged in at least one REU internship at the University of Pennsylvania, and all three referenced the summer experience as the principle reason for applying to, and ultimately attending the University of Pennsylvania for their PhD.

Despite their exceptional record of awarding undergraduate STEM degrees to Black students, as well as their success with encouraging these students to pursue STEM doctoral degrees, HBCUs showed deficiencies with academic rigor. Although the participants did not regret attending a Black college, they all mentioned a purported lack of academic challenge at their undergraduate institution. An alumna of Hampton University stated, "I probably wasn't challenged at any point." Likewise, an alumnus of North Carolina A&T claimed, "Besides chemistry most of the classes weren't too hard." Interestingly, all of the students defended the lack of academic difficulty experienced at their respective HBCUs. A Dillard University alumna clearly articulated the general consensus, "the teachers had to teach to the average ... because the purpose of an HBCU is to kind of try to put everyone on the same level. So many people are coming from different backgrounds and are not as strong in some subjects."

Discussion

Although participants' experiences differed at the baccalaureate level, there were a number of notable similarities throughout their educational journey. All of the students lauded the caring attitude and accessibility of the faculty members at their respective institutions. The majority of the participants stated that was one of the most rewarding experiences of attending an HBCU. All of the participants described professors that were concerned with their academic performance, as well as encouraged them to pursue graduate study and programs that would improve their skill set.

Participants unanimously agreed that the relationship they built with faculty members was one of the most valuable benefits of attending their HBCU. Most described encountering instructors that were sincerely concerned with their academic well-being in addition to vigorously encouraging their pursuit of a STEM doctoral education, both directly and indirectly. Study participants were encouraged verbally regarding their academic performance and influenced to participate in STEM enrichment programs. Additionally, the accessibility to Black professionals who attained the level of success these students envisioned for themselves served as role models and a consistent reminder that their aspirations were achievable. This is critically important for the future possible selves of students, especially Black students. Observing Blacks who have been successful in accomplishing goals reflecting the possible selves these students have conceptualized, in addition to serving as role models, allowed participants to reconcile negative and positive notions about their actual and perceived characteristics (Oyserman et al., 1995). Oyserman et al. (1995) suggest that Black students potentially "focus on strategies to avoid problems, pitfalls, and failures" (p. 1222) more than majority students and having role models affirms that future possible selves are obtainable.

Participants' enrollment in a STEM discipline, and subsequently earning an undergraduate STEM degree, allowed them to challenge the notion that they are unable to succeed in these fields (Oyserman et al., 1995) when imagining their future possible selves. Additionally, they were able to personally observe the scarcity of Blacks pursuing advanced study in STEM fields, which allowed them to formulate specific plans to accomplish what they viewed as their possible selves (Pizzolato, 2007). Likewise, their participation in STEM coursework and laboratory experiences served as their introduction to the scientific process and the beginning of their socialization into STEM professions.

Of the numerous research programs in which participants were engaged, it was clear that the REU internships were most beneficial to all of the students in a number of ways. First, participation in REU internships solidified each of their decisions to pursue a career as a research scientist and earn a PhD. Second, all of the students discussed developing a salient mentor relationship, with at least one of their REU internship supervisors that has persevered throughout their graduate school experience. Third, they all credited their REU experiences with providing them with a thorough understanding of what it means to be and what is expected of them as a research scientist in STEM.

Participation in all of the undergraduate research programs reaffirmed the possible selves that each of the participants had formulated by providing role models, exposure, and experience. Additionally, this was often the most critical means of socializing the participants into the culture of science. Through this socialization process they were introduced to the normative functions of being a scientist; developed mentor relationships with individuals who were able to provide both formal and informal advice; and were offered meaningful involvement in the scientific process. These programs offered the key elements of socialization: knowledge acquisition, investment, and involvement (Weidman et al., 2001). These programs also allowed students the opportunity to develop possible selves anchored in realistic expectations regarding what to anticipate as professional scientists (Pizzolato, 2007).

Unfortunately, all of the participants were underwhelmed by the STEM curriculum at their respective universities. Most reported not being introduced to a solid research background at their undergraduate institution. This is one of the most detrimental aspects of the STEM socialization process for minority students (Gasman et al., 2009; Ulloa & Herrera, 2006). Some participants seemed to offer a vigorous defense of their inadequate training. However, all conceded that their university accepted this notion of teaching to the margins; in essence, assuming all students arrived on campus with inherent mathematics and science deficiencies. Surprisingly, most of the participants were supportive of this paradigm and declared the purpose of an HBCU is to provide an education to those traditionally marginalized by the educational system.

These institutions must continually assess the needs of not only those students that are underperforming and underprepared, but those who are performing beyond expectations, as well. Likewise, if HBCUs maintain their mission of educating students that span the spectrum of preparedness, it is also their responsibility to develop curricula that correlate with the scope of students attending these institutions. The inability to accomplish this may result in irreparable harm to the reputation of these institutions and the quality of education received by their students.

Of greater concern is the negative impact this situation may have on students' development of possible selves. The formulation of possible selves relies on students' intrinsic motivations to establish action plans that encourage the persistence and completion (Oyserman et al., 2002) of STEM education. Likewise, the inability to challenge these students academically may possibly inhibit their ability to be socialized in STEM. Without exposure to adequate instruction these students may experience difficulty acclimating to a STEM environment at the graduate school level and professionally.

In closing, it became clear that encouragement and exposure, provided by faculty members, were two of the most valuable factors regarding the persistence of Black students in STEM education. All of the participants were confident they would not have encountered either of these in the same way at a PWI. This is what makes HBCUs a unique and important component of the U.S. higher education system. There is an inherent culture that exists at HBCUs that liberates faculty and students from the negative notions about the academic ability of Black students. Despite the shortcomings of HBCUs, their students are able to conceive of a future self without boundaries, to move forward with confidence, and to maintain a firm belief that their race does not define who they can become and what they can accomplish.

References

Allen, W. R. (1992). The color of success: African-American college student outcomes at predominantly White and historically Black public colleges and universities. *Harvard Educational Review, 62*(1), 26–44.

Allen, W. R., & Jewell, J. O. (2002). A backward glance forward: Past, present, and future perspectives on historically Black colleges and universities. *Review of Higher Education, 25*(3), 241–261.

American Association for the Advancement of Science. (2001). *In pursuit of a diverse science, technology, engineering, and mathematics workforce: Recommended research priorities to enhance participation by underrepresented minorities.* Washington, DC: Author.

Anderson, E., & Kim, D. (2006). *Increasing the success of minority students in science and technology.* Washington, DC: American Council on Education.

Atwater, M. M. (2000). Equity for Black Americans in precollege science. *Science Education, 84*(2), 154–179.

Babco, E. L. (2003). *Trends in African American and Native American participation in STEM higher education.* Washington, DC: Commission on Professionals in Science and Technology.

Committee on Equal Opportunities in Science and Engineering. (2006). *Biennial report to Congress.* Washington, DC: National Science Foundation.

Bonous-Hammarth, M. (2001). Pathways to success: Affirming opportunities for science, mathematics, and engineering major. *Journal of Negro Education, 69*(1/2), 92–111.

Bowman, S. L., & Tinsley, H. E. A. (1991). The development of vocational realism in Black American college students. *Career Development Quarterly, 39*(3), 240–252.

Brown, M. C., Donahoo, S., & Bertrand, R. D. (2001). The Black college and the quest for educational opportunity. *Urban Education, 36*(5), 553–571.

Carter, D. F. (1999). The impact of institutional choice and environments on African-American and White students' degree expectations. *Research in Higher Education, 40*(1), 17–41.

Cokley, K. O. (2000). An investigation of academic self-concept and its relationship to academic achievement in African American college students. *Journal of Black Psychology, 26*(2), 148–164.

Crawford, I., Suarez-Balcazar, Y., Reich, J., Figert, A., & Nyden, P. (1996). The use of research participation for mentoring prospective minority graduate students. *Teaching Sociology, 24*(3), 256–163.

Fries-Britt, S., & Turner, B. (2002). Uneven stories: Successful Black collegians at a Black and a White campus. *Review of Higher Education, 25*(3), 315–330.

Gasman, M., Lundy-Wagner, V., & Vultaggio, J. (2009). *Preparing underrepresented students of color for doctoral success: The role of undergraduate institutions.* Paper presented at the Annual Meeting of the American Educational Research Association (AERA). San Diego, CA.

Goodchild, F. M. (2004). The pipeline: Still leaking. *American Scientist, 92*(2), 112–114.

Guiffrida, D. A. (2005). Other mothering as a framework for understanding African American students' definitions of student-centered faculty. *Journal of Higher Education, 76*(6), 701–723.

Hall, E. R., & Post-Kammer, P. (1987). Black mathematicians and science majors: Why so few? *Career Development Quarterly, 35*(3), 206–219.

Heck, R. H. (2006). Conceptualizing and conducting meaningful research studies in education. In C. F. Conrad & R. C. Serlin (Eds.), *The Sage handbook for research in education* (pp. 373–392). Thousand Oaks, CA: Sage.

Hrabowski, F. A. (2003). Raising minority achievement in science and mathematics. *Educational Leadership, 60*(4), 44–48.

Hubbard, S. M., & Stage, F. K. (2009). Attitudes, perceptions, and preferences of faculty at Hispanic serving and predominately Black institutions. *Journal of Higher Education, 80*(3), 270–289.

Hunter, A., Laursen, S. L., & Seymour, E. (2007). Becoming a scientist: The role of undergraduate research in students' cognitive, personal, and professional development. *Science Education, 91*(1), 36–74.

Hurtado, S., Cabrera, N. L., Lin, M. H., Arellano, L., & Espinosa, L. L. (2009). Diversifying science: Underrepresented student experiences in structured research programs. *Research in Higher Education, 50*(2), 189–214.

Hurtado, S., Eagan, M. K., Cabrera, N. L., Lin, M. H., Park, J., & Lopez, M. (2008). Training future scientists: Predicting first-year minority student participation in health science research. *Research in Higher Education, 49*(2), 126–152.

Jibrell, S. B. (1990). Business/education partnerships: Pathways to success for Black students in science and mathematics. *Journal of Negro Education, 59*(3), 491–506.

Jones, L. S. (1997). Opening doors with informal science: Exposure and access for our underserved students. *Science Education, 81*(6), 663–678.

Kim, M. M., & Conrad, C. F. (2006). The impact of historically Black colleges and universities on the academic success of African-American students. *Research in Higher Education, 47*(4), 399–427.

Ladson-Billings, G. (1997). It doesn't add up: African American students' mathematics achievement. *Journal of Research in Mathematics Education, 28*(6), 697–708.

Latiker, T. T. (2003). *A qualitative study of African American student persistence in a private Black college.* Paper presented at the Annual Meeting of the American Educational Research Association (AERA). Chicago, IL.

Lawrence-Lightfoot, S., & Davis, J. H. (1997). *The art and science of portraiture.* San Francisco, CA: Jossey-Bass.

Leggon, C., & Pearson, W. (1997). The baccalaureate origins of African American female Ph.D. scientists. *Journal of Women and Minorities in Science and Engineering, 3,* 213–224.

Lewis, B. F. (2003). A critique of literature on the underrepresentation of African Americans in science: Directions for future research. *Journal of Women and Minorities in Science and Engineering, 9,* 361–373.

Lewis, B. F., & Collins, A. (2001). Interpretive investigation of the science-related career decisions of three African-American college students. *Journal of Research in Science Teaching, 38*(5), 599–621.

Markus, H., & Nurius, P. (1986). Possible selves. *American Psychologist, 41*(9), 954–969.

Maton, K. L., Hrabowski, F. A., & Schmitt, C. A. (2000). African American college students in the sciences: College and post college outcomes in the Meyerhoff scholars program. *Journal of Research in Science Teaching, 37*(7), 629-654.

Maxwell, J. A. (1998). *Qualitative research design: An interactive approach.* Thousand Oaks, CA: Sage.

Mullen, A. L. (2001). Gender, race, and the college science track: Analyzing field concentrations and institutional selectivity. *Journal of Women and Minorities in Science and Engineering, 7,* 285-300.

Myers, C. B., & Pavel, D. M. (2011). Underrepresented students in STEM: The transition from undergraduate to graduate programs. *Journal of Diversity in Higher Education, 4*(2), 90–105.

National Center for Education Statistics. (2008). *Digest of education statistics, 2007* (NCES 2008-022). Washington, DC: Author.

Oakes, J. (1990). Opportunities, achievement, and choice: Women and minority students in science and mathematics. *Review of Research in Education, 16,* 153–222.

O'Brien, V., Martinez-Pons, M., & Kopala, M. (1999). Mathematics self-efficacy, ethnic identity, gender, and career interests related to mathematics and science. *Journal of Educational Research, 92*(4), 231–235.

Outcalt, C. L., & Skewes-Cox, T. E. (2002). Involvement, interaction, and satisfaction: The human environment at HBCUs. *Review of Higher Education, 25*(3), 331–347.

Oyserman, D., Bybee, D., & Terry, K. (2006). Possible selves and academic outcomes: How and when possible selves impel action. *Journal of Personality and Social Psychology, 91*(1), 188–204.

Oyserman, D., Gant, L., & Ager, J. (1995). A socially contextualized model of African American identity: Possible selves and school persistence. *Journal of Personality and Social Psychology, 69*(6), 1216–1232.

Oyserman, D., Terry, K., & Bybee, D. (2002). A possible selves intervention to enhance school involvement. *Journal of Adolescence, 25*(3), 313–326.

Palmer, R. T., Davis, R. J., & Maramba, D. C. (2010). Role of HBCUs in supporting academic success of underprepared Black males. *Negro Educational Review, 61*(1–4), 85–106.

Palmer, R. T., & Gasman, M. (2008). "It takes a village to raise a child": The role of social capital in promoting academic success for African American men at a Black college. *Journal of College Student Development, 49*(1), 52–70.

Pascarella, E. T., Wolniak, G. C., Pierson, C. T., & Flowers, L. A. (2004). The role of race in the development of plans for a graduate degree. *Review of Higher Education, 27*(3), 299–320.

Pearson, Jr., W., & Fechter, A. (Eds.). (1994). *Who will do science?* Baltimore, MD: Johns Hopkins Press.

Perna, L. Lundy-Wagner, V., Drezner, N. D., Gasman, M., Yoon, S., Bose, E., & Gary, S. (2009). The contribution of HBCUs to the preparation of African American women for stem careers: A case study. *Research in Higher Education, 50*(1), 1–23.

Pizzolato, J. E. (2006). Achieving college student possible selves: Navigating the space between commitment and achievement of long-term identity goals. *Cultural Diversity and Ethnic Minority Psychology, 12*(1), 57–69.

Pizzolato, J. E. (2007). Impossible selves: Investigating students' persistence decisions when their career-possible selves border on impossible. *Journal of Career Development, 33*(3), 201–233.

Research Experiences for Undergraduates (REU). (n.d.). Retrieved from http://www.nsf.gov/funding/pgm_summ.jsp?pims_id=5517&org=NSF.

Russell, M., & Atwater, M. (2005). Traveling the road to success: A discourse on persistence throughout the science pipeline with African American students at a predominately White institution. *Journal of Research in Science Teaching, 42*(6), 691–715.

Russell, S. H., Hancock, M. P., & McCullough, J. (2007). Benefits of undergraduate research experience. *Science, 316*(5824), 548–549.

Sedlacek, W. E. (2004). *Beyond the big test: Noncognitive assessment in higher education.* San Francisco, CA: Jossey-Bass.

Seymour, E., & Hewitt, N. M. (1997). *Talking about leaving: Why undergraduates leave the sciences.* Boulder, CO: Westview Press.

Southern Education Foundation (SEF). (2005). *Igniting potential: Historically Black colleges and universities and science, technology, engineering and mathematics.* Atlanta, GA: Southern Education Foundation.

Summers, M. F., & Hrabowski, F. A. (2006). Preparing minority scientists and engineers. *Science, 311*(5769), 1870–1871.

Taylor, E., & Antony, J. S. (2000). Stereotype threat reduction and wise schooling: Towards the successful socialization of African American doctoral students in education. *Journal of Negro Education, 69*(3), 184–198.

Tobias, R. (1992). Math and science education for African-American youth: A curriculum change. *NASSP Bulletin, 76*(546), 42–48.

Toma, J. D. (2006). Approaching rigor in applied qualitative research. In C. F. Conrad & R. C. Serlin (Eds.), *The Sage handbook for research in education* (pp. 405–424). Thousand Oaks, CA: Sage.

Triesman, U. (1992). Studying students studying calculus: A look at the lives of minority mathematics students in college. *College Mathematics Journal, 23*(5), 362–372.

Ulloa, E. C., & Herrera, M. (2006). Strategies for multicultural student success: What about grad school? *The Career Development Quarterly, 54*(4), 361–366.

Weidman, J. C., Twale, D. J., & Stein, E. L. (2001). *Socialization of graduate and professional students in higher education: A perilous passage?* (ASHE-ERIC Higher Education Report, Vol. 28, No. 3). San Francisco, CA: Jossey-Bass.

Wenglinsky, H. H. (1996). The educational justification of historically Black colleges and universities: A policy response to the U.S. supreme court. *Educational Evaluation and Policy Analysis, 18*(1), 91–103.

Wenglinsky, H. H. (1997). *Students at historically Black colleges and universities: Their aspirations & accomplishments.* Princeton, NJ: Educational Testing Service.

8

COMMUNITY BUILDING

Minority Serving Institutions and How They Influence Students Pursuing Undergraduate STEM Degrees

Alonzo M. Flowers and Rosa M. Banda

According to a report by the National Academy of Sciences (2007), scientific and technological innovation can only be secured with individuals' success in science, technology, engineering, and mathematics (STEM). Because STEM remains White and male-dominated, programs that focus on increasing the participation of female and minority students have been of great interest to organizations, universities, and national agencies (e.g., National Science Foundation [NSF], 2007) alike. Ways to increase students' interest, participation, matriculation, and completion of STEM undergraduate degrees has been discussed throughout the scholarly community—from primary to secondary to postsecondary school officials and researchers. To be fair, discussions on how to improve success in STEM disciplines remains as complex and multifaceted as ever. Certainly, a *single* approach will not remedy the issue at hand. Rather, several explanations and solutions will need to be implemented if the United States wishes to increase students' success in STEM.

With this in mind, this chapter seeks to further expand the conversation on how to increase students' success in STEM. More specifically, we focus on the role of community building and how minority serving institutions (MSIs) influence students pursuing undergraduate STEM degrees. First, the underrepresentation of minorities in STEM programs is illustrated. Second, the increasing need for STEM education is detailed. Third, we discuss how MSIs are impacting STEM programs. Next, we offer an alternate viewpoint that focuses on the role of community building, more specifically, in terms of knowledge, support, and vision, which, we contend, are integral for students' success in STEM. Last, we offer a number of recommendations that are necessary for creating a community that will encourage and sustain STEM success for underrepresented students who choose to pursue such fields of study.

Minorities Underrepresentation in STEM

The increasing need for STEM education and more importantly, degree completion and subsequent entry into the STEM workforce is vital for the future of the U.S. economy. According to the National Science Board (2007), women and minorities, more often than other students, choose not to persist in their studies in STEM disciplines. While it is important to boost STEM participation for both genders and all races/ethnicities, it is vital to note that population projections indicate that women and minorities will comprise a preponderance of the future STEM workforce (Hyde & Kling, 2001; Walsh & Heppner, 2006) hence, the need to increase women and minorities' decisions to pursue and persist in STEM disciplines.

Even though females were awarded 57% of all bachelor's degrees in 2008–2009 (National Center for Education Statistics, 2011), they remain underrepresented in *most* undergraduate STEM disciplines such as physical science, engineering, and technology (Amelink, 2009). In 2006, females were awarded 23% and 22% and males 77% and 78% of computer and information science and engineering undergraduate degrees, respectively (NSF, 2008). Females, in 2008, were awarded more undergraduate degrees when compared to males in biological and agricultural sciences and psychology (NSF, 2011a).

Likewise, minorities also earn fewer undergraduate STEM degrees than their counterparts. The NSF (2010) posits that even though Blacks, Hispanics, and other minorities comprise approximately 24% of the U.S. population only 13% of minorities earn a bachelor's degree and a mere 10% of minorities constitute the science and engineering workforce. In 2006, only 16.7% of underrepresented minorities were awarded bachelor's degrees in science and engineering while Whites were awarded 64.7% of these degrees (NSF, 2009). More specifically, Asian/Pacific Islanders, American Indian/Alaska Natives, Blacks (used interchangeably with African Americans), and Hispanics were awarded, respectively, 9.3%, .7%, 8.3%, and 7.7% of all undergraduate degrees in science and engineering in 2006 (NSF, 2009).

Increasing Need for STEM Education

The vitality of the U.S. economy "is derived in large part from the productivity of well-trained people and the steady stream of scientific and technical innovations they produce" (National Academy of Sciences, 2007, p. 1). Such scientific and technical innovations are highly contingent on student success in mathematics and science, which also serve as reliable indicators of later success in STEM disciplines (National Academy of Sciences, 2007). More important is the need to not only increase STEM education but to also increase student success in STEM. Student success in STEM and thus an increasing need for effective STEM education is necessary for many reasons, although only two will be explored. First, a brief examination of primary and secondary students' performance in mathematics and science is discussed. Second, the need to someday replace the aging STEM workforce is detailed. Both of the aforementioned reasons further cement the urgency to increase student success in STEM disciplines.

When compared to economically similar countries, U.S. students lag behind in mathematics and science performance (National Center for Education Statistics, 2011a, chapter 6). A Trends in International Mathematics and Science Study (TIMSS) is conducted every 4 years and compares mathematics and science scores of U.S. fourth and eighth graders to fourth and eighth graders from economically similar countries, such as, China, Singapore, Japan, and England. In 2007, U.S. fourth graders scored lower in mathematics than eight educational systems, all of which were located in Asian or European countries (National Center for Education Statistics, 2011a). Eighth graders faired a bit better but still scored lower than five educational systems—all located in Asia. Although U.S. eighth graders performed better than fourth graders in mathematics, U.S. students' performance in science declines over time. While fourth graders, in 2007, scored lower than four educational systems located in Asia, eighth graders fared worse as they scored lower than nine educational systems which were all found in Asia or Europe (National Center for Education Statistics, 2011a, chapter 6). Tracking students' performance in mathematics and science—even measuring assessments internationally—provides insight into how successful U.S. STEM education might or might not be. Even though U.S. students improve in mathematics when compared to other countries from fourth to eighth grade, their performance in science, as students' progress four grade levels, is troubling at best as scores seem to deteriorate. Creating student interest and success in mathematics and science provides a snapshot of how the United States will fare in scientific innovations in a global world.

The need to increase STEM education and more importantly, the need to improve student success in STEM education is also crucial because of today's STEM workforce. According to the NSF (2010), between 4.3 and 5.8 million people were employed in the science and engineering workforce in 2006. Even though the science and engineering workforce has steadily grown, its sustained workforce will begin to grow at a slower rate primarily because of "changes in degree production, immigration, and retirement patterns" (NSF, 2010, pp. 3–6). In other words, the decline in STEM college graduates, the increase in the number of international students who come to the United States to study STEM disciplines, and the nearing retirement of a workforce that, despite its youthfulness, will begin to retire at faster rates than can be replaced if individuals do not choose to pursue STEM education, are certain to reduce the future U.S. science and engineering workforce. The demographics of the science and engineering workforce are important to note. Women, for instance, despite earning 40% of engineering and science degrees in 2006 are disproportionately employed in such occupations when compared to degree completion (NSF,

2010). Like women, in terms of disproportionate representation, Blacks and Hispanics remain underrepresented in the science and engineering workforce (NSF, 2010). The need to increase the participation of women and minorities in STEM education, college completion, and entrance in the workforce is crucial because there are indicators that the U.S. share of the global science and engineering workforce continues to decline (NSF, 2010).

Minority Serving Institutions and STEM Education

Increasing student participation and success in STEM disciplines, especially amongst women and minorities, remains a viable area of interest for the United States. In order to mitigate this issue, the National Academy of Sciences (2007) detailed hundreds of programs and funding that target student success in mathematics and science; a precursor identified as necessary if the United States wishes to remain abreast of scientific and technological innovations. To be sure, there are various universities that are feverishly working with local schools and creating partnerships with nearby communities as a means to try to increase female and minority interest and success in STEM disciplines. However, we will only be discussing the role that MSIs play in regard to STEM education.

MSIs are colleges and universities where the majority student enrollment is comprised of minorities. Hispanic serving institutions (HSIs), historically Black colleges and universities (HBCUs), and Tribal colleges and universities (TCUs) are all considered MSIs (Bridges et al., 2005). According to the Alliance for Equity in Higher Education (2004, as cited in Bridges et al. 2005), MSIs enroll one-third of all Hispanics, Blacks, and American Indian students in the United States. Chubin et al. (2005) posit that, "*Where* minority graduates earn their undergraduate degrees in STEM fields is more than a curiosity. They are a professional lifeline for many and, given the demographic future, they loom large in the production of the nation's technical workforce" (p. 76). Indeed, MSIs are certainly playing an active role in increasing the interest and success of underrepresented minorities in STEM.

While several MSIs are implementing programs to help diversify students pursuing undergraduate STEM degrees, only two universities will be discussed here. In order to peak student interest at an early age, the University of Texas at San Antonio (UTSA), an HSI, created the San Antonio Prefreshman Engineering Program (SAPREP). This collaborative program was founded in 1979 by Dr. Manuel Berriozábal and is designed to encourage middle and high school students, specifically from underrepresented populations, to prepare for career paths in science and engineering. SAPREP, which collaborates with local school districts and universities and has numerous educational and corporate sponsors, is an 8-week summer program that gives students the opportunity to study mathematics for four summers. Students are awarded one elective credit hour for their participation in the program. Since its inception, approximately

14,574 students have participated in SAPREP ("San Antonio Prefreshman Engineering Program," 2011). Of the 5,605 former participants of SAPREP who responded to a 2010 annual survey, 99.9% graduated from high school, 85% are college graduates, and 44% graduated with science, engineering, or mathematics degrees ("San Antonio Prefreshman Engineering Program," 2011). The program continues strong today.

Like UTSA, other universities, such as Clark Atlanta University (CAU), an HBCU, also recognize the importance of support for minority students, specifically in regard to research. CAU created a Research Center for Science and Technology that works to facilitate collaborative and interdisciplinary research among federal, national, industry (e.g., both large and small minority companies), and other universities (Division of Research and Sponsored Programs, 2008). This center has 200,000 square feet and houses various laboratories and conference space, among other entities. Research conducted focuses on, to name a few, cancer research, nanotechnology, and biomedical research. The mission of the center is to establish leadership positions and collaborative partnerships among faculty, the institution, and various stakeholders as well as technology transfer for the purpose of commercialization. Among many other services the center assists in finding funding opportunities, coordinating research partnerships, and providing education and training programs (Division of Research and Sponsored Programs, 2008).

The approaches of UTSA and CAU are distinctly different, but both universities understand and have noted the needs of their community. For UTSA, it is concerned with increasing student participation in STEM as they target middle and high school students through an 8-week summer program. The Center at CAU focuses on sustaining and supporting students and faculty once they arrive on their campus. Both the need to increase interest and the possibility of pursuing a STEM undergraduate degree and the support needed to sustain student (and faculty) success in STEM disciplines, offer two different support beams that build the same bridge; that is, the bridge of how to increase the success of underrepresented students in STEM disciplines. Both universities recognize the importance of creating partnerships with communities that are near and far in terms of proximity.

Creating programs that can successfully work to achieve diversity in the STEM workforce has become a priority for several universities. After reviewing several successful programs, an Initiative of the Council on Competiveness, known as Building Engineering and Science Talent (BEST, 2004) suggests that there are eight principles that universities must follow in order to increase student success in STEM. First, *institutional leadership* must be one that encompasses and welcomes inclusiveness of the student body. Second, *targeted recruitment* must capitalize on a feeder system from K-12 that ultimately attracts the most talented students to pursue STEM fields of study. Third, *engaged faculty* is necessary in order to develop student talent beyond the classroom. Fourth, *personal attention* via the use of residential programs, tutoring, and mentoring is crucial for underrepresented students in STEM. Fifth, *peer support* is indispensable because it facilitates mutual support for undergraduate, graduate, and even postgraduate students as well as opportunities for peer teaching. Sixth, *enriched research opportunities* provide underrepresented students in STEM with research experiences that are further nourished throughout internships and after internships by sustaining influential mentoring relationships. Seventh, *bridging to the next level* suggests that universities must be cognizant that after higher education students enter the workforce and as a result, universities must facilitate the seamless transition of its students into the workforce. Eighth, *continual evaluation* suggests that it is important for programs to be continually assessed to determine what is working and what is not working. Trends in K–12 and higher education STEM development, coupled with demographic and workforce trends, point to a serious challenge not only for institutions of education but also for the communities they serve. Understanding the nature and needs of communities will provide institutions of education with a holistic insight into the multifaceted approaches needed to provide well-developed STEM programs.

The Notion of Community

A community serves to guide, maintain, and provide support for individuals who reside within it. The term *community* is not a new concept. The practice of people living in a shared area providing each other with continuing support has long been part of the social fabric of the world. Cobb (1992) posits:

> In a community, people take responsibility for collective activity and are loyal to each other beyond immediate self-interest. They work together on the basis of shared values. They hold each other accountable for commitments. In earlier centuries, a person was born into a community and a set of reciprocal obligations. Now, those who seek an identity as part of a larger whole must invent community by voluntarily committing themselves to institutions or groups.
>
> *(p. 2)*

Yet, the continued growth of urbanization has forced the community to be more nuclear family centered (Goode, 1982). In other words, community is not necessarily always about the world itself but rather the individual families who comprise the world. However, one cannot focus only on the parts (e.g., families) without taking into account the whole (e.g., community). As such, communities of knowledge, support, and vision must become a working reality in the entire spectrum needed to increase participation and success in STEM related fields. The following are elaborations of what a community of knowledge, support, and vision should entail.

Community of Knowledge

Now more than ever, it is vital to reduce educational inequalities that continue to decrease opportunities for college degree completion, especially in the STEM disciplines. More importantly, it is imperative that MSIs continue to build academic communities and pipelines that support knowledge attainment and a collective vision for underrepresented students who are pursuing STEM fields of study. Researchers in the area of STEM education warn that the United States should be in a state of educational emergency. Callan (2006) suggests:

> What is needed is a sense of urgency among policy leaders, educators, and business leaders comparable to the policy emphasis that other countries are placing on higher education—as reflected in shifting international rankings…. The current level of performance will fall short in a world being reshaped by the knowledge-based global economy. Our country… needs to educate more people with college-level knowledge and skills.
>
> *(p. 5)*

Unfortunately, the method of improving the STEM educational pipeline remains one of the most politically and socially complex processes. In his 2009 speech about the future of America's leadership, President Obama proclaimed:

> The key to meeting these challenges—to improving our health and well-being, to harnessing clean energy, to protecting our security, and succeeding in the global economy—will be reaffirming and strengthening America's role as the world's engine of scientific discovery and technological innovation. And that leadership tomorrow depends on how we educate our students today, especially in those disciplines that hold the promise of producing future innovations and innovators. And that's why education in math and science is so important.
>
> *(Line 31)*

While nationally, there has been increased dialogue concerning STEM education, it remains an issue with global implications. As a result, STEM disciplines and careers have continued to attract an audience that does not reflect America's diversity. While the goal remains to improve the quality of education and increase the learning opportunities for all students, there remains an inequitable educational system based on social and racial divisions. Research has shown that the education system has historically been less responsive to and supportive of the needs of students of color (Harvey, 2008; Moore & Owens, 2008). The key is for MSIs to lead the way to the future. This can be achieved through a collaborative effort between universities and K-12 school systems by establishing programs that seek to create a *community of knowledge* about STEM education and the college pipeline.

Examples of this type of collaboration are P-16 STEM initiatives, which are programs that target students as early as preschool, and from various socioeconomic backgrounds, to enlighten them to STEM majors. Ultimately, the intent of these programs is to expose students to the world of STEM education and the related career opportunities that exist. Effective P-20 programs are marked by the following characteristics: (a) high standards for program students and faculty, (b) personalized attention for students, (c) interaction with role models, (d) peer support, (e) college-/community-based program schools, (e) financial aid and scholarship assistance, and (f) focus on problem-based curricula (Cech, 2008). These administrative and instructional practices could serve as preparatory tools for underrepresented students in their navigation of the educational pipeline, especially in engineering disciplines.

According to Howard (2007), increasing the number of underrepresented students in STEM disciplines has important implications, as previously noted, for America's competitiveness in the global marketplace because STEM disciplines are critical drivers of economic growth and development. Howard (2007) recommended that educators and policymakers consider encouraging the following changes to the education system: (a) improve teacher quality for underrepresented minority students, (b) encourage more African American males to enroll in college preparation courses, particularly in mathematics and science, (c) hold lawmakers and Congress accountable for ensuring that minority students have access to appropriate resources to finance their college education, and (d) encourage more effective collaboration between colleges and local secondary schools to foster minority students' academic preparedness for college to reduce barriers to college access. Innately, to develop a community of knowledge requires collaboration from both the institution and the various stakeholders (e.g., schools, parents, community officials) that impact student learning and development.

Creating a Community of Support

For underrepresented students, interactions with faculty members are essential to their successful transition to the college environment. Minority students who are emotionally connected with faculty and staff members in the institutional environment have higher retention rates (Grier-Reed, Madyun, & Buckley, 2008). As stewards of public good, MSIs have the responsibility to promote intellectual development and provide underrepresented students with opportunities for academic growth. This goal can be obtained by establishing mentoring initiatives that create partnerships among the institutions, the communities, and the students.

Research has shown that mentoring can significantly influence the academic success of students of color (Allen & O'Brien, 2006; Sutton, 2006). Mentors are identified as persons with recognized success who help others to interpret and learn to navigate unfamiliar environments (Daloz, 1986). According to Sutton (2006), mentoring has the potential to decrease students' feelings of marginality, increase their sense of personal significance (that they "*matter*"), and provide important validation of belonging to the campus environment. A mandatory mentoring program could enhance development of self-concept, self-esteem, and self-confidence within underrepresented students, especially first generation students. In addition to mentors aiding in mentees' achievement of academic excellence and social integration on campus, increased retention in STEM academic programs can also occur. Underrepresented students who interact with faculty members are more likely to develop a stronger ability to cope with the academic rigor of college (Frank, 2003). Frank (2003) contends that underrepresented students aspire to achieve the status of their minority mentors; thus, faculty who are mentors act as academic, social, and career guides for this student population.

Creating a Community of Vision

A vision is an abstract concept; one cannot mass create one vision that will influence all schools. Rather each school must create its own collaborative vision. Essentially, there are two parts to consider: (a) What does a vision entail? (b) What are the steps necessary to create a proactive vision? Before explicating our conceptualization of what a community vision should entail, it is important to note that we cannot, by any means, address *every* aspect of *every* vision possible. What we do hope is that we can unite individuals in a shared vision that forces stakeholders within the STEM community to establish a framework for others to build their own respective vision. More specifically, we want to address the interconnection between communities of knowledge and support which will work to reify and create a unified community of vision.

A vision is a viable tool that provides direction for which change should occur (Hoyle, 2007). Vision requires one to look past the idealistic notion in regards to any goal. For instance, the vision might be to triple STEM participation and success among underrepresented students within 3 years. Certainly, the vision is admirable but many facets must be considered before the vision can become more than an abstract notion. One must consider the individual desires and needs within the specific context of each community. Therefore, one must be willing to acknowledge the multiple layers that exist within an environment. A vision might be abstract in nature and only be realizable when social contexts are considered. In addition to creating a vision, the environment and the leader of the environment must be committed to the same vision. Equally important as the leader, is the plan that will be implemented in order to achieve the vision. What steps will be taken? Who will take them? What resources are needed? How can the community be involved? Is the timeline for this vision feasible? While a plan is certainly important to a vision, it is also a necessity to create criteria that measure the effectiveness of the plan. All of these facets, among others, must be methodologically planned in order for a vision to become reality.

What Does a Vision Entail?

A vision entails creating comprehensive programs that seek to increase the knowledge and support for underrepresented minority students in STEM programs. This vision requires that MSIs implement and evaluate the ways in which they provide services for this student population. In addition, MSIs must reexamine the processes in which they work collaboratively with other stakeholders within the community and local schools to minimize the achievement gap within STEM education as it affects minority students. While minority enrollment in STEM programs continues to remain an issue, it is critical that MSIs also reexamine their effectiveness in increasing the opportunity of minority students to gain access, improve matriculation, and increase undergraduate completion in STEM disciplines.

What Are the Steps to Create a Proactive Vision?

There are indeed numerous ways to create a proactive vision, but our approach is the culmination of the necessity to build active communities of knowledge and support. As previously noted, creating a community of knowledge is a basic and vital aspect of introducing and peaking student interest as regards the possibilities when pursuing STEM related disciplines. For example, many students, at a young age, might not embrace being an engineer because they simply do not know what engineers do. In other words, knowledge can not only be taught in practical terms but the teaching of knowledge, especially in STEM disciplines must also be applicable in nature. More importantly, such knowledge must be facilitated through continuous and genuine support from stakeholders found both inside and outside the classroom context.

A vision, regardless of how grand or small, must have unwavering support from stakeholders from within primary, secondary, and postsecondary communities; this support should come from not only school officials but also from corporations, mentors, and university officials. For instance, MSIs must serve as a bridge between all the different members that comprise various entities needed in order to ensure the vision of each respective community. This bridge is already being built by many MSIs as they have established summer programs that target minorities' interest, recruitment, and enrichment in STEM-related fields. Further, MSIs must actively find monies from local, state, and federal levels that support the fulfillment of their STEM vision for minority students. The National Science Foundation (2011) and other nonprofit foundations, for instance, typically provide grants and other financial incentives for institutions to establish STEM related programs that seek to increase minority participation in such disciplines.

Recommendations

In order to build a shared vision of student growth in MSIs, such institutions should be dedicated to proactively building collaborative partnerships with different types of communities. Since institutions of higher education are the gateway to the workforce, institutions should be at the forefront in bridging partnerships at all levels. Because researchers are cognizant of the disparities in racial/ethnic and gender underrepresentation in STEM fields, MSIs must capitalize and ensure, by all means possible, the success of its students, particularly those who pursue undergraduate STEM degrees. Ultimately, the goal of MSIs should be to reshape student education in a manner that works to achieve a shared vision. What follows is a list of recommendations that MSIs should consider as foundational suggestions in which they should tailor and expand to meet their specific needs.

1. *Establish a Shared Vision and Create Goals.* This process enables institutions to establish their aim and focus by creating programs that increase gender and racial/ethnic minority representation in STEM disciplines. Such visions and goals are contingent on the specific needs and context of each institutional environment. More importantly, institutions must take stock of their own needs that ultimately seek to benefit nearby communities and impact the global community. For instance, if a majority of their student population is Hispanic then their focus should be on increasing Hispanic success in STEM fields. This vision should differ if the institution is an HBCU or TCU.

2. *Create a System of Accountability.* Accountability is an assessment measurement that determines if the institution is meeting particular goals. This process must be ongoing and must provide an overview of program development, program implications, and program findings. A system of accountability ensures that an institution's goals are aligned with the outcomes that have resulted from the actions of the program. More importantly, institutions must recognize that neither accountability tools nor measures are generalizable in nature. Rather each institution must develop its own tools to assess the success or lack thereof, of any given program.

3. *Take Stock of Resources.* Resources are integral to the development of STEM programs. University officials must take stock of the available resources within their systems as well as their individual campuses. Universities must remain knowledgeable about current information regarding the availability of human (e.g., faculty, staff, mentors, etc.), financial (e.g., monies

allocated for certain programs), and environmental (e.g., lab equipment, technology updates) resources. By taking stock and capitalizing on the resources readily available, university officials can begin to maximize the resources they have and simultaneously begin to develop plans to acquire resources that are lacking.

4. *Proactively Search for Funding Opportunities.* Because funding opportunities have been limited in current economic times, networking and partnerships will allow for greater insight into the availability of external funds for STEM program development. To be sure, there remains an ample amount of funding opportunities from agencies such as the National Science Foundation. Therefore, it is the responsibility of universities to proactively seek and apply for monies that help further the success of underrepresented students in STEM. In other words, universities must think ahead if they are to be viable competitors in regard to monies awarded by federal agencies.

5. *Create Multifaceted Communities.* In addition, for universities to dispel the "ivory tower" myth, universities must also work hard to become transparent to surrounding communities in order to create genuine partnerships. These partnerships require a committed collaborative partnership that seeks to eliminate the systemic issues that occur in STEM education. More specifically, universities must begin to listen to surrounding communities and capitalize their resources. Equally as important to creating partnerships is the need for universities to not only expand but also extend vertically its resources with communities outside of the institution. Universities must expand and share their communities of knowledge, support, and vision with their partners in order to increase STEM success of underrepresented students.

Conclusion

The need to increase minority participation and success in STEM disciplines has become an increasing issue of importance for universities and a matter of national interest (Museus, Palmer, Davis, & Maramba, 2011). While several universities have implemented programs that target minorities and females, they, despite small increases, continue to be underrepresented in STEM fields (NSF, 2009). The changing demographics and slowing growth rate of the current STEM workforce are catalysts for MSIs to build communities that capitalize on and cultivate students' STEM talent. As such, MSIs must proactively create communities of knowledge, support, and vision to establish genuine partnerships that promote collaboration between various stakeholders. The success of underrepresented students in STEM-related disciplines not only affects the workforce but also, if they are not successful, jeopardizes this country's ability to be globally competitive.

References

Allen, T. D., & O'Brien, K. E. (2006). Formal mentoring programs and organizational attraction. *Human Resource Development Quarterly, 17*(1), 43–58.

Amelink, C. (2009). Literature overview: Gender differences in science achievement. *SWE-AWE CASEE Overviews.* Retrieved from http://www.AWEonline.org

Bridges, B. K., Cambridge, B., Kuh, G. D., & Leegwater, L. H. (2005). Student engagement at minority-serving institutions: Emerging lessons from the BEAMS project. *New Directions for Institutional Research, 125,* 25–43.

Building Engineering and Science Talent (BEST). (2004). *A bridge for all: Higher education design principles to broaden participation in science, technology, engineering and mathematics.* Retrieved from www.bestworkforce.org

Callan, P. (2006). *Measuring up 2006: The national report card on higher education.* (National Center for Public Policy and Higher Education Report #06-5). Washington, DC: National Center for Public Policy and Higher Education.

Cech, S. J. (2008). P-16 councils bring all tiers of education to the table. *Education Week, 40,* 6–9. Retrieved from http://www.edweek.org/ew/articles/2008/ 06/05/40 overview.h27.htm

Chubin, D. E., May, G. S., & Babco, E. L. (2005). Diversifying the engineering workforce. *Journal of Engineering Education, 94*(1), 73–86.

Cobb, C. W. (1992). *Responsive schools, renewed communities.* San Francisco, CA: ICS Press.

Daloz, L. (1986). *Effective teaching and mentoring: Realizing the transformational power of adult learning experiences.* San Francisco, CA: Jossey-Bass.

Division of Research and Sponsored Programs. (2008). *Research centers and focus areas.* Retrieved from http://www.cau.edu/Academics_Research_and_Sponsoreed_Prog.aspx

Frank, A. (2003). If they come, we should listen: African American education majors' perceptions of a predominantly White university experience. *Teaching and Teacher Education, 19*(7), 697–717.

Goode, W. J. (1982). *The family.* Englewood Cliffs, NJ: Prentice-Hall.

Grier-Reed, T., Madyun, N., & Buckley, C. (2008). Low Black student retention on a predominantly White campus: Two faculty respond with the African American student network. *Journal of College Student Development, 49*(5), 476–485.

Harvey, W. B. (2008). The weakest link: A commentary on the connections between K12 and higher education. *American Behavioral Scientist, 51*(7), 972–983.

Howard, T. (2007). The forgotten link: The salience of pre K-12 education and culturally responsive pedagogy in creating access to higher education for African American students. In J. F. L. Jackson (Ed.), *Strengthening the African American educational pipeline: Informing research, policy, and practice* (pp. 17–36). Albany, NY: SUNY Press.

Hoyle, J. (2007). *Leadership and futuring: Making visions happen* (2nd ed.). Thousand Oaks, CA: Corwin Press.

Hyde. J. S., & Kling, K. C. (2001). Women, motivation, and achievement. *Psychology of Women Quarterly, 25,* 364–378.

Moore, J. L., & Owens, D. (2008). Educating and counseling African American students: Recommendations for teachers and school counselors. In L. Tillman (Ed.), *The Sage handbook of African American education* (pp. 351–366). Thousand Oaks, CA: Sage.

Museus, S. D., Palmer, R. T., Davis, R. J., & Maramba, D. C. (2011). *Racial and ethnic minority students' success in STEM education* (ASHE Higher Education Report, Vol. 36, No. 6, pp. 1–140). San Francisco, CA: Jossey-Bass.

National Academy of Sciences. (2007). *Free executive summary: Rising above the gathering storm: Energizing and employing for a brighter economic future.* Retrieved from http://www.nap.edu

National Center for Education Statistics. (2011a). *Digest of education statistics, 2010* (NCES 2011-015). Washington, DC: Author.

National Center for Education Statistics. (2011b). *Enrollment in postsecondary institutions, fall 2009; graduation rates, 2003 & 2006 cohorts.* Washington, DC: Author.

National Science Board. (2007). *A national action plan for addressing the critical needs of the U.S. science, technology, engineering, and mathematics education system.* Arlington, VA: National Science Foundation.

National Science Foundation, Division of Science Resources Statistics. (2009). *Science and engineering degrees by race/ethnicity: 1997–2006* (NSF 10-300), Table 1. Washington, DC: Author.

National Science Foundation, National Center for Science and Engineering Statistics. (2011). *Women, minorities, and persons with disabilities in science and engineering: 2011.* Special report NSF 11-309. Arlington, VA: National Science Board.

National Science Foundation, National Center for Science and Engineering Statistics. (2011). *Science and engineering degrees: 1966–2008* (NSF 11-316). Arlington, VA: National Science Board.

Obama, B. (2009, November). Educate to innovate—Campaign for Excellence in Science. Technology, Engineering & Math (Stem) Education. Speech presented at the White House, Office of the Press Secretary, Washington, DC.

San Antonio Prefreshman Engineering Program. (2011). *San Antonio prefreshman engineering program.* Retrieved from http://www.prep-usa.org/portal/saprep/

Sutton, E. M. (2006). Developmental mentoring of African American college men. In M. J. Cuyjet (Ed.), *African American men in college* (pp. 95–111). San Francisco, CA: Jossey-Bass.

Walsh, B. W., & Heppner, M. J. (2006). Career counseling for women in science, technology, engineering, and mathematics (STEM) fields. In W. B. Walsh & M. J. Heppner, *Handbook of career counseling for women* (2nd ed., pp. 427–452). Mahwah, NJ: Erlbaum.

9

ACADEMIC AND SOCIAL INTEGRATION FOR STUDENTS OF COLOR IN STEM

Examining Differences between HBCUs and Non-HBCUs

Idara Essien-Wood and J. Luke Wood

In 2005, the U.S. Government Accountability Office (GAO) released a report indicating that there is a need to train more higher education students in the fields of science, technology, engineering, and mathematics (STEM) if the United States is to remain a leader in the global market economy. The report noted that the federal government has invested billions of dollars in efforts to develop more STEM graduates; however, these efforts have not drastically increased the overall number of STEM degree holders. As a result, the government has initiated programs to cultivate women STEM majors and STEM majors of color from the United States as these populations have much room for degree production growth.

A large portion of the degrees awarded to African Americans in these fields comes from historically Black colleges and universities (HBCU). In fact, 20.7% of all STEM degrees awarded are from HBCUs. Further, Perna and colleagues (2009) noted that 17 out of the top 20 postsecondary institutions producing the highest number of Black STEM graduates were HBCUs. In addition to production levels, Fries–Britt (1998) explained that HBCUs have higher graduation rates among Black students in STEM in comparison to PWIs. Though a large number of STEM degrees come from HBCUs, the vast majority of Black (and other students of color) who graduate with degrees in STEM are from non-HBCUs (Hoffman, Llaga, & Synder, 2003).

With the high production of STEM graduates from HBCUs, the researchers were interested in whether this differential success in graduate production is a byproduct of differential experiences. In particular, experiences relevant to students' integration into the campus setting were of interest. Thus, the purpose of this chapter was to examine whether first-time students of color majoring in STEM had differential academic and social integration experiences at HBCUs in comparison to non-HBCUs. This research employed a two-stage design, comparing integration experiences between these institutional types; the usefulness of institutional type in predicting integration experiences was then determined while employing relevant controls.

Relevant Literature

While millions of students attend college every year, it is known that not all students will succeed. Nearly a century of inquiry has been dedicated to understanding what enables some students to persist in college where others fail. Numerous theories have been advanced using organizational, environmental, economic, psychological, and sociological models to provide insight into the retention phenomena, the predominant being Tinto's interactional theory (Braxton, 2000; Braxton & Hirschy, 2005; Braxton, Hirschy, & McClendon, 2004). Tinto's (1988, 1993) sociological theory views student persistence from a longitudinal perspective. Tinto (1988, 1993) suggests that colleges have academic and social systems that students' interact with on a continual basis. When students interact with these systems, the result is a constant modification of academic goals as assessment of dedication to the institution. Tinto (1988, 1993) noted that increased levels of involvement in college result in greater commitment to the institution; further, enhanced commitment leads to an increased likelihood of completion. Integration into the campus setting is fostered through both formal and informal engagements. His theory was informed by Durkheim's theory of suicide which proffered that individuals are more likely to commit suicide when they are not sufficiently integrated into society. As such, Tinto (1988, 1993) stated that when students become more involved in the academic and social milieu of an institution, they are more likely to persist.

In the 1980s, research from Pascarella and Terenzini (1980) led to the refinement of constructs relevant to academic and social integration. Specifically, Pascarella and Terenzini (1980) and Terenzini, Lorang, and Pascarella (1981) identified the following constructs as being indicative of integration: peer–group interactions, faculty–student interactions, students perception of faculty concern for students' success and their commitment to teaching, student satisfaction and interest in their academic and intellectual development, and institutional commitment. Contemporarily, these constructs have been operationalized where academic integration refers to experiences which foster academic development and motivation. Often this includes analyses of teacher–student interaction on academic matters or personal matters, student participation in study groups, and usage of academic support services such as the library, computing services, tutoring, counseling, and career centers. Social integration refers to experiences that lead to psychosocial development and involvement in the social fabric of a campus environment. Usually, social integration is measured through student interaction with peers on-campus/off-campus and participation in campus activities including: Greek life, clubs/organizations, student government, athletics, and cultural activities (Dougherty & Kienzl, 2006; Gonzalez & Ting, 2008; Jones, 2010; Severiens & Schmidt, 2008).

Extant research on STEM majors at HBCUs has affirmed the importance of Tinto's (1988, 1993) framework. For instance, Palmer, Davis, and Peters (2008) suggested that the success of Morgan State University's STEM programs are a result of the programs' adherence to Tinto's (1998, 1993) framework. They stated that several programs at the campus foster students' integration by providing a nurturing/supportive environment, faculty to peer mentoring, peer to peer mentoring, establishing high expectations, creating student support groups, and by providing advice and tutoring services. Similarly, Palmer, Davis, and Thompson (2010) highlighted four STEM initiatives at HBCUs noting that the strength of these programs were their focus on facilitating the academic and social integration of students. This was evident in programming which aids students in transitioning to the highly rigorous expectations of STEM programs and exposing them to support resources to facilitate their success. They noted that these efforts were accomplished through research training and mentoring.

Fries-Britt, Burt, and Franklin (2012) examined the experiences of Black male physics majors at HBCUs. Their investigation found that establishing relationships with faculty, students, and campus administration served to facilitate their success in college. Further, they noted that students who had previously attended non-HBCU campuses noted differential interactions with faculty. In particular, these students described having distant relationships or feeling "put down" by faculty at non-HBCUs. In contrast, faculty at HBCUs approached students first, engaged them in discussions, and motivated them to perform rigorously. Students in their study also described the importance of peer interactions, noting that peers encouraged one another, shared information on navigating coursework and policies, and tutored one another. A. M. Flowers' (2012) investigation of Black male engineering males attending HBCUs illustrated findings in line with those from previous academicians. He stated that "participant's ability to integrate academically and socially in their engineering programs was a critical factor in their success" (p. 169). In his study, engineering majors created communities of learners where they worked collaboratively and established friendships. Specifically, Flowers highlighted the importance of faculty–student interactions stating that faculty mentored students, created a supportive environment, tutored students, helped students network, and provided career advice. Overall, previous research on STEM majors in HBCUs seems to indicate that integration experiences are fostered.

Methods

This study employed the L. A. Flowers (2006) study of social and academic integration as a methodological framework. Flowers (2006) examined social and academic integration experiences between Black male students in 2- and 4-year degree granting institutions. In the first stage of his analysis, he compared mean scores (using independent t-tests) of background characteristics and integration variables to determine whether institutional type resulted in differential integration patterns. In the second phase of his analysis, Flowers employed a composite measure of academic and social integration to determine the effect of institutional type on integration. These analyses were conducted using ordinary least squares regression and employed the background characteristics and several other variables as statistical controls. This study will employ a similar analytic process as used in the Flowers study.

Data Collection

The intent of this chapter was to understand whether differential academic and social integration experiences existed between students of color in STEM in HBCUs and non-HBCUs. To explore these integration experiences, data were drawn from the Beginning Postsecondary Students Longitudinal Study (BPS). BPS is a national survey of collegians conducted by the National Center for Education Statistics (NCES). The purpose of BPS is to provide information on the postsecondary experiences of collegians. Specifically, BPS provides researchers and policymakers with information on topics that include, but are not limited to: student demographics, attendance patterns, course taking, persistence and attainment, financial aid, community service, and student goals (Cominole, Riccobono, Siegel, Caves, & Rosen, 2008).

BPS is a panel study which follows a cohort of first-time collegians over a 6-year period. The study is conducted in three waves; in the first wave students are surveyed at the end of their first year in college. The second and third wave followed up with collegians after years 3 and 6, respectively (Cominole, Riccobono, Siegel & Caves, 2010; Wine, Cominole, & Caves, 2009). Of particular focus in this study were the integration experiences of first-time students after their first year of enrollment. This study employed data from first-time students from two separate BPS cohorts, the 1995–1996 initial survey year and the 2003–2004 initial survey year. Using data from two panels allowed the researchers to examine integration experiences which were not solely limited to one period of time.

From these BPS cohort populations, data were delimited by race and major. Respondents included in the analyses were students of color, defined in this research as including all non-White students. Data were further delimited to students who, during their initial response year, were majoring in programs in life sciences, physical sciences, mathematics, computer or information sciences, and engineering. As a result, the sample populations included in these analyses were limited to 600 students from the 1995–1996 cohort and 800 students from the 2003–2004 cohort.

Variables

Multiple outcome variables across the 1995–1996 and 2003–2004 BPS were used to investigate integration. This study employed two types of variables, single item responses and composite scales. These variables were coded on an ordinal scale ranging from 1 to 3, coded as never (1), sometimes (2), and often (3). With respect to academic integration, four single item variables and one composite variable were collected during 1995–1996 and 2003–2004. The four academic integration variables included: (a) *met with advisor,* the frequency in which a student met with their academic advisor during their initial year in college; (b) *social contact with faculty,* the frequency in which students had social/ informal interactions with faculty which did not occur in the classroom or in faculty members' offices; (c) *participation in study groups,* the frequency in which student engaged in study groups which occurred outside of the classroom; and (d) *talked with faculty,* the frequency in which students discussed academic matters with faculty outside of class time. The composite variable employed, the academic integration index, was a measure of all academic integration items.

Unlike the academic integration variable, many social integration measures differed across the 1995–1996 and 2003–2004 panels. While the 1995–1996 panel had five single item variables and one composite variable, the 2003–2004 panel had three single item variables and one composite variable. One single item variable was the same across panels; *participated in school clubs,* which indicated the frequency in which students participated in student government, clubs/organizations, services activities, and religious organizations. In the 1995–1996 panel, students responded to integration questions including: (a) *participated in fine arts,* the frequency with which students engaged in fine arts (e.g., music, choir, drama) and related activities; (b) *played intramural sports,* the frequency with which students participated in nonvarsity, club, or intramural (intercampus) sports; (c) *played varsity sports,* the frequency of students' participation in intercollegiate athletics; and (d) *went places with friends,* the frequency with which students went out (e.g., concerts, eateries, sporting events, movies) with their friends. Also included in the 1995–1996 data was a composite scale which measured frequency of participation in social integration activities. The 2003–2004 had more limited options for variables than the 1995–1996 data. However, the variables included in this cohort panel were: (a) *participation in fine arts,* the frequency with which respondents attended fine arts activities including music, choir, drama, or other arts-based activities. Note that this question is concerned with attendance at fine arts activities while the previous panel was interested in respondents' participation in fine arts; and (b) *participated in club sports,* indicating the frequency with which students participated in nonvarsity, club, or intramural (intercampus) sports as well as intercollegiate athletics. BPS 2003–2004 also included a composite scale that measured participation in social integration activities.

In addition to the aforementioned variables, several control variables (also referred to as background characteristics) were employed in this study: (a) age, (b) income percentile rank, (c) high school grade point average, (d) admissions test scores, (e) highest degree expected, and (f) hours worked per week.

Analytic Technique

Data in this study were analyzed in two stages with the first using independent samples t-tests and the second employing ordinary least squares regression. Several statistical controls were employed in this study which may impact students' level of integration or ability to integrate into the campus setting. These controls included: age, income percentile rank, high school grade point average, SAT/ACT composite score, educational aspirations, and number of hours worked per week.

Results

Background characteristics examined in this study illustrated *some* differences between student of color STEM majors at HBCUs and non-HBCUs. In terms of the 1995–1996 cohort, HBCU STEM majors tended to be younger than their non-HBCU counterparts, $t = -3.70$, $p < .001$. Also, HBCU STEM majors had higher degree goals, $t = 2.83$, $p < .01$ than their non-HBCU counterparts. No other between group differences were evident. In terms of the 2003–2004 cohort, HBCU STEM majors of color still tended to be younger than their non-HBCU counterparts, $t = -5.09$, $p < .001$. Further, HBCU students also had significantly lower admissions test scores than their peers attending non-HBCU institutions, $t = -2.71$, $p < .01$. Differential work patterns were also evident between institutional types. Students attending HBCUs worked fewer hours than students attending non-HBCUs, $t = -2.57$, $p < .01$. Unlike students from the 1995–1996 panel, no significant differences existed by highest degree expected

Findings from this study revealed that first-time, student of color STEM majors have differential integration experiences at HBCUs and non-HBCUs. This was apparent by higher mean scores in every academic and social integration category examined across both the 1995–1996 and 2004–2006 waves. Academic integration of first-time STEM majors of color illustrated important differences between students at HBCUs and non-HBCUs. In the 1995–1996 cohort, the only nonsignificant mean difference identified was specific to social

TABLE 9.1 *Background Characteristics: STEM Majors of Color at HBCUs and Non-HBCUs*

	HBCUs		Non-HBCUs	
	Mean	*SE*	*Mean*	*SE*
1995–1996				
Age first year	18.1	0.31	20.6★★★	0.60
Income percentile rank	41.5	3.65	37.8	2.43
HS GPA	5.8	0.38	5.8	0.13
Admissions test scores	817.6	44.1	856.1	16.7
Highest degree	6.1★★	0.24	5.3	0.15
Hours worked per week	14.0	2.74	16.4	1.53
2003–2004				
Age first year	18.7	0.29	21.6★★★	0.49
Income percentile rank	35.3	5.29	37.9	1.31
HS GPA	5.6	0.26	5.9	0.06
Admissions test scores	872.8	24.0	955.4★★	18.8
Highest degree	5.9	0.29	5.5	0.09
Hours worked per week	9.8	2.30	16.1★★	0.84

Note: ★ = $p < .05$, ★★ = $p < .01$, ★★★ = $p < .001$

contact with faculty (see Table 9.1). As a result, the null hypothesis that students would have no differences in their frequency of academic engagement (excluding social/informal interactions with faculty) was accepted. In contrast, all the remaining items illustrated statistically significant differences in academic integration. For example, STEM majors at HBCUs were significantly more likely to meet with academic advisors, $t = 2.88$, $p < .01$, participate in study groups outside of the classroom, $t = 7.45$, $p < .001$, and talk with faculty about academic matters, $t = 3.93$, $p < .001$.

Data on academic integration from the 2003–2004 BPS illustrated a similar pattern as that from the 1995–1996 cohort. First-time students of color majoring in STEM fields were more likely to benefit from enhanced academic integration experiences, with two of the four items examined illustrating significant differences. While these students were not found to be significantly more likely to meet with their academic advisors ($p = $ ns) or to participate in study groups ($p = $ ns), they were more likely to interact with faculty members. Study findings indicated that STEM majors of color at HBCUs were significantly more likely to have social/informal contact with faculty outside of the classroom or office hours than their non-HBCU counterparts, $t = 5.27$, $p < .001$. Further, HBCU students were also significantly more likely to discuss academic matters with faculty outside of class time than non-HBCU students, $t = 5.25$, $p < .001$.

Findings from this study's analyses illustrated that there were some social integration differences between students of color in STEM in HBCUs and non-HBCUs. With respect to the 1995–1996 panel, two of the five single item variables were significant. For example, while STEM majors of color had higher mean participation in school clubs, playing intramural sports, and playing varsity, none of these differences were statistically significant (p = ns). Thus, in these cases, we failed to reject the null hypotheses. However, STEM majors of color were more likely to participate in fine arts-related activities (e.g., music, choir, drama) at HBCUs than at non-HBCUs, t = 4.62, p < .001. Further, these students were also more likely to go places (e.g., concerts, eateries, sporting events, movies) with friends, t = 3.61, p < .001.

The 2003–2004 cohort illustrated no significant differences on social integration experiences during their first year of college. STEM majors of color at HBCUs were not significantly more likely to participate in school clubs, attend fine arts activities, or participate in school sports (e.g., varsity, nonvarsity, club) (p = ns).

In stage 2 of the research design, this study sought to determine the effect of institutional type (e.g., HBCU vs. non-HBCU) on academic and social integration among STEM students of color. To examine the predictability of institutional type, composite measures of academic and social integration were employed. In all cases (even with the social integration index from the 2003–2004 cohort which illustrated no single item differences) significant differences were detected. Significant differences were detected in the academic integration measures from the 1995–1996 cohort, t = 3.50, p < .001 and 2003–2004 cohort, t = 4.28, p < .001. Differences were also identified in social integration measures from the 1995–1996 cohort, t = 3.34, p < .001 and 2003–2004 cohort, t = 2.12, p < .05.

Four regression models were created to examine the effect of institutional type on integration. Controlling for factors that could influence integration patterns, this study found that students attending HBCUs reported significant more academic integration experiences than their peers attending non-HBCUs in both the 1995–1996 (b = 33.103, p < .001) and 2003–2004 (b = 27.622, p < .001) cohorts. However, the effect of institution type on social integration did not illustrate similar findings. While institutional type was minimally predictive of social integration in 1995–1996 (b = 16.645, p < .05), no effect was seen among the 2003–2004 cohort (b = 8.255, p = ns). While the regression analyses indicated significant findings across the 1995–1996 and 2003–2004 cohorts on academic integration and the 1995–1996 cohort on social integration, the R^2 illustrated that the models accounted for only 13% to 16% of the variance in integration. As a result, approximately 84% to 87% of the variance in academic and social integration among STEM majors of color is not attributable to institutional differences between HBCUs and non-HBCUs.

TABLE 9.2 *Academic Integration among Students of Color in STEM, 1995–1996 and 2003–2004*

	t-value	HBCUs		Non-HBCUs	
		Mean	*SE*	*Mean*	*SE*
1995–1996					
Met with advisor	2.88★★	2.3	.12	1.9	.07
Social contact with faculty	1.71	1.8	.10	1.6	.06
Participation in study groups	7.45★★★	2.3	.27	1.8	.09
Talked with faculty	3.93★★★	2.3	.09	1.8	.09
2003–2004					
Met with academic advisor	.77	1.0	.12	.9	.05
Social contact with faculty	5.27★★★	1.0	.09	0.5	.03
Participation in study groups	1.71	1.0	.10	.8	.06
Talked with faculty	5.25★★★	1.3	.07	.9	.03

Note: ★ = $p < .05$, ★★ = $p < .01$, ★★★ = $p < .001$

Discussion and Implications

Overall, findings from this study illustrated that STEM majors of color attending HBCUs benefit from significantly greater levels of academic integration than their non-HBCU peers. Academic integration findings, particularly from the 2003–2004 cohort, illustrated that faculty interactions on academic and nonacademic matters is greater at HBCUs. This finding echoes research from previous scholars which extol HBCU faculty members' dedication and high levels of interaction with students (Flowers, 2012; Fries-Britt et al., 2012; Palmer, Davis, & Peters, 2008; Palmer, Davis, & Thompson, 2010). Specifically, Fries-Britt et al.'s (2012) study provided comments from students who had attended HBCUs and non-HBCUs who suggested that faculty members at HBCUs were more dedicated and supportive of students than those at other institutions. This research has affirmed these comments using national-level data across two cohorts of BPS.

There are a number of tenable factors which could lead to explain why differential interactions with faculty take place at HBCUs. However, two primary factors seem most relevant. First, Fries-Britt et al.'s (2012) study noted that minority students felt "put down" by faculty at non-HBCUs. Possibly, these "put downs" are evidence of racial microaggressions at non-HBCU institutions. Sue and colleagues (2007) defined racial microaggressions as "brief and commonplace daily verbal, behavioral, or environmental indignities, whether intentional or unintentional, that communicate hostile, derogatory, or negative racial slights and insults toward people of color" (p. 271). Key to this notion is that microaggressions are a form of racism which is subtle in nature (Delgado,

1987; Goodstein, 2008; Harwood, Huntt, & Mendenhall, 2009). Research from Essien-Wood (2010) indicated that microaggressive behaviors may be one explanation for differential integration experiences with faculty. Essien-Wood interviewed Black female STEM majors attending a large PWI. She noted evidence of pervasive microaggressions from faculty, who questioned students' academic abilities, intelligence, encouraged students to change their majors to social science and health-related fields, and largely avoided contact with students on campus and during office hours.

Second, another possible explanation for differential integration experiences has less to do with a negative environment at non-HBCUs and more with the supportive environment fostered at HBCUs. Many scholars have cited the supportive, familylike, and nurturing campus environment fostered at HBCUs (Allen, 1992; Allen, Jewell, Griffin, & Wolf, 2007; Berger & Milem, 2000; Bonous-Hammarth & Boatsman, 1996; Fleming, 1984; L. Flower, 2002; Fries-Britt & Turner, 2002; Kim, 2002; Outcalt & Skewes-Cox, 2002; Palmer & Gasman, 2008). Further, given the historical role of HBCUs in serving the needs of students of color and creating an environment specifically dedicated to their success (Palmer & Wood, 2012), students may be more predisposed to interacting with faculty at these institutions than at non-HBCUs.

Regardless of the rationale for differences in faculty interactions, there is much that non-HBCUs can learn from this study. Non-HBCUs must encourage their faculty to interact more with students of color.

- *In the classroom*: Often, the first domain in which students and faculty interact is in the classroom. Faculty must use classroom time to establish a rapport with students. Wood and Turner (2011) suggested four steps for positive faculty–student classroom interaction that may be useful: (a) faculty should be friendly and caring from the onset, expressing a genuine interest in students and their goals (e.g., academic, personal, career); (b) faculty should monitor students' progress, using classroom time to proactively discuss academic performance; (c) faculty should solicit and listen to students' concerns, illustrating their care for students by responding to issues raised; and (d) faculty, at all times, should be encouraging, illustrating their belief that students will be successful.

- *Office hours*: Faculty should regularly invite students to office hours. For example, students in the A. M. Flowers (2012) study noted that faculty maintained open-door policies, where students felt welcome to come to faculty offices for questions or support. If students attend office hours, faculty should use these opportunities to learn about students personally. The goal of all interactions should be to further students' academic self-efficacy, interest in their identified profession, and belief that faculty members are committed to their success.

- *Walking on campus*: This study noted that informal interactions differed significantly between HBCUs and non-HBCUs. When on campus, in the hallways, or even off campus, faculty can acknowledge students' presence, and illustrate welcoming and affirmative body language. Preferably, faculty should stop to talk with students, using informal interactions to establish/ maintain rapport with students, illustrate authentic care, and discuss nonacademic matters (when appropriate). Exchanges should go beyond the superficial. Faculty can use out of class conversations to provide students with feedback on their contributions in class, discuss opportunities to participate in research projects, or to encourage students to pursue internships in industry.

As illustrated by study findings, there is much that non–HBCUs can learn about students' integration in STEM fields from HBCUs. In all, these recommendations may serve as a starting point to better facilitate the academic integration of STEM majors of color at non-HBCUs.

Limitations and Future Research

As with any research, this study had limitations. First, the data presented represent two distinct points in time (1995–1996 and 2003–2004). As a result, findings may not be applicable to first-year students of color in STEM beyond the years examined. Further, the L. A. Flowers (2006) investigations of BPS integration constructs revealed low coefficient alphas, .72 for academic integration and .59 for social integration. As a result, individual items examined should be considered and interpreted in and of themselves as opposed to as part of fully developed integration constructs. Further, due to sample size limitations among students of color in STEM, analyses were not conducted which disaggregated students by racial/ethnic affiliation (e.g., Black, Hispanic, Asian) or STEM majors type (e.g., life sciences, physical sciences, mathematics, computer/information sciences, and engineering). Thus, there may be nuances to students' integration experiences that were not captured. Finally, the measures of social and academic integration in this study focus on the frequency of interaction; however, they do not measure the quality of the interactions. As such, this study does not account for the meaningfulness of integration.

Further research should be conducted which investigates why differential integration occurs between HBCUs and non-HBCUs. This research can be qualitative in nature, eliciting the voices of STEM majors of color to better understand barriers and supports to their academic integration. Given sample limitations, this study was unable to explore the effect of institutional type on integration within specific STEM fields. Further research can use primary data to explore whether integration varies among field. This would allow academicians to better understand academic and social integration patterns in fields with more limited student enrollment (e.g., physics, astronomy). Any primary research conducted should consider employing a greater number of social and academic integration items, this would enable researchers to go learn more than the minimal number of BPS integration variables provides. Further, having more (and possibly better) measures of integration may account for greater variance than existed in the models produced in this study.

References

Allen, W. R. (1992). The color of success: African-American college student outcomes at predominantly White and historically Black public colleges and universities. *Harvard Educational Review, 62*(1), 26–44.

Allen, W. R., Jewell, J. O., Griffin, K. A., & Wolf, D. S. (2007). Historically Black colleges and universities: Honoring the past, engaging the present, touching the future. *Journal of Negro Education, 76*(3), 263–280.

Berger, J. B., & Milem, J. F. (2000). Exploring the impact of historically Black colleges in promoting the development of undergraduates' self-concept. *Journal of College Student Development, 41*(4), 381–394.

Bonous-Hammarth, M., & Boatsman, K. (1996). *Satisfaction guaranteed? Predicting academic and social outcomes for African American college students.* Paper presented at the Annual Conference of the American Educational Research Association, New York.

Braxton, J. M. (2000). Introduction: Reworking the student departure puzzle. In J. M. Braxton (Ed.), *Reworking the student departure puzzle* (pp. 1–8). Nashville, TN: Vanderbilt University Press.

Braxton, J. M., & Hirschy, A. S. (2005). Theoretical developments in the study of college student departure. In A. Seidman (Ed.), *College student retention: Formula for student success* (pp. 61–87). Westport, CT: Praeger.

Braxton, J. M., Hirschy, A. S., & McClendon, S. A. (2004). *Understanding and reducing college student departure* (ASHE-ERIC Higher Education Research Report No. 3). San Francisco, CA: Jossey-Bass.

Cominole, M., Riccobono, J., Siegel, P., & Caves, L. (2010). *2007–08 National Postsecondary Student Aid Study (NPSAS:08): Full-scale methodology report* (NCES 2011-188). Washington, DC: National Center for Education Statistics, U.S. Department of Education. Retrieved from http://nces.ed.gov/pubsearch

Cominole, M., Riccobono, J., Siegel , P., Caves, L., & Rosen, J. (2008). 2008 *National postsecondary student aid study* (NPSAS:08): *Field test methodology report* (NCES 2008-01). Washington, DC: National Center for Education Statistics, Institute of Education Sciences, U.S. Department of Education.

Delgado, R. (1987). The ethereal scholar: Does critical legal studies have what minorities want? *Harvard Civil Rights-Civil Liberties Law Review, 22,* 301–322.

Dougherty, K. J., & Kienzl, G. S. (2006). It's not enough to get through the open door: Inequalities by social background in transfer from community colleges to four-year colleges. *Teachers College Record, 108*(3), 452–487.

Essien-Wood, I. R. (2010). *Undergraduate African American females in the sciences: A qualitative study of student experiences affecting academic success and persistence* (Unpublished doctoral dissertation). Arizona State University, Tempe.

Fleming, J. (1984). *Blacks in college: A comparative study of student success in Black and White institutions.* San Francisco, CA: Jossey-Bass.

Flowers, A. M. (2012). Academically gifted Black male undergraduates in engineering: Perceptions of factors contributing to their success in a historically Black college and university. In R. T. Palmer & J. L. Wood (Eds.), *Black men in college: Implications for HBCUs and beyond* (pp. 163–175). New York: Routledge.

Flowers, L. (2002). The impact of college racial composition on African American students' academic and social gains: Additional evidence. *Journal of College Student Development, 43*(3), 403–410.

Flowers, L. A. (2006). Effects of attending a two-year institution on African American males' academic and social integration in the first year of college. *Teachers College Record, 108*(2), 267–286.

Fries-Britt, S. (1998). Moving beyond Black achiever isolation: Experiences of gifted Black collegians. *Journal of Higher Education, 69*(5), 556–576.

Fries-Britt, S., Burt, B., & Franklin, K. (2012). Establishing critical relationships: How Black males persist in physics at HBCUs. In R. T. Palmer & J. L. Wood (Eds.), *Black men in college: Implications for HBCUs and beyond* (pp. 71–88). New York: Routledge.

Fries-Britt, S., & Turner, B. (2002). Uneven stories: Successful Black collegians at a Black and a White campus. *Review of Higher Education, 25*(3), 315–330.

Gonzalez, L. M., & Ting, S. R. (2008). Adjustment of undergraduate Latino students at a southeastern university: Cultural components of academic and social integration. *Journal of Hispanic Higher Education, 7*(3), 199–211.

Goodstein, R. (2008). What's missing from the dialogue on racial microaggressions in counseling and therapy. *Journal of American Psychologist, 63*(4) 276–277.

Harwood, S., Huntt, M. B., & Mendenhall, R. (2009) *Racial microaggressions and the University of Illinois at Urbana-Champaign: Preliminary analysis of focus groups with students of color living in university housing.* Urbana-Champaign, IL: Center on Democracy in a Multiracial Society.

Hoffman, K., Llaga, C., & Snyder, T. D. (2003). *Status and trends in the education of Blacks.* Washington, DC: National Center for Education Statistics.

Jones, W. A. (2010). The impact of social integration on subsequent institutional commitment conditional on gender. *Research in Higher Education, 51*(7), 687–700.

Kim, M. M. (2002). Historically Black vs. White institutions: Academic development among Black students. *Review of Higher Education, 25*(4), 385–407.

Outcalt, C. L., & Skewes-Cox, T. E., (2002). Involvement, interaction, and satisfaction: The human environment at HBCUs. *Review of Higher Education, 25*(3), 331–347.

Palmer, R. T., Davis, R. J., & Peters, K. A. (2008). Strategies for increasing African Americans in STEM: A descriptive study of Morgan State University's STEM programs. In N. Gordon (Ed.), *HBCU models of success: Successful models for increasing the pipeline of Black and Hispanic students in STEM areas* (pp. 129–146). New York: Thurgood Marshall College Fund.

Palmer, R.T., Davis, R. J., & Thompson, T. (2010). Theory meets practice: HBCU initiatives that promote academic success among African Americans in STEM. *Journal of College Student Development, 51*(4), 440–443.

Palmer, R. T., & Gasman, M. (2008). 'It takes a village to raise a child': The role of social capital in promoting academic success for African American men at a Black college. *Journal of College Student Development 49*, 52-70.

Palmer, R. T., & Wood, J. L. (Eds.). (2012). *Black men in college: Implications for HBCUs and beyond.* New York: Routledge.

Pascarella, E. T., & Terenzini, P.T. (1980). Freshman persistence and voluntary dropout decisions from a theoretical model. *Journal of Higher Education, 51*(1), 60–75.

Perna, L., Wagner-Lundy, V., Drezner, N. D., Gasman, M., Yoon, S., Bose, E., & Gary. S. (2009). The contribution of HBCUs to the preparation of African American women for STEM careers: A case study. *Research in Higher Education, 50*(1), 1–23.

Severiens, S. E., & Schmidt, H. G. (2008). Academic and social integration and study progress in problem based learning. *Higher Education, 58*(1), 59–69.

Sue, D. W., Capodilupo, C. M., Torino, G. C., Bucceri, J. M., Holder, A. M. B., Nadal, K. L., & Esquilin, M. (2007). Racial microaggresions in everyday life: Implications for clinical practice. *American Psychologist, 62*(4), 271–286.

Terenzini, P. T., Lorang, W. G., & Pascarella, E. T. (1981). Predicting freshman persistence and voluntary dropout decisions: A replication. *Research in Higher Education, 15*(2), 109–127.

Tinto, V. (1988). Stages of student departure: Reflections on the longitudinal character of student leaving. *Journal of Higher Education, 59*(4), 438–455.

Tinto, V. (1993). *Leaving college: Rethinking the causes and cures of student attrition* (2nd ed.). Chicago, IL: University of Chicago Press.

U.S. Government Accountability Office (US GAO). (2005). *Higher education: Federal science, technology, engineering, and mathematics programs and related trends.* Washington, DC: Author.

Wine, J., Cominole, M., & Caves, L. (2009). *2004/09 Beginning Postsecondary Students Longitudinal Study (BPS:04/09) field test* (NCES 2009-01). Washington, DC: National Center for Education Statistics, Institute of Education Sciences, U.S. Department of Education.

Wood, J. L., & Turner, C. S. V. (2011). Black males and the community college: Student perspectives on faculty and academic success. *Community College Journal of Research & Practice, 35,* 1–17.

10

BROADENING PARTICIPATION IN STEM

Policy Implications of a Diverse Higher Education System

Lorelle L. Espinosa and Carlos Rodríguez

From practically every vantage point, our nation and our world are increasingly dependent on scientific and technological innovation and those policies that support the implementation of innovative solutions to our toughest societal challenges. One need only assess our everyday use of technology to appreciate just how reliant on it we have become. In addition to modern day devices, we seek a world in which medical research can pave the way for an increasingly healthy and disease-free society, a world where we can develop effective tools to keep our natural resources sustainable for future generations. The security of our nation via advanced military technology and information systems also rests on our capacity for innovation. Indeed, every aspect of our lives is touched by science, technology, engineering, and mathematics (STEM).

While there is a great need to expand innovation in STEM fields, there is a current policy dimension to this story; one that is both necessary and urgent. If we do not equip the whole of society with opportunities to prepare for and succeed in STEM fields, America will not meet its human capital and technological needs; in fact, we are already seeing signs that this is the case. Over the last 50 years, more than half of our country's economic growth has resulted from the growth of STEM fields (Babco, 2004), with computer and mathematics disciplines growing by 78% between 1997 and 2007 (U.S. Department of Labor, 2007). Not surprisingly, 17 out of the 20 fastest growing occupations are also in STEM (U.S. Bureau of Labor Statistics, 2010), and will continue to represent some of the highest paying jobs in the country today (Carnevale, Smith, & Melton, 2011).

Linking this to a rapidly changing American demographic, it becomes immediately apparent that in order to meet the nation's growing need for

STEM professionals we must accelerate the supply of STEM degrees and credentials from America's own. Racial and ethnic minorities, women and men, are the largest untapped pool of STEM talent in the United States. Compared to what might be expected based on census estimates and despite significant public and private investments in STEM at the postsecondary level, women and men remain seriously underrepresented in educational pathways to STEM careers (Museus, Palmer, Davis, & Maramba, 2011).

It is not, however, as if we have covered no ground. There has been noteworthy progress in graduating more underrepresented minority (URM) students, in particular, in recent decades. Part of this movement can be attributed to federal investment in STEM educational outreach and retention programs and part to a number of other factors including general increases in college-going rates and the strengthening of targeted outreach by institutions of higher education. Yet, while such progress is observable, it remains woefully inadequate given the rapid growth of racial and ethnic minority populations and our scientific and technological needs as a nation. To deny this is to deny that U.S. STEM workforce preparation among diverse populations is not in crisis and does not need improvement. Reframing the conceptual and practical steps to diversity and equity in STEM are thus necessary and must be at the core of the scientific enterprise.

From a concrete perspective, this means aggressive and ongoing assessment of America's higher education institutions across the spectrum of 2- and 4-year colleges and universities, those that serve critical masses of racial and ethnic minorities as well as those that do not. All institutions are thus challenged to expand and enhance their capacity to graduate more minority students in STEM. While the authors acknowledge that higher education is not the only critical player in increasing the number of diverse STEM graduates, the post-secondary community *is* the most equipped to respond and fundamentally change the trajectory of underrepresented students seeking to enter the STEM workforce.

It is with this imperative in mind that we collaborated on the Broadening Participation in STEM project, with funding from the National Science Foundation (NSF)[1] and with the support of a diverse advisory board of STEM professionals, higher education thought leaders, and education officials. The project's objectives were to inform NSF's approach to broadening participation in STEM disciplines, particularly at the undergraduate level, through a number of mechanisms including data analysis and focused input and discussion by key higher education stakeholders. While NSF is not the only federal agency that invests in diversity-focused education programs, it is perhaps the most visible entity because of its years of giving to the minority serving institution (MSI) community and for the agency's recent proposal to restructure this funding.

Background

Diversifying STEM: The Current Political Landscape

In March of 2010, then NSF director Dr. Arden Bement proposed to the House Science and Technology Subcommittee on Research and Science Education the elimination of several NSF-funded programs: the historically Black Colleges and Universities-Undergraduate Program (HBCU-UP),[2] Tribal Colleges and Universities Program (TCUP),[3] and Louis Stokes Alliance for Minority Participation (LSAMP).[4] Instead of funding these programs as distinct entities, Bement proposed a combined or "comprehensive" model and with it a modest funding increase for NSF's Education and Human Resources (EHR) directorate so that it could further support Hispanic serving institutions (HSIs)[5] as part of this comprehensive program; this despite the fact that HSIs and other MSIs would be competing not only with each other, but also with predominantly White serving institutions. According to NSF officials, this effort was one component of a larger strategic imperative to strengthen EHR's mission and promote innovation at the institutional level through incentives associated with a competitive proposal process.

Director Bement further suggested that the strategy would ensure global acceleration of the United States in STEM fields through broad representation of the nation's individuals, geographic regions, and types of institutions educating current and future STEM professionals by promoting collaborations across colleges through required institutional partnerships (Testimony of Dr. Arden L. Bement, Jr., 2010). Some in the policy community suspected pressure from the Office of Management and Budget (OMB) to seek rapid progress in strengthening STEM education. OMB may have assumed that the consolidation of these programs would better leverage the federal return on investment in MSIs. This action, however, was perceived to overlook the historical and emerging place of these institutions in promoting underrepresented student access and success in higher education.

While this recommendation to merge programs may have been well-intentioned, the postsecondary education community—particularly the MSI sector and its supporters—responded with swift criticism. Constituents expressed frustration and deep concern that hard-fought momentum would be dismantled or otherwise diverted as a result, and thus lead to further loss of diverse STEM talent. In an open letter to NSF, the National Association for Equal Opportunity in Higher Education (NAFEO) stated:

> The Proposed merger would eliminate the complimentary, diverse approaches to increasing minority participation in STEM that has been yielding measurable results. The current, separate and distinct programs are targeted to meet and have been meeting the unique needs of HBCUs, the unique needs of TCUs and other MSIs as well as the unique needs of

the underrepresented student groups currently provided for in the separate programs.

(NAFEO, 2011)

NAFEO was not alone. Institutions and their associations across the MSI spectrum were quick to criticize the proposed consolidation and cited the disproportionately high number of minority STEM graduates produced by the MSI sector relative to its size.

The congressional response to NSF's proposal to merge minority-serving institutional programs was also swift. In its report to Congress, the Senate Committee on Appropriations denied NSF's request to merge the HBCU-UP, TCUP, and LSAMP programs. Contributing to this decision were comments made by Edie Bernice Johnson (D-TX) before the subcommittee on research and science education:

> In 2007, I offered an amendment which was incorporated in the original America COMPETES law which "directs the National Academies of the Sciences to compile a report, to be transmitted to the Congress no later than one year after the date of enactment of this Act, about barriers to increasing the number of underrepresented minorities in science, technology, engineering and mathematics fields and to identify strategies for bringing more underrepresented minorities into the science, technology, engineering and mathematics workforce." It concerns me and others on this committee that nearly three years later this report is yet to be seen.
>
> (Testimony by Edie Bernice Johnson, 2010)

As Johnson's account implies, without in-depth empirical understanding of both the challenges and successes experienced by the MSI community, as well as those encountered by the predominantly White institution (PWI) sector, it is a difficult task to effectively support all institutions.

The discussion, and at times fierce debate, among NSF officials, the MSI community, and congressional leaders, is indicative of just how important the advancement of STEM fields, and thus growth of America's scientific workforce, is to our national interest as a global player, as well as to the sensitive nature of broadening participation in STEM. President Obama and other presidents before him have placed great political attention on growing America's scientific and technological industries. Yet perhaps not since Sputnik have we seen such broad, sustained political and public attention to ensuring the prominence of American universities, federal agencies, and private industry in producing human capital and cutting-edge technology in support of the scientific enterprise. Via a Facebook town hall meeting in April 2011, President Obama stated, "We've got to lift our game up when it comes to STEM education.... That's hopefully the greatest legacy I can have as President of the United States."

Indeed, President Obama has reinvigorated the national conversation on

STEM productivity, not only through words but through action. According to John Holdren (2011), the Assistant to the President for Science and Technology and Director of the Office of Science and Technology Policy, the policy community has not seen such strong STEM presence amongst leadership in the administration, including first-time posts of Chief Information Officer and Chief Technology Officer in the Obama White House and an incredibly productive President's Council of Advisors on Science and Technology.

Moving beyond administration leadership, a number of new STEM education initiatives have begun with direct support of the White House, including *Change the Equation*, a nonprofit, nonpartisan CEO-led initiative that seeks to improve U.S. STEM education and *Educate to Innovate*, a youth-focused campaign with the support of leading companies, foundations, nonprofits, and science and engineering societies. Also publicly lauded by presidential appointees—including Secretary of Education Arne Duncan and Undersecretary of Education Martha Kanter—are STEM initiatives coming out of higher education associations in Washington, including the Association of American Universities (AAU), Association of Public and Land Grant Universities (APLU), and American Association of Colleges and Universities (AACU).

The political will that has been built just in the last 2 years has been great and it is not only for President Obama's emphasis on STEM education. Congressional leaders from both sides of the aisle have hosted major convenings on STEM education and the workforce and have introduced legislation to improve math and science education, some of which has been directed specifically at STEM diversity efforts. State-level activity has also increased as states are looking to their STEM enterprise for economic development and job creation. National state associations, including the National Governors Association, have procured funds to support the development of STEM talent at the state level and several individual states have already made great gains; including the states of Ohio, Massachusetts, Texas, Washington, and North Carolina. And yet, for great federal and state investments in STEM education, there remains the need to identify practices that if scaled up correctly could produce rapid gains. It is with this backdrop that the current project finds itself as a research and policy effort whose execution and findings may have great bearing on the future of STEM education policy in this country.

Broadening Participation in STEM Project

The Broadening Participation in STEM project's overarching purpose has involved undertaking a process of mixed methods analyses to enhance and improve upon NSF's approach to diversifying the STEM fields with ultimate bearing on other federal investments. Our objectives were to learn, understand, and recommend promising practices in attracting, enrolling, retaining, and completing more women, racial/ethnic minority, and students with disabilities in science and engineering at the 2- and 4-year levels; with an emphasis on 2-year retention and degree completion for the purposes of transfer. To do this, the project team engaged in four major activities, the first two of which are the focus of the current chapter:

1. A comprehensive trend analysis of STEM enrollment and graduation at 2- and 4-year institutions across the minority serving and nonminority serving institution spectrum;[6]
2. The convening of key stakeholders, including those from MSI and non-MSI communities, to discuss perceived challenges and successes in increasing the number of underrepresented students graduating with STEM degrees;
3. A policy roundtable with officials from the current administration, Department of Education, Department of Energy, NASA, National Institutes of Health (NIH), and other agencies that conduct outreach and otherwise support undergraduate STEM education;
4. The review and synthesis of literature specific to broadening participation program evaluation.

It is through these combined activities that the project team has arrived poised to provide NSF with the rationale, objectives, and suggestions for strengthening STEM education in colleges and universities across the country. More immediately, it is hoped that this work will complement and further extend NSF's intent to gather expert and stakeholder input that informs the foundation's broadening participation efforts.

Understanding the impact of broadening participation on increasing STEM diversity must take into account contextual factors as well as quantifiable, rigorous data. As such, the project team sought to both: (a) present longitudinal trend data on the progression of underrepresented populations in STEM over nearly 20 years, and (b) shed light on the meaning behind this data via guided interpersonal exchange amongst STEM education stakeholders. The project's focus on ensuring and elevating voices of faculty, staff, and institutional leaders out of the MSI community is especially important given the unique role that MSIs play.

Why MSIs?

While our project seeks to inform federal funding provided to both MSIs and non-MSIs, it is our belief that MSIs fill a critical niche in the preparation of minority students for the STEM workforce. It is further our belief that understanding this niche, and those educational practices that promote student success in STEM fields at MSIs, can ultimately strengthen the STEM education infrastructure for minority students in institutions of higher education writ large. Those institutions struggling to strengthen STEM education while simultaneously seeking to meet the educational and social needs of underrepresented groups are in search of models that schools of science and engineering can bring to scale. In this way, MSIs are in the position to inform institutions of all types.

National Center for Education Statistics (NCES; 2008) statistics show that between fall 1984 and fall 2004, minority undergraduate enrollment increased from 1.9 to 4.7 million across all institutions of higher education; a growth rate of 146%. During this same time period, the MSI sector grew to account for almost one-third (32%) of all degree-granting Title IV institutions; primarily due to growth by the HSI and predominantly Black institution (PBI) sectors. Across the higher education landscape, this increase in MSI presence is evident when considering their levels of minority student enrollment. In 1984, MSIs as a whole enrolled 38% of all minority students; in 1994, this proportion increased to 47%, and by 2004, more than half (58%) of minority students were enrolled in MSIs. In fact, HSIs enrolled approximately one-half of all Hispanic undergraduates in 2004 and these same institutions also enrolled 19%, 13%, and 11% of the total college enrollment of Asian American/Pacific Islander, American Indians, and Blacks, respectively. What these data clearly show is that minority students are making conscious choices to attend MSIs, and in large numbers.

Students are also entering community colleges—a large proportion of which are MSIs—in numbers never before seen. Community colleges represent the fastest-growing major segment of postsecondary education in the United States, and they are making great strides in diversifying the STEM workforce. In addition to granting terminal 2-year degrees and certificates, community colleges act as a bridge for students who want to attend 4-year institutions, and many if not most, would classify as an MSI by virtue of their minority student enrollments alone. Among minority students, many STEM graduates earned credits at community colleges toward their degrees and are often simultaneously enrolled in both 2- and 4-year institutions (NCES, 2008).

The aforementioned trend data produced by the Broadening Participation in STEM project point to the pivotal niche MSIs occupy in STEM degree production. As Figures 10.1 and 10.2 show, when compared to other institution types, HBCUs and HSIs graduate a higher percentage of Blacks and Hispanics, respectively, with STEM bachelor's degrees.

While STEM degree attainment by Black students has remained relatively steady, HBCUs continue to award the highest percentage of STEM degrees to Blacks (see Figure 10.3). So too, HSIs perform similarly when it comes to Hispanic STEM graduates (see Figure 10.4).

These and other stories have emerged from the many scholarly and practitioner chronicles on the role of MSIs in educating youth and adult minority student populations. Yet, we also know that MSIs cannot go it alone: If we are to make true gains in STEM degree production amongst our nation's

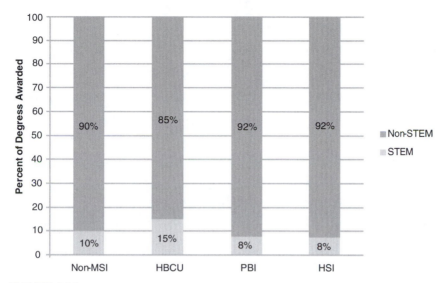

FIGURE 10.1 Percent of STEM bachelor's degrees awarded to Blacks by institution type, 2009

most underrepresented populations, then all institutions of higher education will need to greatly increase their capacity to educate students seeking STEM degrees; and they must also graduate these students in much higher numbers. The Obama Administration knows this, as does NSF and other federal agencies that both support and benefit from institutional efforts to produce more, diverse STEM graduates. Yet, given their recent history and unique role in funding MSIs to achieve these gains in particular, NSF has a rational and moral obligation to ensure their funds are being directed to the right institutions and are being utilized in the most effective way possible.

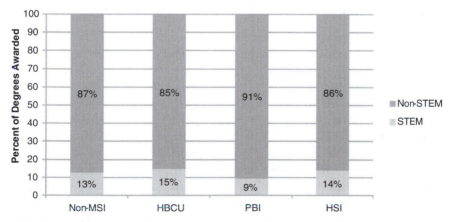

FIGURE 10.2 Percent of STEM bachelor's degrees awarded to Hispanics by institution type, 2009

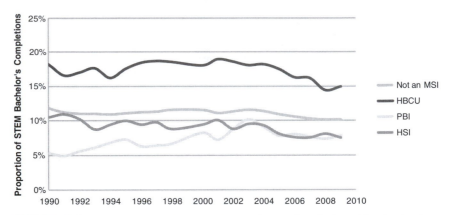

FIGURE 10.3 Percent of STEM bachelor's completions for Blacks, within institutions

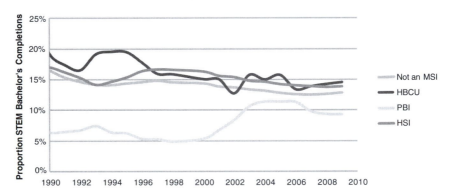

FIGURE 10.4 Percent of STEM bachelor's completions for Hispanics, within institutions

Stakeholder Voices

While national trend data is essentially descriptive in nature and thus reflective of outcomes alone, qualitative data provides a contextual backdrop to the stories that emerge from the statistics we provided NSF (of which a very small portion have been shared here). As experts in research, policy, and practice that promote attracting, retaining, and completing underrepresented groups in STEM fields at the postsecondary level, we know that learning from those working with students on-the-ground is critical to solving the STEM education crisis our nation is confronting. In conceptualizing the stakeholder convening portion of the project—our primary qualitative data source—we were intentional about ensuring that nearly all voices were heard: STEM faculty and department chairs, student affairs staff, academic deans and directors, STEM education researchers and scholars, those who employ STEM graduates, including leadership from national laboratories and major industries, professional STEM organizations, and leaders in STEM education thought.[7]

In early 2011, invitations to attend one of two springtime weekend convenings were sent to colleges and universities based on their inclusion in a sample drawn from a 2009–2010 restricted-access IPEDs dataset housed at the Institute for Higher Education Policy. The sample (n = 252) was drawn from a population of public and private 2- and 4-year institutions (N = 2,655) using four key institutional-level characteristics: (a) degree of urbanicity; (b) size (full-time equivalent undergraduates); (c) census region; and (d) presence of a medical school. This process oversampled for MSIs[8] and 2-year institutions and excluded institutions that graduated only a small number of STEM students. The final list was cross-referenced with a list of HBCU-UP, TCUP, and LSAMP participant campuses provided by NSF. To ensure adequate representation of these programs, the research team hand-selected additional institutions, taking into consideration the makeup of the sample to date (e.g., sector, location, etc.).

Hard-copy letter and e-mail invitations were sent to the chief academic officer on campus (most often the provost). The letter suggested that he or she either attend themselves or forward the invitation to someone on their campus who could best speak to issues of broadening participation in STEM. The letter further stated that if the campus participated in one of NSF's Broadening Participation programs, the provost may choose to send the principal investigator or program coordinator. Given a lack of initial response by campuses, the sampling technique described earlier was duplicated and institutions were contacted by project team staff via phone and e-mail. The selection of individuals not representing institutions was made based on project team knowledge of those organizations and individuals who have contributed to the diversity in STEM conversation on a national scale.

In the end, the following sectors were represented across the two weekend convenings as shown in Table 10.1.

TABLE 10.1 Profile of Stakeholder Convening Attendees

	Receive NSF Funding	Do Not Receive NSF Funding	Total
Total Institutions	35	40	75
HBCU	19	0	19
TCU	6	0	6
PBI	0	3	3
HSI	4	19	23
PWI	6	18	24
Thought Leaders			10
Advisory Council			8
Industry and Orgs			11
Students			1
Total Attendees			106

Of the 75 institutions present, 29 were community colleges and 46 were 4-year institutions from the following states: Alabama, Arizona, California, Delaware, Denver, District of Columbia, Florida, Georgia, Hawaii, Illinois, Kansas, Louisiana, Maryland, Massachusetts, Mississippi, Missouri, Montana, New Mexico, New Jersey, New York, North Carolina, North Dakota, Oregon, Pennsylvania, South Carolina, South Dakota, Tennessee, Texas, Washington, West Virginia, and Wisconsin. College and university faculty and staff attendees included: three assistant deans, four associate deans, 14 full deans, five provosts, nine vice presidents, and numerous assistant professors, associate professors, full professors, endowed professors, and program directors.

Given the diverse backgrounds of those individuals who were invited and ultimately participated in the weekend convenings, we sought to ensure a variety of participatory environments, so that individuals could both build upon what they heard from others and offer contrary evidence. This approach led to the facilitation of over 38 discrete, small focus group sessions of approximately 10 people each.[9] Participants were divided across the groups such that there were opportunities to talk amongst peer institutions (e.g., groups made up of HSIs or 2-year campuses alone), colleagues (e.g., groups made up of faculty or student affairs staff alone), and in some cases, STEM disciplines (e.g., groups made up of engineers alone). Representatives from professional organizations and STEM education thought leaders were most often placed across group settings. In addition to focus groups, the weekend convenings included presentations by the project team on preliminary quantitative findings and subsequent generative large group discussions.

As we conceived the protocol for our focus groups, we tried to keep in mind those questions that would lead to discussion of both expected similarities as well as differences across institutions. Focus group conversation took shape around three substantive lines of inquiry as it concerns broadening STEM higher education:

1. The relationship between national goals—namely, the production of more STEM graduates by colleges and universities—and the ways in which higher education measures success and is accountable to such aims;
2. The role of higher education, including the distinct role of discrete MSI sectors, PWIs, community colleges, and research institutions; and
3. The role of the federal government, and the National Science Foundation in particular, in ensuring an increasingly diverse STEM workforce.

It was our hope that by bringing together individuals working toward the same or similar goals in similar and different settings, learning would take shape for participants in real time with the potential for ongoing discussion and collaboration following the meeting.

Findings from Stakeholder Exchange

If there was one overarching take away from the hours of discussion amongst a wide variety of STEM higher education stakeholders over the weekend convenings in spring of 2011, it was that there is no singular directive for our nation's postsecondary institutions when it comes to diversifying STEM fields. Instead, there must be recognition and acknowledgment by federal and state governments, private industry, researchers, and all education practitioners, that different institutions play very different and unique roles in broadening STEM education and workforce. Parallel to this argument is a required understanding that all higher education institutions are complex organizations. MSIs are not less complex because they serve a majority of students who share similar cultural, ethnic, linguistic, racial, and other origins of diversity. So too, mainstream institutions of higher education represent a vast array of stand-alone colleges and universities with differing missions and academic and cultural climates. Two-year institutions face challenges and experience success in ways that are quite different from the challenges and experiences of their 4-year neighbors and vice versa. In short, from a complex higher education landscape emerges a complex set of institutional types within which there exists further diversity in terms of faculty, leadership, student body, and student outcomes.

Common Perspectives

There was agreement on a number of issues raised by focus group facilitators. First, as it concerns how policymakers should measure progress in broadening participation, participants expressed the need to look beyond degree attainment rates. While completion is important, it fails to address the multiple pathways that students take to receive STEM degrees and is unrepresentative of whether students progress into STEM careers once they leave the college campus. Participants argued that if the true outcome of the nation's great investment in STEM education is a representative cadre of STEM workers, as our nation's political and industry leaders claim, then there must exist broad measurements of institutional- and student-focused milestones in addition to degree outcomes. Suggestions to expand the definition of success included the representation of women and minority students across:

- *Attainment and transition*: 2- to 4-year transfer, attrition to non–STEM majors, course completion, acquisition of discrete skills, and percentage of students accepted to STEM graduate programs;
- *Student disposition and attitude*: intention to pursue a STEM career and relevance of coursework to career prospects;
- *Institutional measures*: faculty qualifications, number of tenured faculty, course quality as perceived by students and graduates measured against gainful employment; and

- *Resources:* availability of state of the art equipment, and research and internship opportunities.

Participants further contended that the baseline from which institutions begin to achieve these and other measures of success (including degree attainment) is incredibly varied. As such, any measure of success must be further couched within the context of institutions and institutional systems. Context measures may include student demographic characteristics such as socioeconomic and full- and part-time status; as well as institutional measures such as teaching and research capacity, research infrastructure, history and sources of funding, and gains made after an influx of funds. Once the appropriate benchmarks are established, they can be used to group institutions with others like them, allowing policymakers to make more accurate comparisons of progress for the purposes of resource distribution; including awards made by NSF and other federal agencies.

Another common sentiment across focus group sessions was the need for greater institutional accountability. As it concerns NSF funding, in particular, most stakeholders agreed that higher and more consistent accountability is needed for ongoing gains. Moreover, resources granted by NSF should include the capacity for proper evaluation. Criteria for such evaluation should be made clear in requests for proposals, and in response, institutions should be required to develop accountability plans as part of the proposal process. As already maintained, indicators of success must go beyond retention and graduation rates to include specific, measureable, and clearly documented outcomes. Said outcomes must be further couched within the unique contextual and cultural factors of individual institutions with distinctions made across departmental performance (i.e., instead of measures of institutions on the whole).

General consensus was also reached on readdressing the federal definition of underrepresented populations. In addition to targeting women, URMs, and persons with a disability, stakeholders suggested an expanded view of "underrepresented" as including students from low socioeconomic backgrounds and those with first-generation college-going status. Many felt that including these indicators across gender and racial/ethnic subgroups would provide a more comprehensive picture of what it means to successfully broaden participation in the STEM fields.

MSIs and Unique Points of Practice

Of the various types of institutions represented at the two stakeholder convenings, two sectors stood out from the rest. Throughout focus group sessions, faculty and staff representing community colleges and TCUs (which are predominantly 2-year institutions) shared perspectives and experiences that were clearly unique—for their interaction with the surrounding community, the types of students served, and their overall academic and social climate. Both sectors serve a majority–minority population (over half of the community colleges present were also minority serving); these students often representing other forms of "nontraditional" status such as low-income, adults, first-generation, or non-native English speakers who work at least part-time. Both also face challenges in educating a student body that is largely underprepared for college credit-bearing courses and thus in need of remediation in math, English, and science disciplines.

The TCU group set themselves apart even further given their institution's role in the larger American Indian community. Several of the TCUs present are located on or near a reservation and are thus integrated into a community that faces great educational challenges. The college-going rate for American Indians is amongst the lowest of America's minority groups for reasons beyond inadequate high school preparation and income barriers; although these also are factors. TCU practitioners expressed the need to help alleviate deep cultural challenges that their students carried to campus on a daily basis. This included breaking down the negative stigma associated with seeking higher education and the need to make curriculum relevant to the everyday lives of students; all within an environment that is necessarily high-touch and intentionally tailored to meet the academic, social, and cultural needs of each individual.

This level of attention that TCU faculty and staff pay to students is remarkable given the fact that these campuses are also some of the most underresourced in the country. When asked how they do it, participants pointed to the ability of TCUs to be cost-efficient and nimble with their educational offerings:

> One of the strengths of TCUs is that we are generally very lean and fast. We can go in a direction if that's the way the wind's blowing. [Others] can't do that … we can move our programs really fast. If a new workforce need arises, we can adapt to that.
>
> I think one of the unique niches and strengths of TCUs is that they have been working on education models successfully with nontraditional students. Nontraditional students are becoming the norm everywhere, and TCUs already know how to handle them. And they can share that body of knowledge, even [research institutions], aren't able to do that.

As for educating STEM students, in particular, one TCU practitioner pointed to the unique approach that faculty must take: "We're at the point of developing students in STEM. They often haven't considered STEM, but we get them interested. They take courses that build their capacity, not weed them out." This statement was in sharp contrast with those expressed by PWI 4-year college faculty who termed their approach to first year courses as ascribing to a "culture of attrition."

Non-TCU community colleges were also more integrated into their surrounding community than many of the 4-year institutions present at the meeting. Two-year schools respond to a multitude of localized needs: providing terminal 1- and 2-year degrees in technical and health fields; educating displaced workers and returning adults; providing students with skills required by the region's core industries; and serving as a beginning point for those seeking to transfer to a local 4-year college or university. Participants were prompted to speak mostly to this last role (of preparing students to transfer) given NSF's desire to focus on this particular role of the 2-year sector; yet they were quick to point out the need for NSF and others to recognize their ongoing balancing act of roles and responsibilities as driven by institutional mission.

Moving past these two sectors, participants representing 4-year MSIs spoke of varying strengths and challenges as compared to those serving a predominantly majority or "traditional" student population. Like the 2-year schools, many of the HBCU participants expressed strong linkages between their institution and the surrounding community, including engagement with local high schools—a mission-driven connection that seemed to serve them well. Another commonality across HBCUs was their use of honors colleges as an environment-specific mechanism for building academic talent within their STEM student body. These colleges receive great support from their president and provost, a seemingly necessary requirement for effectiveness. Other promising practices sited by HBCUs included invasive advising, mentoring, and academic and social support, including peer mentoring and tutoring; undergraduate research opportunities with faculty mentorship; summer bridge programs; and learning communities.

One campus provided financial resources to faculty for their participation in a summer research and mentoring program for undergraduate students. Such programs are augmented during the academic year with problem solving workshops, complementary tutoring, or supplemental instruction strategies. Learning communities were also common. One campus learning community consisted of student "clusters" who share three courses for which the corresponding faculty (English and math) work together on integrated assignments. Another campus had faculty that worked across math and science by providing what the participant called "vertical and horizontal integration of the curriculum."

Participants from both TCUs and many HSIs expressed the need to work with families to educate them on the value of sending their son or daughter to college, the value of a STEM degree in particular, and the need for family to support their children if not financially then emotionally. According to one HSI participant, "Our bridge programs also offer assistance to the families about children leaving the home. So we start with smaller durations away from home [while the student is still in high school], to prepare parents for transitions ... to educate the families." This need to integrate family into the STEM educational experience of their children is explicated in the literature (Andrade, 2007; Carlone & Johnson, 2007; Grandy, 1998; Hurtado et al., 2007; Russell & Atwater, 2005) and is something we found reinforced in small group discussions.

HSIs also found success with learning community models. Several spoke about peer led team learning (PLTL), a practice often associated with introductory STEM courses (Brown, 2010; Horwitz et al., 2009; Preszler, 2009; Smith et al., 2004; Tien, Roth, & Kampmeier, 2004). According to one participant, "The PLTL program is very successful, when done correctly. It creates a feedback triangle between student, mentor and faculty member. Even students who aren't participating in tutoring benefit, because faculty receive feedback and can adjust accordingly." Such adjustments by faculty seemed relatively rare on PWI campuses while MSI participants spoke about faculty who volunteered their time to engage with students in transformative learning settings (like PLTL).

Implications for Policy, Practice and Research

The learning that took place across focus group settings during two weekend convenings as part of the Broadening Participation in STEM project is representative of potential intrainstitutional learning on a much larger scale. Although NSF's proposal to eliminate stand-alone programs for the MSI community in favor of a broader competitive grant program was deemed misinformed and lacking transparency, Bement's underlying premises may have been correct—learning across institutions has the potential to strengthen America's production of more diverse degree holders. Yet just how this learning should take shape is up for discussion.

Not up for discussion is the well-articulated argument by federal and state entities and the STEM academic and industry community, for greater production of STEM degrees and the antecedent need to engage underrepresented communities in STEM education. And while we have made great progress as a nation, we have yet to fully meet this challenge in part because our higher education system has failed not only to help prepare and attract STEM talent but also retain and grant degrees to students who have expressed interest in pursuing STEM careers. Even when students are academically qualified, large numbers of STEM majors either change into other disciplines or leave college all together. The opposite is true as well; students requiring remediation on their way to credit-bearing STEM curricula are often discouraged by poor teaching and lack of systemic support. Both of these scenarios are playing out on 2- and 4-year campuses across the country. Despite these challenges, however, there are isolated success stories and institutional practices that are beating the odds. And it is those practices that must be shared and scaled up.

We are hopeful that our efforts will further enhance the understanding of promising practices and necessary steps to diversifying the so-called STEM pipeline as viewed by those investing in STEM education—the overall federal agency community, congressional leaders, and state and institutional policymakers. So too, STEM faculty, and those who support STEM students whether on a formal or informal basis, can draw meaningful lessons. It is our belief that we require a collective understanding of what students need to succeed in STEM across a broad spectrum of higher education institutions if we are to reach national goals. But it must not stop there. Outside the scope of this project, but necessary for rapid gains in STEM degree production, is the sharing of intrainstitutional learning across the federal agency community. The National Science and Technology Council's 2006 recommendations for improving the impact of federal investments in STEM education research must be seriously considered. The Council pointed to NSF, as well as the U.S. Department of Education and National Institutes of Health, as agencies core to the understanding of where ongoing education research gaps exist. These gaps must be filled and their findings disseminated to policymakers at all levels.

Beyond strict national economic interests in a STEM workforce are social priorities that drive the work of many institutions, including a number of those discussed here. Upward social mobility of underserved populations is in itself a top policy priority. Think beyond national production to the income of individuals with skills that meet the demand of today's technology-driven economy. The Georgetown Center for Education and the Workforce (2011) notes that, "the demand for STEM certificates, certifications, and degrees is a proxy for underlying competencies" (p. 9). These competencies yield a high wage premium, and thus have the potential to mobilize our minority communities and strengthen our civic fabric in the process.

Finally, our historical legacy teaches us that when demographic or other great societal changes have occurred in our nation, as they are now occurring, so too are there great opportunities to benefit from this transformation. From the broadening participation landscape across the nation, great genius and talent resides to create the innovation needed to enhance our quality of life and national prosperity. Our stakeholders challenged all higher education institutions to embed STEM literacy amongst all of their educational goals and to infuse STEM entrepreneurship as a core educational outcome among its STEM graduates. With a technologically and scientifically literate populace comes a more engaged society for this millennium, a benefit that goes beyond dollars and across borders.

Notes

1   Grant No. 1059774. Any opinions, findings, and conclusions or recommendations expressed here are those of the authors and do not necessarily reflect the views of the National Science Foundation.

2   HBCU-UP provides awards to develop, implement, and study innovative models and approaches for dramatic improvement in the preparation and success of underrepresented minority students in STEM (NSF, 2011).

3   TCUP provides awards to Tribal colleges and universities, Alaska Native serving institutions, and Native Hawaiian serving institutions to promote high quality STEM education, research, and outreach (NSF, 2011).

4   LSAMP is aimed at increasing both the quality and quantity of students successfully complet-

ing STEM bachelor's degrees, and increasing the number of students interested in, qualified for, and matriculating in STEM graduate programs (NSF, 2011).

5   Federal law defines an HSI as a public or private nonprofit postsecondary institution with 25% or more total undergraduate Hispanic full-time equivalent student enrollment; with no less than 50% of Hispanic students meeting low-income or first-generation to college student criteria (Santiago, 2006; Stearns & Watanabe, 2002).

6   The Integrated Postsecondary Education Data System (IPEDS) was our primary data source. IPEDS provides annual institutionally reported and verified data on student enrollment and completion for institutions receiving federal Title IV funds. The research team captured trends in enrollment and completion during a nearly 20-year period, from 1987 to 2008, which roughly corresponds to the timeframe when the NSF strengthened its emphasis on increasing the number of underrepresented students completing STEM degrees.

7   A noteworthy limitation of our stakeholder convenings is the lack of student voices. The project team attempted to bring a representative number of students to the meetings, yet after recruiting and receiving RSVPs from four students across the two meetings, only one student was ultimately able to attend.

8   As defined by the Office for Civil Rights and U.S. Department of Education.

9   Each group had at least one facilitator and one note-taker; all groups were recorded.

References

Andrade, E. J. (2007). *Latino college students: A study of collaboration and community building in a math first year experience* (Unpublished doctoral dissertation). California State University, Dominguez Hills.

Babco, E. (2004). *Skills for the innovation economy: What the 21st century workforce needs and how to provide it.* Washington, DC: Commission on Professionals in Science and Technology.

Bement, A. L., Jr. (2010, March 10). Testimony before the House Science and Technology Subcommittee on Research and Science Education, 111th Congress.

Broadening Participation in STEM: Hearing before the Subcommittee on Research and Science Education, Committee on Science and Technology of the House of Representatives. 111th Cong. 2 (2010). Retrieved from http://www.gpo.gov/fdsys/pkg/CHRG-111hhrg55843/pdf/CHRG-111hhrg55843.pdf

Brown, P. J. P. (2010). Process-oriented guided-inquiry learning in an introductory anatomy and physiology course with a diverse student population. *Advances in Physiology Education, 34*(3), 150–155.

Carlone, H. B., & Johnson, A. (2007). Understanding the science experiences of successful women of color: Science identity as an analytic lens. *Journal of Research in Science Teaching, 44*(8), 1011–1245.

Carnevale, A. P., Smith, N., & Melton, M. (2011). *STEM.* Washington, DC: Georgetown Center for Education and the Workforce.

Grandy, J. (1998). Persistence in science of high-ability minority students: Results of a longitudinal study. *Journal of Higher Education, 69*(6), 589–620.

Holdren, J. P. (2011). Science, technology, engineering, and math indication in the Obama administration ... with a focus on the "E". *Remarks for the 2011 Engineering Public Policy Symposium.* Retrieved from http://files.asme.org/asmeorg/NewsPublicPolicy/GovRelations/Programs/29875.pdf

Horwitz, S, Rodger, S. H., Biggers, M., Binkley, D., Frantz, C. K., Gundermann, D, & Sweat, M. (2009, March 4–7). Using peer-led team learning to increase participation and success of under-represented groups in introductory computer science. *Proceedings of the 40th ACM Technical Symposium on Computer Science Education,* Chattanooga, TN.

Hurtado, S., Han, J. C., Saenz, V. B., Espinosa, L. L., Cabrera, N. L., & Cerna, O. S. (2007). Predicting transition and adjustment to college: Biomedical and behavioral science aspirants' and minority students' first year of college. *Research in Higher Education, 48*(7), 841–887.

Museus, S., Palmer, R. T., Davis, R. J., & Maramba, D. C. (2011). *Racial and ethnic minority students' success in STEM education.* Hoboken, NJ: Jossey-Bass.

National Association for Equal Opportunity in Higher Education (2011). *Comments on the NSF proposed comprehensive broadening participation of undergraduates in STEM program* (July 28, 2010). Retrieved from http://www.nafeo.org/community/web2010/documents/NAFEO_Comments_RE%20NSF%20CAP-US.pdf

National Center for Education Statistics. (2008). *Characteristics of minority-serving institutions and minority undergraduates enrolled in these institutions* (NCES 2008-156). Washington, DC: U.S. Department of Education.

National Science Foundation: Testimony before the House Science and Technology Subcommittee on Research and Science Education. 111th Cong. 2 (2010). Retrieved from http://gop.science.house.gov/Media/hearings /research10/mar10/Bement.pdf

Preszler, R. W. (2009). Replacing lecture with peer-led workshops improves student learning. *Life Sciences Education, 8*(3), 182–192.

Russell, M. L., & Atwater, M. M. (2005). Traveling the road to success: A discourse on persistence throughout the science pipeline with African American students at a predominantly White institution. *Journal of Research in Science Teaching, 42*(6), 691–715.

Santiago, D. A. (2006). *Inventing Hispanic-serving institutions (HSIs): The basics.* Washington, DC: Excelencia in Education.

Smith, A. C., Stewart, R., Shields, P., Hayes-Klosteridis, J., Robinson, P., & Yuan, R. (2004). Introductory biology courses: A framework to support active learning in large enrollment introductory science courses. *Life Sciences Education, 4*(2), 143–156.

Stearns, C., & Watanabe, S. (2002). *Hispanic-serving institutions: Statistical trends from 1990–1999* (NCES 2002–051). Washington, DC: National Center for Education Statistics, U.S. Department of Education.

Tien, L. T., Roth, V., & Kampmeier, J. A. (2004). Implementation of a peer-led team learning instructional approach in an undergraduate organic chemistry course. *Journal of Research in Science Teaching, 39*(7), 606–632.

U.S. Bureau of Labor Statistics. (2010). Occupational outlook. *Handbook, 2010–11.* Retrieved from http://www.bls.gov/oco/oco2003. htm.

U.S. Department of Labor (2007). *The STEM workforce challenge: The role of the public workforce system in a national solution for a competitive science, technology, engineering, and mathematics (STEM) workforce.* Prepared for the U.S. Department of Labor, Employment and Training Administration by Jobs for the Future. Retrieved from http://www.doleta.gov/Youth_services/pdf/STEM_Report_4%2007.pdf

11

ACTION RESEARCH

An Essential Practice for 21st Century
Assessment at HSIs[1]

*Alicia C. Dowd, Misty Sawatzky, Raquel M. Rall,
and Estela Mara Bensimon*

Colleges and universities in the United States are being called on by legislators, educational advocacy organizations, accrediting agencies, and philanthropic organizations to use data to improve the quality of their educational programs and increase the numbers of students earning postsecondary degrees and credentials. Special urgency is expressed in regard to degrees in science, technology, engineering, and mathematics (STEM), because the social and economic need for scientists, technologists, and engineers is outpacing the supply of skilled workers and professionals. Further, Hispanic students[2] as well as Black students, Native Americans, and Southeast Asian Americans, are severely underrepresented among STEM professionals and degree holders (Chapa & De La Rosa, 2006; Chubin, May, & Babco, 2005; National Science Board, 2010). To respond to these needs, it is necessary for minority serving institutions (MSIs) to support their respective student populations, fostering access and success in STEM fields.

In the aggregate, underrepresented minorities comprised 28% of the U.S. population, but only about 9% the STEM workforce in 2006 (Committee on Science Engineering and Public Policy, 2010). Despite growth in Latina/o undergraduate enrollment over the past decade, Latinas/os were awarded only 8.6% of baccalaureate degrees in STEM fields in 2008, compared with the 66.1% share of degrees awarded to White students. Among graduate degree recipients, only 5.3% of all master's degrees in science and engineering from 2000 to 2008 were awarded to Latinas/os. At the doctoral level, 1,162 science and engineering degrees were awarded to Latina/o students in 2008, compared to 14,220 to White students (National Science Foundation [NSF], 2011). This represents minimal growth of Latina/o participation at the graduate level from

2% of total enrollment in 1976 to 6.2% in 2008 (Aud, Fox, & KewalRamani, 2010).

To address this shortfall of Latina/o STEM graduates, Hispanic serving institutions (HSIs) must play a leading role because HSIs enroll the majority of Latina/o students (Mercer & Stedman, 2008; Santiago, 2011). Despite comprising only 10% of the colleges and universities in the United States, HSIs enroll 54% of Latina/o undergraduates (Horn, 2006). HSIs are also contributors to the supply of Latina/o doctoral recipients, which is notable given that low levels of graduate degree attainment are particularly problematic in the STEM fields and advanced degrees are generally a prerequisite for access to professional careers. Of 25 institutions that produced the largest number of Latina/o baccalaureates who later earned science and engineering doctorates in the period from 1997 to 2001, eight were HSIs (Contreras, Malcom, & Bensimon, 2008; Dowd, Malcom, & Bensimon, 2009; National Science Foundation [NSF] , 2004).

There have been various strategies to address the underrepresentation of Latinos in STEM. The predominant approach, both at HSIs and non-HSIs, has been to implement special programs on campus to help historically underrepresented minority students enhance their academic skills and become socially integrated into college life. These special programs typically support students through tutoring, career guidance, and undergraduate research opportunities. The mentoring relationships developed between students and faculty and staff through these interactions can be a valuable source of support for Latino students majoring in STEM fields, but these programs typically serve only small numbers of students and are highly dependent on available funding. Further, special programs and targeted mentoring programs tend to focus on giving students the "know how" or cultural capital to navigate difficult and unfamiliar terrain rather than attempting to bring about changes at the institutional level to create more culturally inclusive programs and practices.

While the label "Hispanic Serving" suggests that HSIs have a special mission to serve Hispanic students, this is not the case. HSIs were not founded with the express purpose of overcoming the exclusionary practices of segregation in postsecondary higher education or the inequities in funding. The federal category of HSI was created in 1992 when, as a result of a provision in the reauthorization of the Higher Education Act, over 200 institutions that were regular community colleges, 4-year colleges, and regional universities received the designation of Hispanic serving institution. With HSIs lacking a historical legacy that clearly defines purpose, policies, and values, it is necessary to ask: What does it entail for members and leaders of Hispanic serving institutions to transform an accidental identity into a mission and values that would guide academic decision making, resource allocation, selection, and retention criteria of institutional leaders, faculty, and staff, and assessment of institutional performance and equity in student outcomes in ways that are truly Hispanic serving?

Researchers from the Center of Urban Education (CUE) at the University of Southern California (USC) previously illustrated how HSIs can use data monitoring and benchmarking tools, such as the Equity Index of the Center for Urban Education's Equity Scorecard, to assess whether Latina/o students are graduating with STEM degrees in equal proportion to their representation in the college student population[3] (Contreras et al., 2008; Dowd et al., 2009). For colleges with inequitable participation of and degree completion by Latina/os in STEM fields, the next step, beyond benchmarking performance, is to use action research as a component of institutional self-assessment and improvement. Action research, engaged in by "practitioners as researchers" (Bensimon, Polkinghorne, Bauman, & Vallejo, 2004), is a valuable approach to develop a local and contextualized understanding (Pena, Bensimon, & Colyar, 2006) of the institutional supports necessary to promote Latina/o STEM degree completion.

Action research can be utilized to encourage the adoption of innovative practices (Patton, 2011) that are "race conscious" in a positive way (Bensimon & Malcom, in press).When conducted from this critical, race conscious perspective, action research is the appropriate research methodology to use when seeking to bring about cultural change. Seeing one's own cultural assumptions—for example, about which students are "talented," "deserving," "meritorious," or "high quality"—is an aspect of inquiry, the purposeful use of data for reflective practice and experimentation with new educational practices to solve problems of practice. There are multiple approaches to inquiry in the various action research traditions. Those that are collective (involving communities of practice) and critical (in the sense of investigating dynamics of power and cultural dominance) are referred to as participatory critical action research. Those that involve individuals in reflective practice to improve on problems of practice in their own professional lives—what are sometimes called "indeterminate situations" (Polkinghorne, 2004)—are referred to as practitioner research or action inquiry (Greenwood & Levin, 2005; Noffke, 1997; Reason, 1994). These traditions provide appropriate guidance, data collection, analysis methods, and assessment strategies for institutions engaged in cultural transformation and educational innovation.

Accordingly, CUE has been developing action research tools to promote inquiry with attention to racial/ethnic inequities, using design-based implementation research (Penuel, Fishman, Cheng, & Sabelli, 2011). These action research tools—referred to as self-assessment inventories (SAIs)—are designed to be used as a routine part of institutional assessment. This chapter describes two SAIs and their application to developing culturally inclusive practices in STEM.

Despite some pockets of progress, the process of cultural transformation from a dominant, monocultural STEM curriculum to culturally inclusive pedagogy and practices has arguably yet to begin in earnest in U.S. higher education

(Augustine, 2005; Augustine et al., 2010; Committee on Science Engineering and Public Policy, 2010; National Academy of Sciences, 2011). Institutional self-assessment using action research and culturally inclusive indicators of pedagogy and practice holds the potential to bring about cultural change because change processes require practitioners—faculty, administrators, and counselors—to see their own cultural assumptions in a new light (Kezar & Eckel, 2002; Schein, 1985; Seo & Creed, 2002). Action research is pertinent, timely, and necessary in the reform of postsecondary STEM education for Latinas/os because it moves us beyond mere discourse of valuing student backgrounds, experience, and diversity to the implementation of purposeful and insightful action toward the goal of equity in STEM. As stated by Rendón (1994):

> Diversity in nature is a strength. So is diversity among college students. The challenge is how to harness that strength, and how to unleash the creativity and exuberance for learning that is present in all students who feel free to learn, free to be who they are, and validated for what they know and believe.
>
> *(p. 51)*

By not relegating diversity to simply a trait to be celebrated, but instead taking collaborative action to use it as a resource to enact meaningful and demonstrative change, action research aligns beliefs with intentions and subsequent action implementation to improve access, retention, and graduation outcomes for Latina/o students.

The consideration of what is needed to bring about organizational change toward greater cultural inclusiveness is as relevant to the context of HSIs as it is at predominantly White institutions (PWIs). Without adequate role models and advocates in administrative positions, HSI policies often reflect exclusionary practices based on ethnicity and language status. Second, the proportion of the Hispanic student body at HSIs ranges from 25% to 99% of full-time equivalent students.[4] Therefore, Hispanic students are not necessarily the largest ethnic group at HSIs. And, even where Hispanic students are numerically in the majority, the culture at an HSI can still reflect normative, Anglo values, artifacts, academic content, and lack a Hispanic serving identity (Contreras et al., 2008). Past research has found little difference between HSIs and predominantly White non-HSIs in terms of faculty attitudes and institutional practices (Stage & Hubbard, 2009). Cultural transformation is unlikely without greater numbers of Hispanic faculty, counselors, and administrators who have engaged in professional development beyond their traditional academic socialization. Action research provides such an opportunity because it involves a process of collaboration, knowledge production, and institutional reorganization.

This chapter is organized in five sections including this introduction. The next section discusses the theoretical foundations of the development of CUE's culturally inclusive self-assessment instruments. The third section draws on research from historically Black colleges and universities (HBCUs), which are recognized for producing disproportionate numbers of Black STEM degree holders, to consider the organizational characteristics of MSIs founded with a mission focused on a particular population. We juxtapose this with what we have learned about the HSI STEM culture through a case study of HSIs. The fourth section describes indicators useful in assessing whether practitioners are acting as "institutional agents" (Stanton-Salazar, 1997, 2001, 2010) and incorporating culturally inclusive pedagogy and practices (Gay, 2000; Ladson-Billings, 1995a, 1995b; Tate, 1995). Two of CUE's SAIs are presented to illustrate how to use such indicators as part of action research, action inquiry, and institutional assessment. Finally, we conclude by discussing why these approaches are of particular importance in the HSI context.

Theoretical Foundations of Culturally Inclusive Self-Assessment Instruments

Action research and inquiry using race conscious institutional self-assessment practices provide strategies to support campus cultural change in response to the racism that pervades American institutions. Efforts to create a more culturally inclusive campus can be developed, measured, monitored, and evaluated through routine institutional self-assessment. At HSIs, to establish a Hispanic serving mission, this entails a focus on Latina and Latino students' access to economically and vocationally rewarding fields of study, such as STEM, and on advanced degree completion.

Both SAIs presented below are designed to be used as protocols for action research (collectively pursued) or action inquiry (individually pursued). The objective is to enable practitioners to investigate and reflect on their own practices to discover how their cultural assumptions, artifacts, beliefs, attitudes, and practices can be *remediated* to become more culturally inclusive. *Remediation* is a term rooted in cultural historical activity theory (Cole, Engeström, & Vasquez, 1997; Engeström, 2008) which highlights the fact that educational artifacts all have culture and history (Dowd, Bishop, Bensimon, & Witham, 2011).

The first of the two SAIs presented in this chapter, the Institutional Agents Self-Assessment Inventory for Increasing Latina and Latino Participation in STEM Fields, draws from Ricardo Stanton-Salazar's research (1997, 2001, 2010) on the characteristics and roles of institutional agents and on our own studies of "transfer agents." Transfer agents are defined as those institutional agents engaged in improving equity in community college to 4-year institution transfer pathways (Bensimon, 2007; Bensimon & Dowd, 2009; Bensimon, Dowd, Alford, & Trapp, 2007; Dowd, 2010; Dowd, Bensimon, Gabbard, et al., 2006; Dowd, Bishop, et al., 2011). Ricardo Stanton-Salazar's (2010) article "A Social Capital Framework for the Study of Institutional Agents and Their Role in the Empowerment of Low-Status Students and Youth" provides a full description of the characteristics and roles of institutional agents. Found in a variety of settings (e.g., social workers, educators, and informal mentors), institutional agents are individuals who utilize their own status and authority, resources, and networks, to the service of economically disenfranchised students.

It is important to note that institutional agents do more than serve as a role model or provide psychological support to students. It is clear that students achieve success by receiving not merely moral support but also institutional support and resources. Psychological support complements what institutional agents do, but does not substitute for the crucial behaviors that provide students with access to resource-rich practitioner networks and knowledge bases. As noted above, these resources may be allocated directly to the student, such as a faculty member inviting a Latina/o student to a research conference; or distributed to other institutional agents in support of a Latina and Latino students; for example, an administrator advocating for increased institutional support for Latina/o programs in STEM. Institutional agents provide a variety of forms of support to help their students negotiate success in their institutional environments. For example, an institutional agent may share his or her "funds of knowledge" about applying to graduate school while providing constructive feedback about academic writing. In sum, institutional agents are individuals at educational institutions who use their status, resources, and networks on behalf of historically disenfranchised students.

A practitioner may wish to act as an institutional agent but be hampered by unconscious assumptions and beliefs about students' abilities, aspirations, or motivations. As Sue and his colleagues (2007) have demonstrated, even well-meaning individuals can communicate "racial microaggressions," assaults, insults, and invalidations of various forms that create discriminatory learning environments. The culturally relevant pedagogy literature (Gay, 2000; Ladson-Billings, 1995a, 1995b; Tate, 1995) provides insights on how practitioners can behave in their interactions with students to provide direct support. This literature, similar to the literature on institutional agents, provides guidance on educational practices that empower students to be successful. Equally important, it highlights the importance of communicating respect, validation, and high expectations to students, particularly racially minoritized students who are subject to discriminatory microaggressions, overt acts of racism, and stereotyped assumptions.

Therefore, the second tool presented in this chapter is CUE's Culturally Inclusive Policies and Practices Self-Assessment Inventory (CIPPs-SAI) protocol. It draws on the culturally relevant pedagogy literature to incorporate indicators of culturally inclusive practices in an SAI that guides practitioners through a document analysis process intended to promote self-reflective practice on the messages communicated to students through common educational documents such as admissions applications, financial aid forms, program announcements, and syllabi.

Insights from Empirical Studies at HBCUs and HSIs

To understand and illustrate the relevance of the culturally relevant pedagogy literature in relation to postsecondary STEM education at HSIs, it is useful to draw on lessons from research conducted at HBCUs, which are acknowledged for an "HBCU effect" that produces a disproportionately high number of Black[5] scientists and engineers (McNair, 2009, p. 90). The data indicate that HBCUs offer an example of a context in which a minoritized racial/ethnic group, in the HBCU case—African Americans—are able to achieve results unmatched at other institutions. In 2006, approximately one-third of all Black science and engineering doctorate recipients received their baccalaureate degrees from HBCUs (National Science Board, 2010), a proportion that far outstrips the 3% share of HBCUs among institutions of higher learning institutions in the United States (Palmer & Gasman, 2008). Several studies indicate these numbers are possible because of the culturally inclusive practices at HBCUs. Such practices acknowledge and counter the fact that the learning experiences of Blacks in the STEM disciplines is highly racialized, with race and racism recurring as normal constructs in the everyday experiences of Black students (Terry, 2010). Similar acknowledgment is not typical at HSIs with respect to the experiences of Hispanic students in STEM.

In the absence of a robust literature on culturally inclusive STEM practices and pedagogy at HSIs, a number of the indicators of culturally inclusive practices on CUE's CIPPs-SAI are derived from the research literature on HBCUs. Four broad insights emerge from our review of this literature. First, HBCUs demonstrate the expectation that the educational community will engage in respectful discussion of the history and contemporary experiences of discrimination, racism, and marginalization. One of the primary functions of HBCUs is to acknowledge not only the African Diaspora history, but also the history of social hostility (Brown & Davis, 2001). LeMelle (2002) puts forth that the mission of HBCUs is to produce highly competent Black students who have no ambivalence about who they are and how they should use their skills and talents to maximize their own and their community's interests because the "college for the Negroes has a double responsibility. It must prepare the youth for good lives as American citizens and it must also fit them to tackle their peculiar racial problems with intelligence and courage" (p. 193).

Second, HBCUs show an expectation that student success will be a collaborative effort among the student, peers, faculty, administrators, counselors, students' families and communities. Freeman, Alston, and Winborne (2008) showed this through one of their participants in a study on motivation at an

HBCU. "We felt more confident. At least we tried and worked it through with others. If you're wrong, you're wrong together" (Freeman et al., 2008, p. 227). One interviewee highlighted in the qualitative study at an HBCU in Palmer and Gasman (2008) said that "There's ... staff and sometimes I forget they work here because they are so kind, and so generous ... they just take you under their wing ... if you do not do well, it will not only hurt you, but it will hurt them. You become more concerned about not hurting them that you try so hard. Those things helped me, having administrators that actually care ..." (p. 60).

Third, HBCUs show evidence of a desire to help students succeed, and fourth, a belief that all students are capable of obtaining high educational goals. For example, in *HBCU Perspectives and Research Programs: Spelman College as a Model for Success in the STEM Fields,* McNair (2009) highlights the importance of the initiation of prefreshman summer programs, collaborative peer support programs, faculty development, and research opportunities via the pursuit and receipt of external resources from agencies such the National Aeronautics and Space Administration (NASA), National Institutes of Health (NIH), and the National Science Foundation (NSF). McNair (2009) further asserts that: "There is never the negative, unspoken undertone that one may not succeed" and that a culture of excellence is maintained through the implementation of research training programs, seminar series, mentoring programs, and tutorial and academic support programs (p. 93).

A study by Palmer and Gasman (2008) illustrates the importance of faculty displaying empathy and support. One student in the study commented that the faculty at HBCUs "are usually harder, because they know that you have the potential and they'll push you, and drive you, which of course will only help you in the long run" (p. 58). Additionally, Fries–Britt and Turner (2002) found that high-achieving Black students at HBCUs perceived campus practitioners as going out of their way to meet their individual needs and to achieve greater inclusiveness through expansion of campus activities and traditions. These campus efforts help to build student confidence, make meaningful connections with faculty and peers, and cultivate student energy (Fries–Britt & Turner, 2002). Students interviewed by Fries–Britt and Turner (2002) explained that Black students at HBCUs were better integrated academically and socially than their counterparts at PWIs because they experience intense academic support from practitioners who are convinced that they can be successful and do not give up on them. In sum, the literature on HBCUs illustrates the work that needs to be done at HSIs and PWIs to "promote the inclusion of minority ways of doing and knowing into classroom practices" (Nasir & Hand, 2006, p. 452).

Based on findings from a multi-institutional case study of HSIs (Stanton-Salazar, Macias, Bensimon, & Dowd, 2010) that have a higher than expected share of Latinas/os earning bachelor's degrees in STEM fields, we see that institutional agents at HSIs are engaged in creating an "HSI effect" analogous to the HBCU effect. We found that among the faculty of Hispanic serving 4-year colleges there were STEM faculty members who possessed a critical consciousness and understanding of sociopolitical inequities affecting students of color, particularly the underrepresentation of Latinas and Latinos in STEM fields. As mentioned earlier, individuals who are in positions of power and influence based on rank, reputation, national standing, or formal roles within their own institutions, and have control of resources have the potential to take the role of institutional agents—if they are intentional about using their status and power, influence, and resources to expand educational opportunities for Latina and Latino students.

Results from our interviews with nearly 100 purposefully selected respondents provided examples of institutional agents who used their positions to facilitate opportunities for students who on paper may not have appeared eligible for the kinds of activities that help them see themselves as future scientists. For example, Professor Martinez[6] spoke about Julia, a student starting out on her PhD and working in his lab, in ways that reflected his high expectations and belief that she could be successful. Julia, who had been selected to attend a prestigious conference in Germany, "on first reading … wasn't eligible, but we put in an application for her and she got in." Similarly, speaking about another Latina who at first "struggled" in biology and did only "average" work, Professor Martinez said "some students who do average in coursework have excellent potential … so this young lady struggled very hard [and] on the last exam, which is standardized, she did very well." He added, "You can tell [when] the lights are going off and on and they're excited by the material. Those are the kind of students that I want to attract to conduct research because the research experience can tell these students, 'you can do this kind of professional work given the chance'."

Professor Martinez's efforts at bringing Latina and Latino students into his lab and connecting them with his network of STEM professionals represents an ideological commitment to increasing Latina/o students' access to higher education and transforming HSIs to actualize their mission. Like Professor Martinez, Professor Diaz used his professorial position as well as his administrative role overseeing research laboratories to provide summer research experiences for Latina/o high school and community college students. "Because I was the director I could target students from certain areas," he said, explaining that students like "Alicia Contreras, [who] started off at some community college then … came to my lab, she is graduating with her PhD this semester." A third professor interviewed, Professor Ramirez, expanded the networks of Latino STEM undergraduates by cooking dinner for them and his former students who had earned their PhD's. "In that way" he said, "we develop the community and they [undergraduates] can see it is possible [to go on to the PhD]." Professor Tovar, a chemistry professor and department chair, helped Latinas/os who were transferring from a community college to qualify for a research-based scholarship that was contingent on having a STEM advisor from the university. "Some students feel threatened to approach a faculty member," he explained. "This is when I talk to the faculty member, 'will you please take this person for a week or two in your lab, see how it goes … and then she will [qualify for the scholarship] and transfer."

In what ways do these professors act as institutional agents? And how did they become institutional agents? One thing these four professors have in common is their Latino heritage and even though they vary in age, discipline, and their countries of origin, they share with Latina/o students the experience of being "outsiders" who also struggled to make it in the academy. They see themselves as that "average" Latino or Latina and they use their positions and academic networks to create opportunities that usually are given to students who have accumulated academic and social advantage.

While the four individuals featured as institutional agents happen to all be Latino, not all Latinos are institutional agents. In addition, non–Latinos can also function as institutional agents. The problem is that there are not enough institutional agents, even in HSIs. A small number of institutional agents are not likely to be able to carry out a broad scale cultural change at an institution steeped in established academic norms and dominant traditions.

Building a critical mass of faculty and staff who can take on the role of an institutional agent cannot be left up to chance. Given the scarcity of new faculty positions and an aging tenured faculty, it is even more urgent that leaders in HSIs, particularly department chairs and deans, learn how to create the structures and processes to assist current faculty and staff to develop the values, knowledge, and practices possessed by professors Martinez, Diaz, Ramirez, and Tovar. The body of research produced over the last 10 years by CUE's researchers provides evidence that the methods and tools of action research offer a viable and practical strategy to develop more institutional agents. Action research engages academic actors in a process of inquiry that leads them to reflect on their own practices and to ask themselves: In what ways am I a facilitator, an advocate, a broker … for Latino and Latina students? Needless to say, the development of institutional agents is a complex process. We do not pretend that the tools we describe in this chapter will result in a sudden abundance of institutional agents. We do, however, offer these tools as a critical starting point to jump-start sorely needed efforts to establish viable pathways for Latina and Latino students in STEM fields.

Institutional Agents Self-Assessment Inventory (SAI) for Increasing Latina/o Participation in STEM Fields

CUE's Institutional Agent Self-Assessment Inventory (SAIs part of the CUE's STEM Toolkit), was developed based on Stanton-Salazar's (1997, 2001, 2010) construct of institutional agents. It helps to facilitate reflective practice regarding one's own actions and behaviors as well as the broader institutional practices and resources that serve Latina/o students at a given institution. More specifically, this tool may be used by instructors, administrators, counselors, and campus leaders focused on increasing access and success for Latina/o students in these fields. CUE's Institutional Agents SAI serves to encourage practitioners to reflect on her or his own behavior in support of Latina/o students in the STEM fields.

Following the literature on social workers (Hepworth, Rooney, & Larsen, 2006), Stanton-Salazar (1997, 2001, 2010) classified the multiple institutional agent role types into four groupings of roles that can be enacted by an individual: (a) direct support, (b) integrative support, (c) system developer, and (d) system linkage and networking support. The various roles that individuals play are organized into these groups according to the kind of support that institutional agents provide to racialized students. The "direct support" group includes roles that involve institutional agents in interacting with students and providing them with direct support. Direct forms of support to students are provided through multiple roles: by providing personal and institutional resources (resource agent), performing academic advisory duties, and conveying knowledge about the educational system (knowledge agent and advisor), advocating on behalf of students' needs (advocate), and helping students learn to network (networking coach). When enacting the direct support role types, the institutional agent acts in ways similar to that of a mentor or academic advisor.

The other three groups include roles that involve institutional agents in activities where they interact not only with students but with others at the institutional, system, or community level to gather resources and support for racialized students within the institution and the community. Examples include the role of recruiter, in which faculty or administrators recruit students through communications with students, but also take steps at their own institution or in collaborating across institutions to ensure that Latinas/os are included in the recruitment pool. At times, institutional agents enact the roles in these three groups without interacting with students at all. An example is the role of program developer, in which the agent develops programs that will embed students—some of whom the individual will never meet—in a system of agents, resources, and opportunities.

These support and advocacy roles, when enacted at the systems level rather than in direct support to students, are representative of the distinguishing characteristics of an institutional agent in contrast to (or above and beyond) the roles of mentor and role model. In addition, institutional agents who act at a systems and structural level tend to articulate an explicit agenda to use resources and support structures within their areas of authority to increase the educational opportunities of racialized students.

In sum, institutional agents possess a high degree of human, social, and cultural capital that can impact the social mobility of racial and ethnic groups that are underrepresented in higher education in general, and STEM in particular. HSIs can create greater benefits for their students and the nation by building a network of institutional agents who can provide "privileges, institutional resources, opportunities for career mobility, wealth creation, political empowerment, and school achievement" (Stanton-Salazar, 2011).

Focusing on professional accountability, the Institutional Agent SAI requires practitioners to identify institutional agent behaviors she or he has engaged in and rank the frequency of those behaviors "over the past semester." Practitioners are then asked to write in any comments or obstacles they face regarding these institutional agent behaviors. For instance, the following sample SAI indicator describes a variety of behaviors indicative of direct support to all students, "I've been actively involved in helping a significant number of students assess problems, gather information, and make appropriate decisions related to their success within the institution and within the educational system." There are 15 items of this type. Each item is followed by the question, "To what extent have you done this specifically for Latina/o students?" thereby encouraging cognition surrounding Hispanic-serving practices, explicitly. A second indicator reflects the work of knowledge agents: "I've been actively involved in providing a significant number of students with forms of knowledge and information essential to (1) effectively navigating through the educational system, and to (2) overcoming the obstacles and challenges commonly experienced by students." Lastly, assessing how often and in what way practitioners act as advocates for Latina/o students, the SAI includes indicators such as the following, "I've acted to intercede and defend the rights of my students to have access to key forms of resources an opportunities necessary for their success within the college/university."

The purpose of CUE's SAI, however, goes beyond reflection surrounding practitioners' own past actions. It also serves to motivate future behavioral awareness when opportunities for service arise, and, ultimately, move individuals toward behavioral change (e.g., an increased likelihood of allocating resources to Latina/o students in the future). Overall, the SAI serves to assess practitioners' own behaviors surrounding her or his support of Latina and Latino students, while fostering cultural change toward a Hispanic-serving mission.

Culturally Inclusive Policies and Practices SAI

The Document Analysis for Self-Assessment of Culturally Inclusive Policies and Practices (CIPPs-SAI) is designed for individual and collective practitioner use to facilitate self-assessment of the ways a college or university uses (or could use) culturally inclusive practices[7] to assist minoritized students in navigating through college. It is designed to be used as a necessary but not sufficient part of a series of steps to guide campus practitioners (administrators, student affairs professionals, and faculty) in inquiry, self-assessment and action planning.

In most settings, this document analysis will follow an in-depth review of student success and persistence with close attention being paid to various pivotal milestones in a matriculation process (e.g., application, assessment testing, admissions, placement in a curriculum) or in a curriculum pathway (e.g., gateway courses, credit accumulation, courses required for a major or degree completion, timely graduation). Ideally, a group of practitioners serving in diverse roles on campus (e.g., admissions/matriculation, administration, faculty, student affairs) will agree to assess a sampling of the documents they use in their specific department/post communicating with students as "artifacts of culture" in order to look at the sampled documents "with fresh eyes" to consider the type of cultural assumptions they may hold.

The assessment process requires a number of steps. First, practitioners will collect a sampling of materials that reflect their educational practices and that communicate expectations of and information to students. Faculty are asked to examine documents like course syllabi, class handouts, and assignments; admissions and enrollment professionals are asked to examine application forms, financial aid forms, and web pages; and program administrators and institutional leaders are asked to provide descriptions of student eligibility, mission statements, and program goals.

Second, participants are reminded that printed materials are only one important medium through which practitioners communicate with students on campus. Individual discussions, in class presentations or group discussions, campus gatherings, artwork, and the physical space are other important forms of communication. (The Center for Urban Education offers other protocols for self-assessment of practices represented in other types of media and settings.) Third, practitioners will examine the materials to familiarize or refamiliarize themselves with the contents of the documents. Finally, with the documents in hand, practitioners will complete the four-column worksheet while pointing to specific telling language in the sampled documents that will serve as the "data" for the interpretation.

When the group convenes, practitioners are encouraged to keep in mind that the communication intent of the document's author may differ from the intention perceived during the document review activity. Therefore, the language utilized in this protocol aligns with the receipt of constructive feedback from a colleague sitting beside you. This process is important because it reminds us that self-assessment differs from evaluation in that it is focused on problem-framing and solution generation, not on evaluating practitioner performance. Through this process, practitioners come to realize that whether intentionally or unintentionally, documents communicate educational practices that are shaped by campus cultures and ultimately communicate campus norms. Those things that most surprise practitioners about the documents reviewed in this assessment may run counter to prevailing cultural practices. The final component to the activity is that each participant volunteers ideas to draft an action plan to strengthen culturally inclusive practices on the campus drawing on the reflections from the activity.

Practitioners investigate currently held cultural assumptions by studying the various forms of documentation used to communicate with students in order to view these artifacts with fresh perspectives. Initially, each participant in the protocol individually assesses (via the prompts for self-reflection included on the protocol) their own documentation that they use with students. The response columns alongside each of the indicators ask whether the CIP represented by the indicator is reflected in the document, whether it should or could be (if not already), whether the person completing the review would be *willing* (addressing any personal barriers) to take the steps to change the document if changes are warranted, and whether the practitioner would be *able* (addressing any institutional barriers) to make the changes. Next, the individuals join groups in which they discuss what they noted, learned, or thought about during the document review. The practitioners convene and share ideas geared toward an action plan aimed to strengthen culturally inclusive practices on the campus. By providing an organized setting where practitioners can discuss race as a group with the aid of an outside researcher, inquiry around institutional documents helps practitioners develop racially intentional language and thorough examination of practitioner biases and assumptions (Dowd et al., 2011).

The Culturally Inclusive Policies and Practices Self-Assessment Inventory (CIPPs-SAI) is designed for individual and collective practitioner assessment to investigate the ways in which a college or university utilizes (or could utilize) culturally inclusive practices to ensure underrepresented minority students succeed in college. The Document Analysis inquiry activity emphasizes that the "best way to learn new information ... is in the context of shared, mutually engaging activity" (Dowd et al., 2011, p. 7). Behaviors are influenced by the attitudes, beliefs, intentions, and perceived control of an individual (Ajzen, 1991; Fishbein & Ajzen, 2010). As applied to college documents, this suggests that those practitioners who believe they have the ability to integrate culturally inclusive practices in their documentation, and thereby increase equity within the campus environment, will do so.

Assessment as Professional Accountability for HSIs

Historically, HSIs developed from a coalition of institutions, the Hispanic Association of Colleges and Universities (HACU), formed in 1986 to improve access for Hispanic students in higher education and increase funding for their institutions (Santiago, 2006). Consequently, HSIs are not Hispanic serving in the same historical sense as HBCUs or Tribal colleges and universities, which were established, designed, and staffed for the express purpose of serving Black and American Indian students, respectively (Benitez, 1998; Mercer & Stedman, 2008). HSIs are nascent in their development; they are still in the process of self-invention relative to other MSIs. Further, institutional self-assessment is of particular importance for HSIs because accountability structures ensuring service to Hispanic service have been lacking. Federal policy does not require HSIs that receive federal dollars reserved for HSIs to demonstrate programmatic foci on supporting Latina/o students, much less organizational culture change.

We conducted a content analysis of 80 College Cost Reduction and Access Act-Hispanic-Serving Institutions (CCRAA-HSI) programs that received funding in 2008–2009 (Malcom, Bensimon, & Davila, 2010). The results revealed a lack of intentionality in service to Latina/o student populations. Program descriptions generally focused on improving STEM programs for "STEM students," and those that did mention Latina/o students sometimes utilized deficit-minded language. According to Malcom et al. (2010), one program abstract stated "(Our college) is challenged by a large number of underprepared Hispanic and low-income students...too few of them successfully complete STEM course work or transfer to four-year universities" (p. 4). Consistent with the CCRAA funding objectives, programs concentrating on transfer and articulation agreements (84%) were most prevalent, with academic advising for all STEM students the modal strategy for achieving greater transfer access. Over half of grant recipients proposed this focus. In contrast, strategies centered on assessing the Hispanic serving mission, culture, or Hispanic student outcomes were uncommon. Only a small proportion of CCRAA programs aimed to engage in changes in campus culture (2%), benchmarking of improvements in student outcomes (16%), or assessment/data collection to gauge progress (9%). Greater accountability to spend HSI funds in service to Hispanic student success is needed particularly in light of recent legislation directing $1 billion in federal dollars over the next 10 years toward HSI-STEM funding (Malcom, Dowd, & Yu, 2010).

Without external policy incentives, a culture indicative of service to Latina/o students must come from within the institution. Consequently, it is the responsibility of the community of practitioners within institutions to hold themselves professionally accountable to their student populations. Through individual and institutional assessment practices, campuses are able to identify problems in the current culture and create change. Action research supports assessment to bring about cultural change on both the individual and organizational levels (e.g., department, college, university). CUE's IA-SAI and CIPPs-SAI described above serve as campus-level assessment inventories to observe where these cultural change processes are occurring, and to support intentionality in engaging in a change process where they are not. Practitioners mindful of culturally inclusive practices are self-reflective (Harris, Brown, Ford, & Richardson, 2004) and seek to establish learning environments that are responsive to student needs (Ford, 2005). Moreover, action research provides a foundation for practitioners to investigate and construct culturally inclusive practices through an active process of introspection and self-examination in recognition that everyone harbors stereotypes (Johnson & Inoue, 2003; Richards, Brown, & Forde, 2007). Thus, action research and action inquiry promote the ability to assess and change individual beliefs and behaviors through reflective practices that lead to broader institutional change.

Latina/o students represent a wealth of untapped potential in STEM higher education. In order to better serve the Latina/o students who enroll in HSIs, action research is recommended as an essential practice for 21st century assessment at HSIs, with the objective of supporting the development of institutional agents and developing culturally inclusive pedagogy and practices.

Notes

1 We are grateful for support of the National Science Foundation for our research on the role of institutional agents in STEM fields at Hispanic serving institutions (Grant No. 0653280). The use of National Science Foundation data or funding does not imply National Science Foundation endorsement of the research, research methods, or conclusions contained in this report. Any opinions, findings, and conclusions or recommendations expressed in this material are those of the author(s) and do not necessarily reflect the views of the National Science Foundation.

2 The authors wish to thank Dr. Ricardo Stanton-Salazar for developing the institutional agents' roles and collaborating with them to adapt these to the higher education context, with particular reference to postsecondary STEM education. Inquiries about this chapter may be directed to Alicia Dowd at adowd@usc.edu: Center for Urban Education, Waite Phillips Hall, Suite 702, Los Angeles, CA 90089.

3 Consistent with federal terminology, we use the term *Hispanic* to refer to Hispanic serving institutions and data,

4 Or, setting a higher bar for Hispanic representation, relative to the high school graduate or enrolled high school student populations.

5 Federal law defines HSIs as public or private nonprofit postsecondary institutions with 25% or more total undergraduate Hispanic full-time equivalent student enrollment; with no less than 50% of Hispanic students meeting low-income or first-generation college student criteria (Benitez, 1998; Stearns & Watanabe, 2002).

6 The terms *Black* and *African American* are used interchangeably in this chapter.

7 All names are pseudonyms.

8 Term derived from concepts adapted from culturally responsive, culturally relevant, or culturally inclusive pedagogy; see, for one key reference, Ladson-Billings (1995b).

References

Ajzen, I. (1991). The theory of planned behavior. *Organizational behavior and human decision processes, 50*(2), 179–211.

Aud, S., Fox, M., & KewalRamani, A. (2010). *Status and trends in the education of racial and ethnic groups.* (NCES 2010-015). Washington, DC: U.S. Government Printing Office.

Augustine, N. R. (2005). *Rising above the gathering storm: Energizing and employing America for a brighter economic future.* Washington, DC: National Academy Press,

Augustine, N. R., Barrett, C., Cassell, G., Grasmick, N., Holliday, C., & Jackson, S. A. (2010). *Rising above the gathering storm, revisited: Rapidly approaching Category 5.* Washington, DC: National Academy of Sciences, National Academy of Engineering, Institute of Medicine.

Benitez, M. (1998). Hispanic-serving institutions: Challenges and opportunities. In J. P. Merisotis & C. T. O'Brien (Eds.), *Minority-serving institutions: Distinct purposes, common goals* (New Directions for Higher Education, No. 102, pp. 57–68). San Francisco, CA: Jossey-Bass.

Bensimon, E. M. (2007). The underestimated significance of practitioner knowledge in the scholarship of student success. *Review of Higher Education, 30*(4), 441–469.

Bensimon, E. M., & Dowd, A. C. (2009, Winter). Dimensions of the "transfer choice" gap: Experiences of Latina and Latino students who navigated transfer pathways. *Harvard Educational Review*, 632–658.

Bensimon, E. M., Dowd, A. C., Alford, H., & Trapp, F. (2007). *Missing 87: A study of the "transfer gap" and "choice gap."* Long Beach, CA: Long Beach City College; Los Angeles, CA: Center for Urban Education, University of Southern California.

Bensimon, E. M., & Malcom, L. E. (2012). *The equity scorecard in theory and practice.* Sterling, VA: Stylus.

Bensimon, E. M., Polkinghorne, D. E., Bauman, G. L., & Vallejo, E. (2004). Doing research that makes a difference. *Journal of Higher Education, 75*(1), 104–126.

Brown, M. C., & Davis, J. E. (2001). The historically Black college as social contract, social capital, and social equalizer. *Peabody Journal of Education, 76*(1), 31–49.

Chapa, J., & De La Rosa, B. (2006). The problematic pipeline. *Journal of Hispanic Higher Education, 5*(3), 203–221.

Chubin, D. E., May, G. S., & Babco, E. (2005). Diversifying the engineering workforce. *Journal of Engineering Education, 94*(1), 57–72.

Cole, M., Engeström, Y., & Vasquez, O. (1997). *Mind, culture, and activity: Seminal papers from the Laboratory of Comparative Human Cognition.* Cambridge, England: Cambridge University Press.

Committee on Science Engineering and Public Policy. (2010). *Expanding underrepresented minority participation: America's science and technology talent at the crossroads.* Bethesda, MD: Author.

Contreras, F. E., Malcom, L. E., & Bensimon, E. M. (2008). An equity-based accountability framework for Hispanic serving institutions. In M. Gasman, B. Baez, & C. Turner (Eds.), *Interdisciplinary approaches to understanding minority serving institutions* (pp. 71–90). Albany, NY: SUNY Press.

Dowd, A. C. (2010). Improving transfer access for low-income community college students. In A. Kezar (Ed.), *Recognizing and serving low-income students in postsecondary education: An examination of institutional policies, practices, and culture* (pp. 217–231). New York: Routledge.

Dowd, A. C., Bensimon, E. M., Gabbard, G., Singleton, S., Macias, E. E., Dee, J., & Gile, D. (2006). Transfer access to elite colleges and universities in the United States: Threading the needle of the American dream. Retrieved from http://www.jkcf.org/

Dowd, A. C., Bishop, R., Bensimon, E. M., & Witham, K. (2011). Accountability for equity in postsecondary education. In K. Gallagher, R. Goodyear, & D. Brewer (Eds.), *Introduction to urban education* (pp. 170–185). New York: Routledge.

Dowd, A. C., Malcom, L. E., & Bensimon, E. M. (2009). *Benchmarking the success of Latina and Latino students in STEM to achieve national graduation goals.* Los Angeles, CA: Center for Urban Education, University of Southern California.

Engeström, Y. (2008). *From teams to knots: Activity-theoretical studies of collaboration and learning at work.* Cambridge, England: Cambridge University Press.

Fishbein, M., & Ajzen, I. (2010). *Predicting and changing behavior: The reasoned action approach.* New York: Psychology Press.

Ford, D. Y. (2005). Welcome all students to room 202: Creating culturally responsive classrooms. *Gifted Child Today, 28*(4), 28–30.

Freeman, K., Alston, S., & Winborne, D. (2008). Do learning communities enhance the quality of students' learning and motivation in STEM. *Journal of Negro Education, 77*(4), 227–240.

Fries-Britt, S., & Turner, B. (2002). Uneven stories: Successful Black collegians at a Black and a White Campus. *Review of Higher Education, 25*(3), 315–330.

Gay, G. (2000). *Culturally responsive teaching: Theory, research, and practice.* New York: Teachers College Press.

Greenwood, D. J., & Levin, M. (2005). Reform of the social sciences and of universities through action research. In N. K. Denzin & Y. S. Lincoln (Eds.), *Handbook of qualitative research* (3rd ed., pp. 43–64). Thousand Oaks, CA: Sage.

Harris, J. J., Brown, E. L., Ford, D. Y., & Richardson, J. W. (2004). African Americans and multicultural education. *Education and Urban Society, 36*(3), 304–341.

Hepworth, D. H., Rooney, R. H., & Larsen, J. (2006). *Direct social work practice: Theory and skills.* Pacific Grove, CA: Brooks/Cole.

Horn, L. (2006). *Placing college graduation rates in context: How 4-year college graduation rates vary with selectivity and the size of low-income enrollment.* Washington, DC: National Center for Educational Statisitics.

Johnson, K., & Inoue, Y. (2003). Diversity and multicultural pedagogy. *Journal of Research in International Education, 2*(3), 251-276..

Kezar, A., & Eckel, P. D. (2002). The effect of institutional culture on change strategies in higher education: Universal principals or culturally responsive concepts? *Journal of Higher Education, 73*(4), 436–460.

Ladson-Billings, G. (1995a). But that's just good teaching! The case for culturally relevant pedagogy. *Theory into Practice, 34*(3), 159–165.

Ladson-Billings, G. (1995b). Toward a theory of culturally relevant pedagogy. *American Educational Research Journal, 32*(3), 465–491.

LeMelle, T. J. (2002). The HBCU: Yesterday, today and tomorrow. *Education, 123*(1), 190–196.

Malcom, L. E., Bensimon, E. M., & Davila, B. (2010). Hispanic serving institutions moving beyond numbers toward student success. *Iowa State University: Education Policy and Practice Perspectives, Special Issue 6.*

Malcom, L. E., Dowd, A. C., & Yu, T. (2010). *Tapping HSI-STEM funds to improve Latina and Latino access to the STEM professions.* Los Angeles, CA: University of Southern California Press.

McNair, L. D. (2009). HBCU perspectives and research programs: Spelman college as a model for success in the STEM Fields. *In Memoriam.* New York: Grafton Press.

Mercer, C. J., & Stedman, J. B. (2008). Minority-serving institutions: Selected instiutional and student characteristics. In M. Gasman, Baez, B., & Turner, C.S.V. (Eds.), *Interdisciplinary approaches to understanding minority-serving institutions* (pp. 28–42) Albany, NY:SUNY Press.

Nasir, N. S., & Hand, V. M. (2006). Exploring sociocultural perspectives on race, culture, and learning. *Review of Educational Research, 76*(4), 449-475.

National Academy of Sciences. (2011). *Expanding underrepresented minority participation: America's science and technology talent at the crossroads.* Washington, DC: National Academy Press.

National Science Board. (2010). *Science and engineering indicators 2010.* Arlington, VA: National Science Foundation.

National Science Foundation. (2004). *Women, minorities, and persons with disabilities in science and engineering.* Arlington, VA: National Science Foundation.

National Science Foundation. (2011). *Women, minorities, and persons with disabilities in science and engineering.* Arlington, VA: National Science Foundation.

Noffke, S. E. (1997). Professional, personal, and political dimensions of action research. *Review of Educational Research, 22*, 305–343.

Palmer, R. T., & Gasman, M. (2008). "It takes a village to raise a child": The role of social capital in promoting academic success for African American men at a Black College. *Journal of College Student Development, 49*(1), 52–70.

Patton, M. Q. (2011). *Developmental evaluation: Applying complexity concepts to enhance innovation and use.* New York: Guilford.

Pena, E. V., Bensimon, E. M., & Colyar, J. (2006). Contextual problem defining: Learning to think and act. *Liberal Education, 92*(2), 48–55.

Penuel, W. R., Fishman, B. J., Cheng, B. H., & Sabelli, N. (2011). Organizing research and development at the intersection of learning, implementation, and design. *Educational Researcher, 40*(7), 331–337.

Polkinghorne, D. E. (2004). *Practice and the human sciences: The case for a judgment-based practice of care.* Albany, NY: SUNY Press.

Reason, P. (1994). Three approaches to participative inquiry. In N. K. Denzin & Y. S. Lincoln (Eds.), *Handbook of qualitative research* (pp. 324–339). Thousand Oaks, CA: Sage.

Rendón L. I. (1994). Validating culturally diverse students: Toward a new model of learning and student development. *Innovative Higher Education, 19*(1), 33–51.

Richards, H. V., Brown, A. F., & Forde, T. B. (2007). Addressing diversity in schools: Culturally responsive pedagogy. *Teaching Exceptional Children, 39*(3), 64–68.

Santiago, D. A. (2006). Inventing Hispanic-serving institutions (HSIs): The basics. Retrieved from http://www.edexcelencia.org/research/inventing-hispanic-serving-institutions-basics

Santiago, D. A. (2011). HSIs 2009–2010: Hispanic serving institutions. Retrieved from http://www.edexcelencia.org/research/hispanic-serving-institutions-2009-2010-factsheet

Schein, E. H. (1985). Understanding culture change in the context of organizational change. *Organizational Culture and Leadership*, 244–310.

Seo, M. G., & Creed, W. E. D. (2002). Institutional contradictions, praxis, and institutional change: A dialectical perspective. *Academy of Management Review, 27*(2), 222–247.

Stage, F. K., & Hubbard, S. M. (2009). Attitudes, perceptions, and preferences of faculty at Hispanic Serving and predominantly Black institutions. *Journal of Higher Education, 80*(3), 270–289.

Stanton-Salazar, R. D. (1997). A social capital framework for understanding the socialization of racial minority children and youths. *Harvard Educational Review, 67*(1), 1–40.

Stanton-Salazar, R. D. (2001). *Manufacturing hope and despair: The school and kin support networks of U.S.-Mexican youth.* New York: Teachers College Press.

Stanton-Salazar, R. D. (2011). A social capital framework for the study of institutional agents and their role in the empowerment of low-status youth. *Youth and Society, 43*(3), 1066–1109.

Stanton-Salazar, R. D., Macias, R. M., Bensimon, E. M., & Dowd, A. C. (2010). *The role of institutional agents in providing institutional support to Latino students in STEM.* Paper presented at the 35th annual conference for the Association for the Study of Higher Education, Indianapolis, IN.

Stearns, C., & Watanabe, S. (2002). *Hispanic serving institutions: Statistical trends from 1990–1999* (National Center for Education Statistics Report No. NCES 2002–051). Washington, DC: U.S. Department of Education.

Sue, D. W., Capodilupo, C. M., Torino, G. C., Bucceri, J. M., Holder, A. M. B., Nadal, K. L., & Esquilin, M. (2007). Racial microaggressions in everyday life—Implications for clinical practice. *American Psychologist, 62*(4), 271–286.

Tate, W. F. (1995). Returning to the root: A culturally relevant approach to mathematics pedagogy. *Theory into Practice, 34*(3), 166–173.

Terry, L. M. (2010). Prisons, pipelines, and the president: Developing critical math literacy through participatory action research. *Education Faculty Scholarship, 1*(2), 73–104.

12

ASIAN AMERICAN AND NATIVE AMERICAN PACIFIC ISLANDER SERVING INSTITUTIONS (AANAPISIs)

Mutable Sites for Science, Technology, Engineering, and Math (STEM) Degree Production

Robert T. Teranishi, Dina C. Maramba, and Minh Hoa Ta

Introduction

One of the most urgent challenges facing the United States in the 21st century is to increase the proportion of Americans with a high-quality postsecondary credential. This can only be achieved through the participation of all Americans, including underrepresented racial minority groups, low-income students, immigrants, and language minorities. It is within this context that we highlight the relevance and untapped potential of Asian American and Native American Pacific Islander serving institutions (AANAPISIs), which are institutions federally designated and funded as minority serving institutions (MSIs), in order to improve access and outcomes of low-income and underserved Asian American and Pacific Islander (AAPI) students. This chapter focuses on the ways in which AANAPISIs are critical for understanding and responding to the unique experiences and outcomes of AAPI students in science, technology, engineering, and math (STEM).

A recent study by the National Commission on AAPI Research in Education (2010) discusses the importance of the AANAPISI federal program: First, the program acknowledges the unique challenges facing AAPI students in college access and completion. Second, the AANAPISI program represents a significant commitment of much-needed resources to improving the postsecondary completion rates among AAPI and low-income students. Third, the program acknowledges how campus settings can be mutable points of intervention—sites of possibilities for responding to the impediments AAPI students encounter.

With a focus on the need for a national effort to improve the production of degrees in STEM, this chapter discusses the following: (a) a background on AAPI students and their position within broader discourse and policy efforts related to STEM priorities in higher education; (b) a background on the AANAPISI federal program; (c) a discussion of the ways in which AANAPISIs respond to the unique needs and challenges of AAPI students to increase access to and success during college; and (d) a case study of a specific STEM program at an AANAPISI campus, City College of San Francisco. Ultimately, this chapter will provide lessons that can be learned from AANAPISIs that contribute to the collective strength of MSIs in responding to gaps in STEM degree production in U.S. higher education.

AAPIs and the Broader Discourse on STEM Degree Production

Racial and ethnic minorities are important to national STEM degree production. The sheer size and changing demography of our nation, which has as its fastest growing groups people of color, immigrants, and English language learners, must be at the forefront of how we think about higher education and our nation's future. Despite a growing recognition of the importance of minorities in broader federal higher education priorities, AAPIs are often not considered underrepresented minorities in federal programs that address minority access and degree attainment in STEM. According to the National Science Foundation (NSF), a significant engine for minority STEM efforts, AAPIs are not considered an "underrepresented group" thereby excluding them from grants, fellowships, and efforts to support minority-serving institutions (NSF, 2008, 2011). The exclusion of AAPIs from federal programs that support minority advancement in STEM is also true of other federal agencies and other federally funded organizations, including the National Academies and the National Institutes of Health.

The perceptions and treatment of AAPIs as a successful minority group has a number of negative consequences for the student population. First, the exclusion of AAPIs in broader efforts to address demographic changes in the nation are overlooking the ways in which demographic trends for the total higher education population are fueled, in part, by the AAPI population. A population projected to reach nearly 40 million persons (National Commission, 2011), AAPIs are a large and growing segment of U.S. higher education enrollment—AAPI enrollment grew five-fold between 1979 and 2009. College enrollment is projected to increase for all racial groups, but AAPIs will experience a particularly high proportional increase of 35% over the next decade (National Commission, 2011; see Table 12.1).

Second, the perception and treatment of AAPIs as a nonminority, minority overlooks a significant sector within the population that experiences educational challenges. Aggregated data on AAPI conceals a high degree of heterogeneity that exists within the population. The AAPI racial category consists of 48 different ethnic groups that occupy positions along the full range of the

TABLE 12.1 AAPI Undergraduate Enrollment, 1979–2019

Year	AAPI Undergraduate Enrollment
1979	235,000
1989	550,000
1999	913,000
2009	1,332,000
2019	1,698,000

Source: NCES, IPEDS (as cited in National Commission on Asian American and Pacific Islander Research in Education, 2011).

socioeconomic spectrum, from the poor and underprivileged, to the affluent and highly skilled. AAPIs also speak 300 different languages and have wide variation in immigration histories, cultures, and religions (National Commission, 2011).

Third, because the AAPI population is unlike any other major racial group with regard to their heterogeneity, incidences of low educational attainment are concealed within aggregated data. Consider that 55 to 65% Southeast Asian and Pacific Islander adults have not enrolled in any postsecondary education (National Commission, 2011). Moreover, 40% of Southeast Asians have not completed high school. Among AAPI students who do attend college, it is important to recognize that they attend a wide range of postsecondary institutions. While there are large numbers of AAPIs attending 4-year colleges and universities, many AAPIs are also attending community colleges and other sectors of higher education. In fact, the largest concentration of AAPI college enrollment is in community colleges, which is also where AAPIs are experiencing the greatest growth (National Commission, 2011).

The high concentration of AAPI enrollment in community colleges means we need to do a better job of understanding who these students are and what they are experiencing during college. For example, compared to AAPIs in 4-year colleges, AAPI community college students are more likely to enter college with lower levels of academic preparation, delay matriculation after high school, attend college as part-time students, work while attending college, and enroll in remedial education. AAPI students at community colleges are also more likely to come from low-income backgrounds and be the first in their families to attend college (Teranishi, 2010).

Finally, differential access to different types of postsecondary institutions has a number of implications for the likelihood of degree attainment. Approximately half of Southeast Asian (Vietnamese, Hmong, Laotian, and Cambodian), and Pacific Islander (Native Hawaiian, Guamanian, Samoan, and Tongan) students leave college without earning a degree, which is 3 to 5 times the likelihood of dropping out compared to East Asians (Chinese, Korean, and Japanese) and South Asians (Asian Indian and Pakistani; Table 12.2).

Conversely, East Asians and South Asians have a greater likelihood of having a college degree and continuing on to earn an advanced degree. These data represent the significant challenges that exist among marginalized and vulnerable groups of AAPI students.

The perception of universal academic success among AAPIs results in AAPI students being underserved and excluded from a number of important efforts to address disparities in minority STEM production. This is despite the fact that we need all minority students to improve their participation and completion in STEM fields. According to a report by the Higher Education Research Institute at UCLA (2010), STEM undergraduates across all ethnic groups, including AAPIs, have substantially lower degree completion rates than their same-race peers who enter other academic disciplines. Teranishi (2010) found that while AAPIs are more likely to enter college as a STEM major, they also have the highest rate of switching majors to a non-STEM field. Additionally, the perception of a high representation of AAPIs in STEM is misleading because of

TABLE 12.2 Educational Attainment Rates of AAPI Adults (25 Years or Older), by Ethnicity, 2006–2008

	Have Not Attended College	Percentage Among College Attendees			
		Some College, No Degree	Associate's Degree	Bachelor's Degree	Advanced Degree
Asian American					
Asian Indian	20.4%	8.2%	5.0%	40.5%	46.3%
Filipino	23.8%	26.6%	15.4%	46.9%	11.1%
Japanese	27.8%	21.5%	14.4%	43.9%	20.2%
Korean	29.3%	18.1%	9.4%	46.8%	25.8%
Pakistani	30.2%	12.7%	8.1%	42.6%	36.5%
Chinese	34.5%	12.5%	8.5%	39.2%	39.7%
Thai	36.0%	20.7%	14.3%	40.9%	24.1%
Vietnamese	51.1%	33.7%	15.7%	34.3%	16.3%
Hmong	63.2%	47.5%	22.1%	25.2%	5.1%
Laotian	65.5%	46.5%	19.7%	26.6%	7.2%
Cambodian	65.8%	42.9%	20.7%	28.8%	7.6%
Pacific Islander					
Native Hawaiian	49.3%	50.0%	17.2%	22.7%	10.1%
Guamanian	53.0%	47.0%	20.6%	25.0%	7.5%
Samoan	56.8%	58.1%	20.2%	14.3%	7.4%
Tongan	57.9%	54.0%	15.0%	24.8%	6.2%

Source: American Community Survey, 3-year Public Use Microdata Sample (PUMS; cited in National Commission on Asian American and Pacific Islander Research in Education. (2011).

international students from Asia who often share the classroom with domestic students in U.S. higher education, a trend that conceals trends that occur among AAPI students in STEM (Teranishi, 2010). In fact, a 2011 NSF report further reinforces the notion of AAPI overrepresentation when it stated, "Asians are not considered underrepresented because they are a larger percentage of science and engineering degree recipients and of employed scientists and engineers than they are of the population" (p. 2). Statistics in 2006 indeed show that 9.3% of AAPIs attained bachelor's degrees in science and engineering, which is higher than the national average (4.6%; Museus, Palmer, Davis, & Maramba, 2011). However, this figure is misleading because it does not recognize the diversity and specific underserved groups in the AAPI category (Museus et al., 2011, Teranishi, 2010). Finally, while some AAPI subgroups, such as Chinese and Indians, are earning degrees in STEM fields at a higher rate than for all students, this is certainly not the case for all AAPIs. Some groups, including Southeast Asians and Pacific Islanders, have very poor representation in STEM fields (National Commission, 2010).

We assert that if we are to achieve a higher rate of degree production in STEM, we need to be mindful of the barriers that are impacting access to and degree completion for all students, including AAPIs. This is particularly the case for institutions serving high concentrations of low-income AAPI students. AANAPISIs are an instructive site through which to understand the unique needs of low-income AAPI students pursuing STEM degrees. The following section provides a brief background on the AANAPISI federal program in order to provide a context for their role in addressing the needs of AAPI students in STEM.

A Background on AANAPISIs

AANAPISIs are the newest of MSIs. Similar to other MSI programs that serve particular racial and ethnic minority groups, AANAPISIs are critical for responding to the unique needs and challenges of low-income AAPI students. Yet, making a case for, and the existence of AANAPISIs did not come without challenges. There were a number of reasons AANAPISIs faced difficulty in coming to fruition. First, one of the challenges was the stubborn and persistent racialization of AAPIs as a model minority—a group with academic achievement whose students do not have needs or concerns worthy of attention by researchers, policymakers, or practitioners. Second, the aggregated data AAPIs made it difficult to paint an accurate picture of individual ethnic groups to gain an understanding of the unique needs of underserved AAPI subgroups.

Park and Teranishi (2008) discussed the ways in which the establishment of AANAPISIs occurred in a series of events and legislation stages. A key starting point to the formation of the AANAPISI federal program was an interim 2001 report distributed by the White House Initiative on Asian Americans and

Pacific Islanders that encouraged a federal designation for "Asian American and Pacific Islander Serving Institutions and Organizations" (Park & Teranishi, 2008, p. 114) which would emphasize the encouragement of partnerships between the federal government and community based organizations. Although reports such as this were important factors in creating AANAPISIs, it was in May 2002 (U.S. Congress, H.R. 4825) that Congressman Robert Underwood (D-Guam) formally proposed that the Higher Education Act of 1965 be amended to include funding for colleges and universities that served AAPI students (Park & Teranishi, 2008). This was introduced again as H.R. 4825 in the House of Representatives and eventually reached the Senate as H.R. 333 introduced in the House by Congressman David Wu (D-OR). Finally, in 2005 it was presented as H.R. 2616 by Senators Barbara Boxer (D-CA) and Daniel Akaka (D-HI) as a Senate companion bill S. 2160, the Asian American and Pacific Islanders Serving Institutions Act (Park & Teranishi, 2008).

A few years later, the College Cost Reduction and Access Act of 2007 included the instituting of the AANAPISI federal program (National Commission, 2010). This program provides resources to postsecondary institutions serving at least 10% enrollment of AAPI students, a minimum threshold of low-income students, and lower average educational and general expenditures per student (National Commission, 2010, 2011). As of FY2011 there were 52 institutions with the AANAPISI designation, of which 15 that have been funded and 64 more that meet the criteria, but were not designated, nor funded.[1]

AANAPISIs as Mutable Sites of Opportunity

The formation of AANAPISIs is one of the most important federal policy initiatives for the AAPI community relative to higher education. The federal AANAPISI program is a programmatic effort that enables institutions to respond to the false assumption that AAPIs are not relevant in broader efforts to address significant challenges that exist within U.S. higher education.

As of June 2011, there were 15 postsecondary institutions that had been funded through the AANAPISI program (Table 12.3). The first 15 funded AANAPISIs were in states that include California, Hawaii, Illinois, New York, Massachusetts, Maryland, Texas, Washington, and the U.S. territory, Guam. It is also notable that more than half of the institutions were public, 2-year colleges.

One of the reasons the MSI policy strategy works for AAPI students is that they are highly concentrated in a small number of postsecondary institutions. As of 2009, for example, nearly two-thirds of AAPI undergraduate enrollment was concentrated in 200 institutions. The first 15 funded AANAPISIs combined enrolled nearly one in 10 AAPI undergraduates. This is in sharp contrast to their enrollment of 1.5% of the nation's total undergraduate population. In 2009 these 15 institutions enrolled nearly 89,000 AAPI undergraduates and awarded nearly 9,500 associate's and bachelor's degrees to AAPI students.

TABLE 12.3 Asian American and Native American Pacific Islander Serving Institutions, 2008–2010

Institution	State/ Territory	Higher Education Sector	Cohort Year
City College of San Francisco	CA	Public, 2-year	2008
De Anza College	CA	Public, 2-year	2008
Guam Community College	Guam	Public, 2-year	2008
South Seattle Community College	WA	Public, 4-year	2008
University of Hawaii at Hilo	HI	Public, 4-year	2008
University of Maryland-College Park	MD	Public, 4-year	2008
CUNY Queens College	NY	Public, 4-year	2009
Santa Monica College	CA	Public, 2-year	2009
Coastline Community College	CA	Public, 2-year	2010
Laney College	CA	Public, 2-year	2010
Mission College	CA	Public, 2-year	2010
Richland College	TX	Public, 2-year	2010
University of Guam	Guam	Public, 4-year	2010
University of Illinois at Chicago	IL	Public, 4-year	2010
University of Massachusetts-Boston	MA	Public, 4-year	2010

Sources: U.S. Department of Education. (n.d.). Asian American and Native American Pacific Islander Serving Institution Program Awards. Retrieved June, 2011 (as cited in Teranishi, 2011).

It is also important to note that the students they are serving are disproportionately immigrants and non-native English speakers, from low-income backgrounds, and the first in their families to attend college. A report by the Congressional Research Services (2009) found that the institutions that met the criteria for AANAPISI funding enrolled 75% of the low-income AAPI students in U.S. higher education in 2007. In other words, AANAPISIs provide resources for institutions that enroll the highest concentrations of low-income AAPI students. More importantly, AANAPISIs utilize their resources to respond to the unique needs of their students and engage in a range of initiatives that aim to increase access to and success in college.

Federal funding is also incentivizing institutional reform on AANAPISI campuses by supporting programs to increase *access* (increase in enrollment) to and *success* (persistence, degree attainment, and transfer) in college for AAPI students. While each one of the 15 funded AANAPISIs is using the funding in unique ways, several commonalities exist among the programs. These services were concentrated around academic and student support services, leadership and mentorship opportunities, and research and resource opportunities.

Academic and Student Support Services

AANAPISI funding is increasing access to and utilization of academic counseling, learning communities, financial aid counseling, and tutoring programs, which are helping students to be more academically engaged and improving both retention and degree attainment.

Leadership and Mentorship Opportunities

AANAPISI funding is providing students with greater leadership development and mentorship opportunities, which is increasing both academic and social engagement among AAPI students and improving their academic and career trajectories.

Research and Resource Development

AANAPISI funding is being used to improve the quality of statistical information on AAPI students. This is more accurately reflecting the variations that exist between AAPI ethnic subgroups and developing better systems for tracking student progress and degree attainment rates.

The following is an example of how one funded AANAPISI implemented programmatic initiatives within their campus. As discussed earlier, each AANAPISI has utilized its funding in different ways. Along the same spirit of understanding that the AAPI student population is diverse, each funded AANAPISI identified specific needs particular to the needs of their institution. We present the City College of San Francisco as a case study and describe their programmatic approaches to successfully serving AAPI students.

Case Study of the AANAPISI STEM Achievement Program (ASAP)

City College of San Francisco (CCSF) is one of the oldest and largest community colleges in the nation. CCSF is also one of the largest postsecondary institutions, each year enrolling roughly 100,000 students and offering over 4,700 course sections at nine campuses. The college provides educational access to an extremely diverse student population, including a large percentage of AAPI students (38%; and see Table 12.4).

The CCSF Office of Research and Planning collected data in 2010 which indicated important characteristics of City College of San Francisco students. Seventy-four percent of entering students are placed in developmental education. AAPIs and Latinos are heavily represented in the Non-Native English Speaking category (23% of the 54,000 degree-seeking students). While 83% of the degree-seeking students are part-time (less than 24 units a year), a total of

TABLE 12.4 Demographics of CCSF Credit Students (degree applicable), 2008–2009

Ethnicity	Percent of CCSF Credit Population
American Indian/Alaskan Native	1 %
African American	8 %
Hispanic/Latino	15 %
Asian American	27 %
Filipino	7 %
Pacific Islander	1 %
Southeast Asian	3 %
White (Non-Hispanic)	27 %
Other (Non White)	3 %
Unknown/No Response	9 %

Data Source: Teranishi, R.T. (2011).

30% of credit bearing students receive financial aid. In addition 61% received one to three matriculation services such as testing, orientation, and counseling. Students who enter CCSF placed in developmental education experience a lower rate of persistence and degree completion. For example, 65% full-time non-basic-skills students graduated or transferred in 6 years as compared to 17% part-time basic skills students.

While an assumption persists that AAPI students outperform others in math and science, a close examination of AAPI students at CCSF reveals a complex and volatile picture, with many students struggling in the critical areas of STEM. More specifically, Filipino and Pacific Islander populations are among the students who have the lowest degree attainment and transfer rates compared to other AAPI subgroups and White students.

This trend is repeated across all the STEM disciplines at CCSF. Data collected at CCSF reveal that while a high percentage of AAPI students enroll in remedial math, only 56% continue to the next level, and only 30 to 35% reach transfer-level mathematics. The average passing rate for college level chemistry is 46 to 47%.

With the assistance of the $1.6 million funded by the U.S. Department of Education, the AAPI STEM Achievement Project (ASAP) Center was created in 2008. The objective of ASAP is to increase the number of degrees and transfers for disadvantaged AAPIs at CCSF such as Southeast Asians, Filipinos, Pacific Islanders, and other underserved students in the disciplines of STEM. In the first year, the first task was to find a viable location on campus for the ASAP Center. With the support of the CCSF administration, a center was established to house a computer lab, study area, and office space for instructional and counseling faculty to mentor and advise students. An advisory group was formed that included professionals from the Pacific Gas and Electric Company, faculty from the University of California at Berkeley, San Francisco State University, and community members from underrepresented AAPI communities.

A project manager was assigned to ASAP to work in collaboration with department chairs and faculty from nine STEM disciplines. Together they identified and created 41 academic transfer pathways covering over 50 specific majors to the University of California at Berkeley and San Francisco State University. This collaboration was important as one of ASAP's objectives was to assist students to transfer successfully to a 4-year university, and ASAP created a STEM website specifically to provide students with information in regard to the transfer process. The progress-to-degree process was further streamlined through the addition of 10 sections which included high demand courses such as biology, chemistry, and mathematics classes.

The second task was to launch an outreach and media campaign on campus. By the beginning of the second semester of its existence, the ASAP Center coordinated an open house and recruited 272 underrepresented students. The students included 54% male and 46% female. Eighty-five percent of the AAPI population in ASAP consists of immigrants. While 88% of the underrepresented students in ASAP entered CCSF with a high school diploma, 22% earned a GED degree. In addition, 33.3% had or were taking English as a second language (ESL) classes and 66% worked while attending school. The students included 38% Chinese, 21% Filipino, 11% Vietnamese, 2% Pacific Islanders, 7% other Asian ethnicities, and 21% were first generation college students. The majority of the students were biology, biochemistry, or chemistry majors, with engineering ranking second, followed by computer science, geology, astronomy, and mathematics, respectively.

In the third and fourth semesters of the grant implementation, CCSF also involved students to assist with the ASAP Center. First, they created a student ambassador program. Student ambassadors were trained to do outreach for CCSF and disseminate information about STEM career paths to 1,000 CCSF students and 5,000 high school students. ASAP also hired CCSF alumni and current AAPI students in STEM, to provide tutoring at the ASAP Center and other retention centers located at the college: the African American Scholastic program (AASP), the Latino/a Services Network (LSN), and the Asian Pacific American Student Success Retention Center (APASS). ASAP provided a study hall and student center to foster instruction, tutoring, and discussion in an informal, relaxed atmosphere. Students who participated in the program were provided with tutorial services, faculty assistance, and supplemental instruction. In addition, tutoring services offered at several locations across the campus emerged as an important facet in the ASAP Center's success.

To prepare students who enrolled in chemistry, a faculty-led one-day boot camp session titled "Making Multiple Meanings of Central Scientific Terms

Meaningful" was designed and implemented. In addition, workshops offered during the winter and summer breaks introduced students to the concept of vectors and demonstrated how concepts/terms used in all mathematics and science courses are interrelated. Students participated in a book loan program, as well as field trips to National Aeronautics and Space Administration (NASA), high tech companies in the Silicon Valley, and the Academy of Art. In addition, participating students were funded to attend STEM-related conferences such as Pre-Med, Women Engineering, National Engineering, the National Chemical Society, as well as science fairs throughout the San Francisco area. Students were also encouraged to join professional STEM societies and associations. Furthermore, National Science Foundation scholarships were made accessible to all eligible STEM students.

To track and support student retention and transfer rates, all recruited students were required to meet with an academic counselor at the APASS or the ASAP centers at least once per semester. Caseloads were generated each semester and the students' academic progress was monitored. The project manager also maintained communication with ASAP participants via e-mail. In addition, the STEM website was updated every month and provided information to the students about priority registration and other STEM-related services.

By spring 2012, 119 (42%) of STEM participant students transferred to a 4-year university. Moreover, AAPI students who started as STEM majors and participated in the support services such as supplemental instruction and tutorials had completion rates of 50 to 60% respectively. By comparison, nonparticipants who began college as a STEM major had completion rates of 15 to 20%.

The AANAPISI funded Asian Pacific American STEM Project at CCSF has provided valuable and successful support to students in the last 3 years. Furthermore, the funding allowed the institution to update some of its aging science lab equipment, and inadequate supplies. The funding also made it possible for faculty to examine and improve student learning experiences and campus-wide teaching techniques.

Lessons Learned from AANAPISIs

There are a number of lessons that can be learned from AANAPISIs that contribute to the collective strength of MSIs, including a response to gaps in STEM degree production in U.S. higher education. Based on the case study of CCSF, we can glean a number of lessons from a funded AANAPISI. First, AANAPISIs effectively address the issue of aggregation of the AAPI population. In CCSF's ASAP, one of their objectives included that they recognize and pinpoint underserved AAPI populations in their institutions. In their disaggregation of data, they specifically identified Southeast Asian, Filipino, and Pacific Islander as populations of concern. Second, CCSF acknowledged the critical need to support these particular populations especially in STEM fields.

Third, AANAPISI funding afforded the institution to provide support services that worked toward recruiting, retaining, and transferring students to a 4-year university. CCSF's ASAP, effectively used student ambassadors, peer tutoring, supplemental instruction, interaction with faculty, participation in STEM related conferences, and additional academic advising as strategies for fostering persistence of its participants.

More importantly, these findings have a number of larger and far reaching implications for higher education institutions, federal agencies, and federally funded organizations. They play an important role in accountability and have undue influence in establishing more equitable environments and policies for AAPIs. First, the racialization and unrelenting association with the image of the model minority must continue to be challenged and dismantled at these institutional and federal levels. Second, it is irrefutable that the aggregation of AAPI data is a barrier toward having a clearer understanding of the needs of diverse groups within the AAPI category. Hence, what and how AAPI data is collected and analyzed is critical for the effective disaggregation of AAPI data. This cannot work effectively without a mandate by the federal government. Third, federal agencies and funded organizations must formally recognize that the AAPI population is indeed a group in need of critical examination and services. This is important because federal organizations and agencies play a pivotal role in funding programs and activities that invest in creating equitable opportunities for the AAPI population. The AANAPISI federally funded program is one such example of an effort toward active implementation of addressing issues that affect AAPIs especially with regard to fostering successful STEM participation. Finally, as substantiated from the CCSF case study, AANAPISIs are optimal sites for bringing attention to and addressing the complexity of the AAPI population and the subsequent glaring need for stronger collaboration among higher education institutions and federal agencies and organizations especially with regard to fostering the success of underserved AAPI students in STEM.

Note

1 To receive AANAPISI designation and funding, higher education institutions are required to go through an application process.

References

Congressional Research Service. (2009). *Memorandum regarding the number of institutions potentially eligible to receive grants under the assistance to Asian American and Native American and Pacific Islander-serving institutions program.* Washington, DC: Author.

Higher Education Research Institute, University of California, Los Angeles. (2010). *Degrees of success bachelor's degree completion rates among initial STEM majors.* Los Angeles, CA: Author.

Museus, S. D., Palmer, R. T., Davis, R. J., & Maramba, D. C. (2011). *Racial and ethnic minority students' success in STEM education* (ASHE–Higher Education Report Series, Vol. 36, No. 6). San Francisco, CA: Jossey-Bass.

National Commission on Asian American and Pacific Islander Research in Education. (2010). *Federal higher education policy priorities and the Asian American and Pacific Islander community.* New York: Author.

National Commission on Asian American and Pacific Islander Research in Education. (2011). *The relevance of Asian Americans and Pacific Islanders in the college completion agenda.* New York: Author.

National Science Foundation. (2008). *Broadening participation at the NSF: A framework for action.* Arlington, VA: Author.

National Science Foundation. (2011). *Women, minorities, and persons with disabilities in science and engineering: 2011.* Arlington, VA: Author.

Park, J. J., & Teranishi, R. T. (2008). Asian American and Pacific Islander serving institutions. In M. Gasman, B. Baez, & C. S. V. Turner (Eds.), *Understanding minority serving institutions* (pp. 111–126). Albany, NY: SUNY Press.

Teranishi, R. T. (2010). *Asians in the ivory tower: Dilemmas of racial inequality in American higher education.* New York: Teachers College Press.

Teranishi, R. T. (2011). Office of Research and Planning. San Francisco: Community College of San Francisco.

13

COLLABORATIVE PARTNERSHIPS IN ENGINEERING BETWEEN HISTORICALLY BLACK COLLEGES AND UNIVERSITIES AND PREDOMINANTLY WHITE INSTITUTIONS

Christopher B. Newman and M. Bryant Jackson

For over 40 years, historically Black colleges and universities (HBCUs) and predominantly White institutions (PWIs) have maintained collaborative partnerships through dual degree programs, with a majority of these programs situated in engineering. In this chapter, we examine the ongoing role of HBCUs and the historical challenges these institutions have faced with regard to establishing engineering education for African Americans. We then look specifically at a few examples of dual degree programs and highlight the main parameters of the partnerships. We conclude this chapter by probing some of the key advantages and disadvantages of maintaining these dual degree programs in engineering.

Vital Role of HBCUs

HBCUs were created in large part because of racial segregation in higher education and the resulting unmet needs of newly freed African Americans in Southern states (Anderson, 1988; Palmer & Gasman, 2008). The institutions of higher education established to educate African Americans in the United States played a pivotal role in producing professionals in highly technical areas like science and engineering (Trent & Hill, 1994). Moreover, HBCUs still confer a large portion of bachelor's degrees in science, technology, engineering, and mathematics (STEM) among African American students (Leggon & Pearson, 1997; National Science Foundation [NSF], 2011). HBCUs comprise only 3% of the nation's 4-year colleges and universities (Palmer & Gasman, 2008; Palmer & Wood, 2012); yet, these institutions confer baccalaureate degrees in STEM subjects on a large portion of this nation's African Americans (NSF, 2011). As presented in Table 13.1, HBCUs, between 2001 and 2009, awarded 21.1%

TABLE 13.1 Examples of Some HBCU and PWI (3–2) Dual Degree Programs in Engineering

	Bethune Cookman	Clark Atlanta	Dillard	Morehouse	Spelman	Xavier
Auburn		X		X	X	
Alabama – Huntsville		X		X	X	
Columbia			X	X	X	
Dartmouth				X	X	
Florida	X	X				
Florida State	X					
Georgia Tech		X	X	X	X	X
Michigan		X		X	X	
Missouri Sci & Tech		X		X	X	
New Orleans			X			X
Notre Dame		X		X	X	X
Rensselaer		X		X	X	
Rochester		X		X	X	
Tulane			X			X

Note: This list is not an exhaustive list of Dual Degree Engineering Programs

of bachelor's degrees in engineering to African Americans (NSF, 2011). This figure is quite high considering the relatively few HBCUs with degree offerings in engineering. Additionally, HBCUs, between 2001 and 2009, conferred 22.8% of bachelor's degrees in the sciences (NSF, 2011). In essence, HBCUs award one in five bachelor's degrees in science and engineering to African Americans. Furthermore, Slaughter (2009) points out that seven of the top 10 bachelor's degree producers of African American engineers are HBCUs. Additionally, over half of African Americans who go on to receive doctoral degrees in most science fields, have earned their bachelor's degrees from HBCUs (Leggon, 2010; Slaughter, 2009).

The success of HBCUs and the significant contributions to the education of African Americans reside in providing an environment, which cultivates talent, affirms a scholastic identity, and fosters mentoring relationships (Allen, 1992; Davis, 1994; Fleming, 2004; Harper, Carini, Bridges, & Hayek, 2004; Palmer & Gasman, 2008; Perna et al., 2009). For example, in a study focusing on standardized test scores, Fleming (2004) found African American high achievers attending HBCUs tended to have higher self-esteem and their academic performance was more consistent with their abilities (i.e., previous academic performances). Conversely, she found African American high achievers at PWIs had more psychosocial challenges, which diverted their attention away from their academic goals. Consistent with Allen (1992) and Davis (1994), Fleming's

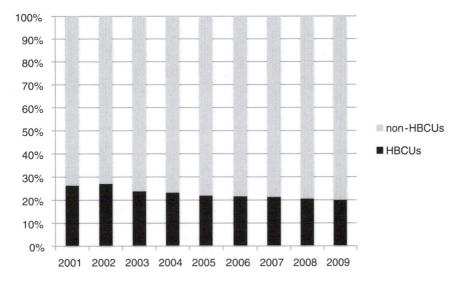

FIGURE 13.1 Bachelor's degrees in the sciences awarded to African Americans by institution type, 2001–2009.

(2004) findings suggest HBCUs provide environments promoting academic achievement and psychological well-being among African Americans.

HBCUs Challenges in Developing and Sustaining Engineering Programs

Since their inception, most HBCUs have struggled to obtain adequate financial resources to build cutting edge facilities, which is a significant disadvantage when trying to establish STEM programs like engineering. PWIs, especially research universities with very high research activity, have received a substantial portion of federal government expenditures with HBCUs receiving a very small portion of federal monies (Suitts, 2003). Additionally, PWI public flagship campuses in Southern states, have historically received a disproportionate amount of state appropriations (Slaton, 2010). In one such state system, Slaton (2010) chronicles the ways in which the University of Maryland denied resources to an HBCU, University of Maryland Eastern Shore, and opportunities to African Americans in engineering education. Slaton (2010) focuses on a number of policies like the inequitable funding of the College Park and Eastern Shore campuses. The disparate funding streams for each campus are emblematic of the social ideologies of then system President Byrd, who propagated social inequality through racist beliefs in the subordination of African Americans in Maryland. He used education policies and practices to ensure African Americans did not participate in highly skilled labor markets like engineering.

In one of many examples of racist policies, the University of Maryland Board of Regents offered African Americans scholarships, beginning in 1932, to attend universities outside of the UMD system (Slaton, 2010). Slaton (2010) chronicles how the scholarships were instituted to support out- of- state study for African Americans who were unable to find suitable college degree programs in the UMD system. Slaton argues:

> The $600 scholarship fund intended to cover the expenses of multiple students at the undergraduate and graduate level, was pathetically small, but represented a decision to fund scholarships instead of improvements at Eastern Shore.
>
> *(p. 29)*

The scholarship fund was a clear indicator of how little the UMD system invested in the education of their African American citizenry and how blatantly the UMD Board of Regents opposed providing equal opportunities to African Americans.

Although, the voucher system was started prior to President Byrd's reign, Byrd launched his own campaign to enhance the opportunities for White Americans at the expense of HBCUs in the state of Maryland. The College of Engineering at the College Park campus became one of President Byrd's most effective "institution-building" enterprises (Slaton, 2010). Slaton states:

> As Byrd developed engineering programs at College Park, he systematically denied the need for any such agenda at Eastern Shore, a setting he saw as removed from UMD's main branch both geographically and conceptually.
>
> *(p. 34)*

For example, there were clear disparities in the amount of investment in the infrastructure (i.e., buildings, equipment, and land cultivation) at the College Park versus Eastern Shore campuses; spending at College Park was estimated to be approximately $4 million while Eastern Shore was only $100,000 (Slaton, 2010).

According to Slaton (2010), during the first full decade of Byrd's presidency (1940–1949), Eastern Shore operated on about $500,000, although the UMD system had a budget of nearly $50 million. This datum encapsulates the inequitable resources and allocations of the higher education institution designated for African Americans in Maryland. However, UMD was not the only system operating in a blatantly racist manner. The intentional actions of the education system during this time period severely undermined the long-term capacities of HBCUs to establish and maintain engineering education programs. HBCUs' struggle for an equitable resource allocation is still an ongoing challenge (Palmer, Davis, & Gasman, 2011; Palmer & Griffin, 2009). Dual degree programs have served to fill in the void of the limited availability of engineering education at HBCUs. In the next section, we will highlight a few dual degree programs in engineering.

Examples of Collaborations between HBCUs and PWIs

Collaborative partnerships between HBCUs and PWIs have emerged as a way to increase the number of African American students earning degrees in an engineering discipline. Over the last 30 years there has been an increase in the number of partnerships between HBCUs and PWIs (Jackson, 2007). Some of these partnerships are informal in nature and may provide opportunities for students to interact with students and faculty from PWIs, access to laboratories, and mentorship opportunities. Other partnerships take on a formal nature including specific articulation agreements between universities (Jackson, 2007). One example of these agreements is dual degree engineering programs that allow students to earn a degree from both participating institutions. These dual degree programs typically fall under one of the following classifications: (a) university to university, which is an agreement is reached between an HBCU and PWI; (b) universities within a particular state system of education; (c) a consortium of universities with other universities.

Most of these formal articulations are classified as 3-2 programs. Students in these programs attend their home university, the HBCU, for 3 years then spend their final 2 years at the PWI. Students then earn two bachelor's degrees, one from their home university in an engineering or related field, and the second from the PWI in an engineering discipline. Students have to complete courses at both universities. In Table 13.1 we provide an example of dual degree collaborations between PWIs and HBCUs. This table shows the regional diversity of institutions participating in dual degree programs in engineering. In the next sections, we provide a more in-depth look at a few of these dual degree programs and the parameters of the collaboration.

The Regents of the University of Georgia have created a formal agreement known as the Regents Engineering Transfer Program (RETP) between state colleges and universities and the Georgia Institute of Technology (University System of Georgia [USG], 2012). Under this agreement, which was approved in 1986 (USG, 2012), students attending a state college or university, an institution with a "commitment to public service, continuing education, technical assistance, and economic development activities" (USG, 2012), have the opportunity to attend Georgia Tech, a research university with a "commitment to wide-ranging research, scholarship, and creative endeavors that are consistent with the highest standards of academic excellence."

The Regents have established several parameters for students participating in the program. Students must be U.S. citizens or permanent residents, who are also residents of Georgia (USG, 2012). While there are some general requirements students must satisfy, including prerequisite courses and a minimal 3.0 grade point average, the decision to admit these students is ultimately left up to the discretion of the RETP coordinator at each institution. For example, students at Savannah State are required to spend at least 3 years at that institution before spending their final 2 years at Georgia Tech. Students must complete three-fourths of the required number of hours for a degree at Savannah State (i.e., no more than 25% of credits may be transferred in). Additionally, students must satisfy all prerequisite engineering requirements for Georgia Tech at Savannah State, including the corresponding mathematics and science courses taken by students at Georgia Tech during the freshman and sophomore years.

Once students have met all of the requirements of the program, they earn a bachelor's degree from both institutions. In this example, students are able to earn a degree in one of six majors at Savannah State, chemistry, mathematics, computer science technology, and chemical, civil, electronics, and mechanical engineering technology, and one of 10 engineering majors from Georgia Tech, aerospace, chemical, civil, computer, electrical, industrial, materials, mechanical, nuclear, and textile.

The Atlanta University Center Consortium

The Atlanta University Center Consortium (AUC) is a group of four HBCUs located within a few miles of each other in the state of Georgia (Atlanta University Center Consortium [AUC], 2012). The four institutions that make up the consortium are Clark Atlanta University, a coeducational bachelor's, master's, and doctorate granting institution, Morehouse College, a bachelor's granting institution for men, Morehouse School of Medicine, a coeducational doctorate granting institution, and Spelman College, a bachelor's granting institution for women. The consortium was founded in 1929 as a way for the schools to share resources and provide programs and services for students at all the institutions.

In 1969, after receiving a grant of $265,000 from the Olin Mathieson Charitable Trust, the AUC created the first Dual Degree Engineering Partnership (DDEP) with the Georgia Institute of Technology to increase the participation of African Americans in engineering (AUC, 2012). Over the last 30 years, this partnership has grown to include 11 other schools including public, private, and elite engineering institutions.

All of the partnerships are 3-2 dual degree programs. Students begin at an AUC university and take all of their core classes, pre-engineering courses, and major requirements at their home university and the required engineering courses at the transfer institution (AUC, 2012). Upon successful completion of the requirements students earn two bachelor's degrees; a bachelor's of arts or science from their home institution and a bachelor's of science in engineering from the transfer institution. At Morehouse College for example, students are able to earn a bachelor's degree in science in general science or engineering, depending on the courses they complete.

Students, who participate in the AUC DDEP program, are eligible for other services as a result of their participation. Students have the opportunity to work with a variety of Fortune 500 companies during summer internships, co-ops, and even permanent employment. Students are encouraged to take advantage of these types of opportunities (AUC, 2012). Funding is also available for students and includes both merit based and need based aid. Each year roughly $300,000 is awarded to students. Partners from industry, foundations, and alumni of the DDEP provide these funds.

Institutional Response to Collaborative Partnerships

Scholars have demonstrated that many underrepresented students follow a non-traditional path to a degree in engineering (May & Chubin, 2003; Museus, Palmer, Davis, & Maramba, 2011; Wills, Auerbach, & Hughes, 2006). These pathways can include attending a community college, transferring to another institution, or participation in a 3-2 dual degree program. Wills et al. (2006) contend institutions that are able to recruit students to their programs and help in students' persistence will allow for more students from underrepresented backgrounds to become engineering majors.

Since 1969, Georgia Tech has established several formal 3-2 partnerships with institutions. In 2004, Georgia Tech launched the Partners in Transitioning to Tech (PITT) program to help with the retention of underrepresented students in electrical and computer engineering (Wills et al., 2006). Georgia Tech identified five different strategies to help those students who had transferred into their university from an HBCU: the use of Super-TA graduate student members, PITTStops (i.e., regular study sessions with graduate mentors and faculty), Dual Degree Distinguished Alumni Speaker Series, various professional development workshops, and a host of early assimilation programs. The PITT program seeks to increase retention rates by engaging participants in the field of engineering and through building a community for which students may feel a sense of belonging.

Potential Advantages

There are several advantages for both student participants and collaborative institutions. For students, as a result of completing upper division coursework in two distinct areas (e.g., physics and engineering or mathematics and engineering) students have a much broader educational training (Michael & Balraj, 2003). Additionally, students have access to two institutional networks (Michael & Balraj, 2003). For example a "Morehouse man" can also benefit from the national networks of Columbia, Notre Dame, or the University of Michigan. These networks may play a key role in finding a meaningful internship or career placement. Additionally, due to the PWI having a high research activity, student participants may have more access to research experiences, which may contribute to a better understanding of and familiarity with the research process. These first-hand research experiences could possibly inspire students to pursue graduate education in engineering.

Institutions also receive considerable benefits from collaborative dual degree partnerships. May and Chubin (2003) point out that dual degree programs can build on the success of HBCUs in attracting African American students and developing their talent. As a result, the main benefit for PWIs is receiving access to well-prepared African Americans and other racial minorities, who may not have attended a PWI otherwise. Furthermore, after maintaining these programs for a number of years, institutions can establish a pipeline of students, which may serve as an integrated support structure. For HBCUs, they too may attract students who may not have attended the institution otherwise. For instance, a student may be interested in engineering, but also want to pursue a liberal arts education at a highly prestigious HBCU like Morehouse or Spelman. Given that Morehouse and Spelman do not offer a degree in engineering a student may decide not to attend one of these institutions. Therefore, a student interested in engineering and attending an institution like Morehouse or Spelman can do both through dual degree programs in engineering albeit a slightly truncated experience.

Potential Disadvantages

While there are advantages to both the partnering institutions and the student participants, there are also disadvantages to both the student participants and the collaborative institutions. The main disadvantage to students is their status as a "transfer" student to the PWI institution. Over the course of the first 3 years at their respective HBCUs, students develop social support and they learn how to navigate their respective institution. However, when students enter the PWI they have to begin this process again. The student participants have to develop new social support networks, which may be difficult considering they may now be in courses with students who may have already developed social networks and study groups. Additionally, the participants have to learn the new bureaucracy at the PWI. Tasks, which may have been relatively simple to accomplish at the previous HBCU, may now be relatively more difficult especially if the PWI does not have a program similar to the PITT program at Georgia Tech.

Moreover, racial minority students, who enter a highly selective PWI through a dual degree program, may be stigmatized by their White peers and faculty members who think that the dual degree program provided a back door into the university. A number of scholars have documented the stigma and prejudices levied on racial minorities from White peers and faculty members in STEM fields (e.g., Hurtado, Newman, Tran, & Chang, 2010; Newman, 2011; Seymour & Hewitt, 1997). This stigma may create a more hostile climate, which may create negative psychosocial factors for African Americans pursuing engineering degrees at PWIs. Lastly, participating in a dual degree program may extend the time to degree for students. While most programs are advertised as 5-year programs (3-2), similar to 4-year bachelor's degree programs, the speed students complete this program may vary. This extended time to degree may lead to some increased attrition rates among dual degree participants.

The main disadvantage for the participating institutions is that this dual degree program may be perceived by some to be a new variation of the scholarship program, which Slaton (2010) documented. While this is not the case for private HBCUs, stakeholders at some of the public HBCUs may wonder why their respective state system does not build up an adequate capacity for the HBCU institution to offer engineering programs. While some may argue this is a state coordination of institutional efforts, others may postulate that the dual degree system is a "relic" from a time of discriminatory institutional practices, which disadvantaged HBCUs from garnering the same resources and prestige as their PWI counterparts. Obviously, having a well-resourced college of engineering allows a university to accumulate substantial resources. For example, currently, the top 20 schools/colleges of engineering each has research expenditures of over $100 million. Through indirect cost recovery, institutions are able to build cutting edge research facilities, recruit students with previously high academic achievement, and mobilize resources to attract world-renowned faculty members. Without comparable resources, a public HBCU will have a nearly insurmountable task of accumulating enough resources to compete with public flagship PWIs.

Conclusion

While several dual degree agreements exist between HBCUs and PWIs, the nature of these relationships is ambiguous at best. Some universities have formal agreements, such as the university system of Georgia, with well-defined parameters of participation; while others have what could be classified as "handshake" agreements where both institutions agree to participate but nothing is formalized. Additionally, information regarding these programs is sparse. Most institutional websites, particularly those of the HBCUs have very limited information regarding the programs. Some PWIs contain information about the partnerships, but very little about what students actually had to do to enter into the agreement, with most referring students to undergraduate transfer admissions. Institutions on both sides of these partnerships should do more to publicize these programs' departmental websites. Additionally, PWIs can do more to recruit students from HBCUs and advertise these programs to students during the high school recruitment process as a nontraditional path toward earning an engineering degree.

Moreover, to our knowledge, there are no empirical studies investigating the student experiences within these dual degree programs. Also, researchers should investigate the college choice process and the role of dual degree programs in students' decision to choose an HBCU or not. Future research should pay particular attention to this student population as the expansion of these dual degree programs could considerably improve the pathways for racial minorities to pursue a degree in STEM.

References

Allen, W. R. (1992). The color of success: African-American college student outcomes at predominantly White and historically Black public colleges and universities. *Harvard Educational Review, 62*(1), 26–44.

Anderson, J. D. (1988). *The education of Blacks in the South, 1860–1935.* Chapel Hill, NC: University of North Carolina Press.

Atlanta University Consortium (AUC). (2012). Retrieved from http://www.aucenter.edu/about_overview.php

Davis, J. E. (1994). College in Black and White: Campus environment and academic achievement of African American males. *Journal of Negro Education, 63*(4), 620–633.

Fleming, J. (2004). The significance of historically Black colleges for high achievers: Correlates of standardized test scores in African American students. In M. C. Brown, II & K. Freeman (Eds.), *Black colleges: New perspectives on policy and practice* (pp. 29–52). Westport, CT: Praeger.

Harper, S. R., Carini, R. Bridges, B., & Hayek, J. (2004). Gender differences in student engagement among African American undergraduates at historically Black colleges and universities. *Journal of College Student Development, 45*(3), 271–284.

Hurtado, S., Newman, C. B., Tran, M. C., & Chang, M. J. (2010). Improving the rate of success for underrepresented racial minorities in STEM fields: Insights from a national project. In S. R. Harper & C. B. Newman (Eds.), *Students of color in STEM* (New Directions for Institutional Research, No. 148, pp. 5–15). San Francisco, CA: Jossey-Bass.

Jackson, M. T. (2007). The Atlanta University Center: A consortium-based dual degree engineering program. In L. G. Dotolo & A. J. Larrance (Eds.), *Access to higher education through consortia* (New Directions for Higher Education, No. 138, pp. 19–25). San Francisco, CA: Jossey-Bass.

Leggon, C. B. (2010). Diversifying science and engineering faculties: Intersections of race, ethnicity, and gender. *American Behavioral Scientist, 53*(7), 1013–1028.

Leggon, C. B., & Pearson, W., Jr. (1997). The baccalaureate origins of African American female Ph.D. scientists. *Journal of Women and Minorities in Science and Engineering, 3*(4), 213–224.

May, G. S., & Chubin, D. E. (2003). A retrospective on undergraduate engineering success for underrepresented minority students. *Journal of Engineering Education, 92*(1), 27–39.

Michael, S. O., & Balraj, L. (2003). Higher education institutional collaborations: An analysis of models of joint degree programs. *Journal of Higher Education Policy and Management, 25*(2), 131–145.

Museus, S. D., Palmer, R. T., Davis, R. J., & Maramba, D. C. (2011). *Racial and ethnic minority students' success in STEM education* (ASHE Higher Education Report, Vol. 36, No. 6).San Francisco, CA: Jossey-Bass.

National Science Foundation, Division of Science Resources Statistics. (2011). *Women, minorities, and persons with disabilities in science and engineering: 2011* (Special Report NSF 11-309). Arlington, VA. Retrieved from http://www.nsf.gov/statistics/wmpd.

Newman, C. B. (2011). Engineering success: The role of faculty relationships with Black collegians. *The Journal of Women and Minorities in Science and Engineering, 17*(3), 193–209.

Palmer, R. T., Davis, R. J., & Gasman, M. (2011). A matter of diversity, equity, and necessity:

The tensions between Maryland's higher education system and its historically Black colleges and universities over the office of civil rights agreement. *Journal of Negro Education, 80*(2), 121–133.

Palmer, R. T., & Gasman, M. (2008). "It takes a village": Social capital and academic success at historically Black colleges and universities. *Journal of College Student Development, 49*(1), 52–70.

Palmer, R. T., & Griffin, K. (2009). Desegregation policy and disparities in faculty salary and workload: Maryland's historically Black and predominantly White institutions. *Negro Educational Review, 60*(1–4), 7–21.

Palmer, R. T., & Wood, J. L. (Eds.). (2012). *Black men in college: Implications for HBCUs and beyond.* New York: Routledge.

Perna, L., Lundy-Wagner, V., Drezner, N. D., Gasman, M., Yoon, S., Bose, E., & Gary, S. (2009). The contribution of HBCUs to the preparation of African American women for STEM careers: A case study. *Research in Higher Education, 50*(1), 1–23.

Seymour, E., & Hewitt, N. M. (1997). *Talking about leaving: Why undergraduates leave the sciences.* Boulder, CO: Westview Press.

Slaton, A. E. (2010). *Race, rigor, and selectivity in U.S. engineering: The history of an occupational color line.* Cambridge, MA: Harvard University Press.

Slaughter, J. B. (2009). African American males in engineering: Past, present, and a future of opportunity. In H. T. Frierson, J. H. Wyche, & W. Pearson, Jr. (Eds.), *Black American males in higher education: Research, programs and academe* (pp. 193–208). Lewes, England: Emerald.

Suitts, S. (2003). Fueling education reform: Historically Black colleges are meeting a national science imperative. *Cell Biology Education, 2*(4), 205–206.

Trent, W., & Hill, J. (1994). The contributions of historically Black colleges and universities to the production of African American scientists and engineers. In W. Pearson, Jr. & A. Fechter (Eds.), *Who will do science? Educating the next generation* (pp. 68–80). Baltimore, MD: Johns Hopkins University Press.

University System of Georgia (USG). (2012). Academic and student affairs handbook. Retrieved from http://www.usg.edu/academic_affairs_handbook/section2/C774

Wills, L., Auerbach, J., & Hughes, J. (October, 2006). *Partners in transitioning to tech: Students who follow non-traditional paths to engineering degrees.* Paper presented at the ASEE/IEEE Frontiers in Education Conference in San Diego, CA.

14

CULTIVATING ENGINEERING STUDENT SUCCESS AT AN HBCU

An Empirical Study on Development

Kenneth Taylor and Robert T. Palmer

> Students who master course content but fail to develop adequate academic self-confidence, academic goals, institutional commitment, and social support and involvement may still be at risk of dropping out.
>
> *(Lotkowski, Robbins, & Noeth, 2004, p. vii)*

Introduction

A litany of research has firmly documented the impact that historically Black colleges and universities (HBCUs) have on the academic performance of Black students in general (e.g., Fries-Britt & Turner, 2002; Gasman, 2008; Palmer & Gasman, 2008; Palmer & Wood, 2012) and science, technology, engineering, and mathematics (STEM) specifically (Gasman, 2010, 2012; U.S. Commission on Civil Rights, 2010). Perna et al. (2009) noted that 17 HBCUs rank as the top producer of baccalaureate degrees to Blacks in STEM. Despite resources disparities, and representing merely 3% of the nation's institutions of higher education, they prepare most of the nation's Black leaders in critical areas, such as science, mathematics, and engineering (Palmer & Wood, 2012). In fact, HBCUs are credited with producing 38% of Blacks who receive degrees in biological science, 31% in mathematics, 35% in computer science, and 22% in engineering (Gasman, 2012).

Indeed, given the significant role that HBCUs play in STEM production among Blacks, they are responding to the clarion call by policymakers, political leaders, and researchers, who assert that more efforts must be devoted to increasing the participation and success of racial minorities in STEM (Gasman, 2010; Harmon, 2012; Harper & Newman, 2010; Palmer, Maramba, & Dancy,

2011; Perna et al., 2009). Notwithstanding the success of HBCUs in STEM production among Blacks, data from the National Science Foundation (NSF, 2012) indicate that Latino/as, Blacks, and American Indians make up an aggregate total of 9% of the science and engineering workforce. Given that these populations make up 26% of the general population, more research is needed to increase access and success among racial minorities in STEM (Museus, Palmer, Davis, & Maramba, 2011).

There are a variety of factors responsible for the educational outcomes among Blacks in STEM at HBCUs. According to Fries-Britt, Burt, and Franklin (2012), faculty at HBCUs are more dedicated to teaching, establishing mentor and role model relationships with students, and engaging them in research opportunities compared with faculty at predominantly White institutions (PWIs). In her study on Black females in STEM at an HBCU, Perna et al.'s (2009) research acknowledged the critical influence of supportive faculty and its relationship to retention and persistence for STEM students. In addition to faculty, Perna et al. (2009) also noted that a supportive peer culture and availability of academic support and research opportunities were important to the academic success of these students. While supporting these factors, Gasman (2012) indicated that the STEM curriculum at HBCUs is culturally relevant to the students. She posited, "Seeing oneself in the curriculum makes a difference and research tells us that [Blacks] respond favorably to socially relevant curricula" (para. 4).

While research notes the important role that HBCUs play in STEM production among Blacks, evidence suggests that some students pursuing STEM majors at these institutions experience challenges to their academic success, provoking premature departure either from the institutions or STEM majors (Harper & Gasman, 2008; Institute for Higher Education Policy [IHEP], 2009; Palmer, Davis, & Hilton, 2009; Palmer & Wood, 2012; Strayhorn, 2009). In an effort to provide HBCUs with an additional resource to increase achievement outcomes among Black STEM students, this chapter will discuss the importance of identity development among Black engineering majors. To conceptualize the importance of this study, the subsequent section of this chapter will review literature on Black students in STEM. This review will also encompass a discussion on identity development, academic outcomes, and STEM.

Review of Literature

Most of the research on Black STEM students has delineated factors in K–12 that limit or challenge their participation in STEM majors in college. Indeed, while research has shown a relationship among strong math and science preparation (Bonous-Hammarth, 2000, 2006), engagement in advancement placement courses (May & Chubin, 2003), positive teacher expectations (Bissell,

2000; Collins, 1992), and accessibility to high quality teachers in K–12 and success in STEM in college (Museus et al., 2011), Blacks are more likely than their White counterparts to lack access to these critical supports (Museus et al., 2011). Notwithstanding these challenges, research has provided insight into factors in K–12 that support the preparedness of minorities in STEM. These factors include early exposure to STEM (Seymour & Hewitt, 1997), self-efficacy in mathematics and science (Colbeck, Cabrera, & Terezini, 2001; Perna et al., 2009), culturally relevant teaching (Ladson-Billings, 1995; Tate, 1995), and parental high involvement (Hrabowski & Maton, 1995). Additional studies on Black STEM students have investigated their experiences at PWIs. According to this research, Blacks at these institutions face numerous challenges, which detract from their success in STEM. These challenges include racism, micro-aggressions (Fries-Britt, Younger, & Hall, 2010a, 2010b; Solórzano, Ceja, & Yosso, 2000), and lack of mentorship and research opportunities with faculty (Fries-Britt et al., 2010a; Fries-Britt et al., 2012; Harper & Hurtado, 2007). These experiences are magnified when Blacks are one of a few faces of color in their classes (Fries-Britt et al., 2010a; Palmer et al., 2011). Compounding these experiences in the classroom is faculty's pedagogical practices (MacDonald & Korinek, 1995; Seymour & Hewitt, 1997; Sondgeroth & Stough, 1992). Indeed, while Black students favor collectivistic pedagogical approaches and display a preference for culturally responsive curricula (S. W. Brown, 2002; Johnson, 2007), faculty in STEM courses tend to use lecture based instructional methods and curricula that is Eurocentric (Farrell, 2002; Jarosz, 2003; Perna et al., 2009). Rather than promote the interest and success of Black students in STEM, these instructional approaches limit their success (S. W. Brown, 2002; Farrell, 2002; Jarosz, 2003; Perna et al., 2009).

Research is consistent in the characterization of how Black STEM students describe their experience at HBCUs (Flowers, 2012; Fries-Britt et al., 2012; Gasman, 2010, 2012). While some students discuss not having access to state-of-the-art laboratories for research and classroom projects (Fries-Britt et al., 2012), there is consensus among researchers that Black students in STEM have supportive and engaging relationships with faculty (Flowers, 2012; Newman, 2011; Palmer, Davis, & Thompson, 2010). Research indicates that faculty serve as mentors to students, believe in and enhance their self-efficacy, and engage them in research opportunities (Fries-Britt et al., 2012; Gasman, 2010, 2012; Newman, 2011). In addition to faculty support, peers at HBCUs also work collectively to foster a supportive culture in STEM. Therefore, instead of a culture at HBCUs that encourages individualism, there is a culture of success that values collectivism (Gasman, 2012). Furthermore, the STEM curriculum at HBCUs has been shown to be culturally relevant to students, which as discussed, facilitates their success in STEM (Gasman, 2012; Museus et al., 2011).

Identity Development

Researchers emphasize that student success is a function of both nonacademic and academic factors (Hrabowski & Maton, 2009; Strayhorn, 2009). In some instances, the issues associated with student persistence have more to do with nonacademic factors, such as institutional environment and identity development issues, and less to do with grades (Evans, Forney, Guido, Patton, & Renn, 2010; Lowery, 2010; Maton & Hrabowski, 2004). Lotkowski et al. (2004) reported the importance of several nonacademic factors including level of academic self-confidence, skills management, as well as academic and social integration (Chickering, 2011), all of which are tenets of identity development (American College Testing, 2007; Chickering, 2011). According to Lotkowski et al. (2004), "Students who master course content but fail to develop adequate academic self-confidence, academic goals, institutional commitment, and social support and involvement may still be at risk of dropping out" (p. vii).

Kawczynski's (2009) phenomenological study, using Chickering and Reisser's (1993) theory of identity development, investigated a sample of sophomore STEM students to gain understanding of their experience. Her research emphasized the need for universities to address what has been described as the "sophomore slump." Findings from her research indicated that the participants' experiences were characterized by developmental tasks associated with academics, involvement, peer relationships, time management, and self-identity. These findings provided important implications for universities to provide support in various forms that extended beyond the sophomore year.

Indeed, a number of studies have explored various noncognitive variables (Montgomery, 2009; NiiLampti, 2005; Sedlacek, 2004; Stretch, 2005; Tracey & Sedlacek, 1985; Trenor, Grant, & Archer, 2010) and their relationship to the success of Black students. In fact, Hrabowski and Maton (1995) found that knowledge of skills, personal motivation, faculty support, advisement, and campus integration are key factors identified in research as affecting the success of Black students in science—related fields. Others have investigated the psychosocial development of Black students at PWIs and HBCUs (e.g., Benbow, 2007; Burroughs, 2008; Hagan, 2003; Russell O 'Grady, 1999; Thomas, 2001). Further, some have made comparisons based on gender, academic classification, and grade point average (Cokley, 1998; Johnson, 2002; Williamson, 2007; Winder, 1995). While these studies have advanced the conversation on psychosocial development, there still remain many complex issues that impact the persistence and graduation of minority engineering students (A. R. Brown, Morning, & Watkins, 2005).

May and Chubin (2003) conducted a comprehensive review of these problems and described strategies for promoting minority success in engineering programs. They noted that the literature demonstrated a relationship among student success and both cognitive and noncognitive variables such as pre-college preparation, recruitment programs and practices, admissions policies, availability of financial assistance, and academic support programs. May and Chubin (2003) concluded that there were important gaps in the literature. Specifically, they observed that many of the studies aggregated the results from a variety of STEM disciplines and multiple minority groups (e.g., Black, Latino, and Native American). Consequently, they suggested there is a need for studies to disaggregate STEM disciplines so that programs can be created which better meet the unique needs of individual STEM programs (Shehab et al., 2007). Indeed, based upon Shehab et al.'s (2007) recommendation, this study not only disaggregates STEM disciplines (e.g., engineering), it also examines the identity development of Black engineering students. To this end, the present study examined the identity development of one group of Black engineering students attending an HBCU. Specifically, the study examined the students' identity development and its relationship academic classification (i.e. freshman, sophomore, junior, or senior) for Black engineering students.

Chickering and Reisser's Theory of Identity Development

Chickering and Reisser's (1993) theory of identity development was considered most appropriate to investigate the identity development of Black engineering students. This seven-vector theory asserts that students move through the first three vectors of (a) developing competence, (b) managing emotions, and (c) moving through autonomy toward interdependence during their first 2 years in college. Students generally experience the last four vectors during their junior and senior years in college; these vectors include (d) developing mature interpersonal relationships, (e) establishing identity, (f) developing purpose, and (g) developing integrity. It has been noted that while statistically significant positive correlates have been found with respect to academic performance and other variables, development occurs at varying rates depending on environmental influences (Evans et al., 2010). Chickering and Reisser (1993) asserted that individuals may experience development over the stages at different times, and not necessarily in sequential order.

Researchers have critiqued Checkering's theory because of its insufficient explanation of the development of other ethnic and minority populations (Pope, 1998). Though critiques exist, Chickering is still held as one theorist who has been successful in establishing a developmental theory that has been applied to understanding different minority student groups. Yet research findings reveal the need for future analyses that address the worldview and cultural differences that exist among different ethnic student groups (Kodama, McEwen, Liang, & Lee, 2002). The guiding framework for this study is based on the constructs of the Student Development Task and Lifestyle Assessment (SDTLA; Winston, Miller, & Cooper, 1999), which was developed from Chickering and Reisser's

(1993) identity development model. The SDTLA focuses specifically on three overarching developmental tasks, including (a) establishing and clarifying purpose (PUR), (b) developing autonomy (AUT), and (c) developing mature interpersonal relationships (MIR). These tasks are further divided into subtasks that are based on the Chickering and Reisser (1993) identity vectors.

Establishing and Clarifying Purpose (PUR)

The first task, establishing and clarifying purpose (PUR), is delineated by four subtasks. Each subtask addresses the individual's reported ability to formulate priorities and assess options in an attempt to have clear goals that can be put into action. Specifically, students who have accomplished the educational involvement subtask (EI) have distinct educational plans, are able to decipher resources, and are actively involved in the academic life of the institution (Winston et al., 1999). Accomplished students under the second subtask, career planning (CP), have a demonstrated knowledge of their abilities and limitations. Further, those accomplished individuals are aware of their fit in the surrounding world in reference to job attainment and are able to take the appropriate preparatory steps toward a career (Winston et al., 1999). The third subtask Lifestyle Planning (LP), involves the establishment of personal direction concerning ethical and religious values. Cultural participation (CUP), which is the fourth subtask of PUR, describes individuals who appreciate a variety of cultural events and organizations. These students are noted for having productive leisure time that is spent with cultural activities and performing personal hobbies such as reading (Winston et al., 1999).

Developing Autonomy Task (AUT)

The SDTLA further focuses on the task of developing autonomy (AUT). AUT is outlined by four subtasks, and involves the characterization of a student's ability to recognize their independences and interdependencies (Winston et al., 1999). The first subtask, emotional autonomy (EA), states that students who have achieved this task do not require continuous approval from others. For interdependence (IND), the second subtask, students with high scores are aware of their relationships with the surrounding community, and are able to fulfill their civic duties. High scores on the third subtask of AUT, academic autonomy (AA), imply that students have the capacity to manage doubt and behavior for the purposes of goal attainment (Winston et al., 1999). These individuals can prepare effective plans and perform at a satisfactory academic level with minimal assistance from others. The fourth subtask of AUT is instrumental autonomy (IA). Students with high scores are noted to demonstrate the ability to meet daily demands while solving problems, and managing their time accordingly with little direction from others.

Mature Interpersonal Relationships Task (MIR)

The final task that is assessed in the SDTLA is the mature interpersonal relationships task (MIR). Students with high scores on the MIR are projected to demonstrate the ability to have mature relationships and trust others without the hindrance of being defensive (Winston et al., 1999). This task is divided into two subtasks: peer relationships (PR) and tolerance (TOL). For PR, students with high scores express a change toward greater trust and independence from their peers. They are further able to make decisions without conforming to the actions or standards of others (Winston et al., 1999). The TOL subtask involves students' abilities to accept the cultural and lifestyle differences of others, while remaining able to maintain contact with individuals of different ethnic and social backgrounds.

The SDTLA is designed to assess the changes that are produced when students undergo important life changes, and their resulting accomplishment as measured by the developmental tasks. Participants self-report their feelings and attitudes about the accomplishment of the developmental tasks. As an evaluative instrument the SDTLA is designed to assess what is classified as "normal" behavior, as opposed to understanding or identifying disorders or illnesses (Winston et al., 1999). The SDTLA is not designed to diagnose disorders or personality or any other problem; rather, it provides framework for students to understand where they are (Winston et al., 1999). Further, the SDTLA emphasizes the point that students develop at different rates, and lack of development in one task or another does not mean they should have had more development.

Methodology

Findings in this chapter were drawn from a larger quantitative study that sought insight into the identity development and its relationship to gender, academic classification, and grade point average for Black engineering students at an HBCU. The study quantified human phenomena by relying on survey research methodology. The independent variables in this study were preexisting, thus classifying the current analysis as ex post facto. The eligibility characteristics included students who self-identified as Black, and majored in a STEM program. Specifically, the study included a sample of 90 engineering students; 71% were male, and 29% were female. The largest percentages of the participants were between the ages of 18 and 19, coinciding with 59% of the sample participants being freshmen. Participants completed the SDTLA, a 153–item instrument based on Chickering and Reisser's theory of identity development (Winston et al., 1999).

Multivariate analysis of variance (MANOVA) was employed to ensure the distinction between the relationships of the dependent and independent variables. There were three categorical independent variables and 10 interval dependent variables that correspond to the 10 subcomponent developmental scale scores provided by the SDTLA. The MANOVA analysis used a 2 (gender-male/female) x 4 (academic classification-freshman, sophomore, junior, and senior) x 3 (A = > 3.49, B = 2.50 – 3.49, C = 1.50 – 2.49) design with 10 dependent variables falling under the broad categories (a) establishing and clarifying purpose (PUR), (b) developing autonomy (AUT), and (c) developing mature interpersonal relationships (MIR) as measured by the SDTLA (Winston et al., 1999). For the purpose of this chapter, the results will focus solely on the variables that yielded statistical significance.

Key Findings

The overall MANOVA for academic classification was significant, $F_{(42, 173)}$ = 1.554, p = .026. Figure 14.1 provides the ANOVA results, significant differences were found for Career Planning, $F_{(3, 71)}$ = 5.828, p = .001; Peer Relationships, $F_{(3, 71)}$ = 3.787, p = .014; Emotional Autonomy, $F_{(3, 71)}$ = 3.130, p =.031; Educational Involvement, $F_{(3, 71)}$ = 4.298, p =.008; and Establishing and Clarifying Purpose, $F_{(3, 71)}$ = 3.681, p = .016. To this end, the null hypothesis was rejected for five of the subscale scores, and it was concluded that there are differences in the identity development for Career Planning, Peer Relations, Emotional Autonomy, Educational Involvement, and Establishing and Clarifying Purpose when students are grouped based on their academic classification.

For Career Planning, post hoc analysis determined statistically significantly higher mean scores for freshmen (M = 50.12, SD = 8.35), when compared to seniors (M = 41.16, SD = 9.04). Significantly higher means were determined for sophomores (M = 57.86, SD = 8.50) when matched against freshmen (M = 50.12, SD = 8.35), juniors (M = 47.74, SD = 9.64), and seniors (M = 41.16, SD = 9.04). As shown in Figure 14.1, the analysis in fact revealed that for

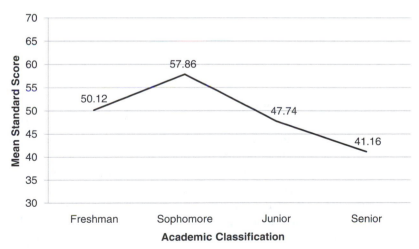

FIGURE 14.1 Mean career planning scores for students by academic classification

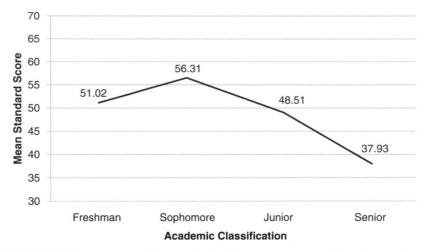

FIGURE 14.2 Mean establishing and clarifying scores for students by academic classification

career planning, the participants' development peaked in the sophomore year and decreased thereafter. Senior scores for career planning fell slightly below the normative sample mean scores.

The results for Establishing and Clarifying purpose task show that seniors (M = 39.37, SD = 10.69) had significantly lower scores than freshmen (M = 51.33, SD = 8.60) and sophomores (M = 56.82, SD = 9.58). Additionally, the results revealed that the mean scores for juniors (M = 46.95, SD = 10.33) were significantly lower than mean scores for sophomores (M = 56.82, SD = 9.58). Figure 14.2 reports a pattern regarding sophomores' development that is consistent with previous significant dependent variables including career planning, emotional autonomy, and educational involvement. Lower scores for seniors are shown in Figure 14.2, than for Career Planning, Emotional Autonomy, and Academic Involvement.

Discussion

The study examined the potential differences among freshman, sophomore, junior, and senior Black engineering students in terms of their identity development. These findings suggest that a noteworthy shift occurs as these engineering students transitioned from being underclassmen to becoming upperclassmen. As shown in the results, there are some areas of developmental concern as they relate to career planning for juniors and seniors.

The results for emotional autonomy were slightly different from the previous variable. Emotional autonomy, a subtask of the Purpose (PUR) task on the SDTLA, is characterized by students' ability to trust their own ideas and feeling free from needing reassurance or approval from others (Winston et al., 1999). Analysis of emotional autonomy revealed significantly lower mean scores for seniors in comparison to freshmen, sophomores, and juniors. Much like the scores for career planning, development for this task decreased as academic classification increased, which is very different from other studies which have generally cited student development on the subtasks to increase as students moved through college. Casanova's (2008) analysis of 284 college students yielded similar trends as the current study in finding that seniors scored lower than underclassmen on emotional autonomy. Both characterizations for career planning and emotional autonomy involve students' capacity to understand, communicate, and have confidence in their skills and fit in the world; thus one could conclude that the findings are consistent with the current study. As defined, students report their ability to formulate their goals and match their abilities with career planning. Thus, the results reveal that transitioning from undergraduate life to graduate school or the workforce presents some level of internal conflict for those students. Educational involvement, much like emotional autonomy, yielded significant mean differences; seniors scored lower than freshmen, sophomores, and juniors. Students who have accomplished this task are characterized as being knowledgeable about resources available to them and actively involved in the university (Winston et al., 1999). These students are capable and qualified for their chosen academic major. Further, they are known to take initiative to actively participate in activities that will enhance their personal group, such as study projects, nonrequired seminars, and interaction with faculty and staff (Winston et al., 1999).

Given that understanding, it is difficult to postulate why seniors would have significantly lower scores in educational involvement than underclassman. However, if we examine the structure of many institutions, support systems are developed and provided for precollege and first year experiences. While support systems and services continue to be available throughout the time students are enrolled, there may be less effort to support seniors. In Kawczynski's (2009) analysis, involvement was identified as one of the significant factors related to the development of sophomore students. Sophomore students were characterized as going through a phase of clarification and change, thus one is left to wonder if enough attention is being placed on their transition to becoming upperclassmen. It is also possible that seniors were in the process of separating from the institution and focused more on graduation and life after college. The question still remains as to whether institutions are focusing enough energy on students who are transitioning out of the institution and into graduate school or the workforce.

The Establishing and Clarifying Purpose task is comprised of four subtasks, including Educational Involvement, Career Planning, Lifestyle Planning, and Cultural Participation. It is not surprising that this task and two of its subtasks had similar significant results. Results show that seniors had significantly lower scores than freshmen and sophomores. Additionally, the results revealed that the mean scores for juniors were significantly lower than mean scores for sophomores, which is what was found with career planning for sophomores and juniors.

Based on the findings from this study, several conclusions were drawn about the identity development of this sample of Black engineering students. Critical development concerns did occur for the engineering students in this study after their sophomore year. In general the development scores that yielded significant differences seemed to peek in the sophomore year and decrease in the subsequent upperclassmen years. It is possible that these critical development concerns may also be evidenced by the drop in the number of students who enroll in engineering programs beyond the sophomore year. Specifically, the concern areas appear to be in the areas of (a) career planning, (b) emotional autonomy, (c) educational involvement, and (d) establishing and clarifying purpose. This revelation directs attention to the need for continued research on the years of development between the sophomore and senior year, and thus support programs could be established.

Implications

The current analysis has extended the discussion on the identity development by providing insight about the development patterns of Black engineering students at one HBCU. Specifically, this analysis extends the knowledge base from simply focusing on programs to an understanding of the need for continued programming as illustrated by student development. Indeed, the most revealing observation from the current analysis was the drastic decline in the mean identity development scores for engineering students as they progressed from being sophomores to seniors. This implies that there is some major change that occurs for engineering students as they near the end of their programming. It could be that those students are in need of some structural programming and guidance as they transition to the next phases of their life. The findings also imply that there is a need to focus on the psychosocial development with specific regard to the identity of engineering students as they matriculate through college and begin to view themselves as professionals.

Interestingly, the findings of this study offer a new perspective. Whereas some studies have found that students majoring in STEM were more likely to persist than students in other majors (e.g., St. John, Hu, Simmons, Carter, & Weber, 2004), the findings of this study imply that there is a shift in development even for this group. Notably, students in STEM have been found to switch majors, and in some instances leave the pipeline after their freshmen and sophomore years (Kawczynski, 2009). This is synonymous with the current findings where there was a developmental decline in several areas for engineering students after their sophomore year. Kawczynski (2009) characterized the sophomore experience as being one of clarification and change. In particular,

Kawczynski (2009) noted that the sophomore year is one where students determine who they are and consider things that are important in their life. Thus, a possible explanation for the decline in development and desire to switch majors comes from an epiphany regarding where these students are versus where they want to be.

The results from this study provide some understanding of the needs of Black engineering students at HBCUs. Based on the results and implications, improvements in the student development can be assisted through purposive programming that provides orientation, advice, and assistance to students not only during the early years of college, but as they advance to graduate school or the workforce.

Recommendations

Policy and Practice

HBCUs that are concerned with effectively determining and addressing the needs of their students in STEM are sure to benefit from understanding their psychosocial development. In particular, the SDTLA was designed to assist with the understanding of student development. This tool is a useful measure for the orientation of students entering a university as well as those transitioning out of the university. The range of benefit would cover counseling, academic advice, student life, and career readiness programs alike. Identifying and understanding the developmental needs could help administrators structure programs that fit the need of the STEM students they support.

Looking at psychosocial factors does not serve to replace understanding academic fortitude, but serves as a supplement to understanding students' developmental needs. Such an analysis of psychosocial development could help to increase the persistence of Black engineering students, and give them insight to the world that is ahead. A broader focus on educating the whole person could yield engineering students that are academically and socially prepared for the challenges and opportunities before them.

Future Research

This study directs attention toward the need for additional research on the identity and psychosocial development of Black STEM students. Specifically, the current analysis focused on engineering students at one HBCU. Though some studies have examined the development of STEM students (e.g., Kawczynski, 2009), much more is needed with regard to understanding the development of Black students. Research is also needed that will compare engineering students' development with other STEM majors to provide a wider analysis for the body of knowledge of psychosocial development.

Moreover, future research could expand beyond the limitations of using one HBCU, and could examine various ethnic groups in engineering programs to determine the level of similarities and differences that may emerge. Further, more investigation on the development for Black engineering students attending both HBCUs and PWIs would add to the knowledge base. Other areas that could provide insight for this topic include increasing the sample size, tracking persistence and enrollment, and also identifying intervention and programs if any that contribute to the development of the participants (i.e. pre-freshmen enrichment programs, and mentoring). Furthermore, to understand the trajectory of STEM and increasing the STEM workforce, an investigation that looks at employment and graduate studies following graduation from these undergraduate programs could provide a significant perspective. Finally, this analysis was based on the quantitative constructs of the SDTLA. Research that examines psychosocial development from a qualitative perspective could serve to triangulate the understanding of Black engineering student development.

Conclusion

This chapter provided understanding for the developmental needs of Black engineering students at one HBUC. Specifically, the results revealed a need to provide programming and developmental support for these students as they enter the upperclassman years of their college experience. Continued research and investigations that seek to uncover the tenets of Black students' psychosocial development could serve to benefit those that are in engineering programs as well as other STEM educational programs. Indeed, this research could result in a framework for increasing the number of Black students that enter STEM programs, persist to graduation, and move forth to the workforce.

References

American College Testing. (2007). *The role of nonacademic factors in college readiness and success.* Iowa City, IA: Author.

Benbow, S. R. (2007). The persistence of African-American college students from three predominantly White universities: A case study of the summer residential pre-college experience programs within the Pennsylvania state system of higher education. *Dissertation Abstracts International.* (UMI No. 3257959)

Bissell, J. (2000). Changing the face of science and engineering: Good beginnings for the twenty-first century. In G. Campbell Jr., R. Denes, & C. Morrison (Eds.), *Access denied: Race, ethnicity, and scientific enterprise* (pp. 61–77). New York: Oxford University Press.

Bonous-Hammarth, M. (2000). Pathways to success: Affirming opportunities for science, mathematics, and engineering majors. *Journal of Negro Education, 69*(1–2), 92–111.

Bonous-Hammarth, M. (2006). Promoting student participation in science, technology, engineering and mathematics careers. In W. R. Allen, M. Bonous-Hammarth, & R. T. Teranishi (Eds.), *Higher education in a global society: Achieving diversity, equity, and excellence* (pp. 269–282). Oxford, England: Elsevier.

Brown, A. R., Morning, C., & Watkins, C. (2005). Influence of African American engineering student perceptions of campus climate on graduation rates. *Journal of Engineering Education, 94*(2), 263–271.

Brown, S. W. (2002). Hispanic students majoring in science or engineering: What happened in their educational journeys? *Journal of Women and Minorities in Science and Engineering, 8*(2), 123–148.

Burroughs, R. (2008). The intersection of athletic and racial identity of Black student-athletes at predominately-White institutions. *Dissertation Abstracts International.* (UMI No. 3296861)

Casanova, A. E. D. (2008). The relationship between creativity and psychosocial development among college honors students and non-honors students. *Dissertation Abstracts International.* (UMI No. 3333654)

Chickering, A. W. (2011). The seven vectors: An overview. Retrieved from http://www.cabrini.edu/communications/ProfDev/cardevChickering.html

Chickering, A. W., & Reisser, L. (1993). *Education and identity* (2nd ed.). San Francisco, CA: Jossey-Bass.

Cokley, K. O. (1998). A comparative study of African self-consciousness, racial identity, and academic self-concept among American college students attending historically Black and predominately White colleges and universities. *Dissertation Abstracts International.* (UMI No. 9839249)

Colbeck, C. L., Cabrera, A. F., & Terenzini, P. T. (2001). Leaning professional confidence: linking teaching practices, students' self-perceptions, and gender. *Review of Higher Education, 24*(2), 173–191.

Collins, M. (1992). *Ordinary children, extraordinary teachers.* Charlottesville, VA: Hampton Roads.

Evans, N. J., Forney, D. S., Guido, F. M., Patton, L. D., & Renn, K. A. (2010). *Student development in college: Theory, research, and practice* (2nd ed). San Francisco, CA: Jossey-Bass.

Farrell, E. F. (2002). Engineering a warmer welcome for female students. *Chronicle of Higher Education, 48*, A31.

Flowers, A. (2012). Academically gifted Black male undergraduates in engineering: Perceptions of factors contributing to their success in an historically Black college and university. In R. T. Palmer & J. L. Wood (Eds.), *Black men in college: Implications for HBCUs and beyond* (pp. 163–175). New York: Routledge.

Fries-Britt, S. L., Burt, B., & Franklin, K. (2012). Establishing critical relationships: How Black males persist in physics at HBCUs. In R. T. Palmer & J. L. Wood (Eds.), *Black men in college: Implications for HBCUs and beyond* (pp. 71–88). New York: Routledge.

Fries-Britt, S. L., & Turner, B. (2002). Uneven stories: Successful Black collegians at a Black and a White campus. *Review of Higher Education, 25*(3), 315–330.

Fries-Britt, S.L., Younger, T., & Hall, W. (2010a). How perceptions of race and campus racial climate impact underrepresented minorities in Physics. In T. E. Dancy II (Ed.), *Managing diversity: (Re)visioning equity on college campuses* (pp. 181–198). New York: Peter Lang.

Fries-Britt, S. L., Younger, T., & Hall, W. (2010b). Lessons from high achieving minorities in physics. In S. R. Harper, C. Newman, & S. Gary (Eds.), *Students of color in STEM: Constructing a new research agenda* (New Directions for Institutional Research, No. 148, pp. 75–83). San Francisco, CA: Jossey-Bass.

Gasman, M. (2008). Minority-serving institutions: A historical backdrop. In M. Gasman, B. Baez, & C. S. V. Turner (Eds.), *Understanding minority-serving institutions* (pp. 18–27). Albany, NY: SUNY Press.

Gasman, M. (2010). Bolstering African American success in the STEM Fields. Retrieved from http://chronicle.com/blogs/innovations/

Gasman, M. (2012). Succeeding in STEM: Lessons from Black colleges. Retrieved from http://www.huffingtonpost.com/marybeth-gasman/black-colleges-education_b_1318328.html

Hagan, W. J. (2003). The influence of African self-consciousness, purpose, and achievement goal orientation on the academic achievement of African American students at a predominately White university. *Dissertation Abstracts International.* (UMI No. 3092442)

Harmon, N. (2012). *The role of minority-serving institutions in national college competition goals.* Institute of Higher Education Policy. Washington, DC: Author.

Harper, S. R., & Gasman, M. (2008). Consequences of conservatism: Black male undergraduates and the politics of historically Black colleges and universities. *Journal of Negro Education, 77*(4), 336–351.

Harper, S. R., & Hurtado, S. (2007). Nine themes in campus racial climates. In S. R. Harper & L. D. Patton (Eds.), *Responding to the realities of race on campus* (New Directions for Student Services, pp. 7–24). San Francisco, CA: Jossey-Bass.

Harper, S. R., & Newman, C. B. (Eds.). (2010). *Students of color in STEM* (New Directions for Institutional Research, No. 148). San Francisco, CA: Jossey-Bass.

Hrabowski, F. A., & Maton, K. I. (1995). Enhancing the success of African American students in the sciences: Freshman year outcomes. *School of Science and Mathematics, 95*(1), 19–27.

Hrabowski, F. A., & Maton, K. I. (2009). Change institutional culture, and you change who goes into science. *Academe, 95*(3), 11–15.

Institute of Higher Education Policy. (2009). *Diversifying the STEM pipeline: The model replication institutions program.* Washington, DC: Author.

Jarosz, J. (2003). Engineering for Native Americans. *Winds of change: A Magazine for American Indians in Science and Technology, 18*(3), 52–57.

Johnson, C. F. (2002). Factors related to mastery and psychosocial development in Black male undergraduate students enrolled in traditionally Black and predominately White institutions. *Dissertation Abstracts International.* (UMI No. 3067056)

Kawczynski, K. A. (2009). The college sophomore student experience: A phenomenological study of a second year program. *Dissertation Abstracts International.* (UMI No. 3378310)

Kodama, C. M., McEwen, M. K., Liang, C. T. H., & Lee, S. (2002). An Asian American perspective on psychosocial student development theory. *New Directions for Student Services, 97,* 45–59.

Ladson-Billings, G. (1995). Toward a theory of culturally relevant pedagogy. *American Educational Research Journal, 32*(3), 465–491.

Lotkowski, V. A., Robbins, S. B., & Noeth, R. J. (2004). *The role of academic and non-academic factors in improving college retention.* Iowa City, IA: ACT.

Lowery, G. (2010). Tougher grading is one reason for high STEM dropout rate. Chronicle Online. Retrieved from http://www.news.cornell.edu/stories/April10/CHERIConference.html

MacDonald, R., & Korinek, L. (1995). Cooperative learning activities in large entry-level geology courses. *Journal of Geological Education 43,* 341–345.

Maton, K. I., & Hrabowski, F. A. (2004). Increasing the number of African American PhDs in the sciences and engineering: A strengths-based approach. *American Psychologist, 59*(6), 547–556.

May G. S., & Chubin D. E. (2003). A retrospective on undergraduate engineering success for under-represented minority students. *Journal of Engineering Education, 92*(1), 27–39.

Montgomery, L. (2009). Case study analysis of the effect of contextual supports and barriers on African American students' persistence in engineering. *Dissertation Abstracts International.* (UMI No. 3380968)

Museus, S. D., Palmer, R. T., Davis, R. J., & Maramba, D. C. (2011). *Racial and ethnic minority student's success in STEM education* (ASHE-Higher Education Report Series, Vol. 36, No. 6). San Francisco, CA: Jossey-Bass.

National Science Foundation, National Center for Science and Engineering Statistics. (2012). Women, minorities, and persons with disabilities in science and engineering. Retrieved from http://www.nsf.gov/statistics/wmpd/tables.cfm

Newman, C. B. (2011). Engineering success: The role of faculty relationships with Black collegians. The *Journal of Women and Minorities in Science and Engineering, 17*(3), 193–209.

NiiLampti, N. (2005). An examination of African American college students on non-cognitive factors of persistence across institution type and athletic status. *Dissertation Abstracts International.* (UMI No. 3203030)

Palmer, R. T., Davis, R. J., & Hilton, A. A. (2009). Exploring challenges that threaten to impede the academic success of academically underprepared African American male collegians at an HBCU. *Journal of College Student Development, 50*(4), 429–445.

Palmer, R. T., Davis, R. J., & Thompson, T. (2010). Theory meets practice: HBCU initiatives that promote academic success among African Americans in STEM. *Journal of College Student Development, 51*(4), 440–443.

Palmer, R. T., & Gasman, M. (2008). "It takes a village to raise a child": The role of social capital in promoting academic success for Black men at a Black college. *Journal of College Student Development 49*(1), 52–70.

Palmer, R. T., Maramba, D. C., & Dancy, T. E. (2011). A qualitative investigation of factors promoting the retention and persistence of students of color in STEM. *Journal of Negro Education, 80*(4), 491–504.

Palmer, R. T., & Wood, J. L. (Eds.). (2012). *Black men in college: Implications for HBCUs and beyond.* New York: Routledge.

Perna, L., Wagner-Lundy, V., Drezner, N. D., Gasman, M., Yoon, S., Bose, E., & Gary. S. (2009). The contribution of HBCUs to the preparation of African American women for STEM careers: A case study. *Research Higher Education, 50*(1), 1–23.

Pope, R. L. (1998). The relationship between psychosocial development and racial identity of Black college students. *Journal of College Student Development, 39*(3), 273–282.

Russell O'Grady, M. (1999). The effect of segregated experiences on the psychosocial development of African-American freshmen at a predominately White university: The influence of group membership. *Dissertation Abstracts International.* (UMI No. 9935658)

Sedlacek, W. E. (2004). *Beyond the big test: Noncognitive assessment in higher education.* San Francisco, CA: Jossey-Bass.

Seymour, E., & Hewitt, N, M. (1997). *Talking about leaving: Why undergraduates leave the sciences.* Oxford, England: Westview Press.

Shehab, R. L., Murphy, T. J., Davidson, J., Rhoads, T. R., Trytten, D. A., & Walden, S. E. (2007). *Academic struggles and strategies: How minority students persist.* Paper presented at the American Society for Engineering Education Annual Conference, Honolulu, HI.

Solórzano, D., G., Ceja, M., & Yosso, T. (2000). Critical race theory, racial microaggressions, and campus racial climate: The experiences of African American college students. *The Journal of Negro Education, 69*(1/2), 60–73.

Sondgeroth, M. S., & Stough, L. M. (1992). *Factors influencing the persistence of ethnic minority students enrolled in a college engineering program.* Paper presented at the American Educational Research Association, San Francisco, CA.

St. John, E. P., Hu, S., Simmons, A., Carter, D. F., & Weber, J. (2004). What difference does a major make? The influence of college major field on persistence by African American and White students. *Research in Higher Education, 45*(3), 209–232.

Strayhorn, T. L. (2009). *Work in progress: Academic and social barriers to Black and Latino male collegians in engineering.* Paper presented at ASEE/IEEE Frontiers in Education Conference. San Antonio, TX.

Stretch, L. S. (2005). Noncognitive variables predicting academic success and persistence for African-American freshmen attending historically Black colleges and universities versus African-American freshmen attending predominantly White institutions. *Dissertation Abstracts International.* (UMI No. 3162473)

Tate, F. W. (1995). Returning to the root: A cultural relevant approach to mathematics pedagogy. *Theory into Practice, 34*(3), 166–173.

Thomas, C. D. (2001). The relationship between psychosocial development and socioeconomic status among Black college students. *Dissertation Abstracts International.* (UMI No. 3014816)

Tracey, T. J., & Sedlacek, W. E. (1985). The relationship of noncognitive variables to academic success: A longitudinal comparison by race. *Journal of College Student Personnel, 26,* 405–410.

Trenor, J. M., Grant, D. R., & Archer, E. (2010). *The role of African American fraternities and sororities in engineering students' educational experiences at a predominantly White institution.* Paper presented at ASEE/IEEE Frontiers in Education Conference. Washington, DC.U.S. Commission on

Civil Rights. (2010). *The educational effectiveness of historically Black colleges and universities: A briefing before the United States Commission on Civil Rights held in Washington, D.C.* Washington, DC: Author.

Williamson, S. Y. (2007). Academic, institutional, and family factors affecting the persistence of Black male STEM majors. *Dissertation Abstracts International.* (UMI No. 3269188)

Winder, J. H. (1995). Feelings of alienation of African American college students at predominately White and historically Black universities: A comparative study. *Dissertation Abstracts International.* (UMI No. 9603397)

Winston, R. B., Miller, T. K., & Cooper, D. L. (1999). *Preliminary technical manual for the student developmental task and lifestyle assessment.* Athens, GA: Student Development Associates.

15

ACHIEVING EQUITY WITHIN AND BEYOND STEM

Toward a New Generation of Scholarship in STEM Education

Juan C. Garibay

Despite tremendous growth in new technologies and advances in science over the last several decades, severe inequities remain throughout the world. The United Nations (2011) estimates that in developing regions 1.4 billion people live in extreme poverty, 837 million are undernourished, 884 million people lack access to clean water, over 2.6 billion people still lack adequate sanitation, and 828 million urban residents live in slum conditions. Additionally, it is estimated that over 22,000 children under the age of 5 die every day mostly from preventable causes (United Nations, 2011). Moreover, racism, sexism, and other forms of discriminatory thought and behavior continue to marginalize people of color, the poor, women, and others both in the United States and abroad. In spite of the persistence of profound inequity, exploitation, and oppression, a large body of scholarship focused on education reform in the fields of science, technology, engineering, and mathematics (STEM) insists that we need to invest more in STEM in order to maintain U.S. global economic supremacy. Interestingly, many scholars who are calling on STEM reform in hopes of creating equitable completion and matriculation rates between underrepresented racial minority (URM) students and their non–URM counterparts have bound equity to economic competition.

Using a relatively narrow framework of equity that solely attempts to achieve equity within STEM, many education researchers tend to focus their efforts on either ensuring appropriate opportunities to learn or understanding the effects of various support programs and classroom processes on traditional measures of success (i.e., scores on standardized exams, retention, and degree completion; Gutstein, 2006). The purpose of this chapter is not to undermine those efforts, but it is necessary to highlight some of the underlying assumptions and issues that arise when equity is tied to market economics in hopes of pushing us forward in STEM educational research, not only to sustainably increase the success rates of URMs in STEM but for disenfranchised groups beyond the walls of higher education. This chapter explores how confining equity in a discourse of domination is shortsighted and problematic especially when many URM students have experienced oppression, and may actually emerge from, have familial connections in, or identify with the plight of those in impoverished nations.

Given that graduates in STEM disciplines will undoubtedly play a critical role in addressing local, national, and global challenges, how we frame the purpose of STEM education will have serious implications for equity in our society. How students in STEM are trained will influence how they respond to these challenges, many of which transcend national boundaries and require global solidarity (Serageldin, 2002). To help eliminate the inequities that marginalized communities continue to face and help everyone become more fully human requires an education that is grounded in the elimination of oppression (Freire, 1970/1998). Indeed, advancement in science and technology should be in the context of improving the human condition throughout the world (Holdren, 2008). Additionally, it requires that the discourse be redefined from threats to U.S. economic competitiveness to addressing the state of poverty and injustice that continues to affect so many people of color, women, working-class, indigenous, and other groups throughout the world.

Issues with Confining Equity to Economic Competitiveness

Many scholars argue that the United States needs to address stark disparities in degree completion rates in STEM between URMs and their non-URM counterparts in order to maintain U.S. global economic competitiveness. Without more scientifically and technically oriented workers to fill workforce roles, it is argued, how can the United States continue to dominate the world economically through scientific innovation? This section highlights several issues with confining equity to economic competition.

Confusion in Whose Interests are Being Served

First, grounding the purpose of STEM education and equity within STEM with an economic competitiveness rationale allows corporate interests to dictate the goals of STEM education (Gutstein, 2006). If we accept an economic rationale for equity, the education students receive can easily serve to socially reproduce the dominant social order. When guided by economic competition and market preparedness the types of competencies that are defined as important in STEM disciplines tend to be scientific and technical literacy and capacity (Gutstein, 2006), which is often at the expense of the development of students' awareness of inequality, social agency, and civic participation. Defining the maintenance of economic dominance as not only the basis for STEM education, but for investing in underrepresented students of color, guides the manner in which the material is taught, the required coursework to earn a degree in STEM, and narrows the socialization process throughout students' STEM trajectories. With the needs of capital as central, education is reduced toward simply producing more productive workers whether they be low-paid basic skills workers or higher-paid "knowledge workers" (Giroux, 1983). Given that college students are the expected "knowledge workers" of the future, higher learning in STEM grounded in the need for capital accumulation and economic competition will emphasize conventional concepts that are essential to an efficient labor process (i.e., effective communication skills, even in more than one language, technical skills, and typical problem-solving skills). While these skills are important even for those working for social change, under the guiding economic argument, such skills are important specifically to help dominate others. Additionally, with many corporations looking to maintain economic dominance by expanding into new and untapped global markets, it is important to ask what then becomes the role of underrepresented students of color?

Indeed, many may argue that an education solely focused on corporate interests is essential because economic growth is necessary to increase the living conditions of all people within a country, including people of color. However, a recent press release by the World Health Organization (WHO) noted that, "without equitable distribution of benefits, national growth can even exacerbate [health] inequities" (WHO, 2008). In order to achieve equity within and beyond STEM education it is imperative that STEM education free itself from emphasizing the maximization of corporate profits above all else (Gutstein, 2006). By prioritizing capital's needs, knowledge of the oppressive aspects of society and skills essential to participating in creating a more just world (Macedo, 1994) are auctioned off for an educational process that is needed for the maintenance of wealth and production. As Gutstein (2006) states, "this is fundamentally in opposition to a social justice agenda that instead places the material, social, psychological, spiritual, and emotional needs of human beings, as well as other species and the planet before capital's needs" (p. 8).

Perpetuating a Dominant, Stagnant STEM Culture

Second, tying the purpose of STEM education with economic competitiveness may further perpetuate a culture within STEM that is not supportive of students' multiple social identities and individual agency (Boaler, 1997). According to Boaler and Greeno (2000), "many students who are succeeding in traditional mathematics classes choose not to continue to study mathematics because they experience a conflict between who they view themselves to be and who they want to become on the one hand, and who they are expected to become in their mathematics classes on the other" (as cited in Cobb, 2004, p. 333). Although there are many factors that contribute to why underrepresented students of color may leave the sciences, a major factor to their disproportionate attrition rates is related to internal conflicts that these students experience with the dominant disciplinary culture (Seymour & Hewitt, 1997).

The dominant disciplinary culture within many STEM departments, which largely reflects White masculine norms, is often at odds with the values and needs of many students of color and women (Seymour & Hewitt, 1997). Conventional research that does not address the inherent culture in STEM departments often results in the development of support programs and initiatives that attempt to socialize diverse students into the dominant STEM culture (Carlone, 2003). Dominant disciplinary cultures of objectivity and exclusivity in STEM require many students of color to negotiate away important aspects of their identity that "don't belong in science" (Carlone, 2003; Tran, 2011). By bonding the purpose of STEM with economic competition education researchers can further perpetuate a dominant, stagnant culture in STEM that does not reflect diverse populations and expects students to become congruent with the prototypical conception of a scientist or engineer.

To address why many students of color leave STEM studies, it is important to understand the interplay between the identity formation of the student and the disciplinary and departmental culture, history, and identity. If not, it may severely restrict the ability of many more students of color, even high achieving ones, to see themselves in it (Boaler & Greeno, 2000; Cobb, 2004). Thus, by restricting the culture of STEM under corporate interests we may perpetuate erroneous deficit-oriented explanations if students of color continue to leave the sciences at high rates. It is important to note that when comparing URM and non-URM students who left STEM during their undergraduate education, Garibay (2011) found that one value that these groups starkly differed on was the value they placed on working for social change. Fifty-nine percent of URM students who left STEM felt working for social change was essential or very important to their future goals compared to slightly over 41% of non-URM students who left STEM (Garibay, 2011). This finding supports previous research that found that URMs often leave the sciences due to the perceived lack of social value, or relevance to improving conditions in their communities (Bonous-Hammarth, 2000).

Although not as wide, Garibay (2011) also found large differences between the proportion of URM students who left STEM and URM students who stayed in STEM who reported working for social change was essential or very important (59% vs. 48.8%, respectively). If we are to increase the number of URM students in STEM and help eliminate injustice beyond higher education, education scholars must not bound the culture of STEM to economic interests, especially at the expense of a culture that is conducive and supportive of students who care about working for social change. It is highly problematic for equity in our society that students who care less about working for social change seem to have greater success in STEM.

STEM Accountability for Preparing Future Leaders

Finally, binding equity and the purpose of STEM education to economic competition limits our ability to critique the role modern Western sciences have played in the existence of current inequities and oppression. Many scholars argue that STEM education has too rarely involved social issues even though science and technology has often been utilized to harm others, perpetuate social inequalities, and destroy the natural environment (Harding, 2006; Lima, 2000; Vaz, 2005). Throughout history many theories claiming the existence of natural inferiority based on race, gender, and other social constructs have emerged specifically from science fields (Harding, 2006).

With respect to race, many American scientists between the 19th and 20th century supported and "validated" the construction of racial inferiority (Washington, 2005), which heavily influenced restrictive immigration policy denying groups categorized as inferior (e.g., Chinese Exclusion Acts, attempts to bar immigrants of African descent during the Depression, and 1924 National Origins Act; see Haney Lopez, 1996), the forced departure of specific groups (e.g., Mexican American repatriation during the Great Depression; see Haney Lopez, 1996), and the living conditions of those groups when able to enter or remain in the United States (Washington, 2005). In the United States, groups categorized by science as racially inferior have a long history of living in areas disproportionately affected by environmental pollution, inadequate sanitation, and industrial waste (Washington, 2005). To achieve social equity education scholars must be able to critique and hold STEM accountable for its contributions to inequities and the "conquer nature paradigm" often employed in many STEM fields (Lima, 2000).

Despite the many instances in which STEM has negatively impacted society and contributed to injustice, many researchers in the scientific community choose not to engage in understanding the social and ethical implications of their work (Beckwith & Huang, 2005). Beckwith and Huang (2005) assert that this "laissez-faire attitude" is cultivated by STEM education as "few students of science receive as an integral part of their scientific education an analysis of the social impact of science and rarely is there any mention of social responsibility" (pp. 1479–1480). Indeed, this culture and socialization process in STEM seems to have an effect on student outcomes related to civic and social responsibility. Garibay (2011) found that majoring in a STEM discipline has a significant negative influence on students' social agency, or the value a student places on improving society and being an active citizen, and that on average STEM students report working for social change is less important to them than non-STEM majors. Nicholls and colleagues (2007) also found that students who pursue STEM majors scored lower in their goal of becoming a community leader, desire to understand other countries and cultures, and desire to keep up with or engage in politics than students in non-STEM majors. Similarly, engineering students have been shown to be less likely than students in other fields to describe themselves as altruistic or socially concerned, to express less of a commitment to promoting racial understanding (Astin, 1993), and have significantly lower levels of commitment to social action (Sax, 2000).

These findings are highly troublesome with respect to creating a more democratic world as STEM education seems to not be preparing many future leaders in STEM who are committed to working for the betterment of society. However, such findings should come as no surprise given the narrow set of competencies that are often valued in STEM departments. As Gutstein (2006) describes for mathematics curricula, "almost all mathematics curricula in the United States today develop functional literacy (which he describes as any competency that does not engender the systematic search for the root causes of inequality and oppression) because schooling tends to reproduce dominant social relations" (p. 7). Perhaps the often narrow socialization process in STEM programs is functioning, as Macedo (1994) writes, to "domesticate the consciousness via a constant disarticulation between the narrow reductionistic reading of one's field of specialization and the reading of the universe within which one's specialism is situated" (p. 15).

Toward the Empowerment of URMs in STEM and Beyond

In order to achieve equity both within and beyond STEM education calls for equity that must not be reduced or cheapened to promote the needs of capital. Prioritizing economic interests creates a dominance-oriented disciplinary culture that guides scientific teaching, learning, and practices and may promote dominance-oriented groups while marginalizing others. Expanding the list of important student outcomes in STEM education to go beyond simply developing "scientific," "mathematical," and "technical" literacies to include the development of critical consciousness (Freire, 1970/1998) and transformational resistance (Solórzano & Delgado-Bernal, 2001) is fundamental to creating a more just and equitable world. Gutstein's (2006) framework for understanding mathematics education for social justice, which can be easily adapted to other STEM disciplines, provides a helpful tool for educators interested in not only helping students of color succeed in STEM fields, but in developing their transformative power to rectify structural inequalities. He describes two distinct sets of pedagogical goals: (a) one focused on mathematics, where student learning, success on exams and in courses, and having a higher orientation to mathematics are necessary to equitably gain access to advanced mathematics and mathematically related careers, and (b) one focused on social justice, where students use mathematics to understand and deconstruct relations of power, inequities, disparate opportunities, and discrimination (reading the world with mathematics); use mathematics to change the world (writing the world with mathematics); and develop positive cultural and social identities.

Two important ways that colleges can support students develop these competencies are through undergraduate research experiences and curricular requirements designed to prepare students for social and civic responsibility (e.g., experiential learning, service-learning, project-based learning, integrative learning, and collaborative inquiry; see Schneider, 2001). These experiences provide students rich opportunities to make connections between academic learning and society, as well as gain a deeper understanding of knowledge and professional practice within their academic discipline. For students in STEM, access to research programs is critical as these programs provide opportunities for students to develop their science identities, and have been shown to positively influence students' graduate school aspirations and enrollment (Barlow & Villarejo, 2004; Bauer & Bennett, 2003; Eagan et al., 2010; Hurtado, Cabrera, Lin, Arellano, & Espinosa, 2009; MacLachlan, 2006; Maton & Hrabowski, 2004; Seymour, Hunter, Laursen, & DeAntoni, 2004). Participation in research can be a catalyst for STEM educational success in the traditional sense and is an important tool for accessing more advanced levels of knowledge in STEM and potential careers in STEM.

Curricular requirements for STEM students that require students to engage with local organizations can help students expand their level of understanding of societal issues while participating in creating a better society. Research on the impact of service-learning has found service-learning courses to significantly increase students' perceived knowledge and understanding of social issues and health disparities (Brown, Heaton, & Wall, 2007), and increase participants' awareness of inequality, concern for the public good, and commitment to social justice (Einfeld & Collins, 2008; Hurtado, 2003). Service-learning courses also increase students' attitudes about working in a diverse community (Gadbury-Amyot, Simmer-Beck, McCunniff, & Williams, 2006) and sense of civic responsibility (Astin & Sax, 1998).

Another way that colleges can support students to better understand science and technology in the larger contexts of society and public policy using curricular requirements is through community-based problem solving (i.e., project-based learning). For example, Worchester Polytechnic Institute, where about 90% of students major in engineering or science, requires all students to complete a series of three projects throughout their undergraduate experience that are designed to help students bridge theory and practice and gain a better understanding of themselves and the world (Vaz, 2005). Through the *Interactive Qualifying Project* (IQP), a junior-year requirement that can be taken either in the United States or abroad, students work in small multidisciplinary teams and are guided by faculty advisors to help solve problems posed by an external sponsor, usually not-for-profit organizations, governmental agencies, and nongovernmental agencies (Vaz, 2005). Educational goals of the IQP include developing students' critical and contextual thinking skills as well as their understanding of the interrelationship between scientific and technological advancement, societal structures, and human need (Vaz, 2005). These opportunities may be able to help students "read and write the world" (Gutstein, 2006) using skills learned from STEM fields—using their skills to create positive change in communities in need—and may contribute to positive cultural and social identities.

Implications for Research and Practice

By redefining student success in STEM to include student outcomes that are integral to an equity-oriented STEM education, we can then begin to research which STEM environments, experiences, and classroom practices positively influence these outcomes and whether STEM programs are meeting these critical goals. In turn, this work can help inform educators and practitioners develop and structure STEM departments, curriculum, and learning environments that are conducive to these measures of student success. Prior research suggests that majoring in a STEM discipline seems to have a negative influence on many important outcomes that have implications for social equity in our society (Astin, 1993; Garibay, 2011; Nicholls et al., 2007; Sax, 2000) and preparing students for participation in a diverse democracy (see Hurtado, 2003). Further research is needed to understand how STEM education develops students' understanding of social issues and inequality, aspirations to work in low-income communities, and their desire to conduct research that will have a meaningful impact on underserved populations. Studies in medical education have shown that medical students have little understanding of underserved populations (Wieland, Beckman, Cha, Beebe, & McDonald, 2010), are less committed to working with underserved populations at the end of medical school (Crandall, Volk, & Cacy, 1997; Crandall, Volk, & Loemker, 1993), and exhibit implicit race and skin tone biases toward Whites and light-skinned groups (White-Means, Dong, Hufstader, & Brown, 2010). These troublesome findings have prompted many educators in the medical field to question whether practices in medical school are actually contributing to health disparities. Similar studies on STEM students are needed throughout different stages in their educational trajectories as these students are called upon in the future to make decisions on critical issues that have large social ramifications.

Addressing the inherent culture in STEM departments, which is created by the actors in these disciplines, also requires an analysis of STEM professors. STEM faculty members serve as important institutional agents in shaping students' educational experiences and trajectories (Landefeld, 2009). STEM faculty members play a key role in the development of departmental structures and cultures, which ultimately facilitate the success of those students who "fit" or thrive most within those organizational arrangements (Seymour & Hewitt, 1997; Turner & Thompson, 1993). For instance, when mentorship opportunities are structured informally, faculty members decide which students to support based on perceptions of a student's motivation and achievement (Ragins,

1999; Ragins & Cotton, 1993; Singh, Ragins, & Tharenou, 2009; Wanberg, Welsh, & Hezlett, 2003) or likeness to themselves (Landefeld, 2009). Such mentorship structures may allow faculty to make decisions based on racial and gender perceptions, in addition to providing limited support for those who may need it the most. Moreover, given that faculty often have the ability to choose which mentoring relationships to participate in, it is important that faculty also value these nontraditional measures of student success. Access to faculty networks is critical for students as faculty can provide access to educational and professional opportunities and resources (Stanton-Salazar, 2010). More research is needed to understand STEM faculty members' definition of the purpose of STEM education, their commitment to social equity, their level of involvement with making a meaningful impact on underserved populations and rectifying structural inequities, whether they provide meaningful support for those students who want to work for social change, and whether STEM faculty members demonstrate implicit racial or gender biases.

Finally, understanding the relationship between institutions of higher education and the larger sociopolitical context of society is a crucial aspect of achieving equity. Minority serving institutions (MSIs) enroll more than half of all minority college students in the United States today, a large proportion of whom are low-income students (Li, 2007). In order to serve these populations more fully, these institutions must hold themselves accountable not only to students of color within their confines, but also to the disenfranchised communities that many of these students and their families live in. Often facing severe financial difficulties, many MSIs will develop partnerships with industries or corporations that negatively impact neighboring working-class communities of color. For example, some MSIs have partnerships with several oil refineries, which negatively impact the health and well-being of adjacent communities (Bowler, Mergler, Huel, & Cone, 1996; Bowler, Ngo, et al., 1997). Oil refineries are often vehemently involved in the political process (often by creating backroom deals with politicians or silencing many community organizations) to protect their financial interests even though their practices have directly contributed to premature deaths and disproportionate disease faced by adjacent low-income communities of color. Increased air pollutant concentrations are associated with impairments in reaction time to visual stimuli and in ability to concentrate (Bullinger, 1989), which are important for educational success. To achieve widespread equity requires finding ways to keep institutions responsible and accountable to disenfranchised communities.

Conclusion

With long-term goals of creating a more just world where life opportunities are not predetermined by race or ethnicity, gender, or class, we must replace the dominant economic rationale for equity within STEM to one that prioritizes the needs of the disenfranchised and values humanity. Given the increase in college students emerging from racially diverse backgrounds (Li, 2007), MSIs will increasingly play a critical role in advancing postsecondary opportunities for students of color. As MSIs continue to actively find ways to serve and increase the success of their students, they must stay true to their mission of educating and advancing the success of underserved populations by keeping STEM disciplines more in tune with the democratic purpose of higher education as opposed to corporate interests.

References

Astin, A. W. (1993). *What matters in college?: Four critical years revisited*. San Francisco, CA: Jossey-Bass.

Astin, A. W., & Sax, L. (1998). How undergraduates are affected by service participation. *Journal of College Student Development, 39*(3), 251–263.

Barlow, A. E. L., & Villarejo, M (2004). Making a difference for minorities: Evaluation of an educational enrichment program. *Journal of Research in Science Teaching, 41*(9), 861–881.

Bauer, K. W., & Bennett, J. S. (2003). Alumni perceptions used to assess undergraduate research experience. *Journal of Higher Education, 74*(2), 210–230.

Beckwith, J., & Huang, F. (2005). Should we make a fuss? A case for social responsibility in science. *Nature Biotechnology, 23*(12), 1479–1480.

Boaler, J. (1997). *Experiencing school mathematics: Teaching styles, sex and setting*. Buckingham, England: Open University Press.

Boaler, J., & Greeno, J. (2000). Identity, agency, and knowing in mathematical worlds. In J. Boaler (Ed.), *Multiple perspectives on mathematics teaching and learning* (pp. 45–82). Stamford, CT: Ablex.

Bonous-Hammarth, M. (2000). Pathways to success: Affirming opportunities for science, mathematics, and engineering majors. *Journal of Negro Education, 69*(1), 92–111.

Bowler, R. M., Mergler, D., Huel, G., & Cone, J. E. (1996). Adverse health effects in African American Residents living adjacent to chemical industries. *Journal of Black Psychology, 22*(4), 470–497.

Bowler, R. M., Ngo, L., Hartney, C., Lloyd, K., Tager, I., Midtling, J., & Huel, G. (1997). Epidemiological health study of a town exposed to chemicals. *Environmental Research, 72*(2), 93–108.

Brown, B., Heaton, P. C., & Wall, A. (2007). A service-learning elective to promote enhanced understanding of civic, cultural, and social issues and health disparities in pharmacy. *American Journal of Pharmaceutical Education, 71*(1), 1–7.

Bullinger, M. (1989). Psychological effects of air pollution on healthy residents: A time-series approach. *Journal of Environmental Psychology, 9*(2), 103–118.

Carlone, H. B. (2003). Innovative science within and against a culture of "achievement." *Science Education, 87*(3), 307–328.

Cobb, P. (2004). Mathematics, literacies, and identity. *Reading Research Quarterly, 39*(3), 333–337.

Crandall, S. J. S., Volk, R. J., & Cacy, D. (1997). A longitudinal investigation of medical student attitudes toward the medically indigent. *Teaching and Learning in Medicine, 9*(4), 254–260.

Crandall, S. J. S., Volk, R. J., & Loemker, V. (1993). Medical students' attitudes toward providing care for the underserved: Are we training socially responsible physicians? *Journal of the American Medical Association, 269*, 2519–2523.

Eagan, M. K., Garcia, G. A., Herrera, F., Garibay, J. C., Hurtado, S., & Chang, M. J. (2010, May). *Making a difference in science education for underrepresented students: The impact of undergraduate research programs*. Paper presented at the Association for Institutional Research Annual Meeting, Chicago, IL.

Einfeld, A., & Collins, D. (2008). The relationship between service-learning, social justice, multicultural competence, and civic engagement. *Journal of College Student Development, 49*(2), 95–109.

Freire, P. (1998). *Pedagogy of the oppressed.* (M. B. Ramos, Trans.). New York: Continuum. (Original work published1970)

Gadbury-Amyot, C. C., Simmer-Beck, M., McCunniff, M., & Williams, K. B. (2006). Using a multifaceted approach including community-based service-learning to enrich formal ethics instruction in a dental school setting. *Journal of Dental Education, 70*(6), 652–661.

Garibay, J. C. (2011, April). *Are colleges socializing future scientists to be apathetic towards societal progress?* Paper presented at the American Educational Research Association Annual Meeting, New Orleans, LA.

Giroux, H. A. (1983). *Theory and resistance in education: Toward a pedagogy for the opposition.* Westport, CT: Bergin & Garvey.

Gustein, E. (2006). *Reading and writing the world with mathematics: Toward a pedagogy for social justice.* New York: Routledge.

Gutstein, E., & Peterson, B. (Eds.). (2005). *Rethinking mathematics: Teaching social justice by the numbers.* Milwaukee, WI: Rethinking Schools.

Haney Lopez, I. F. (1996). *White by law: The legal construction of race.* New York: New York University Press.

Harding, S. (2006). *Science and social inequality: Feminist and postcolonial issues.* Chicago: University of Illinois Press.

Holdren, J. P. (2008). Science and technology for sustainable well-being. AAAS Presidential Address. *Science Magazine, 319*(5862), 424–434.

Hurtado, S. (2003). *Preparing college students for a diverse democracy: Final report to the U.S. Department of Education, OERI, field initiated studies program.* Ann Arbor, MI: Center for the Study of Higher and Postsecondary Education.

Hurtado, S., Cabrera, N. L., Lin, M. H., Arellano, L., & Espinosa, L. L. (2009). Diversifying science: Underrepresented student experiences in structured research programs. *Research in Higher Education, 50*(2), 189–214.

Landefeld, T. (2009). *Mentoring in academia and industry: Vol. 4. Mentoring and diversity: Tips for students and professionals for developing and maintaining a diverse scientific community.* New York: Springer.

Li, X. (2007). *Characteristics of minority-serving institutions and minority undergraduates enrolled in these institutions* (NCES 2008-156).Washington, DC: U.S. Department of Education.

Lima, M. (2000). Service-learning: A unique perspective on engineering education. In E. Tsang (Ed.), *Projects that matter: Concepts and models for service-learning in engineering* (pp. 109–117). Washington, DC: AAHE.

Macedo, D. (1994). *Literacies of power: What Americans are not allowed to know.* Boulder, CO: Westview Press.

MacLachlan, A. J. (2006). *Developing graduate students of color for the professoriate in science, technology, engineering, and mathematics (STEM)* (Research and Occasional Paper Series: CSHE.6.06). Berkeley: Center for Studies in Higher Education, University of California.

Maton, K. I., & Hrabowski, F. A. (2004). Increasing the number of African American PhDs in the Sciences and Engineering: A strengths-based approach. *American Psychologist, 59*(6), 547–556.

Maton, K. I., Hrabowski, F. A., & Schmitt, C. L. (2000). African American college students excelling in the sciences: College and postcollege outcomes in the Meyerhoff Scholars Program. *Journal of Research in Science Teaching, 37*(7) 629–654.

Nicholls, G. M., Wolfe, H., Besterfield-Sacre, M., Shuman, L. J., & Larpkiattaworn, S. (2007). A method for identifying variables for predicting STEM enrollment. *Journal of Engineering Education, 96*(1), 33–44.

Ragins, B. R. (1999). Gender and mentoring relationships: A review and research agenda for the next decade. In G. Powell (Ed.), *Handbook of gender and work* (pp. 347–370). Thousand Oaks, CA: Sage.

Ragins, B. R., & Cotton, J. L. (1993). Gender and willingness to mentor in organizations. *Journal of Management, 19*(1) 97–111.

Sax, L. J. (2000). Citizenship development and the American college student. In T. Ehrlich (Ed.), *Civic responsibility and higher education* (pp. 3–18). Phoenix, AZ: Oryx Press.

Schneider, C. (2001). Toward an engaged academy: New scholarship, new teaching. *Liberal Education, 87*(1), 18–27.

Serageldin, I. (2002). World poverty and hunger: The challenge for science. *Science, 296*(5565), 54–58. Retrieved from: http://www.sciencemag.org/content/296/5565/54.full

Seymour, E., & Hewitt, N. (1997). *Talking about leaving: Why undergraduates leave the sciences.* Boulder, CO: Westview Press.

Seymour, E., Hunter, A. B., Laursen, S. L., & DeAntoni, T. (2004). Establishing the benefits of research experiences for undergraduates in the sciences: First findings from a three-year study. *Science Education, 88*(4), 493–534.

Singh, R., Ragins, B. R., & Tharenou, P. (2009). Who gets a mentor? A longitudinal assessment of the rising star hypothesis. *Journal of Vocational Behavior, 74*(1), 11–17.

Solórzano, D. G., & Delgado-Bernal, D. (2001). Examining transformational resistance through a critical race and LatCrit theory framework: Chicana and Chicano students in an urban context. *Urban Education, 36*(3), 308–342.

Stanton-Salazar, R. D. (2010). A social capital framework for the study of institutional agents and their role in the empowerment of low-status students and youth. *Youth & Society.* Advance online publication. doi: 10.1177/0044118X10382877

Tran, M. (2011). *How can students be scientists and still be themselves: Understanding the intersectionality of science identity and multiple social identities through graduate student experiences.* (Unpublished doctoral dissertation). University of California, Los Angeles.

Turner, C. S. V., & Thompson, J. R. (1993). Socializing women doctoral students: Minority and majority experiences. *Review of Higher Education, 16*(3), 355–370.

United Nations. (2011). The millennium development goals report 2011. New York: Author. Retrieved from http://www.worldbank.org/mdgs/

Vaz, R. F. (2005). Connecting science and technology education with civic understanding: A model for engagement. *Peer Review, 7*(2), 13–16.

Wanberg, C. R., Welsh, E. T., & Hezlett, S. A. (2003). Mentoring research: A review and dynamic process model. *Research in Personnel and Human Resources Management, 21*, 39–124.

Washington, S. H. (2005). *Packing them in: An archaeology of environmental racism in Chicago, 1865–1954.* Lanham, MD: Lexington.

White-Means, S., Dong, Z., Hufstader, M., & Brown, L. T. (2009). Cultural competency, race, and skin tone bias among pharmacy, nursing, and medical students: Implications for addressing health disparities. *Medical Care Research and Review, 66*(4), 436–455.

Wieland, M. L., Beckman, T. J., Cha, S. S., Beebe, T. J., & McDonald, F. S. (2010). Resident physicians' knowledge of underserved patients: A multi-institutional survey. *Mayo Clinic Proceedings, 85*(8), 728–733.

World Health Organization. (2008, August 28). *Inequities are killing people on a grand scale, reports WHO's commission.* Media Centre. Retrieved from: http://www.who.int/mediacentre/news/releases/2008/pr29/en/

AFTERWORD

Shaun R. Harper, PhD

CENTER FOR THE STUDY OF RACE AND EQUITY IN EDUCATION, UNIVERSITY OF PENNSYLVANIA

Collectively, chapters in this book do much to celebrate philosophies and practices that have long enabled minority serving institutions (MSIs) to produce an impressive share of our nation's leaders, especially in the science, technology, engineering, and mathematics (STEM) fields. Because of our presumed inferiority and the deficit lenses through which we are often viewed, the following is communicated (sometimes explicitly) about people of color in the United States: if we just do more of what White people do, we will be successful. MSIs are often viewed in the same way. If only they did more of what predominantly White institutions (PWIs) do, they would attract more high-achieving students of color, their fundraising efforts would be more robust, graduation rates would be higher, and student complaints of administrative dysfunction would be reduced, right? Maybe. But as the authors who have written for this book make clear, if PWIs employed more of the cultural practices and pedagogies that are historically and contemporarily characteristic of MSIs, they would produce more students of color who go on to become scientists, technology developers, engineers, and mathematicians.

I have worked at four PWIs and visited more than 100 others. I often meet students of color who feel an insufficient sense of belonging on those campuses, and I do workshops for faculty and administrators who are struggling to create inclusive environments that produce equitable outcomes for students from all racial backgrounds. I often argue that these institutions could more effectively educate students of color if they responsibly employed many of the practices that are commonplace at Albany State University, the HBCU from which I earned my bachelor's degree. In my view, every institution, no matter how excellent it is perceived to be, can improve its practices by looking at others. For example, the University of Pennsylvania, where I teach, often benchmarks itself against Harvard, Princeton, and other institutions in the Ivy League. But a few years ago when my colleagues here wanted to learn more about environmental conditions that lead to the success of Black women in STEM, they went to Spelman, not Yale. I very much appreciate how this book similarly makes clear that MSIs are sites of excellence in these fields and beyond.

An impressive roster of scholars at Ivy League universities are graduates of HBCUs; for example, Mary Frances Berry (Penn Professor of History), John L. Jackson Jr. (Penn Professor of Anthropology and Communication), and Toni Morrison (Princeton Professor of Humanities) all graduated from Howard University; Angel Harris (Princeton Professor of Sociology) graduated from Grambling State University; Marla F. Frederick (Harvard Professor of African American Studies and Religion) graduated from Spelman College; and William Julius Wilson (Harvard Professor of Social Policy) graduated from Wilberforce University. Likewise, several renowned professors in my field are alumni of HBCUs: Gloria Ladson-Billings (University of Wisconsin) attended Morgan State University; James D. Anderson (University of Illinois) attended Stillman College; James Earl Davis (Temple University) attended Morehouse College; and Vivian L. Gadsden (University of Pennsylvania) attended Fisk University, to name a few. As is the case in the STEM fields, these scholars are proof that HBCUs and other MSIs are important suppliers of extraordinarily talented people of color for various academic disciplines and professions.

Many chapters in this book make a persuasive case for increasing the number of people of color in STEM fields. Undeniably, more of us are needed in labs where scientific discoveries are made and in high-paying technological careers that position our nation at the forefront of innovation. However, I argue here, as I have done elsewhere, that greater representation of influential people of color is needed everywhere. The largest share of doctorates awarded to African Americans is in the field of education. Despite this, there is at present only one full professor of color on the faculty in the Graduate School of Education at Penn. There was one lone African American full professor at the University of Southern California's Rossier School of Education when I taught there 9 years ago; today there are none. I know for sure that full professors at Penn and USC (tenured faculty who are at the highest academic rank) are handsomely compensated. I have reason to believe they earn salaries that exceed or are at least comparable to those of many engineers and scientists. Yet, they too are underrepresented, even in the field where the highest number of doctorates is conferred to us. My point here is that an economic argument is often made to justify the emphasis on expanding the STEM pipeline to include more people of color. I agree with this. Notwithstanding, STEM careers are not the only places where we lack representation at the highest levels of leadership and compensation, nor are they the only jobs that pay well. We are needed everywhere: in the humanities, social sciences, biological and life sciences, and physical sciences. This observation is not intended to undermine the aims of this book or reduce its importance. In fact, I believe that most of the innovative recommendations that authors offer in each chapter can be informative and useful to any academic department that wishes to increase the representation and improve rates of success for students of color.

This timely text joins mine and Christopher B. Newman's volume, *Students of Color in STEM: Engineering a New Research Agenda* (Jossey-Bass, 2010); *Racial and Ethnic Minority Students' Success in STEM Education* (Jossey-Bass, 2011), a monograph cowritten by Samuel D. Museus, Robert T. Palmer, Ryan J. Davis, and Dina C. Maramba; and scores of reports, peer-reviewed academic journal articles, and other publications written in recent years about underrepresented racial minorities in STEM fields. While the problem of the leaky STEM pipeline is not yet fixed, more is now known about it because of the attention devoted to it. Furthermore, the National Science Foundation, the National Institutes of Health, and other entities have made significant investments into initiatives that are intended to increase the representation of people of color in STEM fields. I believe this focus has matured to a point at which other fields can now learn from it. For example, a pitiful number of doctorates are awarded to people of color in the field of economics. If faculty in economics departments were to employ many of the philosophies and practices highlighted in this book; if researchers were to concentrate on better understanding the barriers to student persistence in economics from freshman year through doctoral degree attainment; and if foundations and other funding agencies were to invest in expanding the pipeline for economists of color in the ways that the NSF and NIH have invested in STEM, I comfortably predict that we would see an uptick in the number of PhD recipients of color in economics. In many ways, this book and ongoing national conversations that are concerned with diversifying the STEM professions could serve as a model for diversifying other fields.

This book offers much-needed guidance for all postsecondary institutions, MSIs and PWIs alike. I have consistently argued in my research that those who wish to improve Black male student success in college have much to learn from Black men who have successfully navigated their ways to and through institutions of higher education. In this same way, any discipline that endeavors to elevate the representation and status of students of color can learn much from advancements and innovative practices employed in STEM majors, as well as from minority serving institutions that produce disproportionate shares of people of color in STEM fields.

ABOUT THE EDITORS

Robert T. Palmer is an active researcher and assistant professor of Student Affairs Administration at the State University of New York, Binghamton. His research examines issues of access, equity, retention, persistence, and the college experience of racial and ethnic minorities, particularly Black men as well as other student groups at historically Black colleges. Since completing his PhD in 2007, Dr. Palmer's work has been published in national referred journals, and he has authored well over 60 refereed journal articles, book chapters, and other academic publications in 4 years. His books include *Racial and Ethnic Minority Students' Success in STEM Education* (with Samuel Museus, Ryan J. Davis, and Dina C. Maramba); *Black Men in College: Implications For HBCUS and Beyond* (with J. Luke Wood); *Black Students In Graduate/Professional Education at HBCUs* (Forthcoming, 2012 with Adriel A. Hilton and Tiffany Fountaine), and *Fostering Success of Ethnic and Racial Minorities in STEM: The Role of Minority Serving Institution* (Forthcoming, 2012 with Dina C. Maramba and Marybeth Gasman). In 2009, the American College Personnel Association's (ACPA) Standing Committee for Men recognized his excellent research on Black men with its Outstanding Research Award. In 2011, Dr. Palmer was named an ACPA Emerging Scholar and in 2012 he was recognized as an Emerging Scholar by the American Education Research Association (AERA) for his scholarship on multicultural and multiethnic populations.

Dina C. Maramba is Associate Professor of Student Affairs Administration and affiliate faculty with Asian and Asian American Studies at the State University of New York, Binghamton. She earned her PhD in higher education from the

Claremont Graduate University/San Diego State University, her MS in student affairs in higher education from Colorado State University. Dr. Maramba's research focuses on equity and diversity issues within the context of higher education. Her interests include how educational institutions and campus climates influence access and success among students of color and first generation college students. With over 10 years of experience as a student affairs practitioner, she has worked in many roles including working closely with STEM students and facilitating their success in college. She is also one of the coauthors of an ASHE-Higher Education Report about racial and ethnic minority students in the STEM educational pipeline. Having presented her research at the national and international level, her work includes publications in the *Journal of College Student Development, Journal of College Student Retention, Review in Higher Education* and *National Association of Student Affairs Practitioners.* She is also coeditor of two forthcoming books on Asian Americans and Filipino Americans. Dr. Maramba is a recipient of the 2011 Award for Outstanding Contribution to Asian/Pacific Islander American Research Relating to Higher Education by the Association of College Personnel Administrators (ACPA).

Marybeth Gasman is Professor of Higher Education in the Graduate School of Education at University of Pennsylvania. After 10 years in university and community administration, Dr. Gasman received a PhD in higher education from Indiana University in 2000. She came to Penn GSE as an assistant professor in 2003. In 2006, Dr. Gasman was awarded the Association for the Study of Higher Education's Promising Scholar/Early Career Award for her scholarship. In 2008, she received the University of Pennsylvania's Graduate School of Education Excellence in Teaching Award. In 2009, Dr. Gasman was selected by the Provost as one of eight Penn Fellows. Dr. Gasman is a historian of higher education. Her work explores issues pertaining to philanthropy and historically Black colleges, Black leadership, contemporary fundraising issues at Black colleges, and African American giving. Dr. Gasman's most recent book is *Envisioning Black Colleges: A History of the United Negro College Fund.* She has published several other books, including *Charles S. Johnson: Leadership beyond the Veil in the Age of Jim Crow* (with Patrick J. Gilpin), *Supporting Alma Mater: Successful Strategies for Securing Funds from Black College Alumni* (with Sibby Anderson-Thompkins), *Uplifting a People: African American Philanthropy and Education* (with Kate Sedgwick), *Gender and Philanthropy: New Perspectives on Funding, Collaboration, and Assessment* (with Alice Ginsberg); *Understanding Minority Serving Institutions* (with Benjamin Baez and Caroline Turner), *Historically Black Colleges and Universities: Triumphs, Troubles, and Taboos* (with Christopher Tudico), *Philanthropy, Fundraising, and Volunteerism in Higher Education* (with Andrea Walton), and *A Guide to Fundraising at Historically Black Colleges and Universities: An All Campus Approach* (with Nelson Bowman III).

ABOUT THE CONTRIBUTORS

Rosa M. Banda is a doctoral candidate in the Department of Educational Administration and Human Resource Development at Texas A&M University. Rosa received her bachelor of arts degree in communications with a concentration in public relations and her master of arts degree in higher education with an emphasis on bicultural/bilingual studies, both from the University of Texas at San Antonio.

Estela Mara Bensimon is a professor of higher education and codirector of the Center for Urban Education (CUE) at the University of Southern California, Rossier School of Education, which she founded in 1999. In the last 5 years Dr. Bensimon, in collaboration with faculty and doctoral students affiliated with the Center for Urban Education, has published works about equity, organizational learning and change, and action inquiry, including a 2012 book, *Making Equity Happen In Higher Education: The Equity Scorecard Model in Theory and Practice*. She was inducted as an AERA Fellow in 2011.

Darnell Cole is associate professor of education with an emphasis in higher education and education psychology. He completed his undergraduate work at the University of North Carolina, at Charlotte and received his master's and doctoral degrees at Indiana University, Bloomington. He is on the review board of the *Journal of College Student Development*.

T. Elon Dancy II is assistant professor of adult and higher education at the University of Oklahoma in Norman. Dr. Dancy is editor of *Managing Diversity: (Re)Visioning Equity on College Campuses* (Peter Lang, 2010) and author of the forthcoming book, *The Brother Code: Manhood and Masculinity among African American Men in College* (Information Age Publishing). He has received awards and recognition for his work from the Association for the Study of Higher Education, the American Educational Research Association, as well as the American Enterprise and Thomas B. Fordham Institutes, among others. Dr. Dancy is Senior Editor (with Roland W. Mitchell) of the *College Student Affairs Journal*.

Alicia C. Dowd is associate professor of higher education at the University of Southern California's Rossier School of Education and co-director of the Center for Urban Education (CUE). Dr. Dowd is the principal investigator of a National Science Foundation funded study of Pathways to STEM Bachelor's and Graduate Degrees for Hispanic Students and the Role of Hispanic Serving Institutions.

Lorelle L. Espinosa is a senior analyst with the Social and Economic Policy division of Abt Associates in Bethesda, Maryland, where she examines the effectiveness of higher education and training programs in the fields of science, technology, engineering, and mathematics (STEM). Prior to Abt, Dr. Espinosa served as the director of policy and strategic initiatives for the Institute for Higher Education Policy where she directed the Pathways to College Network and National Coalition for College Completion. Dr. Espinosa holds a master's and doctorate in education from the University of California, Los Angeles; a bachelor's degree from the University of California, Davis; and an associate arts degree from Santa Barbara City College.

Araceli Espinoza is a doctoral candidate and serves as a research assistant for the Center for Higher Education Policy Analysis at the University of Southern California (USC). She is the coauthor of "Examining the Academic Success of Latino Students in STEM Majors" in the *Journal of College Student Development*; "When Gender is Considered: Racial Ethnic Minority Students in STEM Majors" in the *Journal of Women and Minorities in Science and Engineering*; and "The Post-Baccalaureate Goals of Women in STEM," a forthcoming chapter in *Attracting and Retaining Women in STEM New Directions for Institutional Research*.

Idara Essien-Wood is a graduate of Arizona State University (ASU) where she earned her doctorate in educational leadership and policy studies. Currently, Idara serves as adjunct faculty at several colleges and universities. Idara holds a bachelors of science in biological science from University of California, Riverside and a master's in bilingual and multicultural education from California State University, Sacramento.

Alonzo M. Flowers has a doctorate in higher education administration from Texas A&M University. Alonzo holds a master's degree in adult and higher education administration from the University of Texas at San Antonio and a bachelor's degree in political science with a minor in multicultural studies from Texas State University. He is also on the editorial board for the Journal of African American Males in Education. Noteworthy too is his recent article in *TEMPO*, a leading peer reviewed journal for the Texas Association for the Gifted and Talented (TAGT) titled "Becoming Advocates for the Gifted Poor."

Juan C. Garibay is currently a doctoral student in the Higher Education and Organizational Change program at the University of California, Los Angeles (UCLA). He earned his bachelor of science degree in applied mathematics from UCLA.

Shannon Gray is the associate dean of the Pennoni Honors College and Director of the Honors Program at Drexel University in Philadelphia, PA. He received his doctorate degree in higher education management at the University of Pennsylvania's Graduate School of Education.

Dana Hart is a doctoral candidate in higher education administration at Louisiana State University. He has a bachelor's degree in history from the University of Massachusetts at Amherst and an master's in higher education administration from Boston College.

Dimitra Jackson is assistant professor in the higher education program at Texas Tech University. Dr. Jackson's dissertation, *Transfer Students in STEM majors: Gender Differences in the Socialization Factors that Influence Academic and Social Adjustment*, received Honorable Mention from the National Institute for the Study of Transfer Students in 2010. In April of 2011, her dissertation received the 2011 Dissertation of the Year Award from the Council for the Study of Community Colleges (CSCC), which is a branch of the American Association of Community Colleges (AACC).

M. Bryant Jackson is the associate director of Enrollment Management and Student Services in the Rossier School of Education at University of Southern California. Mr. Jackson earned his master's degree in college student affairs from the Pennsylvania State University and his bachelor's degree in mathematics from the University of California, Santa Barbara.

Ginelle John is the admissions director for the Department of Occupational Therapy at New York University. She earned her associate's degree from Nassau Community College, bachelor's degree in human development and family studies from Cornell University, and her master's degree in higher education administration from Teachers College, Columbia University. In 2011, Ginelle earned her doctorate in higher education administration from New York University.

Frankie Santos Laanan is associate professor and higher education program coordinator in the department of educational leadership and policy studies (ELPS) at Iowa State University. Currently, he is interim director of the Center for Excellence in Science, Mathematics and Engineering Education (CES-MEE). In 2005, he founded the Office of Community College Research and Policy (OCCRP), which serves as the research enterprise for the Community College Leadership Program in ELPS. To date, he has received over $3 million in funding from the National Science Foundation, Iowa Department of Education, and The Kern Family Foundation. In 2000, Dr. Laanan received the Emerging Scholar Award from the Council for the Study of Community Colleges. He is past president of the Association for Career and Technical Education Research, and currently is vice president of research and publications for the Council for the Study of Community Colleges.

Katherine D. J. Lloyd is a doctoral student in the Higher Education Administration program at Morgan State University. She is a Fulbright-Hays Scholar and serves as the president of the Graduate Student Association.

Valerie C. Lundy-Wagner is assistant professor and Faculty Fellow at New York University in the Higher & Postsecondary Education Program at the Steinhardt School for Culture, Education, and Human Development. She has coauthored articles, book chapters, and an ASHE Higher Education Report on HBCUs, in some cases addressing gender or STEM. Dr. Lundy-Wagner completed a bachelor's of science in civil and environmental engineering at the University of California, Los Angeles (UCLA), master of arts in education from Stanford University, and doctorate in higher education at the University of Pennsylvania.

Roland W. Mitchell is associate professor in the Department of Educational Theory Policy and Practice at Louisiana State University. He has a bachelor's degree in history from Fisk University, a master's in higher education from Vanderbilt University, and a doctorate in educational research from The University of Alabama. Roland is the Editor of the *College Student Affairs Journal*, Higher Education Section Editor of the *Journal of Curriculum Theorizing*, a member of the Leadership Team of the Bergamo Conference on Curriculum Theory and Classroom Practice, and Director of the Louisiana State University Writing Project's Teaching African American Boys Summer Institute.

Berlisha Morton is a third year doctoral student in higher education administration at Louisiana State University. Her research interests include democracy and spirituality in education, history of catholic education in minority communities, race and gender studies, and historically Black colleges and universities.

Christopher B. Newman is a visiting assistant professor at the University of San Diego School of Leadership and Education Sciences. His scholarship has been published in the *Journal of Social Issues*, the *Journal of Women and Minorities in Science and Engineering*, numerous book chapters, and he is coeditor (with Shaun R. Harper) of the volume, *Students of Color in STEM*. Also, he serves on the advisory board of *InterActions: UCLA Journal of Education and Information Studies*. Dr. Newman earned his doctorate and master's degree in higher education and organizational change from UCLA, his master's degree in leadership studies from the University of San Diego, and his bachelor's degree in Sociology from the University of California, Santa Barbara.

Raquel M. Rall is a Provost Fellow and doctoral student at the University of Southern California. Her research examines issues of the African American student experience, with an emphasis on African American males and science, technology, engineering and math education.

Carlos Rodríguez is a principal research scientist with the American Institutes of Research (AIR) in Washington, DC. He is nationally recognized for his expertise and insight on issues of equity, access, and educational attainment of minority populations across the education spectrum. Dr. Rodríguez holds an appointment as Scholar-In-Residence at American University in Washington DC. He received his doctorate in higher education from the University of Arizona and his master's degree in bicultural and bilingual studies from the University of Texas at San Antonio.

Misty Sawatzky is a doctoral student and Dean's Fellow at the University of Southern California's (USC) Rossier School of Education. She works with Dr. Alicia Dowd as research assistant at the Center of Urban Education (CUE).

Frances K. Stage is professor of administration, leadership, and technology at New York University. She earned her bachelor's degree at the University of Miami and her master's at Drexel University, both in mathematics. Her doctorate is from Arizona State University in Higher Education. Stage is past Vice President for the Postsecondary Education Division of the American Educational Research Association and has won awards for research and scholarship from the Association for the Study of Higher Education and the American Educational Research Association. She spent 1999–2000 as a Senior Fellow at the National Science Foundation and was a Fulbright Specialist at the University of

West Indies, Mona, Jamaica in 2008 and at the University of West Indies, Cave Hill Barbados in 2011. She was Professor of Educational Leadership and Policy Studies at Indiana University, Bloomington from 1986 to 2000 before moving to New York University in 2000.

Soko S.Starobin is Assistant Professor in the School of Education at Iowa State University. Starobin began her higher education in Architecture at Toyota National College of Technology in Japan. As a transfer student, she continued her education and obtained a doctorate in Higher Education from University of North Texas. Starobin joined the Office of Community College Research and Policy (OCCRP) in 2004 and appointed as Assistant Professor at Iowa State University in 2008. She has served as Associate Director at OCCRP since 2007. Her research agenda focuses on gender issues in science, technology, engineering, and mathematics (STEM) fields among community college students. She served as the lead-guest editor of the Special Issue on Community Colleges for the Journal of Women and Minorities in Science and Engineering (volume 16, issue 1, 2010). Her research in STEM fields among community colleges and her early career accomplishments have been recognized as the recipient of the Barbara K. Townsend Emerging Scholar Award from CSCC in spring 2010.

Terrell L. Strayhorn is associate professor of higher education at The Ohio State University, where he also serves as Director of the Center for Higher Education Research and Policy (CHERP), Senior Research Associate at the Kirwan Institute for the Study of Race & Ethnicity, and Faculty Affiliate of the Todd A. Bell National Resource Center for African American Males. He holds joint appointments in the Department of African and African American Studies and sexuality studies. Professor Strayhorn has published five books/monographs, over 30 book chapters, more than 75 refereed journal articles, scientific papers, and reviews. He has received awards from the American College Personnel Association, National Association of Student Personnel Administrators, Association for the Study of Higher Education, and Diverse Issues in Higher Education recognized his early career success, naming him one of the top "Emerging Scholars" in the country. Grants totaling more than $800,000 support his research program, including a 5-year grant from the National Science Foundation.

Minh Hoa Ta is the dean of Chinatown/North Beach Campus and School of International Education and ESL (Office of the Vice Chancellor of Academic Affairs) for the City College of San Francisco. She received bachelor's degrees in social welfare and Asian American studies from the University of California, Berkeley; her MSW in social work education at San Francisco State University, and her doctorate in international multicultural education at the University of San Francisco. She is also active in Community Service and has won several awards, including the Citizen of the Year Award from the Oakland Police Department in 1990.

Kenneth Taylor is a data analyst and education program specialist for the U.S. Department of Education. Dr. Taylor holds a doctorate in higher education administration from Morgan State University. He has worked in several capacities conducting educational research, directing, developing, implementing, and evaluating outcomes for STEM education.

Robert T. Teranishi is associate professor of higher education at New York University and Principal Investigator for The National Commission on Asian American and Pacific Islander Research in Education, a project funded by the College Board and USA Funds. He is also a faculty affiliate with The Steinhardt Institute for Higher Education Policy and a consultant for the Ford Foundation's "Advancing Higher Education Access and Success" initiative. Teranishi is the recipient of the 2010 Martin Luther King, Jr. Faculty Award from NYU and was recently named one of the nation's top "up-and-coming" leaders by Diverse Issues in Higher Education. His most recent book published by Teachers College Press is *Asians in the Ivory Tower: Dilemmas of Racial Inequality in American Higher Education*. In 2011, Teranishi was appointed by Secretary of Education Arne Duncan to the Department of Education's Equity and Excellence Commission.

J. Luke Wood is assistant Professor of Administration, Rehabilitation, and Postsecondary Education at San Diego State University. Dr. Wood is coeditor of the *Journal of African American Males in Education* (JAAME) and Chair of the Multicultural and Multiethnic Education (MME) special interest group of the American Educational Research Association (AERA). Wood has several coauthored and coedited books to his credit, including: *Community College Leadership & Administration: Theory, Practice and Change* (with Carlos Nevarez); *Black Men In College: Implications for HBCUs and Beyond* (with Robert T. Palmer); *Leadership in the Community College: A Case Study Approach for Applying Theory to Practice* (Forthcoming, 2012 with Carlos Nevarez and Rose Penrose); and *Black Males in Postsecondary Education: Examining Their Experiences In Diverse Institutional Contexts* (Forthcoming, 2012 with Adriel A. Hilton and Chance W. Lewis).

INDEX

Page locators in *italics* indicate appendices, figures, and tables.

AANAPISIs. *See* Asian American and Native American Pacific Islander serving institutions (AANAPISIs)
academic advisors: and AANAPISIs, 175; and CCSF AANAPISI STEM Achievement Program, 176–77, 178; and STEM student success, 43
academic and social integration, 116–27; overview, 116–17; and culturally inclusive policies and practices at HBCUs, 156; data collection and analysis, 119–21; literature review, 117–18; of non-White STEM majors, 121–26, *124*; student demographics of non-White STEM majors, *122*; study limitations and future research directions, 126–27
academic preparedness: HBCUs and remedial programs, 36; and MSIs, 18; and retention of REM STEM students, 34; undermatched students and campus climate, 47–48
academic rigor at HBCUs, 96, 98
action research: overview, 149–53; assessment as professional accountability for HSIs, 162–64; Culturally Inclusive Policies and Practices SAI (CIPPs-SAI), 160–62; and culturally inclusive self-assessment instruments, 153–55;

institutional agents self-assessment inventory (SAI) for increasing Latina/o STEM participation, 158–60; studies at HBCUs and HSIs, 155–58
Adams v. Richardson, 6
advisor meetings, academic and social integration, 120, *124*
African American higher education: and African American faculty, 77–83; and Black religious colleges, 75; and importance of HBCUs, 72–73, 75–77; and private liberal arts colleges, 74–75; and Sabbath Schools, 73–74
African American students, perception of campus climate, 48–49
aging STEM workforce, 104–5
Akaka, Daniel, 11, 173
Alabama State University, 76–77
Albany State University, 221
American Baptist Home Missionary Society, 75
American Indian Education Consortium (AIHEC), 9–10
American Indian students. *See* Tribal colleges and universities (TCUs)
American Missionary Association, 75
American Missionary Association (AMA), and establishment of HBCUs, 5
Asian American and Native American Pacific Islander serving institutions (AANAPISIs): and AAPI students, 10–11, 168–72, *170*, *171*;

Asian American and Native American
Pacific Islander serving institutions
(AANAPISIs) (*continued*): City
College of San Francisco (CCSF)
case study, 175–79, *176*; historical
overview, 10–11, 172–73; institutions
with federal funding, 173–75, *174*;
and postsecondary STEM degree
production, 168–69; and STEM
undergraduate degrees, 19–26, *22–23,
25*
Asian American and Pacific Islander
(AAPI) students, 10–11, 168–72, *170,
171*
Atlanta University Center Consortium
(AUC), 185–87
AUT (developing autonomy), Student
Development Task And Lifestyle
Assessment (SDTLA), 196
Avery College, 5

Beginning Postsecondary Student
Longitudinal Study (BPS) data, 51–54,
119, 126
Bement, Arden, 132
Black churches and establishment of
HBCUs, 5
Bluefield State University, 7
Boxer, Barbara, 11, 173
bridge programs, 144
Broadening Participation in STEM
project, 131, 134–35
Brown v. Board of Education: and
educational equality, 6; and HBCUs,
73; and White control of Black
education, 74
Building Engineering and Science Talent
(BEST) initiative, 106–7

campus climate at MSIs: campus climate
study data and analysis, 51–53,
54–55; campus climate study results
and limitations, 53–54; campus
climate theory, 50–51; HBCUs and
STEM student success, 35–37; and
impediments to URM success in
STEM at PWIs, 3; importance of
REM completion of STEM degrees,
33–34; and promotion of REM
success, 41–43; retention of REM
STEM students, 34–35; and structured
mentoring programs, 49–50; student
perceptions and cultural factors,

48–49; survey and interview data
collection, 37–38; survey findings,
38–41, *38, 39*. *See also* student-faculty
interactions and mentoring
Center of Urban Education (CUE) action
research tools: culturally inclusive
policies and practices SAI, 160–62;
described, 151; institutional agents
SAI for increasing Latina/o STEM
participation, 158–60
Change the Equation initiative, 134
Cheyney State University of Pennsylvania,
5, 74
Chickering and Reisser's theory of
identity development, 196–98
City College of San Francisco (CCSF)
AANIPISI STEM Achievement
Program case study, 175–79, *176*
Civil Rights Act of 1964, 6–7
clandestine schools, 5
Clark Atlanta University (CAU), 106,
186
class size and STEM student success,
39–40
classroom time and student integration,
125
climate. *See* institutional climate
College Cost Reduction and Access
Act-Hispanic-Serving Institutions
(CCRAA-HSI), 163
College Cost Reduction and Access Act
of 2007, 11, 173
college pipeline, community knowledge
of, 108–9
community building: and community
accountability, 112; and community
resources, 112–13; and community
vision creation, 110–12; concepts
of community, 107; and funding
opportunities, 113; and multifaceted
communities, 113; STEM and
college pipeline knowledge, 108–9;
and STEM student success, 107–13;
supportive community creation,
109–10
community colleges and two-year MSIs:
and AAPI students, 170; and diversity
in higher education, 142–43, 143–44.
See also STEM student success at
2-year MSIs
community involvement and TCUs, 10
counselors: and STEM student success, 43.
See also academic advisors

cross-racial interactions and STEM
student success, 41–42
Crossing the Finish Line (Bowen, Chingos,
and McPherson), 47
Culturally Inclusive Policies and Practices
SAI (CIPPs-SAI), 160–62
curriculum: curriculum relevance and
TCU students, 143; at HBCUs, 5–6;
and STEM student success, 215–16

degree completion: and AAPI students,
168–71, *171*; Black STEM bachelor's
degree completions, 107, 136–38;
Black STEM bachelor's degrees
by institution type, *137*; and
campus climate, 54–55; disciplinary
STEM culture vs. individual career
goals, 211–12; and economic
competitiveness, 210; and HBCUs,
116; Hispanic STEM bachelor's degree
completions, *138*; Hispanic STEM
bachelor's degrees by institution type,
137; and retention of REM STEM
students, 34–35
Delpit, Lisa, 81
demographics and aging STEM
workforce, 104–5
departmental culture and STEM student
success, 40–41
desegregation and higher education,
6–7
Dillard University, 95, 96
Diné College, 9
direct support, institutional agents, 159
discrimination and U.S. higher education,
72, 183–84
disengagement and retention of REM
STEM students, 34
diversity in higher education: overview,
130–31; Black STEM bachelor's
degree completions, *138*; Black
STEM bachelor's degrees by
institution type, *137*; Broadening
Participation in STEM project,
131, 134–35; current political
landscape, 132–34; Hispanic STEM
bachelor's degree completions, *138*;
Hispanic STEM bachelor's degrees
by institution type, *137*; and MSIs,
135–38, *137*, *138*; policy and research
implications, 145–46; as resource for
meaningful change, 152; stakeholder
focus group findings, 141–45;

stakeholder focus groups, 138–40
doctoral degrees. *See* faculty promotion of
STEM PhD education
Du Bois, W. E. B.: and curriculum at
HBCUs, 5; on influence of Black
thought on American thought, 73;
and pedagogical double-consciousness
(PDC), 79–81
dual consciousness, pedagogical double-
consciousness (PDC), 79–83
Dual Degree Engineering Partnership
(DDEP), 186–87

Education and Human Resources (EHR)
directorate at NSF, 132
Education to Innovate initiative, 134
educational equality court cases, 6
emotional autonomy, 197, 200–201
engineering partnerships between
HBCUs and PWIs: overview, 181,
189–90; advantages of, 187–88; Atlanta
University Center Consortium
(AUC), 185–87; disadvantages of, 188–
89; HBCU challenges in sustaining
engineering programs, 183–85; and
importance of HBCUs, 181–83;
institutional response to, 187; 3–2 dual
degree programs, *182*, 185–86
engineering student success: overview,
192–93, 204; Chickering and Reisser's
theory of identity development,
196–98; future research directions,
203–4; and identity development,
195–96; literature review, 193–94;
policy and practice recommendations,
203; study discussion, 200–203; study
findings, 199–200, *199*, *200*; study
methodology, 198–99
enrollment, and HSIs, 8–9
Equal Protection Clause, 14th
Amendment, 6
equity within and beyond STEM:
overview, 209–10, 217–18, 221–23;
accountability for preparing future
leaders, 213–14; corporate vs.
individual student interests, 210–11;
disciplinary STEM culture vs.
individual career goals, 211–12;
empowerment of URMs in STEM
and beyond, 214–16; research and
practice implications, 216–17
ethnocentrism and establishment of
HBCUs, 74–77

faculty engagement and support:
accessibility and STEM student
success, 94; African American faculty,
77–83; and culturally inclusive policies
and practices at HBCUs, 155–56;
informal interactions and student
integration, 125–26; office hours and
student integration, 125; and STEM
student success, 3, 40, 55, 107, 118;
and student mentoring, 50. *See also*
engineering student success; faculty
promotion of STEM PhD education
faculty promotion of STEM PhD
education: faculty as role models, 87–
90; importance of, 86–87; portraiture
study methodology, 92; and possible
selves theory, 90–91; and socialization
theory, 91–92; study findings,
93–98; study limitations, 93; study
participants, 92–93
family involvement in STEM student
success, 144
federal funding: and increased URM
graduations, 131; and proposed
elimination of NSF-funded programs,
132; and structured mentoring
programs, 49–50
fictive kin, 40
Fighting Words (Hill-Collins), 80–81
fine arts participation, academic and social
integration, 120–21
Freedman's Bureau and establishment of
HBCUs, 5, 75
funding: and 2-year MSIs, 62–63; and
AAPI students, 169; CCSF AANAPISI
STEM Achievement Program, 176–77;
HBCU challenges in sustaining
engineering programs, 183–85; for
HBCUs, 76; and HSIs, 8–9, 150, 163;
proactive search for, 113

Gaines v. University of Missouri Law School, 6
Georgia Institute of Technology, 185–86,
187
global economy and importance of URM
STEM student success, 1–2, 59, 109,
116
goals and community vision creation,
110–12

Hampton University, 5, 94, 95, 96
HBCU Perspectives and Research Programs
(McNair), 156

HBCUs. *See* historically Black colleges
and universities (HBCUs)
Higher Education Act of 1965, 7
Higher Education Act of 1992, 8–9, 150
Highline Community College case study,
64–68
Hill-Collins, Patricia, 80–81
Hispanic Association of Colleges and
Universities (HACU), 162
Hispanic serving institutions (HSIs):
and campus climate theory, 50–51;
and culturally inclusive policies
and practices, 156–58; and degree
completion, 136–38, *137*, *138*; and
diversity in higher education, 144–45;
and federal funding, 8–9, 150, 163;
growth of, 46; historical overview,
8–9; Latina/o enrollment and
graduation rates, 149–51; professional
accountability assessment, 162–64; and
San Antonio Prefreshman Engineering
Program (SAPREP), 105–6; San
Diego City College, 64, 65–68; and
STEM bachelor's degrees, 20–26,
22–23, *25*, 47; and URM STEM
student success, 3, 4. *See also* action
research
historically Black colleges and universities
(HBCUs): and academic rigor, 96,
98; and African American faculty,
77–83; baccalaureate degreees and
persistence and completion of
doctorates, 17; and campus climate
theory, 50; culturally inclusive
practices at, 155–56; declining Black
enrollment, 7; deviation from weed-
out model, 88–89; historical overview,
5–8; importance of, 7–8, 72–73, 76;
increased racial and ethnic diversity
at, 7; institutional climate and STEM
student success, 35–37; and pedagogy
of teaching, 77–83; and STEM
bachelor's degrees, 20–26, *22–23*, *25*,
47; supportive environments at, 125;
and URM STEM student success,
3–4. *See also* academic and social
integration; African American higher
education; engineering partnerships
between HBCUs and PWIs; faculty
promotion of STEM PhD education
Historically Black Colleges and
Universities-Undergraduate Program
(HBCU-UP), 132, 133

HSIs. *See* Hispanic serving institutions (HSIs)

identity development theory, 195–98
informal interactions and student integration, 125–26
institutional accountability: and Institutional Agent SAI, 160; and NSF funding, 142. *See also* action research
institutional agents: and educational equity, 153–54; faculty acting as, 157–58; SAI for increasing Latina/o STEM participation, 158–60
institutional climate. *See* campus climate
institutional leadership and STEM student success, 107
Integrated Postsecondary Educational Data System (IPEDS) data, 19–20, 147*n*6
integration constructs, 117–18
integrative support, institutional agents, 159
interviews: Black doctoral students portraiture study, 92–98; campus climate and STEM student success, 37–38; campus climate study findings, 38–39, *38*, *39*
IPEDS. *See* Integrated Postsecondary Educational Data System (IPEDS)

Johnson, Edie Bernice, 133

knowledge workers, 211

Latina/o students: increased enrollment at HBCUs, 7; perception of campus climate, 48–49. *See also* HSIs
learning communities, 63, 145
Lincoln University of Pennsylvania, 5, 74
literacy and Black community, 74
Louis Stokes Alliance for Minority Participation Program (LSAMP), 49–50, 95, 132, 133
low expectations and Black STEM students, 88

Mathematics, Engineering, and Science Achievement (MESA) Program, San Diego City College, 64–68
McLaurin v. University of Oklahoma, 6
McNair Program, 95
mentoring: and AANAPISIs, 175; and

supportive communities, 109–10. *See also* student-faculty interactions and mentoring
Meyerhoff Program at University of Maryland at Baltimore County (UMBC), 2
microaggression, racial, 124–25, 154
Minority Access to Research Careers (MARC), 95
Minority International Research Training (MIRT), 95
minority serving institutions (MSIs): and diversity in higher education, 135–38, *137*, *138*, 144; and REM bachelor's degrees, 46–47, 51. *See also* community building; STEM education at MSIs; STEM student success at 2-year MSIs; underrepresented racial minorities (URMs)
MIR (mature interpersonal relationships), Student Development Task And Lifestyle Assessment (SDTLA), 197
missionaries and Black higher education, 75
Morehouse College, 186, 187–88
Morehouse School of Medicine, 186
Morgan State University, 118
Morrill Act of 1880, 5
MSIs. *See* minority serving institutions (MSIs)
multifaceted communities, 113

National Association for Equal Opportunity in Higher Education (NAFEO), 132–33
National Association for the Advancement of Colored People (NAACP), 6
National Science Foundation (NSF): and Broadening Participation in STEM project, 131; and growth of STEM occupations, 59; and promotion of REM STEM student success, 33; proposed program mergers and elimination, 132–33; and Research Experience for Undergraduates (REU), 96; and stakeholder focus groups, 138–40, *139*, 142
Native American students and STEM undergraduate degrees, *22–23*, 24, *25*, 26
Navajo Nation, Diné College, 9
nested social practices and Success Literacy, 68

North Carolina A&T State University, 94, 95, 96

Obama, Barack, 76, 133
office hours and student integration, 125
office of Civil Rights (OCR), 7
oppositional knowledge, 80–81
outsider-within knowledge, 80–81

P–16 STEM initiatives, 109
Partners in Transitioning to Tech (PITT), 187
Peabody Education Fund, 75
pedagogical double-consciousness (PDC), 79–81
pedagogy of teaching at HBCUs, 77–83
peer led team learning (PLTL), 145
peer support and STEM student success, 41, 108
perceived goal blockage, 88
perceptions: of AAPI students as successful minority group, 169–70; and retention of REM STEM students, 34; URM student perceptions of PWIs, 51, 55
personal attention and STEM student success, 107–8
Plessy v. Ferguson, 6
portraiture study methodology, 92
possible selves theory, 90–91, 98
practical experience and STEM student success, 89
predominantly White institutions (PWIs): and financial resources, 63; HSIs and AANAPISIs, 18; and impediments to URM success in STEM, 3; and lack of Black student integration, 118; practice recommendations, 125–26; and racial microaggression, 124–25; URM student perceptions of, 51, 55. *See also* academic and social integration; engineering partnerships between HBCUs and PWIs
preparedness. *See* academic preparedness
private liberal arts colleges and Black higher education, 74–75
professionalization and socialization, 91–92
program evaluation: and diversity in higher education, 131; and proactive vision creation, 110–12; and STEM student success, 108. *See also* action research
PUR (establishing and clarifying

purpose), Student Development Task And Lifestyle Assessment (SDTLA), 196, 201–2
PWIs. *See* predominantly White institutions (PWIs)

racial and ethnic minorities (REMs). *See* campus climate at MSIs; underrepresented racial minorities (URMs)
racial microaggressions, 124–25, 154
racial uplift, 76
racism toward transfer students, 188–89
real-world applications, 34
Reconstruction and Black higher education, 4–5
recruitment, CCSF AANAPISI STEM Achievement Program, 177
Regents Engineering Transfer Program (RETP), 185–86
relationships with faculty and STEM student success, 93–98
religious colleges and Black higher education, 75
remediation, culture and history of educational artifacts, 153
Research Center for Science and Technology at CAU, 106
Research Experience for Undergraduates (REU), 96, 97
research opportunities: and diversity in higher education, 144; and STEM student success, 108
retention: mentoring and community support, 110; of REM STEM students, 34–35; and Tinto's interactional theory, 117; and URM STEM students, 211–12
role models. *See* faculty promotion of STEM PhD education
Ronald E. McNair Post-Baccalaureate Achievement Program, 49

Sabbath Schools, 73–74
San Antonio Prefreshman Engineering Program (SAPREP), 105–6
San Diego City College case study, 64, 65–68
scholarship of teaching literature (SoTL), 77–83
school club participation, academic and social integration, 120
second-sight, 80

self-assessment inventories (SAIs): and culturally inclusive policies and practices, 160–62; for increasing Latina/o STEM participation, 158–60. *See also* action research

self-reported data, 93

separate but equal, educational equality, 6

Sipuel v. Board of Regents, 6

The Skin That We Speak (Delpit), 81

social contact with faculty, academic and social integration, 120, *124*

social integration. *See* academic and social integration

socialization theory, 91–92

Spelman College, 186, 188, 222

sports participation, academic and social integration, 120–21

staff support and STEM student success, 40

STEM education at MSIs: AANAPISIs, *29*; growth and diversity of, 105–7; HBCUs, *29–31*; HSIs, *31–32*; research discussion and conclusions, 24, 26; research findings, 20–24, *22–23, 25*; research methodology, 19–20; research needs, 18–19; and socioeconomic status, 17; student persistence and completion of doctorates, 16–17; TCUs, *32*

STEM educational pipeline, community knowledge of, 108–9

STEM PhD education. *See* faculty promotion of STEM PhD education

STEM student success at 2-year MSIs: overview, 59–60, 68–69; and financial resources, 62–63; Highline Community College case study, 64–68; mentors and role models, 62; practice and research recommendations, 69; role and structure of colleges and MSIs, 61–62, 67; San Diego City College case study, 64, 65–68; and student services, 63; Success Literacy framework, 65–66; Success Literacy momentum, 66–67, 68; women and URMs, 60–61

structured mentoring programs, 49–50

Student Development Task And Lifestyle Assessment (SDTLA), 196–98

student–faculty interactions and mentoring: and campus climate, 48–49; campus climate study data and analysis, 51–53, 54–55; campus climate

study results and limitations, 53–54; and campus climate theory, 50–51; and MSIs, 46–48, 62, 67; structured programs, 49–50

student performance in math and science, 104

student services and 2-year MSIs, 63

Students of Color in STEM (Newman), 223

study group participation, academic and social integration, 120, *124*

Success Literacy, 65–68

summer bridge programs, 63, 64, 68

Summer Research Opportunity Program (SROP), 49

survey data collection, 37–39, *38, 39*

Sweatt v. Painter, 6

system developer, institutional agents, 159

system linkage and networking support, institutional agents, 159

talking with faculty, academic and social integration, 120, *124*

targeted recruitment and STEM student success, 107

TCUs. *See* Tribal colleges and universities (TCUs)

teaching: scholarship of teaching literature (SoTL), 77–83. *See also* faculty engagement and support; faculty promotion of STEM PhD education

3–2 dual degree programs, engineering partnerships between HBCUs and PWIs, *182*, 185–86

Tinto's interactional theory, 117, 118

Title III, Higher Education Act of 1965, 7, 10

Title V, Higher Education Act of 1998, 8–9

Title VI, Civil Rights Act of 1964, 6

transfer agents and educational equity, 153–54

Trends in International Mathematics and Science Study (TIMSS), 104

Tribal Colleges and Universities Program (TCUP), 132, 133

Tribal colleges and universities (TCUs): and diversity in higher education, 142–43; historical overview, 9–10; and STEM undergraduate degrees, 20–26, *22–23, 25*; and URM STEM student success, 3, 4

Tuskegee University, 5

twoness and pedagogical double-consciousness (PDC), 79–81, 83

undergraduate research and STEM student success, 89, 95–96, 97–98
undermatched students and campus climate, 47–48
underrepresented racial minorities (URMs): expanded definition of, 142; and importance of STEM student success, 102; and increasing need for STEM education, 103–5, 131; MSIs and STEM bachelor's degrees, 18–19; MSIs and STEM student success, 1–12, 59–61, 105–7; perception of campus climate, 48–49; and structured mentoring programs, 49–50
Underwood, Robert, 11, 173
United States v. Fordice, 6–7
University of Alabama, 76–77
University of Georgia, 185–86
University of Maryland, 183–84
University of Maryland at Baltimore County (UMBC), 2
University of Texas at San Antonio (UTSA), 105–6
URMs. *See* underrepresented racial minorities (URMs)
U.S. economy and increasing need for STEM education, 103–5, 130–31
U.S. higher education, 72–73. *See also* African American higher education

U.S. students, math and science performance, 104

vision and community, proactive vision creation, 110–12

Washington, Booker T., 5
weed-out model, 88–89, 143
West Virginia State University, 7
White House Initiative on Asian Americans and Pacific Islanders (WHIAAPI), 10–11
White House Initiative on HBCUs, 76
White House support for STEM, 133–34
White supremacism, 76–77, 80–81
Wilberforce University, 5, 74
women: importance of mentors for, 62, 193; and racial microaggressions, 125; and STEM student success, 33; and STEM student success at 2-year MSIs, 59–62; and Success Literacy, 65–68; as underrepresented minority, 103
Women in Science and Engineering (WISE), 49
Worchester Polytechnic Institute, 215–16
workforce transition and STEM student success, 108
Wu, David, 11, 173

Xavier University, 95, 96